9/09

Yellowstone and the Snowmobile

Yellowstone and the Snowmobile

Locking Horns over National Park Use

MICHAEL J. YOCHIM

University Press of Kansas

Published by the University Press of Kansas (Lawrence, Kansas 66045),
which was organized by the Kansas Board of Regents and is operated and
funded by Emporia State University, Fort Hays State University, Kansas
State University, Pittsburg State University, the University of Kansas, and
Wichita State University

Library of Congress Cataloging-in-Publication Data

Yochim, Michael J.
Yellowstone and the snowmobile : locking horns over national
park use / Michael J. Yochim.
p. cm.
Includes bibliographical references and index.
ISBN 978-0-7006-1642-8 (cloth : alk. paper)
1. Snowmobiles—Environmental aspects—Yellowstone National
Park. 2. Noise pollution—Government policy—Yellowstone
National Park. 3. Yellowstone National Park. I. Title.
QH545.S6Y63 2009
363.6'80978752—dc22

2008040247

British Library Cataloguing-in-Publication Data is available.

Printed in the United States of America

10 9 8 7 6 5 4 3 2 1

The paper used in this publication is recycled and contains 30 percent
postconsumer waste. It is acid free and meets the minimum requirements
of the American National Standard for Permanence of Paper for Printed
Library Materials z39.48-1992.

For my One

Contents

Acknowledgments

Writing a book is an act of hope, humility, and dedication. It is a creative challenge that constantly reminds one how generous others are with their time and thoughts. From the librarians that come in contact with the author only rarely to those who provide their daily support, many people help to produce a manuscript, and this one was no exception.

Most helpful have been the friends and family members who have listened to me, watched my understanding of this issue evolve and grow, and offered their feedback and support. Deserving particular mention is Ellen Petrick, who has been continually supportive and interested in this project. My parents have also been behind me all the way through graduate school and beyond. Similarly, the Management Assistant's Office staff in Yellowstone continuously supported my work. They were coworkers who also became friends, covering for me during long absences while I traveled to distant research libraries and more recently as I focused upon writing and revising the manuscript. Many more Yellowstone staff members lent their assistance as well; so did the staff at the Greater Yellowstone Coalition, who generously opened their files for my review.

A number of colleagues lent their time and thoughts in reviewing early drafts of this book: Don Bachman, Carol Cole, Sean Eagan, Kevin Franken, Blake Harrison, John Sacklin, Paul Schullery, Denice Swanke, and Lee Whittlesey. Their insights have improved the quality of detail, understanding, and writing in the book. Any lingering errors of writing or judgment are my own.

Librarians at the following institutions lent assistance as well: the Yellowstone National Park Archives; the University of Wisconsin–Madison; Montana State University–Bozeman; the American Heritage Center in Laramie, Wyoming; the Denver Public Library; the National Park Service's Technical Information Center at the Denver Service Center; and the National Archives in College Park, Maryland.

Chapter 4 of this book is substantially derived from the same chapter of my Ph.D. dissertation. As such, the members of my doctoral committee at the University of Wisconsin–Madison deserve credit for their help in reviewing it: my dissertation adviser, Professor Tom Vale, whose weekly chats with me about national parks and the environmental movement I fondly remember, and Bill Cronon, Matt Turner, Bob Ostergren, and Nancy Langston.

Others who have helped at some point include Josh Becker, Tony Britten, Jon Catton, Bill Chaloupka, Kathryn Kirby, David Kirtley, Mutsumi Moteki, Leslie and Ruth Quinn, Kevin Schneider, Hope Sieck, and Rosemary Sucec.

Thanks to all of you.

Yellowstone Winter Road Use

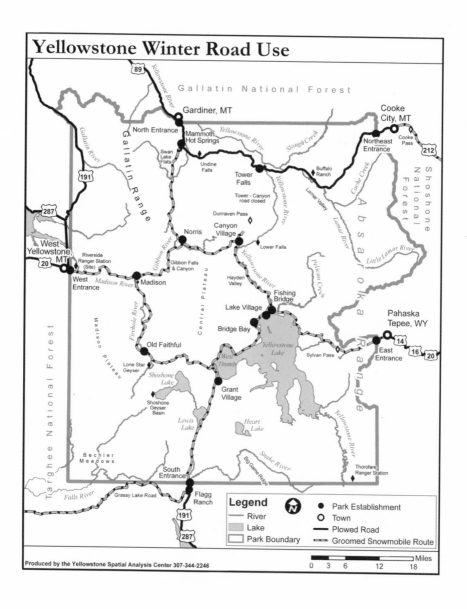

Produced by the Yellowstone Spatial Analysis Center 307-344-2246

Legend
- River
- Lake
- Park Boundary
- Park Establishment
- Town
- Plowed Road
- Groomed Snowmobile Route

Miles
0 3 6 12 18

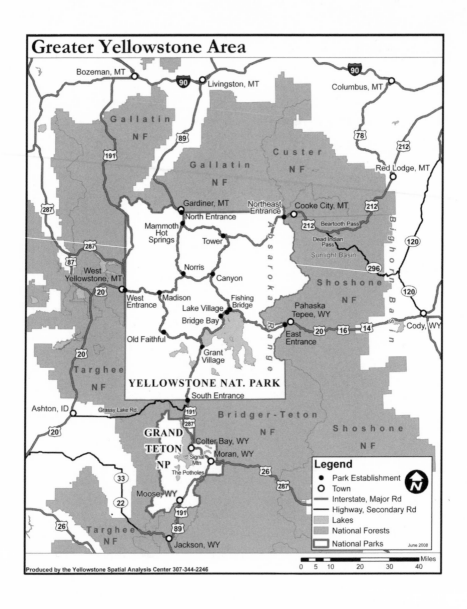

Greater Yellowstone Area

Introduction

Machines in the Winter Wonderland

On some winter mornings at Old Faithful, it can take until noon for the temperature to warm to 10 below. Yellowstone National Park, with the famous geyser as its centerpiece, is one of the coldest places in the states south of Alaska. That cold may repel many people, but it has long attracted both cross-country skiers and snowmobilers.

The earliest visitors to the park found a winter wilderness, with few rangers present or buildings open. They were explorers of a sort, the first to enjoy Yellowstone at its most forbidding time of year. Winter use of the park grew, however, particularly once snowmobiles were invented, and the noise and the damage they caused to the ecosystem grew as well. The use of snowmobiles was already controversial by the early 1990s, and since then the issue has become the focus of one of the greatest controversies involving U.S. national parks. The history of this debate and the evolution of the policies surrounding it reveal an increasing conflict between and among the National Park Service (NPS) and other parties over the appropriate role of motorized recreation (particularly snowmobiling) in Yellowstone, a conflict that in many ways is emblematic of broader public land debates in the American West. This book presents the story of that conflict and examines its implications for Yellowstone and the national park system.

Winter visitors began touring the park in the early twentieth century, initially on skis and eventually in "snowcoaches," vehicles like vans capable of traveling over snow on tracks and skis. The advent of snowmobiles in the 1960s allowed more people to travel the park, enjoying the easy ability to explore a place previously accessible only to those capable of undertaking multiday ski trips. Touring the park on the new vehicles, visitors admired the clash between superheated water and superchilled air, a contrast that produced a winter landscape deserving of the park's historical nickname, Wonderland. Wildlife was abundant, driven by deep winter snows to the lowest elevations, the same places traversed by the park's roads.[1]

By the 1980s, this discovery experience was not as readily available, because over 100,000 people visited annually in winter, enjoying two warm hotels, almost 200 miles of manicured and patrolled roadways, and reliable and comfortable snowmobiles and snowcoaches. Despite the human presence, most still enjoyed their experience, impressed by the thermal scenery and wildlife. To more fully appreciate the sense of discovery that the first motorized winter visitors enjoyed, one had to don cross-country skis (or snowshoes) and embark upon a long ski tour (a journey by ski). Perhaps the best such tour was the trip to Shoshone Geyser Basin, because it contained many of the elements of early explorations: beauty, thermal warmth, remoteness, silence, and risk.

The ski tour to Shoshone was no easy undertaking, and the basin remains one of the less traveled spots in the park, being more than 9 miles by trail up and over the Continental Divide from Old Faithful. The trail climbs immediately away from the geyser, providing skiers with a nice warm-up on frigid mornings. It then passes through areas burned in the 1988 wildfires, followed by evergreen forest and occasional meadows. Frosty bison are sometimes visible as the trail crosses some small creeks and then climbs over Grants Pass. Once over the divide, skiers reach a trail junction about 2 miles from the geyser basin. By February, the trail sign there is often almost buried, indicating about 4 feet of snow. Two months later it usually disappears under snow some 7 feet deep. The trail then follows Shoshone Creek, one of Yellowstone's many creeks kept open—and green with growing aquatic vegetation—by a continuous influx of warm water from hot springs. Such life in the midst of wintry whiteness is one of the magical contrasts of Yellowstone this time of year. Soon, steam in the distance announces the presence of Shoshone Geyser Basin, on the shore of Shoshone Lake.

Warmed by volcanic heat, the trail through the geyser basin remains mostly bare. Snow and ice sculptures abound, especially after clear, subzero nights. Most trees are covered by inch-thick hoarfrost that condenses from steam drifting off hot springs. Other trees feature draperies of frost 6 inches long. On smaller rocks, fantastic ice sculptures form, their delicate fingers pointing in the direction of the nearest hot spring (frost and ice accumulate toward the moisture source). Large snow pillows rest on the bigger rocks, which insulate the frozen moisture from the ground's heat. On clear days, little sparkles of frost highlight anything not otherwise covered in snow. Sundogs, short rainbows of atmospheric ice appearing only in very cold conditions, may accompany the sun once it burns through the last vestiges of fog.

Partway through the basin, the trail traverses a little valley to a view of Shoshone Lake, passing green moss on either side—more winter greenery! Though the ground may be too hot and dry for plants in summer, the moisture and temperatures of winter enable plants and moss to exist, as long as they remain short enough to absorb the heat from below that they need to survive the −50°F frosts. One such plant is Ross' bentgrass (*Agrostis rossiae*), an endemic plant unique to Yellowstone's thermal areas and their unusual growing conditions. Like the moss, it greens up in November, blooms in March, and turns brown by June: more life amid freezing dormancy. The lake overlook presents another oasis cre-

Shoshone Geyser Basin, 1995. In Yellowstone's geyser basins, the clash between superheated water and superchilled air is most evident. Here, trees are coated with hoarfrost from nearby hot springs, with Shoshone Lake in the background and the Red Mountains in the distance. Photo by author.

ated by thermal activity, areas of open water in the otherwise frozen lake. Trumpeter swans are often present, an incongruous sight of natural grace in this otherwise inhospitable place. Otters and Canada geese sometimes appear, along with coyotes, and the coyotes sometimes play a form of tag with the otters in a desperate effort to steal fish. In short, this snowbound place features a whole web of life dependent on earth's warmth.

The Shoshone Geyser Basin ski tour is an experience of all the senses, from the sounds of nature and the sights of life in a frozen landscape to the sharp bite of the inhaled air and the pungency of sulfur from the hot springs. The silence can be especially impressive; the only sounds are gurgling creeks, hissing geysers, winter winds, softly chirping chickadees (that such tiny birds survive in Yellowstone's harsh winter environment is cause for wonder), and the swish of one's skis. Not only does nature assail the senses, but so does the journey's inherent risk. Intense cold, biting winds, remoteness, and lack of other skiers can all turn a delightful day into a survival experience. These conditions demand that the skier pay close attention to time, weather, ski conditions, and his or her own physical state. In sum, the experience can be energy and wildness incarnate, invigorating and refreshing all who make the long journey there with care.

Snowmobiles behind Old Faithful Inn, 1990s. As many as 1,500 snowmobilers would visit Old Faithful per day in the 1990s, bringing problems with noise, air pollution, and wildlife. Photo by author.

Even with hundreds of other visitors and the associated lodges and gas stations necessary to accommodate them, some elements of this experience were still available to nonskiing visitors in the 1970s and early 1980s. By the late 1980s, though, more and more of these special qualities were disappearing; the clean, crisp air of Shoshone, for example, could not usually be found at Old Faithful, and silence was almost impossible to find there. In their place were hordes of snowmobiles, their fumes permeating even one's clothing and their noise ever-present. About 700 snowmobiles per day visited Old Faithful in the 1990s, peaking near 1,500 on the busiest days of Christmas week and President's Day weekend. Instances of snowmobilers harassing wildlife were also common, along with conflicts between skiers and snowmobilers. With so many noisy, polluting machines present, the tranquil, clean experience of nature sought by so many was available only to those strong enough to undertake a long ski tour such as that to Shoshone Geyser Basin.

While stationed at Old Faithful during the winter of 1993–1994, I witnessed these conditions but was fortunate enough to be able to ski to Shoshone. It became my favorite tour because of its beauty and because the basin was one of the few places that seemed reliably free of snowmobile noise. At 5.5 direct-line miles and across the Continental Divide from the nearest road, it was a wilderness refuge from the ever-present machine. However, one cold day that February, while enjoying some sunshine after eating lunch there, I heard something foreign: the faint whine of snowmobiles. Something about that high-frequency, cyclic whine and the calm, cold weather conditions that day enabled the noise to travel across impressive distance and topography to the geyser basin. Even though it was barely audible, the mechanized noise was totally alien; my ears focused upon it, amplifying it beyond its low decibel level. More than any experience I had that winter, the noise illustrated how much snowmobiles had come to dominate Yellowstone and the degree to which their use had compromised the National Park Service's primary mission, preservation. Not even a full-day ski tour over the Continental Divide provided a genuine national park experience; Yellowstone instead resembled a racetrack with pretty scenery. Now, virtually no one could find true, natural silence or come close to discovering the wonderland of earlier years.[2]

The National Park Service has spent more than a decade since that winter, and millions of dollars, attempting to address the problems. Politicians at all levels of government have attempted to influence the outcome, and interest groups and concerned citizens by the thousands have expressed their opinions. As the controversy unfolded in the late 1990s, it became evident that the NPS was struggling to protect its snow-covered wonderland amid growing visitation and increasing entrenchment and bitterness among politicians and interest groups. I became involved in the issue myself, researching its history in graduate studies and eventually working within the NPS itself to aid the agency's efforts to understand the perspectives of all stakeholders. The issue remains unresolved as of this writing in 2008, with divergent interest groups influencing the debate through lawsuits in at least three different courts and with political attention extending to the Office of the Vice President in Washington, D.C. Resolution of the controversy seems a distant hope.[3]

No comprehensive history of this issue exists, and the dearth of information has in some ways hampered the modern debate over what kinds of visitor uses are most appropriate in the winter park. Moreover, the research gap reflects the lack of scholarly attention directed toward winter use of any national park or toward motorized recreation in the parks. Though a few scholars have chronicled the rise of winter recreation in America, they have paid little attention to the winter visitor experience in the national parks specifically, despite the fact that national parks opened some of the first ski resorts in the West.[4]

National parks and the evolution of their general policies, however, have seen considerable scholarly inquiry, particularly by historians and geographers. Some authors have provided broad histories of the NPS and its parks, while others have used histories or case studies of individual (usually major) national parks to explore the tension that the NPS has experienced in reconciling the two halves of its mission.[5] The agency's Organic Act directs it to "conserve the scenery and the natural and historic objects and the wild life therein and to provide for the enjoyment of the same in such manner and by such means as will leave them unimpaired for the enjoyment of future generations."[6] Commentators debate the extent to which the dual mandates of preserving park resources while welcoming visitors to experience them (in a way that ensures the resources are left intact for future generations) conflict or are harmonious. They examine other major themes in national park management as well, such as the role of science therein,[7] the evolving meanings of national parks, and the influence of particular interests upon park management.[8]

Collectively, most of the authors writing on these topics examine the creation of "place" in the national parks, that combination of nature and society expressed therein. In general, they view the parks as primarily natural, with both Native American and historical human influences that at times greatly color their sense of place.[9] Another dimension—time—is incorporated within nature and society: Both change over time, and many writers have examined these temporal changes in the parks. No one, however, has examined the creation of a winter place in Yellowstone or the changes to it over time, a scholarly omission that begs to be rectified.[10] With this book I have attempted to fill this void and to contribute to the contemporary debate by relating the evolution of Yellowstone's winter use policies and the unique winter place affected and created by those policies. It is the story of the struggle that Americans and the NPS have engaged in as they have attempted to determine what the look and feel of Yellowstone in winter should be, whether snowmobiles are appropriate in the park, and who should make those decisions.[11]

Caught in this long-term controversy, the National Park Service has agonized over whether snowmobiles are appropriate in Yellowstone, while interested members of society have promoted alternative, and oftentimes conflicting, visions of nature preservation there. These visions are driven by incompatible societal values and identities, producing a conflict that seems irreconcilable. Promoting many of those different visions have been certain strident personalities and dominant politicians (often one and the same, but not always), with such political influence (along with that of industry) approaching control of NPS policy-making at times. Finally, tardy and confounded science has confused the debate, with stakeholders choosing the science that most supports their preconceived agendas. Throughout, NPS autonomy has withered, despite the agency's improving success at navigating the intersection of politics and nature preservation.

More specifically, with spectacular nature as the stage, Americans have created a winter place like no other. It is a truly remarkable landscape, one that bears not only the strong imprint of nature but also distinct traces of contemporary society.

Americans who care about that landscape have engaged in an eighty-year dialogue with each other and the park's managers about what policies to use in preserving the wonders there and creating the human elements of that place. As this debate has unfolded, sets of fundamental American values have become institutionalized, values that at times conflicted with and at other times complemented national park ideals. These differing visions of park management and landscape meaning have transformed the park into a theater of conflict between fundamental American values, particularly freedom (as embodied in the use of snowmobiles) and reverence for nature (especially in the parks) as a sacred national treasure derogated by the machine. Yellowstone in winter is therefore both contested and cherished, at the same time.

Interest groups and involved individuals—stakeholders in the discourse—have, over time, used federal law, public opinion, and/or political power to defend the values they wish to be expressed in the winter wonderland. Depending on the values and personal or community identities being defended, along with the political and legal context and industry interest in the issue, those defensive attempts have at times challenged the National Park Service, its autonomy, and its ability to protect Yellowstone. Reacting to the power politics of the moment, park managers have been forced to become politically astute. While that shrewdness has resulted in advances for nature protection in Yellowstone, the stakeholder conflicts of the past two decades have taken a toll on the agency and its employees. Increasingly, they find themselves struggling to preserve their resources adequately. Numerous scholars and former NPS directors have suggested that the NPS is vulnerable to political influences that do not always advance nature preservation, with some finding that such influence is increasing; not all, however, have grounded these assertions in specific examples. This book provides extensive documentation of such actions, grounding claims of political manipulations, increasing over time, in reality.[12]

Some politicians, as well as certain park superintendents, have had dominant personalities and correspondingly distinct influences on this history. The park's winter use history and landscape owe much to these individuals, from park superintendents Jack Anderson and Mike Finley to Interior Secretary Gale Norton and Senator Alan Simpson, and this book will examine their influence. Scholars have likened the national parks to fiefdoms controlled by powerful superintendents; this story certainly confirms the truth of that assertion (at least at times), but it also demonstrates that other powerful figures, such as the secretary of the interior and certain elected officials, are influential in national park policy development.[13]

One of the "values" being defended in Yellowstone policy-making has been science. Science plays a particularly confounding force in the later portions of the story, as scientists have disputed the effects of snowmobile travel upon park wildlife. This conundrum demonstrates that the insistence of some authors that park management be based upon science are simplistic;[14] they fail to recognize that scientific opinion is rarely uniform (at least to the extent that it can offer clear management direction), often evolves slowly before producing widely accepted results (when managers must make immediate decisions), and is itself often a societal value. Even though some Americans believe that objective science can resolve disputes like this, the snowmobile story confirms other scholarly claims that science can ultimately be only one of many factors in park decision-making. American society in general professes to believe in science-based decision-making, but most of the time we base our decisions as much or more on other values.[15]

Science is hardly the only confounding factor in this story; indeed, managing a park as vast and beloved as Yellowstone involves a constant effort to balance many factors, both social and natural. Other pressing dilemmas have frequently distracted park managers from the winter use problems, such as the 1988 wildfires and the ensuing policy review. Moreover, for much of Yellowstone's winter use history, its managers have piloted the park into uncharted terrain. Though other national parks welcomed ski resorts and/or snowmobiling in the post–World War II era, most of the resorts eventually closed, and few other parks saw snowmobiling boom to the degree that it did in Yellowstone. Its managers have been forced, often without precedent or direction from above, to accommodate local community pressures and evolving technologies without full knowledge of the consequences. Steering into a policy abyss, park managers have not been able to be as proactive as many of them would have liked. Further, the national structure of the National Park Service has encouraged crisis management; it is present throughout this story.

Finally, the story would be incomplete without a discussion of the sheer fun of winter exploration in Yellowstone. The winter scenery is unique and fascinating, with a combination of heavy snowfall, thermal activity, and abundant wildlife not found anywhere else in America. Additionally amusing are the oversnow vehicles used for winter exploration; these bear little resemblance to the vehicles people see on a daily basis. Their novelty has combined with the awesome scenery to create a memorable experience for visitors unlike any other. Long a story of struggle and conflict, Yellowstone's winter experience is grounded in the park's novelty, beauty, and excitement.

The book begins in the early days of motorized winter travel, when local residents clamored for, and then found, access to a previously closed winter wilderness. In the 1930s, they began to discover the exhilaration of exploring Yellowstone in winter and soon recognized it as a winter wonderland. But how to

Child in snowcoach, 1966. This photograph captures the fun many visitors had touring the park in winter; clearly, the vehicle's owners drew upon that attribute to advertise their tours. As enjoyable as tours by snowcoach were, though, more visitors were drawn to the touring freedom provided by snowmobiles. NPS photo.

explore it? While some regularly called upon Yellowstone management to plow park roads and admit private automobiles, others took advantage of the un-plowed roads and pioneered motorized access with vehicles capable of traveling over snow (today called snowcoaches). By 1960, snowcoach access to Yellowstone was routine, but so was a recurring debate: Was oversnow travel or automobile access via plowed roads the best form of visitor access? Chapter 1 uncovers this dialectic, starting before World War II and ending around 1960. It reveals that park managers had little guidance in determining the appropriate winter use for Yellowstone. Without such policy guidance, it was more a matter of early winter use happening *to* Yellowstone than of the NPS directing the park proactively. By the mid-1960s, adventurism by nearby community members in snowcoaches had laid the foundation of the park's winter use policies; soon, the arrival of the snowmobile would help cement oversnow vehicle tourism into place.

That vehicle arrived in the 1960s, forcing park managers to decide which form of winter use would prevail, oversnow vehicles or automobiles on plowed roads. Chapter 2 examines a congressional hearing, public pressure, and the NPS decision-making that resulted in the agency's move to institutionalize oversnow vehicle use. Directed by a superintendent who seemed to like snowmobiling personally, Yellowstone managers began maintaining winter roads for snowmobiles, opened a lodge in the park's interior, and promoted the new oversnow vehicle program—actions that all took place without the environmental review required by the National Environmental Policy Act, passed in 1970. Park managers were in a difficult position; public pressure seemingly left them little choice between allowing the automobile, which would bring known and feared impacts to the park, or the snowmobile, which seemed to come without those impacts. Throughout the 1970s and early 1980s, managers mostly adhered to their snowmobile solution, with the lack of environmental review perhaps concealing other potential solutions.

With ready access to the park's wonders, the 1980s and early 1990s were golden years for snowmobile enthusiasts in Yellowstone. There were few limits to snowmobiling in the park; visitors could go when and where they wanted on either snowmobile or snowcoach, and the park's wonders were ever-present. However, visitation grew, bringing with it unanticipated problems such as conflicting visitor expectations and wildlife harassment. The primitive snowmobile technologies then in use also led to degradation of Yellowstone's pristine air quality and impairment of its winter silence. Technological change, community expectations in gateway communities, and agency inability to grapple with the growing problems all combined to let winter visitation slip out of control. Hamstrung by a lack of funding to address the problems adequately, park managers gathered what information they could and waited for an opportunity to take a hard look at the situation. Interest groups with distinctive values and sometimes close ties to influential politicians began to take notice of the agency's policy deliberations. Seeing no other way to convince all the stakeholders that there were indeed serious problems in the park, managers hoped for and awaited a crisis. Chapter 3 chronicles this gradual shift from the "good old days" to a tragedy of the commons.

As Chapter 4 details, the crisis finally arrived in 1997, when a harsh winter drove many of the park's emblematic bison outside the park and to their deaths at human hands. Sued by an animal rights group concerned that snowmobile trails contributed to that exodus, the agency agreed to write an Environmental Impact

Statement on winter use. The issue received national press, rapidly transforming it into a national issue. Stymied by a lack of quieter and cleaner technologies and desperate to reduce impacts from the existing machines, park managers believed they had little choice but to propose a ban on snowmobiles. They finalized that proposal under the Clinton administration but quickly learned that such strong actions inspire strong reactions. Snowmobile advocates litigated the ban and soon found political allies in the new George W. Bush administration, which pressured Yellowstone managers to come up with a plan allowing snowmobiling to continue in the park. They reluctantly obliged (insisting upon restrictions that they believed would solve most of the snowmobile problems), but this policy reversal resulted in a litigious and legislative melee. The interest groups disenfranchised by these opposing decisions sued and successfully overturned both, and the politicians sympathetic to the two sides attempted unsuccessfully to resolve the issue in Congress. This era ended in early 2004 with a litigious morass reflecting the conflicting sets of values held by the plaintiff stakeholders: Conservationists[16] wished to preserve the sacredness they perceived in the park, while snowmobilers defended their activity and the freedom and economic enhancement it represented to them, with both groups claiming that science was on their side and public officials seemingly stymied in their policy-making efforts.

Contemplating their few options in early 2004, Yellowstone's planners soon recognized an unusual chance to enact reforms that would address some of the problems while ensuring continued motorized access to the park. Jumping at the opportunity, they made several changes that returned some silence, clean air, orderliness, and tranquil wildlife-viewing to the park. Amazingly then, caught between opposing interest groups and in the midst of intense political scrutiny, park managers were able to make some progress, a credit both to an unplanned stroke of luck and to their increasing political acumen. Chapter 5 records these developments, along with the agency's later attempts to find a compromise that pleased most constituents while protecting park resources. That attempt, concluding as of the writing of this book, settled portions of the debate while stirring others, resulting in still more litigation. Influential personalities, science, and community identities were all important in the recent policy evolution, as they had been previously.

It was at this time that I found myself working for the very agency dealing with this issue. As I had during my academic studies, I was forced to look at it in a logical manner, except that I was now actually trying to resolve it, applying the knowledge gained from my studies to the situation as best I could. I have endeavored to record recent events as objectively as possible, but the reader should know that I was one of the actors in Chapter 5 (if a minor one; most crucial decisions were made without my input). It was also during this assignment that I wrote the majority of this book. The views expressed in this book are mine, not those of the National Park Service or the Yellowstone management staff. The reader will probably perceive that I prefer cross-country skis to snowmobiling, but even more I support affordable public access—in this case, bus transportation—rather than expensive forms such as snowmobiles and snowcoaches. Again, I have attempted to be as objective as possible in examining the positions of the various stakeholders in this book and in recording the story.

As of this writing, the winter use policy debate continues, as it is likely to do for the foreseeable future. Overall, the story of Yellowstone's winter use policy evolution is an account of attempts by interest groups and elected officials at all levels to influence park policy-making and of attempts by the NPS to negotiate this minefield while respecting all views and ensuring Yellowstone's continued preservation. It is a story of deeply held values, of a contested but cherished landscape, of conflicting and confounding science, and of increasing political influence over NPS policy-making. The story illustrates the conflicting points of view we have about our national parks and their policies: Are they nature reserves or recreational playgrounds? Are they also science laboratories or economic engines? Can they be more than one of these? Who gets to decide? And can a solution to the conflicting interests preserve Yellowstone? The answers remain to be seen, but whatever they are, park managers have an intractable situation that few land managers would envy.

1

The Public Wants In

On February 9, 1933 I was a Park Ranger in Yellowstone Park stationed with District Ranger "Al" Bicknell at the old Riverside Ranger Station on the Madison River. On the morning of that date, after a bitter cold night, Bicknell read the minimum thermometer before breakfast and returned to the Station with the news that we had set a record low for the Park.

The official Weather Bureau thermometer was calibrated only to –65 degrees Fahrenheit but the indicator needle on this minimum instrument had dropped down into the bulb. At Ranger Bicknell's request I went to the weather station to verify this fact and we agreed that the best estimate was 66 below zero. The U.S. Weather Bureau later requested that we send in the minimum thermometer in order that they might test it since it had recorded a new U.S. minimum [outside of Alaska]. They mailed us a new minimum thermometer calibrated considerably lower than our old one.

District Park Ranger Frank H. Anderson, 1949[1]

Anderson and Bicknell's discovery on that bitter cold morning—a record that stood for twenty-one years, until Rogers Pass, Montana, recorded a numbing 72 below in 1954—illustrates perhaps better than any other single incident the potential severity of a Yellowstone winter. That same night, other rangers recorded 57 below at Lamar, 56 below at Yellowstone Lake, and 40 below even at Mammoth Hot Springs, the park's "banana belt." Temperatures rivaling these still occur once or twice per winter, although the onset of global warming seems to have made them about 10 degrees warmer.[2]

Such temperatures make one wonder why anyone would voluntarily visit Yellowstone in the winter. Though the park did not have many winter visitors in the 1920s and 1930s, it did have a few—and by the late 1930s a growing number of them. Intrigued by the clash of hot water and cold air and the easy wildlife viewing from roads through low-elevation wintering grounds, an increasing number of regional residents wanted in. From the 1930s on, those residents became visitors as park managers gradually opened Yellowstone's frosty doors. Soon, more and more nonresidents joined the ranks of visitors.

This growth reflected societal changes that gradually overtook the country between the two world wars, changes that became even more pronounced after World War II. By 1960, visitors had discovered Yellowstone's winter wonderland, and winter visitation, though small in number, was well established. The park's managers, however, were not quite sure just where they were going with their new winter use policy. In part, their confusion resulted from an ongoing regional debate about whether they should plow park roads or accommodate oversnow vehicles. The lack of precedent for winter visitor use or guidance emanating from the National Park Service headquarters in Washington, D.C., on the same subject meant Yellowstone managers were plowing new policy ground. For these reasons, this era would close with the park embroiled in conflict over what its winter future should be like.

Yellowstone in Winter before 1930

Yellowstone in winter before about 1930 was a quiet place. With summer tourists gone, hotels were shuttered and roads closed by snow. Park rangers patrolled to guard wildlife, especially bison, from poachers. The annual spring thaw was usually welcomed, though clearing snowy roads was difficult before the park acquired rotary plows in the 1930s. As a few vignettes below reveal, Yellowstone during the winter season at this time was characterized by wilderness isolation, vastness, and travel difficulties. Still, by the late 1920s, the trickle of winter visitors that writer Paul Schullery chronicled in *Yellowstone's Ski Pioneers: Peril and Heroism on the Winter Trail* had begun to increase, albeit very slowly.[3]

Winter visitors before 1920 were certainly the exception, not the rule, as reflected in park policies at the time. According to the "Winter Instructions to Rangers," issued in 1918, the few winter visitors were to "be looked upon with a certain amount of suspicion" and "should be questioned closely in regard to their business in the park and if necessary will be watched until they leave the park." This suspicion was warranted because poachers primarily did their "work" in winter, when fur-bearing animals had long fur for insulation, making their pelts more valuable. Even after 1918, when the newly created National Park Service took over the administration of Yellowstone from the army, poaching continued.[4]

Poaching of the park's bison was especially problematic; by 1900, only about two dozen remained in all of Yellowstone. Concerned for their welfare, in 1902 the U.S. Army administrators convinced Congress to appropriate funds for the purchase of twenty-one bison from captive herds in Texas and Montana. Game warden Charles J. "Buffalo" Jones and his successors guarded, nourished, and ranched these animals and their offspring for the next several decades, mainly at the "Buffalo Ranch" in the Lamar Valley. Under this protection, the bison population reversed its downward trend and grew to more than 1,000 animals by the late 1920s. Through these efforts, Yellowstone bison came to symbolize conservation success. To a degree, they also ironically symbolize wildness. The park's few remaining native bison, rather than perishing as the army had expected, actually clung to life in the Yellowstone wilderness, eventually mixing and interbreeding with the managed captive herd.[5] Today's Yellowstone bison are therefore the only herd of bison in the country that has continuously ranged freely in the wild. These multiple symbolisms would become particularly important in the snowmobile controversy in the late 1990s.

More significant for this era, though, was that bison needed protection, which meant that some soldiers and rangers overwintered in the park interior on the higher plateaus south of Mammoth and Tower, rather than moving down to the park's headquarters at Mammoth, about 1,000 feet lower on the park's northern edge. Those people wintering in the interior found Yellowstone to be a very snowy place, especially if they were stationed in one of its "snow belts" on the south or east sides. There, snow commonly measured as much as 8 or 10 feet deep (130 inches, for example, in March 1925), with 3 to 7 feet elsewhere being more typical. Snowbound rangers were dependent for communication on primitive telephone lines that most cabins had and for transportation on their skis. Most isolated were the rangers at the Thorofare Ranger Station in the park's southeast corner (today the remotest place in the United States outside of Alaska), staffed for several winters during this era. The cabin, already isolated, was even more so in winter, when the distance to the nearest plowed road increased substantially, from "only" 40 miles in the summer to almost 100 miles.[6] Indeed, in the words of one Thorofare ranger, Curtis K. Skinner, "There are many wilderness patrol cabins in Yellowstone National Park, . . . [b]ut none of these has quite the overwhelming power of the wilderness around Thoroughfare [sic] where natural plant and animal life in such abundance reigns supreme with very little disturbance by the minor and temporary presence of man."[7]

Wilderness isolation and coping with winter's endlessness were indeed the norm in the park's interior before 1930. Yellowstone's vastness and the risks inherent in traveling it in winter were especially brought home when army scouts patrolled on skis (called snowshoes at the time), an integral part of their protective duties. Perhaps the most Herculean winter ski trip was one that Scout Peter Holte and an unnamed companion took through the Bechler region (the southwest corner of Yellowstone) in spring 1902 (although spring is the time of snowmelt, the season often has the deepest snow accumulation of the year). The men left the Snake River Soldier Station at the South Entrance on May 12, 1902, and arrived at the Proposition Creek Cabin (about 10 miles west of Snake River) to find its rations entirely gone. After spending a hungry night there, they continued on to the Bartlett Cabin, located near the mouth of Bechler Canyon. Holte's description of their adventure onward from Proposition Creek speaks for itself:

> May 13th Left for Bartlett Cabin. [I]t was warm last night and snow did not crust and shoeing [the expression at the time for cross-country skiing] is very heavy. We fell[ed] trees across the small streams and crossed. We had decided to undress and wade the Bechler. But finding this impossible we fell[ed] dead trees and made a raft[,] tied our snowshoes and packs on securely and paddled across, landing safely some distance below. [T]he country for at least two miles is flooded. [W]e waded where possible but within about five or six hundred yards of the cabin we were compelled to make a detour of more then [sic] two miles. The cabin is nearly surrounded by this Lake, only one narrow ridge leading to it from the west and this ridge is only a few inches above the water[.] We are cut off from warm formation which we intended to visit tomorrow[.] This cabin is in very bad condition the roof having fallen in in two places, and it leaks all over like a sieve[.] [I]t is not safe to use another winter as the roof is to[o] weak to hold up the weight of snow. It contains nothing but the cupboard, stove, axe and eight cans of Emergency rations.
>
> May 14th Rained very heavy all night, raising the water between two and three feet and covered the ridge by which we reached the cabin, leaving us on an Island[.] We found some nails in the cabin and with these we constructed a raft using the logs from an old corral near the cabin.
>
> May 15th Rained all night and is still raining today[.] [T]he water is now within ten feet of the cabin an[d] is rising fast[—]the lake surrounding the cabin is at least three miles across. [T]aking some Emergency rations with us we placed our packs and snowshoes on the raft and with long poles shoved across the lake untill [sic] we reached cascade river where the current carried us swiftly into the Bechler river. We only knew when we reached these rivers by the swift current as the the [sic] entire country is one vast lake. Beaver splashed all around us[,] six Elk swam across cascade in front of our raft[;] they seemed poor and weak. We landed close to the ford on the Bechler river[,] securely fastened the raft and started for mountain ash [creek.] [W]e were continually wading above our knees in snowwater[.] [W]e carefully examined mountain ash creek[;] there are many Beaver colonies on this stream but no sign of them having been molested.

Perhaps not surprisingly, Holte suffered from rheumatism later in that trip, having to spend an extra day at Snake River to recover before proceeding back to headquarters at Mammoth Hot Springs.[8]

By the 1940s, park managers stopped stationing rangers at the more remote winter stations. Rangers did, however, continue to make winter patrols and found that the inherent travel risks had not diminished. For example, Rangers Nathaniel Lacy, Delmar Peterson, and Harry Reynolds skied through the Thorofare area in 1956, staying at the ranger station there before embarking for the South Entrance via the Fox Creek and Harebell patrol cabins. On that ski out, they encountered winter storm after storm and sank up to their knees in snow—while on their skis! Losing precious time amid 10- to 25-foot drifts on Big Game Ridge, they got caught in a sudden blizzard, with winds increasing to hurricane force. Bivouacking for the night, they proceeded westward toward the Harebell Cabin the next day, arriving after dark and finding it only by stumbling across its exposed stovepipe. After digging down to the door and clearing the roof of snow, they skied safely out to the South Entrance the next day. By experiencing a night without shelter, they became the newest members of the "Royal Order of Mountain Men," a tongue-in-cheek group of Yellowstone rangers who had suffered a similar fate at one time or another (the group had no dues, just an exclusive membership rite).[9]

In the frontcountry, all park roads were closed by heavy snowfall between October and early December in most years, with the exception of the road from Mammoth to Gardiner (the latter being even lower than Mammoth), which usually remained drivable by automobiles all winter. Gardiner received daily train service, and the road from Gardiner north to Livingston was usually in good driving condition because it was too low in elevation for much normal snow accumulation. Unusually heavy snowfall, however, could restrict travel from Mammoth to Gardiner to horse-drawn sleighs, an event which occurred in February 1922. Elsewhere in the park, sleighs or skis were the norm. For example, a sleigh traveled the route from Mammoth to Cooke City, a town just outside the park's Northeast Entrance, once or twice weekly all winter to deliver mail and other supplies to the town's miners.[10]

Technology for plowing deep snow was not developed until the late 1920s. Yellowstone managers, for example, owned and used only a horse-drawn plow for winter plowing in the 1920s. As with surrounding states, the lack of effective snowplowing equipment meant that warming spring weather was the primary snow removal agent on high-elevation roads. Even with the tractors and dynamite that managers began using to clear deeper drifts in the 1920s, it was still early July before some roads could be opened to the public. Rotary plows began to change the situation in the late 1920s; Yellowstone managers acquired one in 1932 after leasing one from Idaho and observing its utility (they procured a second one in 1937).[11]

By the late 1920s, a trickle of visitors began to arrive in winter, generally drawn to observe the diversity and large numbers of overwintering wildlife in the Mam-

Ski trail across Yellowstone Lake, 1969. Rangers have long patrolled Yellowstone's backcountry on skis, using patrol cabins for shelter. On Yellowstone Lake, the park's winter vastness is especially evident. Here, the ski trail of a patrol in more recent years is the only evidence of their passage remaining. NPS photo.

moth area. Such visitors could only drive the 5 miles from Gardiner to Mammoth, but that area still offered sightings of elk, deer, bighorn sheep, and pronghorn. The winter of 1926–1927, for example, saw at least 1,438 visitors in 525 cars tour this area. Visitors also had the option of cross-country skiing. One of the first long visitor ski trips had occurred in 1925, when five men from the State College in Bozeman took a nine-day cross-country ski trip through the park. Traveling from Mammoth to Norris, over to Canyon, back to Norris, south to Old Faithful, and then out to West Yellowstone, the men stayed with some of the interior rangers, using their telephones to report their progress to the chief ranger's office every day. While there were other such trips, they were the exception in this era, not the rule.[12]

Though Superintendent Horace Albright reported positively on the five-man venture, he and his successors took a mixed view of public requests for such trips. Generally, the historical record is silent on what qualifications park managers desired in such parties. It appears that they would permit them if they believed the requesting skiers were prepared for Yellowstone's extreme winter temperatures and deep snow. Skiers from outside the Yellowstone area were more commonly denied permission for such trips, perhaps amid fears that they were not familiar with the area's extremes and would succumb to the winter elements. Such conflicting answers toward winter ski trips were evident as late as 1949, when park managers denied permission to some parties of hopeful skiers while granting permission to others. In general, managers did not seem prepared to manage winter visitation, or did not understand the desire for it, making confused or contradictory approaches the norm. Inconsistent winter visitation policies characterize much of the park's history; some might say that winter use happened *to* Yellowstone, rather than Yellowstone managers planning and controlling it in any organized manner, at least in the early decades.[13]

In sum, Yellowstone before 1930 saw winter's forces prevail over human visitation; geography ruled. Rangers experienced isolation, vastness, and risk on their adventurous patrols. Nevertheless, a trickle of visitors soon challenged park managers to recognize that Yellowstone's winter solitude and wilderness conditions were an attraction to some. The automobile and the changes it brought to American society would soon breach Yellowstone's winter fortress.

Automobiles, Tourists, and Round One of Calls for Plowed Roads

In the 1910s, Henry Ford took what had been an expensive novelty for a few years—automobiles—and transformed them into something affordable to the middle class. This development quickly changed not only the primary means of transport for Americans, but also the traveling landscape of America. By 1930, touring by automobile had become the new norm for Americans, relegating the railroads relied upon previously to freight transport, primarily. Sweeping changes came as well to Yellowstone and its surrounding communities, with direct implications for winter visitation.

Before World War I, most Yellowstone tourists arrived by train and stayed in elegant hotels. Because these were expensive tourist luxuries, most visitors then were from society's upper income classes. Automobiles, first formally admitted into Yellowstone in 1915, initially did little to change this situation.[14] By the late 1910s, however, an increasing number of Americans owned automobiles (8 million automobiles by 1920, up from only 458,000 in 1910), and they were beginning to discover their recreational potential. Compared to railroads, automobile travel offered many attractions. Travelers were not confined by railroad schedules or routes; they were free to go anywhere their vehicles could go, at the driver's whim. Touring by car was also daring and fun. Primitive roads and technologies demanded ingenuity in getting a vehicle moving after becoming stuck or breaking down, and motorists often stopped to assist each other and stayed together in the era's automobile camps. As Americans fell in love with their new freedoms, automobile travel grew rapidly in popularity.[15]

Sensing the growing demand for safe and enjoyable cross-country travel, both private organizations and the federal government responded by building and marking the first cross-country highways in the 1910s. One of these, the Lincoln Highway, passed near Yellowstone, through southern Wyoming. By 1924, the country had the beginnings of its national highway system, with 9,700 miles of hard-surfaced highway and almost 100,000 miles of secondary gravel-surfaced roads.[16]

Stephen Mather, the first director of the National Park Service, which Congress had created in 1916, realized that he could use the country's increasing automobile infatuation to boost national park popularity. He conceived the National Park-to-Park Highway, a grand loop route connecting most of the western national parks (Yellowstone, Glacier, Mount Rainier, Crater Lake, Yosemite, Sequoia, Grand Canyon, Mesa Verde, and Rocky Mountain). This highway, and others soon to follow, would bring more visitors to the parks, making them popular and their continued existence more likely before a Congress that sometimes questioned the value of the parks. Other marked highways also featured Yellowstone, including the Atlantic-Yellowstone-Pacific Highway (a transcontinental highway across the country's northern tier and passing through Yellowstone) and the Black and Yellow Trail (from the *Black* Hills to *Yellow*stone—formally opened by Superintendent Albright in 1925). These efforts at organized highway systems were successful at stimulating automobile visitation to the parks, including Yellowstone; by 1922, two-thirds of all Yellowstone tourists arrived by car.[17]

Most of these marked highways passed through Cody, Wyoming, because it had one clear geographical advantage for motorists over the other Yellowstone gateways: The most direct routes between Yellowstone and the populous eastern seaboard all converged there. Visitation through Yellowstone's East Entrance confirmed these geographical benefits, with more visitors traveling by automobile entering via that gate in six years of the 1920s than by any other entrance.[18] So many new visitors began to transform the small town. Motorists were not as wealthy as railroad passengers, but they were more numerous, offering returns of different sorts to those who recognized economic opportunity. Many restaurants, motels, campgrounds, and gas/service stations sprung up in Cody in this era. For example, the Buffalo Bill Campground and Buffalo Bill Village were established in the 1920s, both drawing upon Cody's primary cultural feature, its founder Buffalo Bill, to capture tourist attention and spending.[19]

By the late 1920s, the town hummed with activity for three or four months every summer, but the rest of the year was dusty and quiet, a situation that bothered some local residents. For the moment, they could do little to change that fact. But other regional events in this era would soon give them an opportunity to expand their tourist economy into the winter season.

In the winter of 1930–1931, mild weather enabled the state of Idaho to keep the road from Ashton to West Yellowstone, Montana, open for most of the winter. Idahoans, traveling that route but finding the park closed at the West Entrance, complained and suggested that Old Faithful be opened for winter sports, a request that was in keeping with the long-standing popularity of cross-country skiing in the West's snowbound communities. Their complaints received no immediate redress, but road plowing continued to spread throughout the region in the late 1920s and early 1930s.[20] Montana and Wyoming joined Idaho in keeping their own roads open throughout the winter, with Montana opening U.S. Highway 191 from West Yellowstone to Bozeman in the winter of 1936–1937 and Wyoming opening the first 35 miles of road between Cody and Yellowstone's East Entrance in 1929 (of the three states, Wyoming had the easiest job maintaining a Yellowstone approach road in winter, because the road from Cody to the park was the lowest in elevation and enjoyed the warmest and driest climate of the three [except for Montana's road to Gardiner], particularly in these Dust Bowl years).[21]

Assisting the Wyoming Highway Commission and winter travelers were road improvements between Cody and Yellowstone Park during this era. Before their completion around 1933, this road had been narrow and unimproved. Travelers had to walk ahead or sound their horns to avoid colliding with oncoming vehicles around blind curves; they often became coated with dust from the dirt road; and in the park, they had to navigate a corkscrew bridge built to ease the steep grade going up Sylvan Pass. Starting about 1928, the road received a series of improvements in and out of the park, resulting in a two-lane oiled road with more moderate grades on the pass, making travel on this route more attractive.[22]

Cody citizens celebrated these improvements. Some who had participated in a dedication tour of the National Park-to-Park Highway in 1920 realized there was a potential for greater, year-round accessibility. If a winter transcontinental highway (like the Park-to-Park Highway) could be opened through Cody and Yellowstone, summer tourism benefits could be extended year-round, at least to some degree. The main problem was that Yellowstone roads were unplowed. Soon, the Cody Club, a group of influential town citizens, took the lead in investigating the possibility of such a national year-round road. In 1931, the group appointed local doctor R. C. Trueblood to investigate the cost of plowing Yellowstone's roads by examining what other Rocky Mountain states spent on road plowing. Trueblood estimated that plowing the 140 miles from east to west across Yellowstone would cost about $140,000, a figure that he felt was generous. Trueblood also estimated that 10 percent of the travel on a winter transcontinental route through Flagstaff, Arizona, could be diverted through Yellowstone, and that the $3 Yellowstone entrance fee would more than cover plowing costs there. With the research complete, in 1932 he and the Cody Club called upon park managers to plow Yellowstone's roads year-round, suggesting also that the Lake Hotel be opened to foster winter sports in the park.[23]

The Club quickly generated support throughout Wyoming and the Bighorn Basin (the low topographic basin in which Cody sits). U.S. senators and representatives (from nearby states as well as Wyoming), several chambers of commerce and development associations, some Lions Clubs in the region, and some prominent area ranchers all wrote to the NPS promoting the idea. The Club went throughout the West to gather support, eventually receiving formal endorsements from the states of Wyoming, Montana, South Dakota, and Idaho as well as from chambers of commerce in Sacramento and San Francisco, California.[24]

While the Club may have been persuasive, its idea also reflected the boundless hope of boosterism. Just inside Yellowstone's East Entrance was Sylvan Pass, one of only two natural travel corridors crossing the long Absaroka mountain range. At 8,500 feet above sea level, the pass's narrow topographic trench had open rocky slopes on both sides. Regular travelers there might have noticed numerous avalanche paths on those slopes, many of which crossed the road.[25] Moreover, the pass aligned with prevailing southwest winds, making it extremely windy. Proposing to plow this route was at best an exercise in technological optimism and at worst a proposal of ignorance, especially given the more limited plowing technologies of the era. Either way, it was booster hope, made worse by the fact that Trueblood seemed to use a snowfall figure somewhat below the park's actual snowfall average in making his plowing estimate (perhaps influenced by the ongoing Dust Bowl drought). He used an annual figure of 100 inches, which is only about half the average through Sylvan Pass and much of Yellowstone. His error added to the perception that plowing the 140 miles across the park was feasible.

Boosterism is certainly hopeful; some would call it benignly or even willfully ignorant. In this case, the Club failed to note that much lower east-west cross-country routes were available just north and south of the Yellowstone area. U.S. 10 traveled the low-lying Yellowstone River Valley through southern Montana. The two passes it crossed were both about 3,000 feet lower than Sylvan Pass and had no avalanche danger, due to their lower elevations and lower average snow accumulation. South of Yellowstone, the Lincoln Highway crossed the high desert of southern Wyoming—and it was already open year-round. Today, these two routes are home to Interstate Highways 90 and 80, respectively, a clear indication of their inherent travel feasibility. To think, as the Cody Club certainly seemed to, that people would voluntarily travel through rugged, snowy Yellowstone instead of one of these much easier routes was certainly not geographic common sense.[26]

Horace Albright, who had left Yellowstone in 1929 to become NPS director in Washington, responded to the plowing request discouragingly, but he did ask Yellowstone managers to assemble data on the park's snowpack and snow conditions. He knew that NPS authorities were plowing up to 20 miles of road in Crater Lake National Park in Oregon and in Yosemite National Park in California, but Yellowstone's conditions were quite different. Those two parks had milder winters and less snow drifting than Yellowstone. Albright, the former superintendent of Yellowstone, knew too that its roads "do not have proper surface, they are too narrow, and in many places they are subject to slides." Yellowstone still did not have a rotary plow (both Yosemite and Crater Lake did). The plowed road segments in the other two parks were also much shorter than what the Cody Club envisioned in Yellowstone. Finally, most of the buildings in Yellowstone's interior would need to be winterized, ranger patrols would be necessary for travelers, and gas stations and restaurants would need to be opened. Operationally, Albright knew that opening Yellowstone in winter was a much more serious endeavor than the Cody Club suggested it would be. Given the shortage of federal funds during the Depression, he knew his agency could not come close to funding a winter opening, so he opposed it.[27]

Soon, both Senators John Kendrick and Joseph Carey of Wyoming agreed with him, feeling (in Albright's words) "that this is an entirely impracticable proposal, that there would be a tremendous cost involved in keeping the road open, that there would be actual danger to visitors, and that above all very few people would avail themselves of the opportunity to go west by this northern route in the dead of winter."[28] The calls for plowing met high-level and more informed opposition, so they gradually ceased, at least for a few years. Cody boosters, however, would not sit still for long; by 1940, they would resume their calls for plowing Yellowstone roads.

Winter Recreation Arrives in Yellowstone

In 1932, the United States hosted the Winter Olympics in Lake Placid, New York. That event not only stimulated the country's interest in winter sports (especially skiing) but also eventually led to the development of America's ski industry. Just four years later the country's first large ski resort opened in Sun Valley, Idaho. During World War II, the maneuvers of the Tenth Mountain Division further stimulated interest in the sport. After the war, ski resorts blossomed across the country (many of them pioneered by members of the division), but especially in the West and New England. Soon, the country's new pastime knocked on Yellowstone's door, and park managers began providing an opportunity for people to pursue it, along with viewing the park's wildlife and winter scenery.[29]

The main problem for winter recreationists in Yellowstone before 1930 was access: Very little of the park was open to vehicular travel. This began to change in 1938, when Yellowstone received funding to plow the road from Mammoth to Cooke City year-round. Recall that just the year before, Yellowstone had acquired a second rotary plow, and the surrounding states were plowing most of their highways by this time. Still snowbound, however, were the residents of tiny Cooke City. The state of Montana was unable to reach its residents there by plow via Red Lodge because the Beartooth Highway, which linked the two towns, approached 11,000 feet in elevation, received immense amounts of snow and wind, and was consequently not plowable. In contrast, the road to Cooke City through Yellowstone stayed below 7,500 feet, making it far easier to plow. Sympathetic to the needs of Cooke City's seventy-five or so residents, park managers have provided access to life's necessities through Yellowstone since 1938.[30]

Actually, managers had plowed the road from Mammoth to Tower Falls (20 miles toward Cooke City from Mammoth) several times the winter before, "to encourage winter sports and to acquaint the people with the spectacular wildlife show which the park affords in winter," according to Superintendent Edmund Rogers (Albright's successor in Yellowstone). On the first weekend of January 1938, many Montana residents made the trip, and three weeks later another eighty-eight residents of Cody made the long trip around and through southern Montana for a reprise of the earlier weekend. The agency found another opportunity to provide the fun the next month, when it had to plow the road all the way to the Buffalo Ranch in Lamar Valley (about 15 miles beyond Tower Falls) to remove two cow buffalo and one cow elk for shipment to zoological gardens in Buenos Aires, Argentina. This time, some 500 people from towns throughout the region made the trip. In Rogers's words, "The weather was ideal and all roads leading to the park [via] Gardiner were bare of snow. . . . Several hundred buffalo were at the Buffalo Ranch and in the horseshoe area between the Buffalo Ranch and Tower Falls. Visitors also saw elk, deer, antelope, and mountain sheep. The occasion proved very successful."[31]

The Buffalo Ranch was *the* place to see bison at this time in Yellowstone's history.[32] Having survived their close encounter with extinction in the park, the bison had grown rapidly in number, to the point that by the 1930s, they numbered around 1,000. Park managers continued to manage them much like domestic cattle, performing such ranch-like activities as inoculating them for disease, culling excess animals, and corralling and feeding them in winter. The ranching activities and the animals' habit of migrating to lower elevations in winter, where they would find less snow and more easily obtainable forage, made them highly visible to the ranch's first winter visitors. The attraction of seeing them, as well as the new-found ability to see some winter park scenery, brought increasing numbers of local residents to the park once the road was plowed regularly.[33]

Wanting to be good hosts, park managers soon began to hold an annual celebration of winter, called "Montana Day." Superintendent Rogers described it well in his monthly report for February 1939:

A happy memory to those who attended was "Montana Day" on Sunday, February 19, when 1001 people in 278 cars were checked in through the north entrance. Considerable publicity throughout the State had been given this occasion which was sponsored by the Gardiner Commercial Club in cooperation with the National Park Service. Skiing courses suitable for amateurs as well as experienced skiers had been laid out at the "Little America" ski field [just west of the Buffalo Ranch] and this sport was enjoyed by many. Large numbers of elk, deer, antelope, mountain sheep and buffalo were seen by the visitors, particularly those who traveled the road between Gardiner and the Buffalo Ranch in the morning. Many residents of Mammoth participated in this event in addition to the number mentioned above. Sandwiches and coffee were served free of charge by the Gardiner Commercial Club at the Buffalo Ranch bunkhouse. The event provided an unusual and enjoyable outing for those who made the trip and the first winter "Montana Day" in Yellowstone National Park was chalked up as an outstanding success.

The event continued through 1942, when World War II travel restrictions put an end to it. In the festival's later years, visitors could ride through the bison corrals on a hay sled, go ice skating on a rink at Mammoth, participate in a "game stalk" on skis (a guided cross-country ski tour), observe wildlife through spotting scopes, and take advantage of a portable ski lift near the Northeast Entrance. Up to 2,300 people attended, a large number for the time.[34]

These were banner years for visitors seeking winter fun in Yellowstone, as park managers also opened a downhill ski field on nearby Mount Washburn in spring 1938. Again using their rotary plows, they plowed the first 7 miles south from Tower Falls to the "Mae West Curve" area. They waited until April, when the soft snows of winter had hardened through spring freeze-thaw cycles into a firm, easily skiable surface. The Montana Ski Association advertised the event, and 65 people took advantage of the opportunity, with another 460 people coming to enjoy the spring weather. Superintendent Rogers noted, "Skiing conditions were good at this high altitude and were appreciated by Montana skiers whose local ski courses were not available at this late date due to the melting of the snow at lower altitudes. The ski meet proved so popular that a second similar event was scheduled for Sunday, May 1." The event became an annual spring rite and was the springboard for the Yellowstone Winter Sports Association, a group organized three years later by park employees to promote skiing in the park. In 1941, the group acquired a 300-foot rope tow and installed it on the Mount Washburn slopes. After the war, group members evidently moved the rope tow to Undine Falls, closer to Mammoth Hot Springs, where most of them lived. Though park managers continued to plow out the road to Mae West Curve for spring skiing after the war, the removal of the lift probably doomed the area's popularity; the last record of its use was in 1950.[35]

Until 1994, downhill skiing was available at Undine Falls, sponsored by the same employee group, in later years called the Yellowstone Ski Association. The Undine hill was primarily for locals (it was where Mammoth and Gardiner schoolchildren learned to ski—two went on to become Olympic skiers), though any member of the public could use the facility. During the same period (through about 1990), many other western national parks, such as Rocky Mountain, Mount Rainier, Lassen Volcanic, Sequoia, and Yosemite also had small downhill ski resorts, all generally catering to park and local residents. The situation in Yellowstone began to change by 1993, when the ski association considered replacing the rope tow with a poma lift, a cable with platters attached that skiers sit upon to be hauled up the hill. The new lift seemed inappropriate to many conservationists, partly because it necessitated the removal of some old-growth Douglas-fir trees but also because the downhill ski industry had proliferated throughout the West, making downhill skiing commonly available. The major resorts offered much greater vertical drops than the small national park lifts, most of which had therefore closed over the past ten years. In Yellowstone's case, three major ski resorts were located within 75 miles. Responding to the public outcry, Yellowstone managers removed the Undine Falls development entirely in 1994.[36]

Although times changed and the appropriateness of downhill skiing in national parks came to be questioned, the situation in the late 1930s and 1940s was such that it seemed appropriate. More important is that the availability of down-hill skiing stimulated winter visitation to Yellowstone. By World War II, a winter visitor to Yellowstone could ski, view wildlife, and drive all the way to Cooke City. Still, the visitor had no access to the park's interior and such famous wonders as Old Faithful Geyser and the Lower Falls of the Yellowstone. It was probably inevitable, then, that surrounding communities would want more access to Yellowstone, namely in the form of additional plowed roads. Soon, the park had a déjà vu experience with Cody.

Round Two: Cody Again Calls for Plowed Roads in the Park

Since the matter of plowing Yellowstone's roads had been settled in 1932, the Cody Club had remained anxious to stimulate the town's winter economy. Watching all the winter activities beginning in 1938, the group's desire to see Yellowstone's roads plowed soon came out of hibernation. The next year, members contacted their congressional delegation to request another look at the Yellowstone plowing matter. Initially, Arno Cammerer, Albright's successor as NPS director, responded by stonewalling the requests. Eventually, though, Cammerer had enough congressional pressure that his chief of engineering asked Yellowstone managers to prepare a cost estimate of keeping park roads open throughout the winter. Once again, park managers took a careful look at road plowing, and as before, they would conclude it was not feasible. And again, the conclusion would not entirely satisfy local communities.[37]

To gather information on plowing's feasibility and cost, park managers actually plowed the road from Mammoth to Old Faithful twice in early 1940. Using that experience, Acting Superintendent J. W. Emmert transmitted the cost estimates to Cammerer. Emmert began by making the case for constructing seven permanent road camps throughout the park. After noting that park facilities had never been constructed for winter use (an accurate message that park managers would repeat as future decades brought the same requests), he then explained how severe Yellowstone's climate could be and that the road camps were essential. They could function as bases for the snow-plowing equipment, for the winter ranger patrols, and for visitor services, providing fuel, supplies, and lodging. Winterizing the buildings and purchasing the necessary equipment would total $274,000, with recurring annual costs totaling $101,000, compared to the existing outlay of only $8,400 to plow the northern roads throughout winter and to open the rest of the park's road system in spring. Emmert estimated that the additional entrance fee revenue would defray the annual costs by about $30,000.[38] For the era, these were high figures, and they quickly met with criticism, especially in the

Cody press and from some congressional representatives. Still, the agency defended them, explaining that Cody's weather is not Yellowstone's weather.[39]

This controversy soon reached a climax, albeit a more local (and unexpected) one than the earlier debate's. By 1937, the three local states had formed the Tri-State Yellowstone Civic Association to advocate a longer summer season in Yellowstone. Responding to the Cody Club's request to discuss the plowing matter, the civic association met in Livingston, Montana, on February 17, 1940. However, no one from Cody or its Club was present; their representative, Breck Moran, editor of the *Cody Enterprise,* was delayed in Yellowstone. Rather than driving to the meeting, he had decided to ski through the park on his own to learn about Yellowstone's winter conditions firsthand. Encountering −30°F temperatures and badly blistering his feet, Moran skied until 11:00 P.M. some evenings. Having underestimated how much the soft snow would delay his travel, he arrived in Livingston an hour after the meeting had adjourned and was therefore unable to present his town's case in favor of plowed roads.[40]

Idaho had also failed to send anyone to the meeting, so it was attended exclusively by interests from five Montana cities. Bozeman's delegate began the meeting by stating that it was hard to believe that many people would travel through the park when U.S. Highway 10, by now open through the friendlier route in southern Montana (and Bozeman) in winter, still saw little travel. No one present felt that opening the roads would be economically justified, so they voted unanimously to oppose any Yellowstone road openings at that time (though they noted that future conditions could change the situation). Additionally, a representative of the Northern Pacific Railway defended the park's plowing estimates, arguing that Yellowstone had erred on the conservative side (the railroad was probably interested in preserving itself as the provider of winter transportation).[41]

It is probably no surprise that park managers, who also attended the meeting, were pleased at its outcome and spread the news about it. Moreover, they were disappointed that Moran was absent, for they felt that the Montana representatives would have persuaded him away from his and Cody's proposal to plow park roads.[42]

The civic association may also have been influenced by Yellowstone's promise the previous autumn to extend the summer season longer into spring and fall. The agency did indeed keep that promise, opening some roads as early as late March in 1940, 1941, and 1942. Specifically, those were the mid-elevation roads on Yellowstone's west side, from Mammoth to West Yellowstone and Old Faithful. Plowing was generally more feasible there than on the high-elevation roads on Yellowstone's eastern and southern sides, especially Sylvan Pass and the Lewis Lake Divide on the South Entrance Road. The mid-elevation roads on the west side receive only around 150 inches of snow per winter, compared to 200–300 inches on the east side roads. Despite the early openings, however, few motorists drove the roads, reinforcing park managers' reluctance to plow all winter. As was soon evident, however, the Cody Club's enthusiasm was not fazed.[43]

With Moran's absence at the civic association meeting weakening its position, the Cody Club next proposed a compromise on the issue: that Yellowstone managers plow the west side roads year-round, instead of only opening them earlier in spring. Such a proposal recognized the inherent feasibility of plowing those mid-elevation roads, echoing the park's recent spring plowing efforts. According to the *Cody Enterprise,* the Club's proposal was "an opening wedge" in the discussion, a stepping stone to plowing all park roads. Additionally, the Club successfully persuaded the Tri-State Civic Association to reverse its earlier resolution against plowing and instead support the group's compromise.[44]

The Club was undoubtedly influenced by Breck Moran, who was not persuaded against plowing by his skiing experience or by the Montana delegates' position at the meeting. As the winter progressed, he published a series of articles about skiing in Yellowstone. He drew not only upon his February adventure but also upon a separate trip to Sylvan Pass that same winter. He and his five companions had found it to be in typical condition, "looking and feeling like the gates of hell," with a roaring blizzard in action. Despite that view, he continued to feel that motorized travel through Yellowstone was possible and urged park managers to plow their roads. His enthusiasm for this venture, despite his firsthand knowledge of the winter dangers in Yellowstone and on Sylvan Pass, demonstrated well the town's booster optimism. Cody and its Club seemed to be against basic geography, ignoring the now obvious evidence that plowing roads across rugged Sylvan Pass and extreme Yellowstone was not a good idea.[45]

Still, Yellowstone had done its homework and stood its ground. Acting Director Arthur E. Demaray, writing one of the many congressional representatives lobbying for plowed roads, summarized his agency's position by stating, "In view of the considerable additional cost that would be involved, the severe climatic conditions, the small number of persons who would visit the park in winter, and the small amount of additional revenue that would accrue to the Government, it is not considered advisable to keep the Yellowstone National Park roads open for winter travel." Nevertheless, the agency received quite a bit of political pressure throughout 1941 to alter its position. Perhaps it might eventually have begun some plowing, but the advent of World War II changed all playing fields. The issue died until after the war.[46]

Enter the Snowplanes

Although Yellowstone's managers were reluctant to plow their roads, creative mechanics in the United States and Canada had long dealt with snow-covered roads differently, by developing oversnow vehicles. Soon, entrepreneurs near Yellow-stone began using such vehicles, and it would not take long for some of them to knock on Yellowstone's doors for permission to enter. Actually, park managers themselves were feeling an increasing need for some form of mechanical over-snow transport. These needs and the recreational desires of local residents would soon both be met by an unconventional vehicle known as the "snowplane."

In both 1932 and 1937, winter keepers in the park's interior had come down with illnesses requiring evacuation. The two incidents involved similar rescues. Park rangers and winter keepers contrived patient sleds that they either pulled or harnessed to horses to pull and then proceeded on snowshoes or skis toward Mammoth with the patients. At the same time, managers there sent a rotary plow southward as fast as possible to meet the rescuers. Drifts of snow, cold weather, and a blizzard in the latter case challenged the skiers, but they rendezvoused near Norris Junction and transferred their patients to an ambulance following the plow. The patients then traveled to Livingston, and in both cases successfully re-covered, one from a ruptured appendix and the other from an unrecorded mal-ady. Both cases received national press coverage and illustrated the risks involved in stationing people in areas remote from motorized vehicular travel.[47]

The need for oversnow vehicles was evident not only in Yellowstone. Although the U.S. snowbelt states were plowing most roads by this time, they left some roads unplowed, and storms would close others, stranding people. Some of them coped with the situation by continuing to use horse-drawn sleighs or dogsleds, but others felt that plowing and traditional technologies were not the only ways to contend with snow. In more than one backyard or garage, mechanically gifted in-dividuals devised different versions of oversnow vehicles, usually featuring some kind of passenger box or seat on skis with a motor-driven track or rubber drive (once the latter became available). The earliest such vehicles dated to the late 1800s, and one was even mass-produced in the 1920s. Based on the Model T Ford and produced by Virgil White in New Hampshire, it was called the "Snowmobile." White produced about 25,000 of them before fire destroyed his factory in 1928, ending his foray into oversnow technology.[48]

White's Snowmobile, like most of those produced elsewhere before 1930, was heavy, slow, and utilitarian—a product of his era. Because the modern small and lightweight two-cycle engine was still several decades away from commercial pro-duction, White had no choice but to use a standard four-cycle, and typically heavy, engine. His Snowmobile had a high engine/vehicle weight ratio, which meant the vehicle struggled to go faster than 15 or 20 miles per hour. Such vehi-cles plowed through snow as much as they traveled on top of it—an improvement over an automobile in unplowed conditions, but still slow and cumbersome. Their recreational potential was limited, as was even their utility in the softer, deeper snow found in the Rockies. For these reasons, White's Snowmobile, like all the others produced in this era, was limited to utilitarian purposes and did not revolutionize winter transportation.[49]

That revolution would not fully occur until 1959, though steps in that direction were taken in the 1920s and 1930s by two other mechanics. Joseph-Armand Bombardier and Karl Lorch, inventors operating independently of each other in different parts of Canada, both saw that snow's softness made vehicle weight crucial. So, they took cues from another vehicle in which every ounce mattered—the airplane—for mechanized oversnow travel. In the 1920s both men developed a "snowplane," a vehicle with a one- or two-person cab, set on three or four skis (one or two in front, for steering, and two in back), and a small rear-mounted airplane engine. The vehicles had no wings, so they did not become airborne. However, their powerful engines made them capable of speeds over 100 miles per hour, so they figuratively took off, at least over open snow. Lorch mass-produced snowplanes for thirty-five years beginning in 1928. The vehicles' unguarded propellers limited their practicality for widespread use, but they did still find some buyers, including a few in the Yellowstone area. Bombardier never mass-produced snowplanes, but his later creations (the snowcoach and modern snowmobile) would come to play important roles in Yellowstone's history.[50]

Two other snowplane makers, garage owners from Anaconda, Montana, actually traveled to Yellowstone in January 1939 to demonstrate snowplane advantages to park managers. They drove their home-built 65-horsepower machine back and forth over Swan Lake Flats with a different staff member on board each time, convincing the skeptics that motorized oversnow travel was indeed possible, even in Yellowstone's soft, deep-snow conditions. Park managers witnessed their potential again in March 1942 when they allowed Glen Simmons of the federal Reclamation Service to drive from the South Entrance to Old Faithful in a snowplane (to do some needed work). He made the 80-mile round trip in less than eight hours, spending some of that time trying to get over dry ground in the Old Faithful area. In some areas of Yellowstone, geothermal activity warms the ground enough to melt snow, making steering difficult for oversnow vehicles that steer with skis because they have no purchase on the bare pavement. Such areas would continue to challenge oversnow vehicle travelers, but they were not so extensive that they precluded such travel altogether. Despite the dry ground, the two snowplane feasibility demonstrations soon influenced park managers to adopt the new transportation mode.[51]

A year later, they began using a snowplane themselves. Initially, they used a rented machine to transport patrol rangers from Mammoth to the Norris and Canyon areas. Rangers drove the snowplane to trailheads for ski patrol, rather than skiing the road as well, enabling them to shorten their patrols by several

Snowplane and Colorado Highway Maintenance Supervisor Charlie Shumate at West Thumb Geyser Basin, 1957. Park managers and early visitors used such vehicles for touring Yellowstone. Home-built vehicles, they consisted of a one- or two-person cab mounted on skis with an airplane engine and propeller on the back (left side of photo—propeller is in motion). They could go quite fast but did not become airborne. Shumate was probably in the park as part of the Snow Survey Committee (see page 43). NPS photo.

days. Finding that snowplane travel made everyone's life easier, park managers bought a machine for NPS use the following January. Though they had some initial difficulties with it in powdery snow, they eventually became more experienced with it, grew to depend on it for transportation in the park interior, and bought a second machine to supplement the first.[52]

Managers soon found new uses for the snowplanes. Always captivating to people, Yellowstone was drawing more winter interest from writers and reporters. When reporters and photographers wanted to go into the park interior for winter research, Yellowstone managers summoned their snowplanes. Lowell Thomas, a well-known skier and NBC radio news commentator, and *Look* magazine both published pieces researched via snowplanes. Additionally, park managers made two more rescues of employees stationed in the interior with snowplanes. The ease of these two rescues, thanks to the simplicity of snowplane travel, evidently made them less newsworthy than the earlier two, for no published accounts of them seem to exist.[53]

As with other technologies our society produces for utilitarian purposes, Americans eventually found recreational potential in snowplanes. Once visitors resumed their winter trips to Yellowstone after World War II, and with the press starting to show the park's interior winter wonders to the world, it was inevitable that someone would look upon snowplanes as more than simply utilitarian. Soon, snowplane owners from West Yellowstone and Jackson, two gateway communities with much snowier winters than Cody, would put snowplanes to a new use.[54]

Jackson residents tested the waters first, with thoughts of offering regularly scheduled trips to Old Faithful from Moran, Wyoming (Moran was about 20 miles south of Yellowstone's South Entrance and as close as plowed roads came to Yellowstone from Jackson at the time). In December 1947, the area's rumor mill brought the proposals to the attention of Jackson Hole National Monument (predecessor to Grand Teton National Park) Superintendent John S. McLaughlin, who quickly tipped off Yellowstone Superintendent Rogers to the possibility. McLaughlin additionally warned him that the idea's promoters were "friendly to the National Park scheme of things in Jackson Hole," and that they "will not be easily talked out of [their idea]," even though common sense seemed to suggest to him that Jackson Hole did not get enough winter tourism to make the idea profitable at that time.[55]

The possibility of regularly scheduled trips stirred anxious discussion among park managers. Such visitors would be taking serious risks where little, if any, medical or mechanical help was available. Moving quickly, Acting Yellowstone Superintendent Fred Johnston wrote the regional director requesting advice in the matter. Because the idea was a business proposal, it would (if accepted) more formally condone and welcome winter visitor use of the park's interior than if snowplane owners had merely requested permission to enter the park for personal pleasure. The proposal highlighted the lack of foresight or planning by park managers regarding interior winter visitor use. Because they had successfully resisted Cody's calls for plowing, they may have assumed that visitation to the park interior would not happen. However, snowplanes could change that situation, a fact that park managers had evidently not foreseen.[56]

Sensing the potential precedent in the proposal, Regional Director Lawrence Merriam quickly directed Yellowstone managers not to issue a business permit for regularly scheduled trips. Because private, individual trips would not so clearly welcome travel to Yellowstone's winter interior, Merriam felt that the agency was "hardly in a position" to prevent them. Consequently, if such personal trips materialized, he suggested the travelers register with the rangers at the South Entrance, and that the rangers fully inform them of the risks they were taking.[57] It seems odd that Merriam and Johnston felt helpless to prevent such individual trips into the park, as they had already turned down many a potential cross-country skier. Perhaps they felt more willing to allow motorized use than cross-country skier travel because motorized users had additional lines of defense against winter emergencies (not only could they take refuge in their vehicles, but they could also carry more emergency equipment). Or, perhaps their confusion over the future of winter use explained their seeming helplessness. The only guidance the NPS had issued on a national scale for winter park visitor uses made no mention of over-snow vehicles and deferred policy-making on backcountry skiing until such time as demand warranted it[58] (Yellowstone's managers probably felt that time had already arrived). What was appropriate motorized use in winter, and what was not? And what exactly was safe in the current unstaffed, wilderness-like conditions? Such questions were difficult to answer, and any answer given would soon be challenged by society's tendency to develop other new machines.

As it turned out, snowplane trips from Jackson did not materialize for several more years. Instead, the first private visitor trips by snowplane into the park interior originated from West Yellowstone, which was only half the distance to Old Faithful (30 miles) as Moran. In January 1949, thirty-five visitors entered the West Entrance, most of them traveling to Old Faithful, with one going on to the West Thumb area. Superintendent Rogers wrote, "This is the first winter that snowplanes have entered the park for purely pleasure trips and it appears that this mode of travel is becoming more popular." Such trips continued sporadically throughout that winter and into the 1950s, with Jackson snowplane owners eventually entering through the South Entrance. Never overwhelmingly popular, they did make it possible, and presumably enjoyable, to do something that was never possible before—experience Yellowstone's winter wonderland in motorized oversnow vehicles.[59]

Few records of these early trips survive, but they must have been memorable experiences. Yellowstone's incredible winter landscape was finally available for people to experience without days of arduous skiing: the meadows and mountains covered with snow; the waterfalls encased in ice; the rivers open due to thermal flow and frequented by waterfowl; the bison and elk easily visible from the relatively low-lying roads; the geysers and hot springs sending up plumes of steam and fog; and the forests covered in snow and, in the thermal areas, turned into "ghost trees" with frost condensed from geyser steam. It was a new world to anyone who visited, an almost magical experience made possible by the eclectic snowplane. Those brave enough to visit undoubtedly regaled their friends and families with tales of the wonders they had seen. It is not surprising, then, that some snowplane owners soon began taking annual trips into the park; the unique experiences provided by their vehicles were well worth repeating.[60]

The vehicles were themselves a source of adventure, if for some reason Yellowstone's wonders were not adequately entertaining. Many snowplane models had no brakes, so drivers had to be alert: The friction of passing over snow was the only effective braking action. Protected only by some guard rods, passengers had to mind the dangerous propeller blades. Snowplanes could be fast, too (and therefore fun to many); the late West Yellowstone snowplane owner Walt Stuart recalled zooming across Yellowstone Lake at 140 miles per hour (while his snowplane probably went only half that fast, it undoubtedly felt like 140 mph). He also recalled one incident on the lake where his passenger pointed out that their tracks were filling with water behind them. Stuart said later, "We figured there was probably more ice underneath, but we never stopped to find out!"[61] Fun and fabulous, the Yellowstone winter experience was addictive.

With the snowplane's arrival in Yellowstone, the park entered the second half of the twentieth century as a winter destination. While its status as a destination was not initially obvious, in part because plowing advocates would soon divert attention to another debate on the matter, continually growing visitation would soon make that status clearer.

Round Three: More Calls for Plowing

Not privy to the snowplane fun were the residents of Wyoming's Bighorn Basin, isolated from Yellowstone's interior scenery by the forbidding Sylvan Pass. Residents did, however, take part in the country's increasing fascination with skiing. In 1939, Breck Moran and other Cody residents organized the Shoshone Alpine Club to promote downhill skiing in the area. For them, the best snow existed near the East Entrance at Pahaska Tepee. By March 1939, the group had opened a ski lift there, made accessible by a State Highway Commission agreement to extend plowing to the area. Finding their venture successful, the club soon moved their lifts across the road to the Sleeping Giant area, which had better terrain. Though they had to close the resort during World War II, the availability of skiing so close to Yellowstone would eventually result in yet another request for plowed park roads.[62]

For all Americans, World War II was a significant departure from normal life. Rationing, travel restrictions, and scrap metal drives were obvious signs that the country was experiencing a crisis, although the extent of eventual involvement in the war was not immediately evident. The Cody Club, for example, continued its efforts to see Yellowstone's roads plowed, altering its previous economic reasoning to suggest that the roads be kept open in winter as a defense measure. The Club also wrote Wyoming congressmen to suggest that the armed forces use Yellowstone as a training ground, similar to the way the 87th Mountain Infantry Regiment (predecessor to the Tenth Mountain Division) was training at Mount Rainier National Park in Washington. As the war progressed, however, the Club fell silent, probably because the country's increasing war involvement diverted attention away from such booster causes. Additionally, because the NPS would not allow the 87th to use even ammunition blanks at Mount Rainier, let alone live ammunition, the army moved the regiment to Camp Hale in Colorado in 1942. Removing the military presence from Mount Rainier took the wind out of the Club's sails.[63]

Once the war ended, Cody witnessed many of the same social changes that the rest of the country saw. Wartime rationing and travel restrictions were lifted, prosperity swept over much of America, and Americans found themselves with more vacation time. Tourism boomed; Yellowstone, for example, saw 1 million visitors for the first time in 1948, while its prewar high, in 1941, was only 600,000. The tourism industry responded accordingly, doubling the national number of motor courts between 1939 and 1948. Several opened in Cody during this era, such as today's Parkway Inn. These trends were not only manifested in the summertime; people began to travel more in winter, too, especially as Tenth Mountain Division members opened their ski resorts. Locally, the Shoshone Alpine Club reopened Sleeping Giant late in 1946. A steady number of skiers, now free to travel, visited and participated in races and festivals held there annually. Once there, some took a side trip to the East Entrance for cross-country skiing. Such visits augmented the long-standing desire by area residents to see Yellowstone's roads plowed.[64]

In most ways, this round of pressure to plow Yellowstone's roads was similar to the previous two. Local communities, partly led by Bighorn Basin interests, called upon park managers to plow their roads; Yellowstone managers responded by citing earlier estimates of the cost of plowing; plowing supporters disputed those costs and elevated the debate to their congressional representatives; and the NPS responded with updated plowing feasibility estimates that finally snuffed out the debate.

In some ways, though, this round differed. First, the Gardiner (Montana) Commercial Club played perhaps a more influential role in this debate than the Bighorn Basin interests did. When park roads closed annually in fall, Gardiner residents found that a trip to West Yellowstone or Idaho became over 100 miles longer, because they now had to drive north through Livingston and Bozeman to get around Yellowstone's closed roads. Consequently, Gardiner was especially interested in opening the mid-elevation roads from Mammoth Hot Springs to West Yellowstone (and the side trip to Old Faithful). Though the Greybull (Wyoming) Club was the first to make the call for plowing (in 1946), the Gardiner Commercial Club soon followed, sending representatives throughout southern Idaho and Montana (the two regions most likely to benefit from plowed west side roads) to promote the idea. The Gardiner club was also active politically, writing congressional representatives and rebutting NPS arguments against plowing.[65]

Gardiner's entry into the recurring debate challenged Yellowstone's managers. Because they faced the same longer winter trip to West Yellowstone and beyond as Gardiner residents, they privately sympathized with the request. Additionally, their knowledge of the milder conditions on the park's west side and previous plowing experiments there told them that Gardiner's request was much more feasible than Cody's recurring one.[66] However, they felt that to respond positively to it could open the door to plowing all park roads, because some Bighorn Basin interests seemingly could not understand the difference between the west side roads and "the gates of hell." Attempting to prevent Gardiner's proposal from becoming an opening wedge for the larger proposal, park managers decided to keep the discussion as an all-or-nothing proposal: Plow all of Yellowstone's roads or keep things as they were, plowing only the low-elevation north-side roads. They knew they still had to be prepared to discuss Gardiner's proposal separately, but the entrance of Bighorn Basin interests into the debate the following year successfully kept the focus on the larger plowing question.[67]

In 1948, the Big Horn Basin Clubs[68] (a federation of area commercial clubs, including those in Cody) joined the pro-plowing movement. The Cody Club itself was now divided on the issue, but Breck Moran, still editor of the *Cody Enterprise,* was Cody's representative to the Big Horn Basin Clubs. He continued to editorialize in favor of opening Yellowstone's roads in winter, and he was probably influential in convincing the larger regional group to promote plowing.[69] The entry of the federation of clubs helped to elevate the debate to a more national level. Now, the NPS knew that its 1940 estimates, which it had been using to respond to the plowing demands, would no longer suffice. To prepare new estimates and assess plowing's feasibility, park managers asked the Public Roads Administration (PRA) to review the issue late in 1948.[70] Going for outside review was a smart move for park managers because the country's highway administration was the expert on roads and plowing and would therefore be an objective third party (park managers undoubtedly hoped the PRA would add credibility to their position).

The PRA agreed to do the assessment and solicited information on snowfall, wind, avalanches, emergency traveler facilities, and summer season opening and closing dates from park managers.[71] In early 1949, the agency issued a report entirely affirming the NPS position. In fact, the PRA came up with substantially higher estimates both for upfront equipment purchase and building winterization costs ($505,500) and also for annual recurring costs ($337,000). These estimates were higher partly because the agency included costs for plowing the Beartooth Highway (finished in 1936, the highway was annually cleared of winter snow in the springtime by the NPS).[72] Including it in the estimate exemplified the federal agencies' attempt to frame the plowing questions as an all-or-nothing debate.

Still, the PRA's estimates for plowing the remainder of Yellowstone's highways were consistent with Yellowstone's own 1940 estimates. Further, by examining tourist travel on open roads elsewhere in the region, the PRA estimated that Yellowstone winter travel would be only 5 percent of the summer volume and less during severe winters. That volume would still require shelter houses, road camps, and periodic patrols. Because none of these were currently provided, the agency wrote that "administrative problems of the Park Service would be increased manyfold." Shortly afterward, the state highway directors for Wyoming and Idaho concurred with the report's assessment. PRA Commissioner Thomas MacDonald, in transmitting the report to NPS Director Newton B. Drury, concluded, "The proposal to attempt winter snow removal on the Yellowstone Park Highway System, besides being a hazardous and an impracticable undertaking, is economically unsound."[73] For the muted terms typical of government correspondence, these were strong words.

The report ended the debate. With such a strong affirmation of its position, the NPS quickly discussed the findings with Secretary of the Interior Oscar Chapman. He concurred in its recommendations and decided against plowing Yellowstone's roads. The park then announced the findings and the anti-plowing decision to the area's congressional representatives and the Big Horn Basin Clubs. The commercial clubs responded with few other calls for plowing, at least for another eight years.[74]

As before, the recurring controversy ended with a compromise of sorts. Distancing itself from the failed plowing proposal, the Jackson Chamber of Commerce asked park managers to return to the extended summer plowed road season that they had begun in 1940 (managers had curtailed spring and fall plowing during the war). Other chambers in the Jackson area echoed the chamber's request, as did some residents of Cody. Park managers responded by acquiring a fourth rotary plow in 1951 to open the roads by May 1 on the park's west side and May 25 on the east side. It would not be long before mechanical problems with those plows triggered the fourth plowing controversy. Before that could happen, however, West Yellowstone residents would introduce another oversnow vehicle for visitor use.[75]

Snowcoaches: A Good Tourist Gimmick

Yellowstone, always a source of fascination for Americans, increasingly exerted its pull upon winter visitors. With access to Yellowstone made possible by snowplanes, a small but consistent stream of visitors went to Old Faithful. These brave souls had the park to themselves; compared to summertime, when a million or more visitors toured the park, Yellowstone was practically empty. Enjoying the solitude and scenery, the winter explorers brought back glowing reports. Soon, a few more writers and reporters made the snowplane trip as well. Correspondents and photographers for *Collier's, Life,* and *Natural History* all visited Yellowstone by snowplane in the early 1950s and published articles about the winter wonderland and its snowbound rangers. With their interest stimulated, more and more visitors took advantage of the newly opened winter door, and local entrepreneurs responded by acquiring and offering tours in another type of oversnow vehicle.[76]

Watching the snowplanes and observing the increasing visitation were Harold Young and Bill Nicholls, two motel owners in West Yellowstone. They realized that Yellowstone's winter wonderland could be a "good tourist gimmick." So, they proposed commercial park tours in their snowplanes to Yellowstone managers, who turned them down, just as they would have done with the Jackson entrepreneurs a few years earlier.[77]

Soon, however, Young and Nicholls acquired two "Snowmobiles" manufactured by Bombardier of Quebec. This Snowmobile was just as heavy as White's earlier New Hampshire model of the same name but accommodated up to ten passengers in a large enclosed cab set on skis and tracks. Bombardier had begun producing such machines in 1936, with local authorities there adapting them for use as school buses and mail trucks and doctors using them to make house calls. In Yellowstone, the vehicles had two clear benefits for commercial touring: They had a larger, more comfortable cab that could carry more people than snowplanes, and the unguarded propeller was gone. Effectively, these vehicles could open Yellowstone's interior wonders to more visitors. Today we call them "snowcoaches" to distinguish them from the smaller snowmobiles that would arrive in Yellowstone in a few years.[78]

With their new vehicles, Young and Nicholls again requested permission to offer commercial park tours. In so doing, they were attempting to combine American ingenuity with entrepreneurism to help tourists enjoy Yellowstone's snow-covered roads. The public and other entrepreneurs were knocking on the park's door, begging for permission to enter. Once again, park managers needed to make a decision: Was such use appropriate? Were they ready for it? More broadly, what should winter visitor use in Yellowstone look like? Looking to national policy, they found that winter use guidance had not changed; motorized oversnow uses were still not addressed. Still, even though winter visitors faced some serious risks entering Yellowstone, more and more they wanted to come in anyway.[79]

Yellowstone's managers again refused Young and Nicholls, but the two men would not take no for an answer and continued to request permission annually.

A Bombardier "Snowmobile" (called a "snowcoach" today), 1968. Admitted in 1955, such vehicles could carry up to twelve people in a heated interior. As many as 2,000 visitors per winter enjoyed park tours in these Snowmobiles in the 1950s and early 1960s; some models are still in use in Yellowstone today. In the 1960s, the first Bombardier "ski-doos," modern-day snowmobiles, entered Yellowstone; the Yellowstone Park Company then playfully called this model a "King Size Ski-Doo." NPS photo.

In January 1955, their persistence paid off. The managers granted them a one-year permit for such tours, with several conditions. First, the two men could not advertise their service. Second, they would always have to hold a vehicle in reserve, in the event of a breakdown (the first of which occurred just a year later). And third, they had to carry emergency supplies and basic repair equipment in whatever vehicle was in service. This was an experimental permit, to see if the concept could work.[80] That experimental protocol was evident in the directive against advertising, a proscription that also indicated park managers' uncertainty about the future of winter use.

The managers' approach toward skier requests to tour the park also reflected continued uncertainty, both nationally and locally; the NPS's Washington office had still not issued guidance on such backcountry tours. As before, Yellowstone managers granted some parties permission for tours while capriciously turning others down. They even acknowledged this inconsistency in a 1949 letter refusing permission to one Bozeman party while noting that they were allowing a different party of Boy Scouts from the same area to enter the park. In their defense, park managers noted that the Scouts were taking a safer route (not over 8,800-foot Dunraven Pass, as the other party proposed) and argued that the Scout trip was an experiment to see if well-prepared young men could successfully undertake the park's winter conditions. As it turned out, the Scouts did not make their goal of reaching Old Faithful, but still enjoyed touring the park, and a few years later they did succeed in reaching the famous geyser. It would not be long before park managers regularly allowed such visits, reflecting increasing comfort with winter visitor use and the increasing popularity of cross-country skiing.[81]

Young and Nicholls, with a permit finally in hand, did not share the park managers' uncertainty about whether oversnow vehicle use was appropriate, and their tours quickly became popular. In March 1955, just two months after the tours began, *Parade* magazine featured an article about the tours. About 300 people took the tour that winter, and numbers varied from 300 to 600 over the next few winters. By 1963, the winter total approached 1,000, leading the two men to add more Snowmobiles to their fleet. About that same time they began offering package tours with the Northern Pacific Railway; for one fee, visitors received round-trip railroad transportation from Chicago and two days of touring in Yellowstone and West Yellowstone. Their business lasted some ten years; in 1966, they were forced to relinquish their permit to the Yellowstone Park Company because it began offering its own snowcoach tours. Under the NPS concession rules then in place, the concessioner had the exclusive right to offer transportation in the park.[82]

With the number of winter visitors increasing (see Table 1.1), park managers soon had to accept that winter use was there to stay. They also needed more of their own oversnow vehicles. They had acquired some army Weasels for winter patrols and transportation in the late 1940s (Weasels were tracked vehicles used by the military in World War II for amphibious and snow-covered terrain operations like landing at the beaches of Normandy). One Weasel was stationed at Old Faithful for use by its winter keeper (who, interestingly, laid in over 2 *tons* of food for himself and his family for a winter). A decade later, they also acquired a Tucker SnoCat, a more comfortable, four-track-drive vehicle that they used for special guest trips into the interior.[83]

Still, there is little evidence that park managers gave much thought to, or had much guidance on, winter use or what it should be like in the future. Having defeated calls for plowing three times already, managers probably viewed plowing as the default option for winter transportation. Oversnow vehicles were already popular, but managers probably could not envision a winter visitation program

Table 1.1. Winter Visitation to Yellowstone National Park, 1948–1961

Year	Number of Visitors on Snowmachines	Total Visitation, Dec.–March*
1948–1949	>61	3,888
1949–1950	162	8,077
1950–1951	8 (very mild winter)	8,180
1951–1952	>56	8,198
1952–1953	>59	3,314
1953–1954	171	4,913
1954–1955	631	4,995
1955–1956	580	3,242
1956–1957	533	3,223
1957–1958	>85	2,442
1958–1959	>345	2,679
1959–1960	>265	2,552
1960–1961	508	4,363

*Total visitation includes visitors entering the North Entrance by car; it is unclear why the three winters around 1950 saw such higher use than the other winters.
Source: SMRs from 1948 to 1961, Yellowstone National Park Research Library, Gardiner, Montana.

dependent solely on them—they were viewed as oddities or curiosities rather than modes of transportation, and rightly so. They were expensive and had inherent problems that limited their suitability for widespread use. Conversely, Young and Nicholls demonstrated that others could envision mass transportation over snow. It would not be long before the continuing American interest in winter recreation would combine with American (and Canadian) technological ingenuity to produce an oversnow vehicle that would revolutionize winter travel. At the time, however, the difficulty of predicting the effects of broad American trends on park-level operations (or the local novelty of such vehicles) meant that there was little planning for the future of oversnow vehicle use in Yellowstone. Then, as now, park managers were busy, with little time to ponder such subjects; more commonly, the worries of the day occupied their thoughts. Park budgets were tight, winter equipment was expensive, and the agency struggled to get what it needed. Finally, several scholars argue that the agency valued visitor accommodation more than resource preservation at this time in its history. Such a predisposition would encourage managers to allow winter use, even though they were not well prepared for it.[84]

Improvements in technology brought other unanticipated problems. For example, the oversnow vehicles that were now plying Yellowstone's snow-covered roads compacted the snow over which they traveled. Over the course of a winter, repeated trips turned the snow roads into compacted avenues of near-solid ice, making spring plowing difficult, especially on the busiest tour route between Old Faithful and West Yellowstone. Plow operators responded with creativity, using graders to peel off the ice (as opposed to rotary plows, which worked best in un-packed snow). Such creativity did not solve all problems; another effect of over-snow vehicle use was pavement scarring, caused by Bombardier skis scraping bare pavement in the thermally warmed areas. In the 1970s, park managers began to spread wood chips in such areas to prevent this kind of damage.[85] Still, these were Band-Aid solutions to a problem park managers still did not fully grasp: People wanted to see Yellowstone in the winter, and the tools were now available for them to do so, but park budgets and facilities were not meeting these new demands (nor was winter's severity changing).

Another winter toy soon came to Yellowstone: the modern-day snowmobile. However, another round of questions about plowing preceded it, a round that eclipsed all previous rounds in intensity and duration.

Round Four: Feasible But Not Practical

The 1949 assessment of plowing's feasibility did not settle the issue for long; park managers rested on its conclusions for less than a decade. This time, the recurring controversy began with a natural event, a heavier than normal winter that delayed the spring opening. The delays prompted the state of Wyoming to carry the banner for plowing this time (the presence of a Cody resident in the governor's chair helped elevate the issue beyond the town), and it demanded year-round plowed roads in Yellowstone as the town had previously. Once again, the NPS responded with estimates of plowing costs and demonstrated that park geography and modern tourist patterns could not justify plowing. There were many echoes of the previous controversies, echoes that again provide important insights into the relationship between Yellowstone and its neighbors—and among humans, nature, and geography.

It began surreptitiously, with a heavy winter snowfall that made spring plowing slow and tedious in 1956. As park managers still do today, they began the annual plowing effort at Mammoth Hot Springs, where the plows were overhauled throughout the winter. Beginning in late March, two plows began heading south toward Norris. There, managers doubled their number, with two plows proceeding toward Canyon and on to Lake, while two others plowed to Madison, Old Faithful, and West Yellowstone. All told, these sections of roadway took two or three weeks to plow. At that point, the easy work was done. Continuing south and east toward those respective entrances, the plows began to encounter up to 10 feet

Rotary plow in Yellowstone, 1960s or 1970s. Clearing Yellowstone's roads of the winter snow accumulation in spring takes two or three months, with up to six rotary plows necessary. The Sylvan Pass and Lewis River Divide snowbelts on the East and South Entrance Roads, respectively, present the greatest challenge to the plow crews, with snow depths such as this—and more than twice this amount in certain areas—being common. NPS photo.

of snow on the level. These entrance roads, each about 25 miles long, cross the Lewis River Divide and Absaroka snow belts, respectively, where such snow depths were (and in heavy winters still are) the norm. It would ordinarily take the plow crews up to a month to clear these two roads; exacerbating the difficulties in 1956 were numerous fallen trees on the road. With the plow crews lagging behind on the South Entrance Road, Yellowstone Superintendent Rogers requested assistance from Grand Teton National Park managers. They responded with another rotary plow, but encountered problems with it and had to cease plowing after just 2 miles. Consequently, Yellowstone managers continued with their own plows, supplementing them with bulldozers to blade the deep snow down to rotary plow height. Despite these problems, park staff still managed to open the East Entrance a day early and the South Entrance only two days later than scheduled.[86]

The South Entrance delay, along with some misinformation, resulted in demands that Yellowstone managers open all entrances simultaneously. Some early-season tourists, perhaps believing that the entrance would open on May 15 as the American Automobile Association (AAA) had told them—not May 25 as the NPS had scheduled—had to alter their travel plans. Fred Houchens of the Jackson Hole Chamber of Commerce soon complained to park managers and Wyoming

Governor Milward Simpson. He and Simpson suffered from additional misinformation, believing that the Grand Teton plows were idled not by mechanical problems but by bureaucratic red tape (insufficient funds). They demanded that park managers end their "bureaucratic disregard of Wyoming" and open all entrances simultaneously.[87]

Simpson quickly took center stage in the pro-plowing camp. Having grown up in the Cody area, he had spent some time working in Yellowstone as a young adult. For most of his career, he had practiced law in Cody, additionally serving as president of the University of Wyoming from 1943 to 1954. During the multi-decade effort to create Grand Teton National Park, he played an influential role in defending local ranchers and opposing park creation. He seemed to be particularly aggrieved by the role of John D. Rockefeller, Jr., in that effort: Rockefeller had quietly purchased about 33,000 acres of private ranch land in Jackson Hole for eventual inclusion in the park. Simpson felt that Rockefeller and the NPS had used their wealth and power unfairly to circumvent local desires, and he brought this feeling of unfair treatment with him to the governor's office in 1955. He accused Yellowstone's managers of unfairly directing business toward Montana and Idaho interests, not understanding that regional geography meant that managers in Mammoth found Montana and its businesses much easier to reach than Wyoming. Geography alone, though, cannot change deeply held convictions; Simpson continued to believe that "the time has come for a sweeping clean up in the Park Service. . . . That shake up necessitates the removal of the Rockefeller influence from [the NPS]." Regarding the entrance-opening situation, Simpson felt the NPS was discriminating unfairly against his state.[88]

In response to the criticism over the plowing delay, Rogers and NPS Director Connie Wirth did their best to describe their reasons accurately to Simpson and examined the plowing equipment status and needs in the two parks. The pressure for simultaneous entrance opening spread quickly throughout Wyoming and Montana, with Montana interests insisting that even the Beartooth Highway open with the other entrances (evidently, geographic ignorance, whether benign or willful, was not unique to Wyoming). Yellowstone managers continued to argue their point: that Wyoming's two entrances, unfortunately, were victims of geography, much more difficult to open than the west and north Montana entrances. The Beartooth Highway was impossible to open earlier than about June 1.[89]

An exchange of correspondence in early 1957 between Wirth and Simpson demonstrates Simpson's devotion to Wyoming interests in spite of geographical realities. After Simpson wrote Wirth that he could "see no reason why all Park entrances into Yellowstone should not be opened almost simultaneously," Wirth responded that the "basic facts of geography and weather conditions act together to penalize some of the entrances. Unfortunately from your standpoint, two of these are in Wyoming. The one at the greatest disadvantage is, of course, from Red Lodge, Montana." Simpson replied by stating that opening any roads earlier than the others could subject visitors to dangerous winter conditions, so all openings should be simultaneous, failing to acknowledge that the Montana entrances were lower in elevation than Wyoming's (though Simpson did implicitly acknowledge the extreme conditions on the Beartooth). Wirth's final reply was direct and forceful:

> The answer to all the points you raise is in the fact that the climate in Yellowstone varies greatly. You recognize this by eliminating Red Lodge–Cooke City from your previous recommendations. However, the same line of reasoning should be applied to determine the relative positions of other gateways. As I have explained before, I regret that due to elevations and other factors, this situation penalizes the East and South entrances. The safety factors involved operate in direct relation to the amount of snow that will normally fall in a given area and the climatic conditions as they are affected by altitude. All this adds up to the fact that it is safe, with the equipment and installations we have, to invite the public to use the roads in lower elevations sooner than in the higher. . . . [C]limatological conditions and other factors . . . favor opening the North and West entrances several weeks earlier than the East and South.

Geography and climate, in other words, should decide the bottom line in this case, according to Wirth—but rules in the political world differ, as he would soon find out.[90]

Simpson's devoted attention was even called into question by one of his own lifelong friends in Cody, who wrote Yellowstone Chief Clerk Joe Joffe,

> I see our good Governor has been picking on you again. I suppose it would be heresy for me to say any*thing against his reasoning, but to be perfectly truthful, I can't quite follow it. I learned long ago that it is easier to walk on flat land than to climb a mountain and that the snow goes off faster at a lower altitude than a high one and that just because my neighbor is lucky, it doesn't mean that I must force myself to be lucky too. There are a lot of people down here who feel the same as I do.

Indeed, Simpson was Cody's "Man Against Geography," and some of Cody's own called his bluff, at least privately. Such renouncements, however, did not alter the direction of the debate.[91]

The author of this quote (who went unnamed) reminds us that one person does not speak for an entire town, even if that person is influential. People in Cody had many different opinions on the matter. Unfortunately, these differences of opinion were obscured by the influence that some individuals—like Simpson or members of the Cody Club—exercised. Powerful voices can become the town's voice in any community as influential persons put forward the public face of their town. In that way, Cody, not just Simpson or the Cody Club, became the actor against geography, at least to some degree. Cody was certainly not the only gateway community, however, in which powerful people carried disproportionate influence (likewise, Montana's interest in seeing the Beartooth Highway opened earlier suggests that Wyoming and Cody were not the only opponents of geography).

As Simpson sparred with park managers, Houchens (who had issued the first complaints about the delayed opening of the South Entrance) and others in the Wyoming camp soon changed the debate's focus to a familiar one, plowing park roads year-round. As before, they reasoned that open roads would stimulate travel and tourist spending in their communities, towns that saw their economies slump every fall when tourists went home. The Montana congressional delegation soon joined in requesting an updated analysis of the potential for plowing, though they focused only on the park's west side roads (not because they were easier to plow but rather because plowing them would connect the two Montana communities of Gardiner and West Yellowstone).[92]

Soon, the chorus of pressure on park managers began to pay off. First, Yellowstone managers decided to extend the park's season, opening all park entrances (except the Beartooth Highway) as close to May 15 as possible and keeping them open through the end of October.[93] A longer season would not only please local businesses and politicians but also advance the goals of the newly launched NPS development program called "Mission 66." This program, Director Wirth's brainchild, was designed to provide a way for the NPS to catch up with the rapidly increasing numbers of national park visitors after World War II (47.8 million nationally in 1954—more than twice the number in 1941, the last big prewar year of visitation). Congress had sliced the agency's budget during the war, but failed to increase it afterward to keep up with gains in visitation. Wirth understood the advantage of bundling ten years of necessary developments together in a single package with a slick name (the 66 referred to 1966, the completion date of the program, and the agency's fiftieth anniversary): It stood a better chance of congressional funding than the annual proposals his predecessors had attempted to fund. President Dwight D. Eisenhower and Congress enthusiastically approved the program early in 1956, providing large, rapidly increasing appropriations for such things as new roads, trails, campgrounds, visitor centers, and maintenance facilities. Mission 66 also provided funding for new ranger positions and encouraged longer visitor seasons, as well as winter visitor seasons, to spread out the summer visitation peaks. In Yellowstone, a new superintendent, Lon Garrison, promoted all portions of Mission 66. He had just come from the program's steering committee in Washington, D.C., so responding to public pressure by extending the park's summer season was a natural response for him.[94]

Moreover, by mid-1957 Garrison had gone a step further, responding to the calls for year-round plowing by commissioning another review of the issue.[95] He created the Snow Survey Committee, composed of Yellowstone managers and representatives of the Yellowstone Park Company, the AAA, the Bureau of Public Roads, and the Colorado and California state highway departments. The latter two maintained year-round highways in climates similar to that of Yellowstone; of course, so did Wyoming, Montana, and Idaho, but Garrison and his superiors felt that including these states, whose opinions were already so clearly stated, would risk biasing the committee's findings. Also, though it was not stated, including them would have had the result of empowering those who complained most; park managers did not want to risk their autonomy in such a manner. Still, excluding them carried a different risk, that they would not accept a finding against plowing. To solve this dilemma and to address complaints from Montana and Wyoming about the exclusion, park managers requested "observers" from the three states to participate in committee activities. Observers participated in all ways except in drafting the final report.[96]

As with the previous investigations into year-round plowing, the committee investigated the facilities and equipment needed for winter opening and tabulated the costs of such an endeavor. They examined Yellowstone Park Company buildings to see if any could be opened in winter, finding just one, a new employee dormitory at the Old Faithful Campers' Cabins. Beyond such research, however, they personally traveled all the roads in question three times: in summer, at winter's peak (using the park's Weasels and SnoCats), and in mid-May when the plows were working to open the East and South Entrance roads. Their summer trip included a day on Beartooth Pass, which all agreed should not be plowed in winter and whose spring opening could not easily be pushed to an earlier date. Their winter trip included a day examining Sylvan Pass, where they observed some recent avalanche activity. Personally observing Sylvan Pass at that time of year was an eye-opener; the group agreed that keeping it open would be difficult. Moreover, they realized that their vehicles sat atop the snow, providing good visibility; automobiles would be in a snow trench, providing poor views of the park, at least in certain areas.[97]

After their trip to observe the spring plowing effort, the group finished their report, concluding that plowing year-round was "feasible but not practical." It

Snow Survey Committee at Virginia Meadows, 1958. The Snow Survey Committee was formed to investigate whether plowing park roads year-round was feasible. To gather needed information, the group toured Yellowstone in such vehicles, observing winter conditions firsthand. In front is a Tucker Snow-cat; behind it, four Weasels procured from the U.S. Army. At other times they used snowplanes and Bombardier Snowmobiles. NPS photo.

could be done, but it made little financial or practical sense. Equipment purchases and necessary building construction costs had risen to $2 million, with annual outlays of over $380,000, for an estimated maximum daily traffic load of only 140 vehicles. The committee did feel, though, that it would be worthwhile to extend Yellowstone's summer season, as the park was already considering, and that the extension could be a step toward turning Yellowstone into a year-round park.[98]

Reaction to the committee's report varied by audience. Predictably (and perhaps because his representatives were only observers), Governor Simpson disagreed with it. He continued to urge year-round plowing, as he had done throughout the committee's work. Geographic realities never did impress Simpson; as late as 1958 (his last year as governor) he was still arguing that "there has never been a laudable reason given for . . . delaying the opening of the East and South gates. It is rank discrimination against our Wonderful State of Wyoming." Geographic reality (or rank discrimination) prevailed, at least partly; the park never fully attempted to open its five entrances simultaneously, though it did move the targeted opening date two weeks earlier, to May 1 (which required that plowing had to begin a full month earlier, in late February, from Mammoth). Simpson might not have won the simultaneous opening he requested, but he got something that was, in reality, more valuable: an earlier opening for the Wyoming entrances and therefore a longer business season for Jackson and Cody (courtesy of the substantial costs to the NPS from the earlier start to plowing).[99]

This solution, and Simpson's actions, made at least one observer wonder who really ran Yellowstone Park: the NPS or Wyoming? Fred Martin, editor of the *Park County News* in Livingston, Montana, ran an editorial in August 1958 raising this question. He felt that the agency's failure to examine plowing the park's mid-elevation, west side roads separately from the others was a capitulation to Wyoming. He argued that the likely finding—that plowing from Mammoth to West Yellowstone was both feasible *and* practical—would have invited additional claims of prejudice from the Wyoming interests. Given Simpson's influence, Martin accused Wyoming of unduly influencing the debate. Although NPS authorities dismissed his concerns as impugning their committee's hard work and respectability,[100] Martin did raise an important question: If NPS authorities were cowed into an all-or-nothing stance by a constituent interest group, was the agency truly operating freely and dispassionately? If such decision-making demonstrated that the agency operated in a political world, was that acceptable for park preservation? Similarly, was it acceptable to other communities, especially those that were not as powerful as those connected to Simpson? Such questions went unanswered at the time but have recurred throughout Yellowstone's history. This instance would become one of the first clear examples (at least in this story) of how the agency operated in a political climate that disenfranchised some constituents and that might have clouded objective decision-making about how to use and protect park resources. Over time, the political lens under which the agency operated would intensify, increasing the political micromanagement of the agency and sharply influencing the future winter debate.

In Yellowstone, Superintendent Garrison accepted and agreed with the committee's recommendations, which pushed him to consider the future of Yellowstone winter visitation. Observing that twice in a decade the plowing idea had erupted into a controversy, and with his earlier Mission 66 work having made him receptive to winter park tourism, Garrison argued that "we should frankly recognize that at sometime in the future most of our roads will be kept open the year around. . . . I believe we should immediately incorporate this thinking in our planning." He then suggested that the agency alter its road construction projects to make the completed roads wide enough to plow, and that his colleagues publicly mention plowing park roads for winter tourism as a long-term goal when it released the Snow Survey Report.[101]

Garrison then gave serious thought to the future of winter visitation. His thinking was prodded in part by the Snow Survey Committee, but even so, this may have been the first time a superintendent had thought in broad terms about the subject. However, his suggestions were shot down by NPS Regional Director

Howard Baker, who felt that a public acknowledgment of the likelihood of future winter plowing would continue to stir the pot of discontent in Wyoming and elsewhere. Baker was probably correct, and his feelings prevailed,[102] but by stifling Garrison's realism regarding future winter visitation, he may also have curtailed broader agency planning. In so doing, he deferred to society regarding Yellowstone's future appearance—the same society that would soon develop another oversnow vehicle, one that would revolutionize winter tourism and substantially transform the winter use debate.

That vehicle, the modern snowmobile, made a quiet, almost unnoticed entry into Yellowstone, as the next chapter will reveal. As with their handling of the earlier oversnow vehicles, park managers permitted them to enter without much forethought. They had to do little to accommodate them, since nature provided the snow-covered roads already. They could not have known the full consequences of that decision in advance, however, because the snowmobile appeared so unexpectedly. Appear it would, though, in just a few short years.

Opening the Door

For the forty years through 1960, Yellowstone's gateway communities had engaged in a continuing geographical dialectic over the appearance of Yellowstone in winter. Influenced by their respective geographies, low-elevation Cody and Gardiner routinely envisioned Yellowstone's roads looking like theirs in winter—in a word, plowed, no matter the real-world likelihood that such efforts would not be very successful on the park's east and south sides. Meanwhile, residents of snow-covered Jackson and West Yellowstone responded to winter differently, by acquiring and using vehicles capable of traveling over their snow-covered roads—and those of Yellowstone (this may seem like geographical determinism, but it did not have to be this way; today, for example, Cody is generally an advocate of oversnow travel). By the late 1960s, park managers would have to choose between the two alternatives, finding them to be a zero-sum game. The fact that they rejected the idea of plowed roads four times was perhaps indicative of their future decisions, but that was far from clear in 1960.

Throughout this period, natural and social changes, along with dominant individuals and rudimentary science, influenced the creation of Yellowstone's winter look and feel (its "winter place"). A heavy winter stimulated the fourth round of plowing controversy, while continued technological evolution by society introduced two new means of winter touring, enabling visitors to explore the park safely. Certain key individuals moved the debate in one way or another, with Horace Albright taking a strong stand against plowing and Milward Simpson aggressively promoting it. Finally, in every instance of calls for plowed roads, the NPS successfully countered with science in the form of cost estimates. All of these influences would continue in various forms.

In addition to transforming Yellowstone's winter place from an uninhabited wilderness to a fledgling visitor destination, these same forces also affected the relationship between Yellowstone and its neighbors. Cody, initially a distant town with little influence on Yellowstone, came to exert a strong influence on the park's policies. The town's relationship to the park was at times friendly and at other times hostile or pressured. Cody has maintained its relationship of influence over Yellowstone managers ever since, with such concern varying from noninterest to strong influence, even virtual control at times.

Throughout, the National Park Service, hamstrung by a lack of funding and staffing, reacted primarily with crisis management. There were very real constraints on the ability of Yellowstone managers and their superiors in Washington to envision and direct future visitation, including this pressure from all sides, as well as the other pressing management issues of the day. The lack of direction on motorized use from the NPS director's office in Washington—a likely result of political pressures and the novelty of Yellowstone's winter vehicles—did not help matters. As time would tell, Regional Director Baker's muffling of Garrison's forward-thinking ideas may have hampered the agency's ability to cope with societal changes to its winter operations.

Finally, those who visited during this era may have experienced a greater sense of discovery and exploration than those who would visit the snowbound park later, if for no other reason than because these earlier visitors were experiencing a park that had seen very few winter visitors to date. Later visitors also had more facilities open to welcome them, such as a lodge at Old Faithful. Yellowstone's wonders were unveiled, and visitors thrilled in the discovery of them. With the unique vehicles adding to the attractions, visitors would flock to the park in increasing numbers. In part for that reason, debate about the park's future returned only six years later—but after a revolution in winter travel arrived.

2

A Snowmobile Policy for Yellowstone

There is no question but that we are confronted with a totally new concept of winter use.

Unidentified assistant NPS director, 1966

I think the real question is: What is appropriate park visitor use in Yellowstone in the wintertime?

NPS Director George Hartzog, 1967

In a park we are concerned with the effect of snowmobiles on the spirit of wilderness, on the spirit of the out-of-doors. These mechanical intrusions create a diluted, lukewarm, "concensus" [*sic*] environment. The whole park idea is cheapened.

Jackson Hole conservationist Adolph Murie, 1967 [1]

Although Harold Young's snowcoaches [2] were novel and provided access to Yellowstone's winter wonders, there may have been something missing from his tours—an element of freedom. Visitors were locked into his schedules, confined to round-trips between West Yellowstone and Old Faithful or Canyon. Not only were some of the wonders on Yellowstone's east side difficult to reach, but visitors could not go where and when they wanted; they were confined to group travel. The independence that Americans associated with automobile touring was lacking, because few visitors could afford their own snowcoach.

Joseph-Armand Bombardier, the creative engineer in Quebec, would soon change that with his Ski-Doo, the first modern snowmobile. The Ski-Doo would revolutionize winter in Yellowstone. It made something that was already enjoyable—touring the park—even more fun because visitors were now able to tour independently. [3] Visitation would consequently boom, but residents and politicians of Wyoming, slow to realize the new vehicle's possibilities, continued to focus on plowing the park's roads. The park could not accommodate both snowmobiles and automobiles, so park managers eventually found themselves forced to choose between the two. In some ways, it was a choice between a rock and a hard place. The new superintendent's personal preference, however, along with thirty-five years of resisting calls for plowing, would make the choice relatively straightforward. In admitting snowmobiles rather than automobiles, he and his staff preserved what they felt to be a unique park experience based on Yellowstone's wonders, instead of merely offering pretty scenery to interstate travelers. Though that choice brought some unanticipated problems, managers resolved them as best they could and stuck to their new program. By 1980, Yellowstone had a smoothly operating winter system, drawing thousands of winter visitors.

The 1960s and 1970s were times of change in Yellowstone, with many of the same forces influencing the policy-making as in previous eras. Science, interest groups, politicians, and society would all influence the course of events; park managers, not foreseeing the changing demands for winter travel, reacted as best they could, given their limitations. Still confused and divided over the proper role of motorized winter use in Yellowstone when the snowmobile arrived in the park, the agency and some members of society came to a truce by 1980. However, it was an uneasy and short-lived truce, for it set the stage for increasing problems and conflict—problems some other national parks avoided by examining the environmental impacts of snowmobile use in the 1970s and/or prohibiting such use.

A Totally New Concept of Winter Use

In the 1950s, Canadian snowcoach maker Joseph-Armand Bombardier turned his company's attention away from such vehicles because the Quebec government had begun plowing roads province-wide in 1947. Still, Bombardier continued to look for the technology necessary to mass-produce a faster snowmobile. He fondly remembered the thrill of driving over snow at high speeds in a vehicle he had designed as a child (a propeller-driven sport sled that was so fast and dangerous his father made him disassemble it immediately). He knew that success for such a winter vehicle depended more on its speed and recreational potential than its utility; in a word, it had to be fun. With lighter and more powerful two-stroke engines becoming available in the late 1950s, and prompted by a letter from a northern Canada friend suggesting he develop a smaller vehicle more affordable and practical for a single person to use, Bombardier set to work on that dream.[4]

After a year or two of work, he unveiled the Ski-Doo in 1959. It had all the components of the modern snowmobile: a front-mounted engine that drove a rubber track wide enough to keep the vehicle afloat on soft snow; a variable-speed clutch that made shifting unnecessary; two front-mounted skis that provided steering; and an elongated seat over the track that enabled passengers to use their weight to aid steering. The vehicle was light and could travel up to 40 miles per hour. Bombardier patented his invention, but other mechanics soon copied him, coming up with their own snowmobile versions. Polaris was the first to follow (the company had been experimenting with its own prototypes since 1954), and Arctic Cat and dozens of other companies designed similar snowmobiles in the 1960s.[5]

It was some of the other snowmobiles that first entered Yellowstone. Their entry went almost unnoticed; in his report for January 1963, Superintendent Garrison noted only, "A total of 81 visitors were transported to Old Faithful by Snowmobiles, three snowplanes, and three Polaris Snow Travelers." He provided no explanation of what Snow Travelers were, nor details about the owners or the performance of their machines. This simple statement of fact merely whispered of things to come but again suggested the ambivalence park managers seemed to have toward the future of winter use.[6]

It took a few more years for snowmobiling to catch on in the park. One year after the first three Snow Travelers arrived, six more entered, driven by fourteen people. This time, Garrison provided more details, explaining that a "Polaris is a toboggan with tracks and motor driven—powered oversnow sleds—which many people are buying." In this understated manner, Garrison (perhaps unknowingly) hinted at what was to come: an explosion in Yellowstone snowmobile use, as Americans embraced the "totally new concept."[7]

Events in 1965 and 1966 combined with surging national interest in snowmobiling to stimulate such visitation to Yellowstone. A pioneering two-day snowmobile trip through the park by Monte Wight, a Ski-Doo distributor from Pinedale, Wyoming, demonstrated the vehicle's possibilities. In February 1965, the NPS granted him permission to travel by snowmobile from the West to the South Entrance via Old Faithful with a group of companions. Acting Superintendent J. M. Carpenter, reasoning that such a trip would provide the agency with useful information on how the machines traveled in light snow, sent Park Ranger Dale Nuss along to observe their traveling success firsthand. Driving almost thirty Ski-Doos, the group made the 90-mile trip in two days.

Group participant Jerry Schmier, who soon established a snowmobile rental business in West Yellowstone, remembered that the park was pristine and beautiful, but that the trip was pioneering and difficult. The group ran into trouble after leaving Old Faithful when they opted to drive across Lewis Lake, which appeared to be solidly frozen, windblown, and packed with snow (whereas the road was covered with soft, drifted, and unpacked snow). Unfortunately, some in the party broke through a top layer of ice, coming to rest on more solid ice underneath. Wading in 32-degree water to lift the machines out, the group found that the water froze to the snowmobiles' tracks when they were placed back on a firm surface. Struggling to free the frozen parts, the group continued on to the South Entrance, arriving there at 11:00 P.M. amid subzero temperatures. Despite their struggles, their memorable adventure would be repeated innumerable times in the future (and usually with less trouble).[8]

Wight's trip—the first to go *through* the park, not just into it—demonstrated both the feasibility of snowmobile travel and its touring possibilities. Moreover, it may have given park managers, who would soon be embroiled in another plowing controversy, the idea that snowmobile travel could be an alternative to plowing. Indeed, new superintendent John McLaughlin wrote,

> Undoubtedly more Park travel during the winter months by this type of machine can be expected and should be encouraged. This type of recreation is increasing rapidly in this particular section of the country and its influence has spread to Yellowstone National Park. The machines are now relatively inexpensive and maintenance requirements simple. Much of the terrain of the Park and its features are compatible and attractive to this mode of winter travel.[9]

Attractive and feasible it was; the next few years saw several more such trips, including repeats of Wight's trip, another that went around the park's "Lower Loop" (the 100-mile loop road connecting Old Faithful, West Thumb, Lake, Canyon, Norris, and Madison), and still another from Mammoth to Moran. Today, these are common one-day trips, but at the time, they were precedent-setting. By the late 1960s, it was clear that snowmobiling was gaining popularity rapidly, as people found the machines to be an independent and affordable way to explore previously inaccessible areas. Indeed, park managers noticed a "greatly increased interest and use" of snowmobiles in early 1966. Snowmobiling blossomed throughout the region; visitors began exploring not only the park's major roads, but also the East Entrance area, the mining roads around Cooke City, and the Cave Falls road, in Yellowstone's southwest corner.[10]

By enabling virtually anyone to travel through snow-covered terrain, snowmobiles transformed winter from the season of hibernation to a season in which outdoor activity was not only possible, but enjoyable. As Howard T. Kelsey, owner of what was then West Yellowstone's largest hotel (the Stagecoach Inn), stated, snowmobiles could "make a 60-year-old man feel like a kid again." Recognizing the fun and profit in the machines, several local communities began holding winter carnivals, featuring various kinds of snow activities centered on snowmobile races and contests. With an already long history of motorized winter exploration, West Yellowstone soon developed the most prominent snowmobile carnival in the region (and shortly, the country). Kelsey and his business associate Ray Brandt developed the Western Snowmobile Roundup, held there March 18–20, 1966.

Snowmobiles at West Entrance, 1972. In 1963, the first visitors on modern-day snowmobiles entered Yellowstone, perhaps on some of the Bombardier models in the middle of this line. By the late 1960s, visitation on such machines was growing exponentially. NPS photo.

Participants numbered about 250 on 185 machines that first year and raced their machines in slalom, oval track, obstacle-course, relay, and cross-country racing. The event became an annual celebration, rapidly growing in size, popularity, and diversity of activities. By 1970 it was the largest of its kind in the country, attracting more than 5,000 people with 4,000 machines.[11] Given that success, it was no wonder that West Yellowstone began calling itself the "Snowmobile Capital of the World" at this time.[12]

With Yellowstone National Park right next door, many of the roundup's participants took time to tour it. The second year of the festival about a third of them entered the park on 325 or more machines (a number almost equal to the number of such machines that had entered the park to date that season). Such snowmobile pioneers enjoyed their visits and in so doing helped to imbue the festival with multiple meanings: Not only was it a celebration of snowmobiling and winter fun, but it was also a celebration of Yellowstone and the exploratory freedom that snowmobiling offered. This mixture of meanings was evident in a brochure advertising the third (1968) festival: Its cover included a full-page photograph of Yellowstone's Lower Falls under a mantle of snow and ice—the implicit message being that one could see such fabulous scenery thanks to the snowmobile. Snowmobiles were fun and they opened up new terrain to explore; the town and the park provided the venue for thrills and discovery. From the beginning, then, snowmobiling in the northern Rockies has conflated freedom and fun with Yellowstone and West Yellowstone. This association of meanings would continue to grow in the ensuing decades and become highly important in the controversy that erupted after 1995.[13]

More than any single event to date, the roundups in West Yellowstone garnered publicity and attention, which stimulated more visitation and publicity. Many television channels, radio stations, newspapers, and magazines covered the first event. Subsequent roundups were also consistently publicized, as were Yellowstone's winter wonders. Marlin Perkins, for example, narrated "Winter Comes to Yellowstone," one of his ongoing *Wild Kingdom* series on NBC, on March 14, 1965. Although his show did not feature snowmobiles, it did depict him traveling in an army Weasel into the park interior. Given the show's popularity, it undoubtedly stimulated the imagination of many who would find snowmobiles (often from West Yellowstone) to be their means to personally explore the park in winter. A promotional movie entitled *Winter Vacationland,* produced and distributed by the Wyoming Travel Commission, contributed to increased visitor interest as well, as did the opening of the Jackson Hole ski resort during this era (many skiers took a day off from skiing to explore Yellowstone). All told, winter visitation to Yellowstone grew almost exponentially in the 1960s and early 1970s (see Figure 2.1). Not since the introduction of the automobile had a vehicle so revolutionized visitation.[14]

Bombardier's dream had come true, but it brought unanticipated problems to park managers. Enjoying the perky machines, some snowmobilers banked up onto road cuts and swung back down onto the road, an activity today called "sidehilling." Such activity trampled roadside vegetation. More serious were violations of Yellowstone's requirement to snowmobile only on snow-covered roads. As early as 1966 park rangers found snowmobile tracks in Bechler Meadows, several miles from the nearest road; these violators were difficult to apprehend. Further, cross-country skiers and dogsled operators also wanted to tour the park. Increasingly, park managers granted them permission, reflecting a growing comfort with all winter uses, but conflicts were possible between nonmotorized users and the proliferating snowmobiles. Eventually, these and other problems with snowmobiles would intensify. For now, such problems seemed easy to address through management actions like increased ranger patrols.[15]

To some, such problems were easily dealt with; to others, they begged questions about the future of Yellowstone's winter use. A proposal by the Yellowstone Park Company brought these broader questions to the fore. The company, sens-

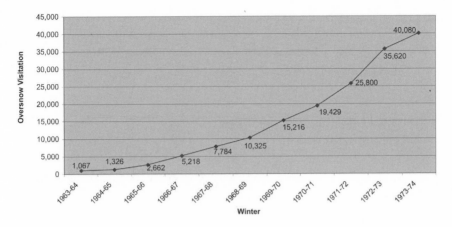

Figure 2.1. Oversnow Visitation, 1963/64–1973/74
Sources: SMRs, 1963–1967, and "Summary Record of Snowmobile Use, Yellowstone National Park," File "Winter Activities," Box K-57, YNPA.

ing the income potential offered by the new activity and associated snowmobiler needs, soon proposed opening hotels at Old Faithful and Mammoth for winter use. While park managers granted permission for the Mammoth Motor Inn to be opened, no hotel at Old Faithful was opened in the 1960s. The Mammoth hotel was open continuously from 1966 through October 1970, when it reverted to closing for the winter seasons because they simply were not profitable, despite the company's hopes. The reasoning against an Old Faithful hotel at this time is not clear, but lingering questions about possible plowing (explored in the next section of this chapter) made the future of interior park operations uncertain. Would the agency be plowing or continuing to allow snowmobiles, and how would either affect demand for Old Faithful accommodations? Should park managers put new regulations in place for winter pursuits, or should they discourage such use? Most fundamentally, what should Yellowstone look like in the winter?[16]

Looking to park policies for guidance, park managers saw that their own "Master Plan," along with Mission 66 policies, directed that such use be encouraged—but those policies and plans were issued before the explosion of snowmobile use. Seeking updated guidance, they still found little to go on. Snowmobiles were neither mentioned in national NPS winter use guidelines nor defined as vehicles under the park's vehicle regulations. Managers wondered if their off-road vehicular travel ban legally applied to snowmobiles. In general, the park was not prepared for the new toy. But who could have been? A winter vehicle as fun, fast, and powerful as the snowmobile had never before existed. Society threw a curve ball at the national parks—and soon the batting performance at Yellowstone would be brought into focus by the fifth (and last) plowing controversy, which had been brewing and festering for several years. Park managers would once again defeat efforts to plow, but only through a compromise that addressed the questions at hand by welcoming snowmobiles.[17]

The Real Question: Snowmobiles, Automobiles, or Other?

A perennial issue in political elections is the economy. With the previous plowing controversy still fresh in the minds of regional politicians, and the belief still prevailing that plowed park roads would stimulate local economies, it was easy for several campaigning politicians to bring up the issue again. Wyoming Senator Gale McGee, in his reelection campaign in 1964, was one of the first to renew calls for plowing. Two years later, Wyoming Governor Clifford B. Hansen joined with Montana Senator Lee Metcalf in calling for plowed roads as they both campaigned for U.S. Senate seats in their respective states. By 1966, the issue was once again on the political radar screen throughout the region, with governors, senators, congressmen, chambers of commerce, and others calling for plowed roads.[18]

Initially, Yellowstone's managers did as they had done before: They resisted the calls for plowing. They again explained that the severity of Yellowstone's climate and the geographical difficulties involved in opening certain road segments were "nature's will, not man's." The six years that had elapsed since the previous controversy had not brought an appreciable change in either the road or building infrastructure needed for winter operations. Most roads were still too narrow (having not been updated from their 1920s standards) to provide room for snow storage, and few of the buildings were winterized. Managers did update their estimates of potential winter traffic and plowing/winterization costs, finding that little had changed. As before, such logic prevailed—but only for a time, for societal and political winds would blow it away in a few years.[19]

Calls for plowing intensified in 1966 with Hansen's and Metcalf's election campaigns. Fred Martin, editor of Livingston's *Park County News,* assisted in keeping the issue hot, repeatedly editorializing and writing his congressional representatives in favor of plowing.[20] With criticism escalating, Yellowstone managers responded by inviting representatives from the three local states to join another committee, this one focusing on some of the problems facing Yellowstone and its visitors. In part, this was an effort to help the plowing boosters understand the larger context within which park managers were operating, such as the park's broader visitation trends and problems. Spending large sums to promote winter visitation, for example, could deprive the much more numerous summer visitors of facilities that were clearly needed. Recognizing the need for more comprehensive planning, Yellowstone's managers at the same time were also beginning the research for a new master plan. They probably hoped that the broader perspective might defuse the plowing pressure. However, the pro-plowing movement's long history and the perception that plowing would stimulate economies would prove to be more influential.[21]

As it turned out, the Tri-State Committee for Recreation and Travel produced little of substance despite meeting five times in 1966 and 1967. The political actors stuck to their pro-plowing positions, and Wyoming even calculated its own estimates—without asking park managers for either permission or their expertise—of plowing the road from Moran to Old Faithful. The committee discussed the plowing question at most of its meetings, but it did not reach resolution on the matter, perhaps because some communities in the area were growing fond of snowmobiling through Yellowstone and preferred that activity to continue rather than any plowing. Combining a playful, novel vehicle with the spectacular Yellowstone scenery and wildlife viewing produced a unique park experience that plowing would destroy. The Tri-State Committee, then, like the Yellowstone Park Company with its discussion of the winter hotel proposal, merely highlighted the brewing conflict between snowmobiling and plowing. Again, the committee's failure to resolve the plowing question suggested the larger question: What should Yellowstone look like in winter?[22]

More public debate on that issue began in February 1967, after several Wyoming chambers of commerce cooperated in a letter campaign directed toward Senator Gale McGee. Three years earlier, the U.S. Senate had passed a resolution calling for a hearing on plowing Yellowstone's roads, but its Committee on Interior and Insular Affairs had taken no action on the matter. McGee, responding to his constituents' demands to investigate plowing, finally decided in March to hold a hearing. His announcement elevated the winter use question, and stakeholders in the issue began considering their positions and organizing their testimony.[23]

Those favoring plowing knew their position well; they had been advocating it for years, and McGee's hearing promised them their day in the sun. For Yellowstone managers, however, the upcoming hearing forced the issue: What was to be their winter use policy? For years, they had maintained that plowing was not feasible for a number of good reasons, most of which had not changed. Additionally, they were more and more adamant that avalanche snowsheds were necessary to permit automobile travel over Sylvan Pass. These would be expensive, costing upward of $10 million to build.[24] Despite these bona fide concerns, park managers had long struggled to advance their own vision of what Yellowstone in winter should be like; they knew what they did not want (plowed roads), but they really did not know what they wanted instead.

The arrival and increasing popularity of snowmobiling meant that now a new, clear position was possible. No longer did managers need to keep the floodgates closed against winter tourism, for snowmobiles seemed to offer a solution to most of the problems plowing presented. They sat on top of the snow, making plowing unnecessary and offering good visibility. Snow would remain on the roads, protecting them from temperature extremes and pavement scarring. Road salting and its impacts upon native vegetation could be avoided.[25] Wildlife would not get trapped upon plowed roads (which would resemble deep trenches in some areas), would not follow the roads, and would not be hit by automobiles. The bison, elk, and other animals of the park also might not suffer the disruption of their behavior, movements, and distribution that park managers believed plowed roads could cause. (Not foreseen at the time was the possibility that wildlife would use hard-packed snowmobile routes in a similar manner. When that came to happen in the 1990s, a concerned interest group raised the same questions.)[26]

Snowmobiles also offered a solution to a larger impact managers feared plowing would have: turning Yellowstone's roads into well-traveled links in the country's coast-to-coast highway system. That outcome is precisely what plowing's boosters wanted, but the construction of the country's interstate highway system at that time may have pushed park managers to consider what plowed roads through Yellowstone would really do. If they were plowed, they could become thoroughfares rather than parkways, especially for the locals who already made up the bulk of early spring and late fall traffic. Though no interstate highway per se would pass through Yellowstone, the U.S. highways already present in the park shouldered some cross-country traffic—and would continue to do so. Yellowstone's complexion would change as it went from a nature retreat to a cog in the country's highway system. Snowmobiles, by contrast, would keep the gates closed against through-traffic while allowing visitors who wished to experience Yellowstone to do just that. Finally, then, after thirty-five years of defending the park against plowing, the automobile, and their feared impacts, Yellowstone's managers had a way to open the park's wonders to the world while simultaneously protecting it from through-traffic impacts.[27]

Also, the NPS director's office had finally weighed in on motorized vehicle use, including snowmobiling. Winter use in general was "highly desirable," and snowmobiling in particular was "a compatible winter use and should be encouraged," subject to the agency's existing laws, which the director felt did indeed cover snowmobile activity (they could use snow-covered roads and, in some places, frozen lakes).[28] With this national guidance promoting snowmobiling, Yellowstone's managers felt increasingly confident adopting a position opposing plowing but welcoming snowmobiling.

Similar realizations were dawning upon those communities experiencing snowmobile travel, particularly West Yellowstone and the Idaho communities southwest of there, located in similarly snowy climates. Because many visitors still did not own private snowmobiles, entrepreneurs in those towns had begun maintaining rental fleets. The rental income, combined with what snowmobilers spent on accommodations and food, was quickly turning winter into a period of economic success; no longer did town economies slumber in winter doldrums. Plowing Yellowstone's roads threatened that new revenue source, and some local residents had begun writing their political representatives to oppose plowing and defend the status quo. More and more, park managers sympathized with them.[29]

Something would need to be done about the problems that came with snowmobiles, however. In addition to the already-known problems, such as more difficult spring plowing (due to snow compaction), snowmobiling had brought other problems, such as littering and inconsiderate human waste disposal. Also, over-snow vehicles pushing against snow for propulsion tended to create moguls, or bumps of snow up to 3 feet tall, on the roads. Such roller-coaster conditions (which intensified as snowmobile use grew) made travel uncomfortable. Some form of snow smoothing would be necessary. Most of these problems could be addressed through management actions, but preventing the park from turning into a thoroughfare vis-à-vis plowed roads would be more difficult. Again, snowmobile visitation seemed more attractive than automobiles and plowing.[30]

To address the inconvenience that local residents faced in their winter travels when Yellowstone's roads were closed, park managers examined the regional road network. Both a winter east-west route from Cody to West Yellowstone and a north-south route between Jackson and Bozeman were desirable. While the shortest such routes both went through Yellowstone, other lower and safer routes were, or would soon be, possible. The state of Wyoming had been improving Dead Indian Pass between Cody and Cooke City for several years and would soon have it modernized enough for winter travel. Plowing this route would be easier than plowing Sylvan Pass and would facilitate travel from Cody to Mammoth. Therefore, Yellowstone managers promised to plow the first 8 miles east of Cooke City to the Wyoming state line (where Wyoming would take over) if the route were indeed finished. Travel from Jackson north to West Yellowstone could occur via the Grassy Lake Road, which was an existing gravel road along Yellowstone's south boundary linking Flagg Ranch to Ashton, Idaho. Such routes would improve the ease of winter travel. Though the crucial link between West Yellowstone and Mammoth Hot Springs would still be closed to autos, the two other routes could take some of the pressure off park managers to plow Yellowstone roads.[31]

Snowmobilers and moguls on the West Entrance Road, 1972. Especially on days with above-freezing temperatures, smooth snow is transformed into such rough surfaces by oversnow vehicles pushing against the snow for propulsion. Park managers knew that smoothing the road surface would be necessary for the public and elected officials to accept their plan to institutionalize oversnow vehicle access rather than automobile access on plowed roads as the mode of winter travel. NPS photo.

These thoughts about plowing versus snowmobiling were foremost in park managers' minds when Senator McGee convened the hearing in Jackson, Wyoming, on August 12, 1967, to debate "the real question" (as NPS Director George Hartzog referred to it at the hearing). McGee began by allowing Hartzog to present the agency's position, which was by this time clear. The park's roads should not be cogs in the nation's highway system, but rather parkways to explore Yellowstone's winter wonders. Snowmobiles would prevent automobile through-traffic and its impacts while providing winter visitor access. Regional (and cross-country) winter travel could be improved by plowing Dead Indian Pass and the Grassy Lake Road. In sum, Hartzog felt that unless evidence to the contrary somehow came to light, oversnow visitation was the appropriate means of travel in the park in the wintertime. Snowmobiles preserved Yellowstone's resources and park-like atmosphere while automobiles would turn it into a thruway.[32]

In contrast, and as expected, the chambers of commerce and political representatives from throughout the region nearly unanimously supported plowing.

The issue attracted widespread attention, with chambers of commerce as far away as Logan and Salt Lake City, Utah, sending statements in support. Even Amarillo, Texas, had a representative personally attend the hearing to support plowing and represent the Highway 287 Association, a group of businesses along that highway advocating its development. By far, the prevailing sentiment at the hearing was in favor of plowing.[33]

The NPS director was not the only one to speak against plowing, however. Representatives from Livingston, Montana, supported snowmobiling for the same reasons as Hartzog. At least one snowmobile advocacy group, the Lander (Wyo.) Snow-Drifters, agreed, as did the two primary Yellowstone concessioners, Hamilton Stores and the Yellowstone Park Company. The concessioners' reasoning reflected an economic concern, that winterizing their buildings would be prohibitively expensive, especially given the small amount of expected revenue that opening them would generate (their earlier thoughts of opening a lodge at Old Faithful were evidently forgotten). Expressing a more resonant economic concern was West Yellowstone's representative, Howard Kelsey. The day before the hearing, the board of directors for his town's chamber of commerce voted against plowing, but the board changed its position on the day of the hearing (probably to be in sympathy with the other chambers). Kelsey, though, still gave an idea of the economic potential inherent in snowmobiling:

> 2 years ago . . . we had, through the west gate, 994 passengers in the large snowmobiles [snowcoaches]. . . . Only 64 people went into the park through the west gate on the small machines. . . .
>
> Now, this last winter—and I think this is quite significant—there were 4,009 passengers on the large snowmobiles, there were 1,823 on the small snowmobiles, representing a total of 5,332 people that came to West Yellowstone who spent an average of two and a half nights. . . .
>
> Now, . . . transforming this into dollars and cents, in 1965, the people who came up for snowmobile rides spent $64,488. This last year they left $296,000 in the community.
>
> . . . If . . . the roads are plowed, this means that the West Yellowstone snowmobile business is a thing of the past, and it's just starting.
>
> I mean, any time you can take a recreational industry and in 2 years project it five times what it was, it is a pretty important index of what can happen.

Kelsey's words would prove to be prophetic, as more and more of his neighbors realized that the snowmobile offered a new winter economy.[34]

The issue got little interest among conservationists, a situation that would change significantly with time. None actually spoke at the hearing, and only four sent written statements. Wyoming conservationist Mary Back and the National Wildlife Federation opposed plowing because it would be too costly to American taxpayers for the few benefits they would receive in return, but neither endorsed snowmobiling as an alternative. Similarly, the Wildlife Management Institute of Washington, D.C., opposed plowing, fearing that automobile travel would cause physiological stress on wildlife, but this group also chose not to endorse snowmobiling. The Izaak Walton League, however, specifically endorsed snowmobiling, feeling that it offered a better park experience than automobile tourism.[35]

The conservationists' response was muted for several reasons. Many of them had prior commitments or were on vacation, enjoying the short northern Rockies summer; they may also have heard of the hearing too late to adjust their plans. A letter from Adolph Murie (a prominent conservationist residing in Jackson Hole) to Stewart Brandborg of the Wilderness Society suggests another reason: Conservationists were confused about the new vehicles and their impacts upon nature preservation. They did not like off-road snowmobile use, which the NPS allowed in the "Potholes" area (an open area on the flats of Jackson Hole) of Grand Teton National Park. Murie (echoing his thoughts at the beginning of this chapter) felt that off-road snowmobile tracks "kill[ed] the spirit of the wild" because they were an obvious human intrusion into the nature experience he valued. It was the machine in the garden—and worse, it was a machine that could go anywhere in the garden. But what if they were restricted to roads? While autos would have known impacts, such impacts from on-road snowmobile use were not yet known. Murie and his associates knew they did not want off-road use, but which vehicle to use on the roads was less clear.[36]

That confusion was again evident the next month, when Yellowstone managers held three other hearings on their proposed master plan. Because these hearings came so soon after McGee's congressional hearing, many attendees offered opinions on winter use. Conservationists seemed united against plowing because they feared it would turn Yellowstone into a thruway, removing its sacrosanct park nature. But they, like the NPS in the years before the hearing, seemed divided on what should be done instead. Many did not offer an opinion, but those who did, such as Mardy Murie of the Wilderness Society, endorsed snowmobiling as long as the machines were confined to park roadways. This position would change with the rapid growth of snowmobiling over the next two decades, but for the time being, conservationists, if pressed to choose between plowing and snowmobiling, reluctantly chose the latter, as long as the machines were restricted to unplowed roadways. (Chambers of commerce and political representatives were again solidly behind plowing at these master plan hearings.)[37]

More than any previous event or debate, these four hearings brought to the fore the pivotal question about Yellowstone's future winter use, demonstrating the divided opinions among the public and forcing park managers to envision their park's winter future. Bombardier's invention offered managers a way out of their persistent defense against plowing. By inviting continued snowmobile use in the park, they could accommodate winter visitation while preserving the park-like atmosphere. Not everyone was excited about the snowmobiling idea; most economy boosters still wanted plowed roads, and some conservationists were beginning to see that snowmobiles were not an untarnished way to salvation. But other economy boosters and conservationists endorsed the potential snowmobile program, and park managers believed they could mitigate any problems with the machines. All told, park managers believed they could use the snowmobile to preserve Yellowstone's serene atmosphere, preventing it from becoming a speedway. They would soon cement that belief into policy.

Revolution Leads to Resolution: A Snowmobile Policy

Directing Yellowstone's winter decision-making over the next eight years was Jack K. Anderson, who arrived in the park in fall 1967. He had been superintendent at Grand Teton National Park, where he had been dealing with similar winter use questions. He was an ex-military fighter pilot and was not afraid of controversy (really, no modern Yellowstone superintendent could, or can, be). He enjoyed exploring new management paradigms, as reflected in a sign over his desk that read, "But that's the way we've always done it." During his tenure in Yellowstone, he instituted many of the provisions of the later-named "natural regulation" policy that are today the hallmarks (and debates) of national park management. One step in that direction was to close the open dumps at which bears fed, which returned the bruins to more natural feeding behaviors. Another step was to institute the prescribed fire policy, which allowed (and still allows) some lightning-caused fires to burn naturally. These moves were all controversial and are chronicled by other authors.[38] His decisions regarding winter use brought change to Yellowstone as well, and eventual controversy after he retired.

Perhaps because it is natural for some to waver in the face of opposition, park managers initially reconsidered their commitment to allow snowmobiling. Just before Anderson took over as superintendent, his predecessor, John McLaughlin, wrote Director Hartzog seeking permission to plow most park roads through the end of December each year, and then convert to oversnow travel. Such a policy could theoretically accommodate both the demands for plowing and the NPS's preference for snowmobiling. Additionally, plowing could be done more easily with the lower snow depths of early winter than with those of late winter. McLaughlin felt that this action would probably make "the Wyoming Congres-

Jack Anderson, superintendent of Yellowstone National Park, 1968–1975. Anderson made the decision to admit snowmobiles rather than to plow park roads. He failed, however, to examine their environmental impacts comprehensively. NPS photo.

sional Delegation settle down for the next several years and maintain some semblance of peace and quiet." Hartzog, however, viewed the idea as a weakening of the agency's position and a clear move toward accommodating demands for an inappropriate form of winter travel, so he denied McLaughlin's request.[39]

In October, Anderson took over as superintendent. With Hartzog's support for continued snowmobile use clear, he and his staff made no changes to the existing snowmobile program for the upcoming winter. Visitors could still tour the park's interior by snowmobile, while only the road from Gardiner to Cooke City was plowed. As winter progressed, the significance of the recent events sunk in for Anderson and his employees. Their director had taken a strong position in favor of oversnow visitation and had reaffirmed that position directly with them. Snowmobiles, not automobiles, would be the mode of travel. Rather than spend their time resisting plowing, they now needed to develop their oversnow program into a viable alternative. It had to be a broad-based winter use program, supported by park employees and the concessioners and backed by NPS rules and regulations.

The first step in that direction was a March 1968 staff meeting that Anderson convened to discuss oversnow operations. About a dozen of his staff discussed the past winter's operation and what would be needed to fully accommodate oversnow visitation. The winter had again seen people enjoying the park via snowmobile. While some problems were present, the focus of visitation was Yellowstone, not transit through the park. Discussing the problems, they produced a list of decisions and recommendations for the next winter.[40]

Over the next three years, Anderson and his staff would take those and other steps to promote oversnow travel, gradually instituting Yellowstone's oversnow program. By 1972, Yellowstone had a relatively smooth-running program, and the park would not see renewed demands for plowed roads for almost thirty years.[41] Anderson would be influential in translating Hartzog's position into reality. It helped that Anderson agreed with Hartzog: He personally enjoyed snowmobiling, especially the freedom that the activity gave people to explore previously inaccessible terrain. To him, snowmobiles were a means to an end, that of touring Yellowstone's "white winter wilderness." He believed that snowmobiling, however, should not be a visitor's principal activity, because that would mean that Yellowstone was nothing more than a snowmobile recreation area (little better than the feared automobile speedway). Consequently, he had his staff explore ways to make Yellowstone an enjoyable place to experience via oversnow vehicles.[42]

The most pressing need was for smoother roadways. Grooming the snow roads (or attempting to do so) was nothing new to Yellowstone; Yellowstone Park Company employees had tried some road grooming since the 1950s. Their methods, however, were primitive, consisting of pulling a heavy wooden "drag" behind a snowcoach. Through its sheer weight and friction, it flattened and packed the snow to some degree, but it scarred the road surface in thermally warmed areas. The explosion of snowmobile use in the late 1960s began to make the company's drag efforts inadequate. In fact, the roads were getting so bad that some inexperienced snowmobile operators injured themselves as they drove too fast for the rough conditions.[43]

Investigating solutions, Anderson sent his chief ranger, Harold Estey, to the International Snowmobile Conference in 1969 and 1970. There, Estey evidently learned how other state agencies and snowmobile clubs groomed snowmobile trails with ski-resort grooming machines.[44] Returning to Yellowstone, he convinced his colleagues that Yellowstone needed such equipment for its roads. By

Snow groomer, 1975. Yellowstone managers acquired such machines in the early 1970s to smooth the snow roads, making them more comfortable for visitors to tour. Park staff still groom most roads several times weekly with such machines. NPS photo.

February 1971, park managers had purchased the necessary pieces and begun grooming the more heavily used snowmobile routes (from Old Faithful to the South Entrance, West Yellowstone, and Mammoth). Eventually, they expanded the grooming to all snow-covered roads (the snowmobile routes), a policy they continue today. Groomed roads not only facilitated visitation but reversed the previous situation wherein rough road conditions tempted snowmobilers to drive off-road. Now the roads were smoother, so most visitors stayed on them.[45]

An increasing number of visitors also wanted to stay overnight at Old Faithful; some were so motivated to spend the night that they camped out in the only open, heated building: the public restrooms (one would assume they at least did not contribute to the human waste problem!). Such demand meant that the time now seemed ripe for a winterized hotel there. A new marketing director for the

Old Faithful Snowlodge, 1972. The NPS and the Yellowstone Park Company opened this building (an employee dormitory and public restaurant for the Old Faithful Campers' Cabins in summer) in December 1971 for winter accommodations near the famous geyser. Note the temporary Snow Lodge sign covering the more permanent Campers' Cabins sign; in 1973 the building was permanently renamed the Snowlodge. With this hotel opened and the NPS welcoming snowmobiles in other ways, the 1970s saw oversnow vehicle touring become institutionalized as the main way to see the park in winter. NPS photo.

Yellowstone Park Company, Richard Ludewig, brought the idea to fruition late in 1971. After touring Old Faithful by oversnow vehicle earlier that year, he recognized the opportunity to provide a unique guest experience by converting the "Campers' Cabins" building (a partially winterized dormitory for summer employees who served several hundred nearby cabins) into a hostel-type dorm.[46] Because it was rustic (most bathrooms, for example, were public), Ludewig argued that advertising should emphasize not the lodge, but rather the experience it would make possible: a convivial atmosphere focused on the pristine and peaceful Old Faithful environment (an advertising thrust that was in line with Anderson's thinking on winter use). Successfully persuaded, the company opened the Old Faithful Snowlodge on December 17, 1971, emphasizing "simple, pleasant and comfortable lodging spiced with hearty western food and beverage and nature's grandest winter display." The lodge was immediately popular—sold out its first Christmas—and remained open for winter seasons through 1998, when it was replaced with a more comfortable lodge that still operates in winter.[47]

Anderson and his staff also realized that they needed to promote their new policy to win over public support. Following the example of the NPS's first director, Stephen Mather, who had promoted the national parks themselves forty years earlier, they issued press releases advertising Yellowstone's wonders and the park's new winter program. They had several public relations successes. The federal Bureau of Outdoor Recreation included the Old Faithful–West Yellowstone trip in a movie on trails open to NPS visitors.[48] Anderson plied his connections in the area to coax Lowell Thomas, the skier and NBC radio news commentator, to visit the park in winter. Thomas toured the park in March 1969 via both snowcoach and snowmobile and gave the country several glowing reports.[49] As hoped, these efforts helped secure the already-growing public interest in snowmobiling through Yellowstone.

Publicity efforts also brought increasing acceptance of Yellowstone's snowmobile program in the political realm. Cliff Hansen, now freshman senator for Wyoming, was the last to make a demand for plowed roads, in 1970. By contrast, most of Wyoming's other political representatives (at both the state and national levels) were by then becoming supportive of the snowmobile program. Governor Stan Hathaway and Senator McGee wrote to George Hartzog early in 1970 to request that the NPS make snowmobile trips from Grand Teton National Park to Old Faithful more feasible by (ironically) plowing the road from Colter Bay to Yellowstone's South Entrance. Without it being plowed, visitors had an additional 17 miles to snowmobile in both directions to reach Old Faithful (for a total of almost 60 miles each way), a distance that prevented many from wanting to try it. Recognizing that granting the request would promote acceptance of Yellowstone's snowmobile program in the powerful Wyoming political community, Hartzog granted it. Grand Teton authorities began plowing the road late that year, an action that turned plowing into a tool to facilitate snowmobiling in Yellowstone.[50]

All these efforts to stimulate snowmobile visits and promote acceptance of the park's new program had their desired effects. As noted earlier, visitation boomed, with most visitors now traveling on snowmobiles. The advent of road grooming, along with West Yellowstone's Snowmobile Roundup, kept growth rates nearly exponential into the early 1970s. There were more than 40,000 oversnow visitors in winter 1973–1974 (about 35,000 arrived by snowmobile and 5,000 by snowcoach, which remained stable in this era). As Park Ranger James E. Fox succinctly summarized, "The key word in snowmobile use within the park . . . is growth." Certainly, the fun and freedom associated with snowmobiling contributed to this trend, as suggested by the fact that snowmobiling was growing rapidly nationally at the same time.[51]

By 1972, then, Yellowstone had a successful snowmobile program, complete with road grooming and a popular lodge in the winter wilderness. Calls for plowing ceased, so managers no longer feared the conversion of their park into a speedway (though more modern events might suggest that perhaps they should have). The pressures of the time had pushed them toward adopting snowmobiling to protect the park, and the plan seemed to be working. However, the solution that preserved the park's atmosphere soon brought yet more problems, which managers again attempted to address as best they could without challenging the basic form of access.

A Diluted Environment and a Pair of Earplugs

The rapid increase in snowmobile visitation in the early 1970s exacerbated the problems that park managers had already experienced (particularly litter, off-road travel, and associated wildlife harassment) and brought some new problems. Of those, snowmobile noise was the most annoying. The earliest snowmobiles were quite loud, regularly emitting more than 80 decibels of noise, a volume about equal to a freight train's.[52] Some snowmobile owners made their machines even louder by altering them to increase their power (such as with an expansion chamber, an after-market device that allowed for increased fuel combustion). Field rangers reported hearing snowmobile noise as far as 5 miles away and complained especially about machines fitted with expansion chambers. Ranger Pete Thompson, for example, noted that when they passed within 20 feet, their noise was "actually painful to the eardrum." His colleague Ranger James E. Fox also complained about the noise being loud enough to be painful, particularly when one had to listen to many of them over the course of a day. Other problems included speeding and exhaust. The latter would accumulate at the West Entrance (prone to winter air inversions, which produce a stable air mass at ground level) to the point that "a foul-smelling blue pall of smoke hangs over [it] for most of the morning."[53]

Rangers were not alone in making these complaints, for a fair number of private individuals wrote the park with similar concerns during this era. For many, snowmobile noise was the dominant concern. Others worried that snowmobile use caused wildlife harassment, both through their noise and their operators' behavior. Most of those filing complaints asked that snowmobiles be banned from Yellowstone, and two specifically suggested that the management restrict travel to snowcoaches only.[54]

Anderson and his staff did their best to address such problems, primarily by adopting and enforcing new targeted regulations. A basic but important step was to make snowmobiles subject to the same regulations as automobiles, an action Anderson accomplished in 1969 in accordance with NPS suggestions. That decision made off-road travel illegal and remedied some concerns about wildlife harassment. Over the next two years, Anderson issued other regulations requiring snowmobilers to dispose of litter properly, to adhere to the speed limit (45 mph), and to use machines emitting less than 78 decibels of noise. Snowmobile manufacturers were making strides at quieting their machines at the same time, an encouraging trend for Anderson and his staff. Putting these regulations in place was a successful move when combined with improved law enforcement (for example, regular staffing at the busier entrances and the Old Faithful Visitor Center). Anderson probably felt he had little choice but to work out the kinks of his snowmobile program; to do otherwise could have reopened the feared door to plowing.[55]

Still, rangers who dealt directly with snowmobile regulation enforcement continued to question the new policy well into the 1970s. Richard T. Danforth, a ranger based in West Yellowstone, argued that snowmobiles, by being recreational vehicles, changed the focus of a winter visit for people from enjoying Yellowstone's wonders to having fun on their machines (one of the problems Anderson had feared). He wrote Anderson,

> The snowmobilers are here for the express purpose of having a good time. They are not here to take in all the joys of Yellowstone in its natural setting. To affirm this, you might talk with the Naturalists at Old Faithful and ask them just how many snowmobilers take in the Interpretive movie or ask anything about the natural features of the park other than "When does Old Faithful go off next."

Danforth feared that "we have allowed ourselves to get into the trap of changing the park from one of the primary natural areas into a recreational area." To turn the emphasis in winter visitation back toward an appreciation of Yellowstone's wonders, he suggested plowing the mid-elevation west side roads, along with the road from Norris to Canyon (so visitors could drive to the Lower Falls) and the road from Old Faithful to the South Entrance (which he acknowledged would be difficult due to snow accumulations there). Plowing, he felt, would not only be less expensive for the agency, but because automobiles were familiar to all Americans, the focus of a winter visit would also be more on the park's wonders, not on having fun with snowmobiles. In short, visitors traveling by car would be more interested in learning about the park and its natural features.[56]

Field-based rangers like Danforth were not the only ones to question the funmobile's appropriateness in Yellowstone. At least one colleague of his in the NPS's Rocky Mountain Regional Office also expressed reservations about the activity to Superintendent Anderson. Lorraine Mintzmyer verbally told Anderson that she thought a fundamentally recreational vehicle like the snowmobile would subtly change the park experience from educational to recreational. As she later wrote, "this intrusion was a recreational activity inconsistent with the purposes of the 'first' National Park. . . . I also knew, from past history, that once a use was started, it multiplies and overwhelms the very resource it occupies."[57] She wrote this in 2007 with the benefit of hindsight, but the verbal warning she and Danforth gave would be considerably more prophetic than they realized at the time. Unfortunately, Anderson seemed to be blinded to this possibility by his fear of admitting the automobile into the park in winter—or by his personal love of snowmobiling (more on this later).

Potential solutions to some of these problems existed, but they were either impractical at the time or ignored. One had already been suggested: restricting winter travel to snowcoaches. Such vehicles had been used successfully in the park for more than a decade and could have been a viable alternative to either plowing or snowmobile travel. However, they did not offer the touring flexibility and freedom that American tourists had enjoyed vis-à-vis the automobile for decades. The snowmobile was the winter equivalent of the auto, offering that freedom and most likely shifting the debate to exclude the snowcoach option. Whether it was snowmobiles or autos, both symbolized freedom, blinding the actors in this ongoing debate to a solution that might have worked for all. It would not be seriously discussed until the 1990s.

Those same two options (snowmobile or automobile travel) could have been altered in other ways to address concerns about them. For example, restricting plowed roads to commercial tour vehicles would have prohibited private vehicle travel, thereby preventing Yellowstone from becoming a thruway and improving safety while allowing visitors to tour the winter wonderland. Alternatively, restricting snowmobilers to guided tours (as suggested by Yellowstone Park Ranger Douglas Riley) would likely have improved driver behavior. However, neither may have been feasible in the political climate of the era. The plowing restriction would have gone against thirty-five years of pressure for highways accessible to all motorists, and the snowmobile restriction would have removed much of the very freedom that made such vehicles so attractive in the first place (though park managers did implement the latter idea in 2004, as detailed in Chapter 5). Both restrictions could have improved the long-term situation, but Anderson probably believed that the feasibility of either was questionable, just like the snowcoach-only option. Situated on the frontline of dealing with strong external plowing pressure, he was most concerned with defending his park against the impacts that plowed roads would presumably bring. As time would tell, he might have been the first to defend the snowmobile policy, but he would not be the last to do so, often for good reasons but in the face of valid public concern.

More and more, such questions were not only being raised in Yellowstone but also throughout the park system and the northern states in general. Taking advantage of the American "infatuation with noise, speed, and the great outdoors," snowmobile manufacturers were very successful in the late 1960s at selling their machines, with total snowmobile numbers ballooning from less than 100,000 in North America in 1965 to almost 2 million less than six years later. With such an increase, the same problems that Yellowstone was experiencing were becoming noticeable throughout the country. Noise was again the most common complaint, along with snowmobile fumes, wildlife harassment (often mentioned were accounts of snowmobilers in other regions chasing coyotes until the animals were crushed by the machines or dead from exhaustion), litter, trespassing on private property, safety, and vegetation trampling.[58]

In response, conservationists and other members of the public demanded regulations to guide snowmobiler activity. Local, state, and federal agencies responded with a wide variety of proposals, ranging from outright bans to restricting snowmobiles to specific trails and curfews on their use. The regulations that resulted helped on local scales, but disparities between and within agencies produced confusion on the ground. For example, Grand Teton allowed some off-road snowmobiling (in the "Potholes" area, as mentioned earlier, and now on Jackson Lake), but Yellowstone prohibited off-road travel, and Glacier was moving toward banning snowmobiling altogether. Concerned citizens demanded more consistent regulation, both from the NPS and from the federal government. Regarding the NPS, they demanded a more restrictive and specific decibel limitation, rather than the agency's comparatively weak regulation requiring only a working muffler on snowmobiles (the 78 decibel limit mentioned earlier was specific to Yellowstone).[59]

The NPS responded in the 1970s by restricting snowmobile models allowed in national parks to those 1973–1975 models that emitted 82 decibels or less (at or near full-throttle at a distance of 50 feet) and to post-1975 models that emitted 78 decibels or less. However, the agency continued to give park superintendents the discretion to allow or prohibit snowmobiling and to determine what areas were open to snowmobiling. The national parks had been created partly because each park was unique, and on some matters, such as off-trail prohibitions, or snowmobiling on lake surfaces, it therefore would have been difficult to devise rules that would apply to all the parks equally. Other matters—such as noise restrictions—were more amenable to national standards. Sorting the policies appropriate for national regulation from those better left to individual park decision-making was sometimes a source of debate among NPS personnel and interest groups, and this continues to be the case. In this situation, conservationists remained unhappy with the off-road provision, and the discrepancies among parks continued to worry them. Actions on the national scale would soon sharpen the focus on the interpark differences, but still without a resolution.[60]

Snowmobiles were not the only off-road vehicles causing concern at the time. Dune buggies and motorcycles were also proliferating throughout the country, broadening the concerns about snowmobiles into national concerns about off-road vehicle (ORV) use in general. Accordingly, members of Congress and the executive branch investigated ORV issues in 1971. The Interior and Insular Affairs Committee held an informational hearing on snowmobiles and other ORVs that May, and the newly formed Environmental Protection Agency (EPA) held more hearings later that year on ORV noise pollution. Interior Secretary Rogers B. Morton investigated the impacts of such vehicle use on federal lands, personally visiting Yellowstone in the winter of 1972–1973 to observe its snowmobiling program. These efforts produced ample evidence of ORV proliferation and associated problems on federal lands. It was obvious that a more consistent approach toward their use had become necessary.[61]

Congress did not provide that direction, but President Richard Nixon soon did, in Executive Order 11644, which he issued in 1972. Entitled "Use of Off-Road Vehicles on the Public Lands," the order intended to manage ORV use such that resources would be protected and conflicts among land users minimized. All federal land managers were required to minimize wildlife harassment, noise, and the trampling of vegetation from ORV use, and national park managers could only allow it if it did not adversely affect the "natural, aesthetic, or scenic values" of their lands. While some executive orders were toothless presidential proclamations, this executive order clarified the purpose and interpretation of the National Environmental Policy Act (NEPA), which Nixon had signed into law just two years earlier. NEPA, which is still in effect, compelled federal agencies to examine the environmental impacts of proposed actions before they were enacted and stipulated that the agencies examine a variety of actions, not single choices. The act is a "look before you leap" requirement: It does not mandate that agencies choose the most environmentally protective option, but it does say they must know what the environmental consequences of an action will be. In Nixon's case, subsequent court cases involving his executive order determined that it had the force of law, though those cases did not define "natural, aesthetic, or scenic values."[62]

Nixon's order prompted a review of snowmobiling in all national parks. The NPS revised its national policy to prohibit the activity in parks unless superintendents specifically opened their parks to it. The "open unless closed" approach therefore changed to a "closed unless specifically opened" approach, suggesting that increasing criticism of snowmobiling in parks was influencing the agency's thinking. Additionally, because the full ramifications of NEPA were now clear (initially, the act seemed to be just a broad statement of policy, but subsequent examination revealed that it had some toothsome requirements), managers realized they had to consider the environmental impacts of snowmobiling in individual parks.[63]

Superintendent Anderson was one of the first to respond. He specifically opened Yellowstone to snowmobiling, designating all unplowed park roads as snowmobile routes (the same routes that had been open to snowmobiling for almost a decade). He noted that he was following the executive order's guidelines, but he did not specifically examine the environmental impacts of his decision as NEPA regulations directed, and as his supervisor, Acting Regional Director Glen Bean, may have directed him to do.[64] Most likely, he felt the examination was unnecessary, because snowmobiling had been allowed in Yellowstone for years and he had already taken many steps to mitigate the activity's environmental impacts. Doing the environmental examination might also have ignited the plowing issue all over again, especially if it found that snowmobiling had unacceptable impacts. Conversely, the environmental inspection might instead have found that plowing would produce more impacts, and/or that snowcoach-only travel or restricted bus travel were workable alternatives. But no evidence of such an assessment—or of the reasoning against doing one—exists.

By contrast, many other national park superintendents either did examine snowmobile impacts on their parks or simply banned the machines to comply with the executive order. Most parks in the snowbelt states had admitted snowmobiles as Yellowstone had; in fact, only a handful had not, largely due to inconsistent snow or lack of unplowed roadways.[65] Responding to the directives, Grand Canyon, Yosemite, Lassen Volcanic, Sequoia/Kings Canyon, and Glacier national parks all banned snowmobiles.[66] Environmental examinations could result in decisions to continue allowing snowmobiles; for example, Rocky Mountain National Park managers decided in 1975 to retain a 10-mile snowmobile trail on the park's west side. Crater Lake, Acadia, Grand Teton, and Mount Rainier national parks also allowed snowmobiling to continue, but the level of environmental compliance in these parks varied from none (Acadia) to adequate (Crater Lake and Mount Rainier) to extensive but delayed (Grand Teton, which did not examine the environmental impacts until the early 1980s). So the executive order resulted in some snowmobiling restrictions, but it did not end the variability in park compliance. To a large degree, this variability reflected the differing conditions in national parks; blanket policies for all parks are not always possible.[67]

When asked about his colleagues' decisions to ban snowmobiles, Superintendent Anderson, in a postretirement interview, said, "I'm a little upset with some of my fellow superintendents. I sometimes think they are getting lazy when they want to ban snowmobiles simply because they are motor-powered vehicles. . . . [T]hey just don't want to get involved because it sets up a debate and . . . creates work for land managers. He'd [sic] much prefer to sit back and rest in the traditionally quiet parts of the year."[68] In that same interview (with Derrick Crandall, trail program coordinator for the Snowmobile Safety and Certification Committee), Anderson made other comments that indicate that he personally liked snowmobiling and may have been blind to its problems. For example, when asked about the snowmobile noise impacts on cross-country skiers, he dismissed the concern by suggesting they ski farther from the roads or use a pair of earplugs. He left little doubt that he enjoyed snowmobiling, stating it was "a great experience and a great sport, one of the cleanest types of recreation I know." Certainly, retirement helped him feel free to express his opinion; his interviewer's connection with the snowmobile industry probably also encouraged sympathy with snowmobilers. Though he was more reserved as superintendent, his actions in that position still earned him the first-ever "International Award of Merit" in 1973 from the International Snowmobile Industry Association (ISIA) for his "enlightened leadership and sincere dedication to the improvement and advancement of snowmobiling in the United States." It is hard to avoid the conclusion that Anderson enjoyed the activity and was recognized for his actions to promote it in Yellowstone.[69]

Reading these quotations, one might also suspect that Anderson was blind to the activity's problems and therefore biased in his snowmobile decision-making. While there is probably some truth to this conclusion, one must remember the context in which Anderson made his decisions as superintendent. He arrived in Yellowstone just as thirty-five years of plowing pressure was culminating. Yellowstone was already leaning toward a snowmobile program; Anderson merely cemented that direction. More important, he was forced to choose between plowing and snowmobiling (with other options, again, being ignored or undesirable). Faced with thirty-five years of pressure to accommodate some form of winter visitation, and sincerely believing that plowing would turn the park into a thoroughfare, the choice for Anderson and some of his contemporaries seemed simple: They *felt* that snowmobiles would preserve the park's retreat-like nature—but feelings do not always square with reality.

For one thing, the snowmobile fun factor and the machine's environmental impacts diminished the special aura of the park's unique natural setting for some. Further, the park's forbidding winter climate would surely have deterred most interstate drivers, keeping wheeled vehicle volumes in Yellowstone low. Also, had Anderson undertaken the review required by NEPA, he and his staff might have realized that they could plow without incurring many harmful impacts. As noted earlier, that review might also have revealed other options that simultaneously protected the park and its special status while allowing people to visit it. Overall, in deciding not to look at the environmental consequences, he may have been simply taking the easy way out, or allowing himself to be blinded by his personal preference. Had Anderson undertaken this review, the park might look very different in winter today.

Anderson can also be criticized for his failure to see that institutionalizing snowmobiling would hamper future superintendents' flexibility to restrict that activity. A study of Yellowstone's own recent history would have revealed instances in which park managers found an established activity difficult to restrict, in part because concerned interest groups rallied to the activity's cause. For example, just ten years earlier, superintendent Lon Garrison had tried to ban motorboats from the arms of Yellowstone Lake to preserve a wilderness atmosphere there. However, he found his efforts stymied by powerful boating interests and sympathetic politicians. Though he did succeed in resolving some of the associated problems, he did not succeed in banning the boats as he desired, mainly because boating had become institutionalized and was aggressively defended by its fans.[70] Snowmobiling in Yellowstone would have a similar history, becoming established over the next quarter century and turning the park into the very speedway Anderson so feared. Had he contemplated the lessons from Garrison's boating controversy or done the environmental review, he might have reconsidered snowmobiling or been more receptive to other ideas, such as allowing only guided snowmobiling or only commercially driven buses and vans on plowed roads.

Anderson retired in 1975, to be replaced by a man who would keep the welcome mat out for snowmobiling. Responding to the welcome and needing to provide for their families at an otherwise economically depressed time of year, snowmobile entrepreneurs would continue to offer more snowmobiles for rent. By the time new Superintendent John Townsley left his post in 1982, these actions meant that snowmobiling in Yellowstone would be entrenched as *the* mode of winter travel.

Institutionalization Brings Power

John Townsley was another career NPS employee, son of Forrest Townsley, a Yosemite National Park ranger. The younger Townsley came to Yellowstone from the National Capital Parks in Washington, D.C. Like Anderson, he was a strong leader in his new post, not afraid of taking on challenging issues. For example, he removed the Yellowstone Park Company (and its owner, General Host) from Yellowstone due to mismanagement of park hotels. In general, though, he was so strong that he seemed to tolerate little feedback from his employees. Whereas almost all of those who knew the two superintendents liked Jack Anderson, they nearly unanimously disliked Townsley, primarily because of his autocratic management style.[71]

In directing Yellowstone's snowmobile program, Townsley continued Anderson's policies, further institutionalizing snowmobiling as the main way (along with a nominal amount of snowcoach travel) to tour Yellowstone in winter. He improved the road-grooming program, having the groomers operate at times in the evening when falling temperatures would refreeze the snow, producing a more durable snow surface. In response to pressure from interests in Wyoming and Cody, he stationed a new grooming machine at the East Entrance to provide more consistent trail maintenance over Sylvan Pass. In that way, that treacherous stretch of road was more predictably open and became somewhat safer to travel (though the snowsheds desired by his predecessors were never built).[72] To provide places for travelers to escape the cold, he opened warming huts at Canyon and Madison junctions. He had his staff comply with national NPS regulations to allow twelve- to fifteen-year-olds drive snowmobiles independently as long as they remained close to adults supervising them.[73] Finally, he had the park concessioner (by then TW Services, thanks to his efforts) reopen the Mammoth Hot Springs Hotel in the winter; it proved to be marginally more profitable than in the 1960s.[74]

When complaints about the program arose, Townsley continued Anderson's policy of defending it and hoping manufacturers would design quieter machines. Similarly, he attempted to deemphasize the snowmobile's fun factor, viewing it instead as a mode of travel that enabled visitors "to see, to enjoy, to understand, and to appreciate the extraordinary animal and thermal resources that are here" in Yellowstone. When a stuntman's lawyer requested permission in 1977 for his client to jump a snowmobile over Old Faithful Geyser during its eruption, Townsley and his staff found the answer easy: They firmly denied the request. Snowmobiling was there to stay not because it was a thrill but because it offered access to the park's winter beauty, at least in policy. Unspoken, but perhaps still fresh in managers' minds, was the fear that plowing could turn the park into a thoroughfare.[75]

The continuing concerns about snowmobiling, particularly in national parks, were not only evident in Yellowstone, but nationally as well. Provoked by conservationist worries, President Jimmy Carter clarified Nixon's earlier executive order with one of his own in 1977. Executive Order 11989 directed federal land managers to close areas or trails immediately where ORV use was found to be causing adverse effects on the soil, vegetation, wildlife or its habitat, or cultural or natural resources. The NPS's agency-wide response to the order, partially drafted by Townsley, was to endorse the vehicles' utility, not their recreational nature: "Snowmobiles are viewed as a mode of transportation which provide an alternate form of access when snow cover interrupts normal vehicular access to a park." Conservationists remained dissatisfied and pressed the agency to ban the machines nationwide. By this time, they more strongly felt that snowmobiles made a national park visit a recreational experience instead of an inspirational one, as

Danforth and Mintzmyer had argued earlier. Still, regarding Yellowstone, conservationists failed (just as they had previously, along with park managers) to present a satisfactory alternative. Despite Carter's attempt to provide more clarity, the disagreement between the agency and conservationists continued.[76]

With Townsley supporting snowmobiling so strongly, West Yellowstone merchants continued to develop their snowmobile economy. They first needed to make snowmobile travel in their community more feasible, because the state of Montana forbade snowmobiling on city streets unless specifically legalized by a municipality. Consequently, in 1968 West Yellowstone's city leaders made snowmobiling on the town's alleys legal, expanding such travel to all city streets five years later (except the two U.S. highways passing through town).[77] Snowmobile boosters opened more and more snowmobile rentals during this era and began grooming trails for them on national forest lands to the south and west of town. From 125 miles of such trails in 1972, the West Yellowstone snowmobile club expanded the trail network to 212 miles by the 1980s, in cooperation with the U.S. Forest Service and state of Montana. Such trails offered access to backcountry areas where off-trail snowmobiling (along with its associated thrills) was allowed, something Yellowstone did not offer. These actions all paved the way for snowmobiling to become the town's winter economic engine.[78]

Advertising was an important part of creating a snowmobile economy in the town. West Yellowstone's ads emphasized the thrill, freedom, and independence of the activity, along with its masculine prowess, control, and camaraderie. Other ads compared snowmobilers to modern-day cowboys, drawing upon the Old West's mystique to promote the activity. The advertising was broad-based, also targeting middle-class families who would be attracted to the package tours that West Yellowstone entrepreneurs developed about the same time. Bars in town proliferated as well, adding to the recreational atmosphere. With the Big Sky Ski Resort opening just 50 miles north at about the same time, such advertising effectively lured some skiers south for a day of snowmobiling, either in Yellowstone or on the national forest trails—but almost always on machines rented in West Yellowstone. In these ways, the town's merchants capitalized upon the snowmobiling craze.[79]

Between West Yellowstone's own efforts and those by Townsley and Anderson, the town's new snowmobile economy quickly developed. West Yellowstone's first bank, the First Security Bank, opened in 1966 and realized its two-year goal of $1 million in total footings in just three months. By 1982, the bank's footings were an order of magnitude greater. Residents directly employed in the snowmobile economy at that time numbered 426 (well over half the town's working-age population), serving 29 hotels, 11 restaurants and bars, 13 gift shops, 6 service stations, 2 lumber or hardware stores, and 4 realtors. By this time, West Yellowstone's economy no longer slumbered in the long winter; it buzzed with activity. As Dean Nelson, president of the bank, succinctly stated, the town's "winter economy *is* the snowmobile" (emphasis in original). It had become so lucrative by the early 1980s that some merchants derived more income in February than in any other month of the year, including the busy summer months, and 75 percent of the town's winter economic returns came from snowmobile rentals and related activity.[80]

West Yellowstone's experiences with snowmobiles during these years, as well as the advertising associated with them, gave the town a distinctive identity. The town and its people grew up with snowmobiles, so the machines were an expression of shared hardship and entrepreneurship. With pride, West Yellowstone merchants continued to advertise their town as the snowmobile capital of the world. Being to winter what the auto was to summer—motorized freedom—snowmobiles gave the town an ambiance of freedom and Western independence, themes that corresponded to core American values. These meanings would come to make any change to the dominance of snowmobiling there difficult, as would be seen in the 1990s.[81]

West Yellowstone's actions dovetailed with Townsley's to heighten the popularity of snowmobiling and cement it into place not only as the town's economic centerpiece but also as Yellowstone Park's mode of winter transportation. By the early 1980s, oversnow visitation had stabilized at about 45,000 per winter (see Figure 2.2), a number that brought the activity increasingly powerful defenders. Signs of that power came in 1981, when NPS budget cuts forced park managers to consider closing Yellowstone completely the following winter. Fearing the loss of their winter activity, dozens of snowmobilers and clubs wrote Townsley to urge he keep the park open. Politicians from the nearby states joined with the snowmobilers in defending the area's winter mainstay, as did Secretary of the Interior James Watt, who personally visited Yellowstone in December 1981 to look into the problem and defend snowmobile use. Sympathizing with the requests, Townsley found less drastic ways to cut spending instead, such as trimming some of the winter road grooming program and the number of seasonal employees hired for winter visitor services.[82] More indications of snowmobiling's newfound strength came from Yellowstone's neighbor to the south, Grand Teton National Park, where snowmobiling was equally institutionalized by the late 1970s. When Grand Teton authorities tried to close the Potholes area to off-road snowmobiling (in part because it was the only off-road snowmobiling area—not a frozen lake surface—in the national park system), they twice found their efforts stymied by snowmobile advocates and sympathetic congressmen in Wyoming.[83] Snowmobiling was *the* mode of transportation, now fully institutionalized and growing rapidly in authority and influence in both Grand Teton and Yellowstone national parks.

Like his predecessor, Townsley received the International Award of Merit from the ISIA. In presenting the award in May 1981, the group's chief executive officer,

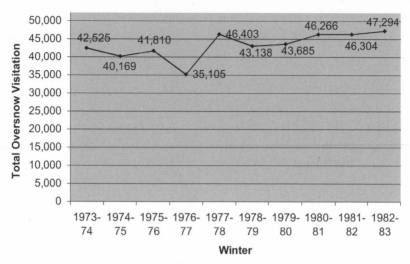

Figure 2.2. Winter Visitation to Yellowstone National Park, 1973/74–1982/83
Source: U.S. Department of the Interior/National Park Service, *Winter Use Plan Environmental Assessment*, November 1990, 88.

M. B. Doyle, noted that "snowmobilers, local tourism industry leaders and other governmental officials" had all recommended him for such appreciation. "They recognize his personal commitment to bringing persons enjoying a variety of outdoor winter activities into harmony with each other and the park resource they are experiencing." He also received the Department of the Interior's Distinguished Service Award for his work in human and public relations, in at least some measure as a result of his efforts in relation to snowmobile use. Such awards were notable, but probably small comfort to him at times, as he was fighting cancer. He soon succumbed to the disease, dying while in office in September 1982.[84]

Townsley left behind the country's largest national park snowmobile program. Visitors enjoyed well-groomed trails, welcoming rangers, and comfortable lodging at two different hotels. The program was basically complete, formalized, and accepted by many national park observers. Yellowstone was not a part of the national highway system, but it was a place set aside, made accessible by Bombardier's unique vehicle and the efforts of two superintendents to develop a winter use program based on snowmobiling instead of plowed roads. Park roads were snow-covered parkways, with some visitors enjoying the animals and winter scenery—and others who simply enjoyed snowmobiling. For Anderson and Townsley, the solution, seemingly so easy, worked for a while, with management actions like noise limits helping to preserve the peace. But, some park employees and observers disagreed, feeling that snowmobiles had fundamentally altered the park experience.

These critics might have argued that easy solutions often carry hidden costs and are easily unraveled—a truth that Townsley's successors would soon come to discover.

A Policy in Place

For thirty-five years, Yellowstone's managers had successfully resisted demands to plow their roads. For most of that time, they struggled to present an alternative vision of what Yellowstone should look like in winter, but the snowmobile's arrival in the 1960s allowed them to choose an option very different from plowing. Feeling that they were forced to choose between plowing and snowmobiling, Anderson and his staff chose snowmobiling for many reasons, all of which were related to protecting Yellowstone while accommodating visitation.

Once the choice was made, managers institutionalized it by addressing the problems that developed through managerial actions, new regulations, and technologies developed by snowmobile manufacturers. These solutions helped for a while, but eventually they became little more than Band-Aids for a problem managers seemingly would not recognize: The snowmobile's recreational nature consistently diverted some tourist attention from the park as they focused on their funmobiles. Attracted by the perky machines and the park, visitors continued to arrive, bringing more associated problems and allowing the snowmobile industry to acquire increasing power. That growth in turn made significant changes to the winter visitation program more and more difficult to implement. Conservationists, initially confused about the machines, gradually grew to dislike them and pressured park managers to ban them—but without presenting coherent alternative visions on how to accommodate park visitation. All in all, the snowmobile solution was tenuous, and it was already beginning to unravel by the early 1980s. Distinctive personalities, conflicting visions of the purposes of the national parks, growing sectors of the region's economy, changing technologies, and evolving societal preferences all influenced the discourse on snowmobiling, with some observers raising more and more well-justified concerns.

In choosing snowmobiling, Anderson and his colleagues were successfully able to resist political pressure and thereby prevent plowing. Pressure to plow the park's roads was enormous, emanating from throughout the tri-state area and even the West in general. That Anderson was able to resist such pressure might surprise some observers of national park history today; other managers, including many of those who succeeded him, were often forced to capitulate to political demands, contrary to their desires. Anderson could sell his decision to regional politicians because it served two commonly sought political ends: economic enhancement in the form of snowmobile rentals (as West Yellowstone experienced, certainly) and motorized access to the park. Anderson was fortunate in that he was able to both protect his park's resources and satisfy regional politicians. Future park managers would envy his fortune, even though they might rue his decision.

However snowmobiles may have resolved the dilemmas park managers faced in the late 1960s, they would eventually turn Yellowstone into the very thing Anderson most wanted to prevent: a motorized speedway. Gradually, insidiously, and quietly (in a manner of speaking), snowmobiles would come to dominate Yellowstone and the visitor experience. The industry and snowmobile advocacy groups would come to profit from the park activity in many ways, not just financially. Anderson might have foreseen that eventuality, but in his hectic day-to-day life as superintendent, he failed to take an important lesson from Yellowstone's own past: Once institutionalized, most recreational activities are impossible to eliminate entirely. He also failed to do the environmental review that was needed and failed to realize that his personal taste for snowmobiling may have clouded his ability to make decisions objectively. Overall, despite his best efforts, the park in the 1990s would be a place far different from what he envisioned, enjoyed, and strove to create.[85] As Richard Danforth had stated prophetically years earlier, "snowmobiling is snowballing faster than we can plan or fund for it."[86]

3
Skating on a Very Thin Edge

We are once again at a critical crossroads and are teetering on the brink—we have the opportunity to help preserve uniqueness or to proliferate a watered down, carbon copy mediocrity we can find elsewhere.

Yellowstone Park Ranger Gerald E. Mernin, 1984

Attempting to band-aid winter requirements at Yellowstone is an invitation to potential tragedy.

NPS Regional Director Lorraine Mintzmyer, 1987

In their wildest dreams, I doubt that anyone could have predicted [that snowmobile use] would grow like it has. But we can't turn back the clock. Winter recreation in Yellowstone is here to stay whether we like it or not.

Yellowstone Superintendent Bob Barbee, 1990[1]

National park scholars have often likened the parks to fiefdoms, each controlled and heavily influenced by its superintendent and their dispositions. Yellowstone's winter use history illustrates this critique. In this case, John Townsley's death would come to signify the closing of an era in Yellowstone's winter use history. The welcome mat for snowmobiling would be pulled back by a new superintendent who viewed the activity more critically.[2]

Additionally, the short memories of Americans meant that the reasons park managers originally embraced snowmobiling would gradually be forgotten; the story would soon see new actors who were not familiar with the issue's past. For these reasons, and because managerial situations change over time, the relatively uncritical acceptance of snowmobiling as Yellowstone's default mode of transportation became more and more untenable. By the mid-1980s, park managers and observers viewed the activity more skeptically and were less willing to make the sacrifices necessary to allow it.

These were the primary reasons for the change in attitudes toward snowmobiling, but the immediate motivation for the more critical approach was something familiar to park managers: resumed growth in winter visitation. Throughout the

1980s and early 1990s, snowmobiling continued to boom, and the boom magnified the problems.

The 1980s also saw increasing attention to the issue by interest groups. Two coalitions, one representing environmental interests and the other snowmobile interests, were founded in this era and soon brought their perspectives and associated values to this issue. Possessing dramatically different visions of what Yellowstone should be in winter, the coalitions pressed their goals and developed the skills and allies necessary to advance them.

Dismayed by the growth in visitation and pressured by the environmental coalition to rein in winter use, Yellowstone's managers began to reexamine their winter use program as best they could. But for fifteen years they floundered in their efforts, partly because snowmobiling was becoming more and more entrenched as the winter economic mainstay of local communities (with increasingly powerful support from politicians and the snowmobile coalition), but also because they could not procure the necessary funding to address the issue. Winter use became a growing, destructive snowball of noise, air pollution, and wildlife concerns. The crisis necessary to give this issue the attention it needed would not arrive until the late 1990s. So the comprehensive critique went undone, and the snowball continued to grow unchecked. By the mid-1990s, the worst fears of many would come true: Yellowstone had become a snowmobiling racetrack. The good old days were gone, and a tragedy of the commons ensued.

A Critical Crossroads: Problems, Questions, and No Easy Answers

In 1983, Robert Barbee became Yellowstone's new superintendent. His previous superintendent appointments had included Cape Lookout National Seashore in North Carolina, Hawaii Volcanoes, and Redwood National Park. At Redwood, Barbee had developed the NPS's premier ecological restoration program, reforesting the heavily logged headwaters areas of Redwood Creek (newly included in the park) to protect old-growth redwood trees downstream. In Yellowstone, his job included improving staff morale, which had sagged under Townsley. Barbee, a friendly, approachable person who trusted the men and women of his staff to do their jobs, was a good man for the task. He had a good sense of humor and was particularly adept at expressing things in quick, memorable sound bites (for example, when passing along the latest gossip from Washington, Barbee said, "I have the newest palace intrigue"). Possessed of political savvy, an understanding of the forces and values behind conflicting views, and an ability to get along with most people, he was capable of dealing with Yellowstone's controversies while supervising his large staff sensitively. Although he is best known for his park stewardship during Yellowstone's record-breaking 1988 wildfires, he was also the first superintendent to tackle—or try to tackle—the developing problems with winter use.[3]

Barbee arrived in Yellowstone to find a winter operation unique among the national parks. With the park's hot springs and geysers clashing with the cold air to create fabulous snow scenes populated by iconic American wildlife, Yellowstone's natural winter geography was distinctive enough. Add to that the necessity of using unusual forms of transportation for access, as well as two hotels catering expressly to winter visitors, and one could experience a place unlike any other in the world. Yellowstone was not the typical open space of the West; geographers would call it a distinct *place*, a combination of natural creations and human imprints not replicated elsewhere. Some visitors felt like early western explorers; others described the experience as quasi-religious. Yellowstone was indeed a place capable of drawing forth powerful feelings.[4]

It was also a place that generated significant economic activity, especially in West Yellowstone. By the mid-1980s, the community was thriving, with hundreds of snowmobiles and hotel rooms available for rent. The community collectively earned an average of $250,000 weekly from its winter visitors. Snowmobiling had become so lucrative that the town began pressuring Yellowstone for an extension of the oversnow travel season later into March, probably to provide attendees of its annual Roundup with Yellowstone access (organizers had moved the event's date to later in March, after Yellowstone typically closed to snowmobiling and began plowing). Park managers were reluctant to comply, mainly because such an extension would delay the spring plowing schedule and possibly affect the opening dates for the other entrances. Also, warming spring temperatures often melted out portions of the snow roads by this time. Nevertheless, they agreed to a one-week extension on the condition that spring weather might trump their efforts. They would not haul snow to those areas melting out, as some in West Yellowstone had evidently requested. The town's request, a reversal of nearly forty years of local pressure for plowed roads and/or a longer summer season, indicated how important snowmobiling had become, not only as the basis of the town's economy, but also as a basis of park policy-making.[5]

Snowmobiling was indeed the centerpiece of winter visitation during this era, as shown in Figure 3.1. Oversnow visitation consistently grew throughout the 1980s, topping out at over 100,000 in the early 1990s (when winter visitation, including those arriving by automobile through the North Entrance, exceeded 140,000). The growth in the mid-1980s was in part due to advertising by TW Services, the park's new concessioner. Having opened the Mammoth Hot Springs Hotel for winter business just before Barbee arrived, the company was disappointed by the response and sought to boost business through advertising. Also

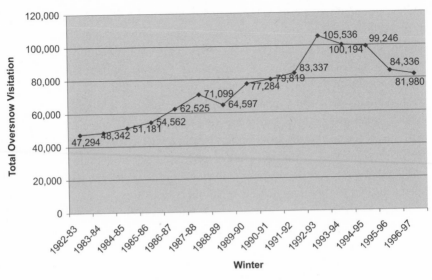

Figure 3.1. Winter Visitation to Yellowstone National Park, 1982/83–1996/97
Sources: U.S. Department of the Interior/National Park Service, *Winter Use Plan Environmental Assessment*, November 1990, 88, and Greater Yellowstone Winter Visitor Use Management Working Group, *Winter Visitor Use Management: A Multi-agency Assessment*, March 1999, 82.

contributing to the increase were improvements in snowmobile reliability and continued advertising by West Yellowstone merchants.[6]

With snowmobile use growing, park managers continued to deal with the associated problems. For example, in the mid-1980s, they banned dogsledding in the park amid safety concerns—namely, those arising from conflicts between dogsledding and snowmobiling.[7] Not unexpectedly, they also continued to receive complaints, most of which centered on snowmobile noise and air pollution, as before, and which arrived roughly in proportion to the number of snowmobiles. For example, Patricia Moon, after visiting Yellowstone in early 1986, complained to Superintendent Barbee, writing, "Wilderness? I am not sure it is because there were so many snowmobiles I felt at times I was back in the city. These machines really do not belong in a *natural* park. They are very noisy and an unattractive sight" (emphasis in original). Visitors were not the only ones concerned about ubiquitous snowmobile use. Kurt Westenbarger, a West Yellowstone resident, echoed Moon's concerns, writing Barbee that "the increased usage of the park causes me, and probably others, to enjoy it less due to the noise and smog." He urged the superintendent to enact pollution and noise limits immediately, before the inexorably growing use further escaped control.[8]

Winter visitors observing Old Faithful Geyser in eruption, 1970s or 1980s. By the late 1980s, more than 100,000 visitors toured Yellowstone every winter. While most enjoyed their visits, they brought increasing problems with noise, air pollution, and wildlife harassment. The photograph suggests the somewhat chaotic, unregulated nature of winter use in this era. NPS photo.

Growing more and more concerned, Yellowstone's managers developed a modest research program intended to assess snowmobiling's impacts on park wildlife. Two of the first research thrusts concluded that snowmobiling was not a major factor influencing park wildlife population size, distribution, behavior, or movements, although it did result in some minor impacts. Additionally, elk and bison tended to run away from cross-country skiers and snowshoers, avoiding them more than they avoided the typical snowmobilers. Such research sent mixed signals to park managers because it conflicted with their perception that cross-country skiing, a traditional activity, harmonized more with park values than did snowmobiling and its air and noise pollution.[9] Should managers ban or put restrictions on cross-country skiing, when most of their complaints and attention were directed at snowmobiling? The answer was unclear and would confound the issue for many years to come.

The complaints, the continual pressure to accommodate more snowmobiling, the activity's resumed growth, and the research worried Barbee. He was the "new kid" in Yellowstone, less inclined than previous superintendents to accept snowmobiling uncritically. The pressure to plow park roads had disappeared, and now the pressure was on to resolve the snowmobile issue. Even if he was unaware of his predecessors' reasons to allow snowmobiles, his situation was different, and the machines were cause for concern. When respected staff members like Gerald Mernin worried that the NPS was only succeeding in preserving "a watered down, carbon copy mediocrity we can find elsewhere," Barbee in turn wondered what Yellowstone should look like in winter, what level of control he had over winter use, and what effects resumed growth in winter visitation would have on park resources.[10]

His attention piqued, he sought a way to provide more direction on the issue of winter use and its probable growth. In 1983, he directed his staff to begin preparing a Winter Use Plan that would address the growth in an orderly and comprehensive manner. Early the next year, the staff met to brainstorm on the issues that the plan should address. Verifying that Barbee's concerns were valid, the group came up with a substantial list of winter concerns, headed with the question, "Is the purpose of Yellowstone National Park only to provide the visitor an opportunity to experience and appreciate the natural and historic values present here, or should we also provide some purely recreational activities?" The question suggests that some in the park still viewed snowmobiling as primarily recreational, a distraction from the park's central missions. Other important issues included the cost of the park experience (including transportation, and whether plowing the park's mid-elevation roads on the west side would defray such costs), the appropriateness of different recreational activities, visitor facilities and services (and the kinds of visitors they would draw), operational matters, research needs, and staffing.[11]

By June, Barbee's staff had a working draft of a Winter Use Plan, a step that was significant for several reasons. First, it was the first coordinated, proactive attempt to grapple with the broad question of what winter visitor uses of Yellowstone were appropriate, along with the associated levels of such uses and necessary services and facilities for them. In fact, the plan acknowledged that "decision making regarding winter use in Yellowstone has been incremental" since the 1960s. Additionally, it was an environmental assessment, the first attempt to subject winter use in Yellowstone to the environmental review required by the National Environmental Policy Act. As part of that review, at least one staff person suggested that park managers develop a program to monitor the impacts from winter visitor use, an idea that would not see fruition until the mid-1990s. Unfortunately, because this effort to examine winter use was neither crisis-driven nor funded, it soon stagnated, along with the proposed monitoring program. Without emergency funding, the Winter Use Plan and its successive documents would be more of a soft glance than a hard look.[12]

Progress on the plan occurred in fits and starts, with most substantive action on it delayed until the end of the decade. In part, it became mired in confusion over how best to address the issues. As they discussed the topic, staff members gradually realized that they had no baseline with which to compare prospective changes; nowhere did they have a comprehensive listing of winter policies. Moreover, such policies often differed from district to district within the park; one district's staff might shovel their walkways for winter visitors while rangers in another simply allowed visitors to pack down the snow on them. A general lack of research on the impacts of winter use on park resources was a concern (there were no air or noise studies to complement the two wildlife studies). Some felt snowmobile impacts like air and noise pollution should be addressed through specific snowmobile limits, while Barbee felt too much detail would attract the disapproval of surrounding elected officials. Finally, few other national parks could provide substantial guidance to Yellowstone; most other parks greatly curtailed their winter services or closed completely. Of those that did welcome snowmobilers, all saw much less use than Yellowstone (Grand Teton, Rocky Mountain, and Voyageurs were the only other parks with significant snowmobile use). For these reasons, Barbee knew that "all eyes were on Yellowstone" to see how he and his staff dealt with winter use.[13]

Those eyes would have to wait until 1989 and 1990 because two unexpected controversies erupted to delay the winter use critique. In the mid-1980s, the Fishing Bridge controversy blew up and occupied much of the park staff's time. Although the complete story of that controversy is beyond the scope of this book, a brief review is warranted because the issue brought a powerful actor into play in Yellowstone policy-making. Barbee and his staff wanted to close the stores and campgrounds around the historic bridge at the outlet of Yellowstone Lake, fearing that the visitors they attracted were causing a high number of unintentional grizzly bear deaths. Residents in nearby Cody, however, fearing that such closure would dampen the flow of tourists through their community, opposed the move and engaged U.S. Senator Alan Simpson (like his father, former governor Milward Simpson, he was from Cody) to defend their interests. Research by the University of Wyoming soon disproved the town's economic worries. However, the research did not do much to change local perception, and Simpson and many Cody residents remained opposed to the closure. Early in 1988, the NPS finalized a compromise, closing only the most bear-sensitive facilities and leaving the RV park in place. This controversy became "an unimaginable energy drain on time and resources" for Barbee and his staff for four years, stalling most progress on the Winter Use Plan. It also had the side effect of attracting political attention to Yellowstone, mainly from Simpson and, to a lesser extent, the rest of Wyoming's congressional delegation.[14]

Just as the Fishing Bridge controversy was ending, freeing up park staff, the 1988 wildfires occurred. From June through October, record drought, high temperatures, and wind caused wildfires to burn almost 800,000 acres (about 36 percent) of Yellowstone. These fires were the largest in Yellowstone's history—indeed, the largest in recent memory anywhere in America—and they occurred in a beloved national park. Park managers spent most of the winter of 1988–1989 organizing recovery efforts, examining their firefighting actions that summer, assisting with a national review of federal-agency fire policies, commissioning an intense research thrust into fire history and ecology, and otherwise preparing the park for the next summer's visitation. As with Fishing Bridge, all park staff resources were consumed in the fire-fighting and recovery efforts, and still more political attention was focused on park managers and their policy-making, again by Simpson, in particular.[15] Consequently, work on the Winter Use Plan again stalled, and political sensitivities were further heightened.

Despite the distractions, Yellowstone's managers were able to take a little time out to address winter use. In February 1987, they cooperated with regional office personnel in a comprehensive evaluation of their winter operations. Regional Director Lorraine Mintzmyer found that the NPS in general was "skating on a very thin edge," with inadequate funding and preparation for its winter use program. She suggested splitting the Winter Use Plan effort into two parts. The first would be the necessary summary of Yellowstone's existing winter policies and needs, while the second would be the Winter Use Plan itself. To secure funding for these endeavors, the group felt that NPS Director William Penn Mott should invite congressional representatives to Yellowstone for a winter visit to observe the situation personally.[16]

Arranging the congressional visit was easier than coming up with the suggested policy summary. In February 1988, three members of the Senate Committee on Natural Resources (which authorizes funding to national parks) visited Yellowstone, touring the park and listening to managers' woes. Barbee, who already knew that curtailing his winter use program, given its economic importance regionally, was not politically feasible, attempted instead to have his existing program adequately funded (a move that would draw criticism from conservationists). He and his staff provided the senators with estimates of the winter funding necessary to properly manage the park: $840,000 for one-time capital-improvement funds, $850,000 for annual recurring costs, and a one-time appropriation of $300,000 for the Winter Use Plan (and several million to build a new Snowlodge, a responsibility that the agency eventually delegated to the park's primary concessioner). Though the three senators were sympathetic, their full committee was less so. Yellowstone received only a one-time allocation of $1.4 million, which park managers used to fund the most desperately needed capital improvements.

As his predecessors had done, Barbee continued to move forward without sufficient funding, doing his best with what time his staff could carve out of their busy schedules. Under those circumstances, the policy examination actually did move forward, however incompletely.[17]

Once the furor over the wildfires had subsided, some of Barbee's staff returned to the assessment of existing policies. In May 1989, they released an 85-page document entitled "Existing Winter Use Management Guidelines, Inventory, and Needs." The document was significant for two reasons. First, it was the first comprehensive summary of Yellowstone's winter use policies and the first formal NPS critique of snowmobiling (including the increasingly decrepit Snowlodge). Second, it was the first time that park managers publicly acknowledged that winter funding was coming at the expense of summer visitors. In listing the funding and staffing necessary to properly operate the park in winter (which included funds for research and monitoring), the document confirmed that winter use was an unwanted child, demanding attention but never receiving an adequate amount of it. Overall, it was confirmation that times had changed: Snowmobiling increasingly took up more than its share of management effort and time.[18]

Completion of the assessment was the first step in trying to get a handle on burgeoning winter use. The next would be the Winter Use Plan itself. But before park managers could complete the plan, they found themselves receiving some unexpected criticism from a new interest group, one that would take a special interest in Yellowstone affairs.

Coalitions of the Willing and Unwilling

Ronald Reagan, Interior Secretary James Watt, and their federal land policies seemed to magnify the persistent threats to Yellowstone's integrity in the 1980s, at least to conservationists. Those threats resulted in the formation of two new interest groups, one dedicated to Yellowstone's protection and another to promoting Reagan's policies. Both, the Greater Yellowstone Coalition (GYC) and the BlueRibbon Coalition, would come to play instrumental roles in the winter use story.

First on the scene was the Greater Yellowstone Coalition, which had its roots in 1981 Reagan administration proposals to increase timber harvests on the national forest lands around Yellowstone and to allow oil and gas drilling in the Washakie Wilderness on the park's eastern boundary (proposing such drilling inside designated wilderness was a precedent-setting threat). John Townsley was still superintendent at that time, and he saw a risk to continued grizzly bear preservation in the proposals. Recognizing that the Yellowstone area was an "ecosystem" (a natural system of animals and plants interrelated with each other and their physical and chemical environment), he believed that grizzly conservation necessitated a more coordinated management approach among the federal agencies in the Yellowstone area. Despairing of any such vision in the Reagan administration proposals, Townsley actually appeared at a public hearing that year to criticize the oil and gas drilling proposal—in his official capacity as superintendent! Such a forward action resulted in a hostile reaction from his Washington superiors. They bawled him out a few days later, telling him not to stick his nose into the management of surrounding lands. Though the logging did occur, resulting in extensive clearcuts on the park's western boundary (which grizzlies avoid to this day), Townsley could take pride in the fact that the oil and gas drilling proposal died.[19]

Even though Townsley had spent his life working for the agency and knew well of its political influences, he was bothered by this experience and felt that something more was needed to ensure long-term preservation of Yellowstone's bruins and other resources. Discussing the matter with Rick Reese, director of the Yellowstone Institute (a nonprofit organization that sponsors educational field trips and classes about facets of Yellowstone's natural history), Townsley planted a seed in Reese's mind that germinated and grew after Townsley died. Reese learned all he could about the incipient ecological subfield of conservation biology (what ecosystems were and how to preserve them). He soon published a book entitled *Greater Yellowstone,* which applied conservation biology concepts to the Greater Yellowstone Ecosystem and argued that federal agencies needed to preserve the ecosystem's functions and resources through wise management actions.[20]

Such education efforts were useful, but Reese knew that action based upon that knowledge was even more necessary, especially in the contemporary political climate. A Greater Yellowstone Sierra Club was needed, an organization that could speak and act independently to promote conservation in the Yellowstone region, just as the Sierra Club had long done for Yosemite National Park. Consequently, in 1983 Reese and several of his colleagues in the area met at the Teton Science School (another field school similar to the Yellowstone Institute) in Jackson Hole, Wyoming. There, they organized the Greater Yellowstone Coalition, an alliance of existing local, regional, and national organizations, all with the common mission of "protection of the Greater Yellowstone ecosystem in its natural condition" through education and citizen action. Chartering the group were thirty-five such organizations; today, the GYC has several dozen member groups and several thousand individual members (it went public in 1984).[21]

The group was an immediate success, mainly because it was a highly motivated group of individuals who applied a new and powerful concept to an already beloved place. Its message was widely received, accepted, and promoted, at least initially. For example, just two years later, NPS Director Mott gave a speech discussing the ecosystem concept and calling for coordinated management in the Yellowstone area, and by early 1991 (according to Reese), some 170 articles and books had been published promoting the idea, along with specials on all the country's major television networks and several conferences. The Congressional Research Service soon argued that the Greater Yellowstone Ecosystem was an "identifiable landform," and even President George H. W. Bush referred to the idea in a 1989 speech, back at the Teton Science School.[22]

Words are one thing, but actions are another. Initially, the group's actions seemed idealistic. One of its first steps was to propose federal legislation to preserve the Greater Yellowstone Ecosystem. The group soon found that such wide-ranging proposals could backfire. The word "ecosystem" was not yet found in the lexicons of most local politicians. The Wyoming state legislature, perceiving a threat to traditional ways of managing federal lands there, almost passed a resolution condemning the concept—and the GYC. Learning as it went, by the latter part of the decade the Coalition began to focus on specific local issues that threatened its loftier goal. Such an approach offered more tangible results; it was easier to affect the outcome of a small local issue than to pass revolutionary legislation in Congress (particularly given Wyoming's attitude). Moreover, each success or failure offered the group an opportunity to emphasize its message, something it did well into the 1990s. As a result, the GYC was recognized as one of the most effective conservation groups in the country during this era.[23]

As winter use was one of those more local issues at this time, the GYC dabbled in it almost immediately. Concerned that snowmobile use stressed wildlife at an already demanding time of year and that little research had assessed its potential impacts, the group nervously watched park managers' actions in the 1980s. When Superintendent Barbee presented his wish list of financial needs to the congressional committee, the GYC became alarmed, fearing he was putting "the cart before the horse," asking for construction and acquisition funds before the impacts of those developments on Yellowstone's natural resources had been assessed. The group was further upset that park managers had not solicited any public opinion on winter use or on the issues that the proposed plan should address, as suggested by NEPA. Consequently, the GYC, the Wilderness Society, and the National Parks and Conservation Association all wrote to Yellowstone questioning what they viewed as a predetermined approach to winter planning and demanding both research into the effects of winter use and the opportunity for public comment. Networking like this with other groups was natural for the GYC, since it was already an alliance itself.[24]

In truth, Barbee and his staff were already planning to gather public input on the scope of the Winter Use Plan, so the conservationist demands were easily met. In spring 1989, park planners held six open houses in the Yellowstone area, invit-

Snowmobiles on Dunraven Pass, 1979. By the 1980s, snowmobiling (with some snowcoach visitation) was institutionalized as the means to visit Yellowstone in winter. All park roads not plowed were open to snowmobile visitation, including this route, which the NPS later closed due to avalanche danger. During this era, snowmobiling came to have both detractors and promoters, especially the Greater Yellowstone Coalition and BlueRibbon Coalition, respectively. NPS photo.

ing residents to discuss winter use issues with them. Many participated, and another 250 groups or persons, including the GYC and several other interest groups, mailed their comments to the agency.[25]

Conservationists touched upon all of the growing concerns with snowmobiling, including noise and air pollution, the need for research and monitoring into winter recreation's impacts upon wildlife and other resources, and the need for comprehensive planning. Of the organized groups, the GYC provided the most extensive and perhaps the most thoughtful comments. GYC Program Assistant Don Bachman challenged the NPS to define the essence of Yellowstone in winter, arguing that it was "winter beauty, raw threatening cold, and silence." In suggesting that all winter visitor use should be guided by this concept, the group's efforts complemented the park managers' recent actions, though they were perhaps more articulate in presenting what made the winter wonderland such a distinctive place. To them, Yellowstone's beauty, risk, and natural quiet were manifestations of the park's inherent sacredness. The GYC would increasingly draw upon this American value in advocating for snowmobile removal from Yellowstone.[26]

On behalf of the GYC, Bachman specifically urged critical investigations into two issues that were brewing at the time, both of which would become primary concerns in the NPS planning process. The first was whether Yellowstone should open winterized lodging at Canyon Village, which had a lodge with several hundred cabins nearby. At the time, the cabins there were not winterized, but park planners were (separately) considering improvements to them. If the cabins were winterized, members of the public would have easier access to great cross-country skiing, such as trails to overlooks of the spectacular Lower Falls. The other issue was whether Grand Teton authorities should permit construction of a new snowmobile trail through their park that would connect to Yellowstone. Bachman and his associates feared that both of these ideas would encourage more visitor use of the parks, which in turn would exacerbate existing noise and safety problems (such as the lack of efficient oversnow rescue machinery, a problem at the time) and distract from the area's winter beauty. Consequently, the group opposed both development ideas.[27]

Countering the conservation community, in particular with regard to the snowmobile trail, was a consortium of political, economic, and recreation interests. The trail was to be called the Continental Divide Snowmobile Trail (CDST) and would connect Lander, Wyoming (where the idea originated), to Yellowstone's South Entrance, about 350 miles away. Part of the route, however, involved building a new 45-mile trail through the northeastern portion of Grand Teton National Park, either on the shoulder of the main highway from Moran to Yellowstone or on a utility corridor parallel to that same road but east of it and in the backcountry. Both ideas were strained interpretations of NPS policy, which restricted road use to either snowmobiles or automobiles (allowing snowmobiles on the shoulder of a plowed road put the two kinds of vehicles in dangerous proximity to each other) and which precluded public snowmobile use in the backcountry. Even though Grand Teton already had a precedent for violations of national policy by allowing off-road snowmobiling in the Potholes area, park managers there were reluctant to consider another such violation.[28] Still, with the strong support of the state of Wyoming, its congressional representatives, many chambers of commerce, both Grand Teton National Park hoteliers, and many different snowmobile advocacy groups, the trail possibility and the Winter Use Plan of which it was a part moved forward.[29]

One of the advocates of the CDST was the other coalition, the BlueRibbon. Its letter to the NPS endorsing the trail was only one page long, so it did not stand out among the many commenters.[30] However, just like the original snowmobiles that entered Yellowstone, this group may have been quiet in its entry but would come to have a loud voice in the winter use story. Understanding its background is just as important as knowing the GYC's.

Polarizing policies, such as those of Reagan and Watt, not only had their critics but also their supporters. If the GYC was a backlash in defense of Greater Yellowstone's preservation and national environmental laws, "Wise Use" groups were a backlash against a decade of progressively stronger federal land protection under the environmental laws passed in the 1960s and 1970s. Motorized recreational vehicle users especially disliked the 1964 Wilderness Act and Executive Order 11644 because they restricted off-road travel in some areas. With Watt's and Reagan's encouragement, these constituents organized interest groups dedicated to the "wise use" of the country's federal lands. To them, such use included liberal motorized use regulations on those lands. Many such groups were based in the rural West and drew financial support from resource extraction industries, whose leaders advocated the same cause: loosened federal land restrictions.[31]

The BlueRibbon Coalition was one such group, organized by Clark Collins, a southern Idaho electrician. He sympathized with the Wise Use movement because he enjoyed riding his dirt bike on the extensive federal lands in his region and had seen some favorite areas placed off-limits to off-road vehicle use. In the mid-1980s, he complained about the increasing restrictions to Idaho governor John Evans. Evans, who supported wilderness designation in Idaho, replied that "motorized recreationists are politically insignificant." Clearly, he was not sympathetic to Collins's concerns, but his dismissive, if frank, remark served to galvanize Collins (there are few things more motivating than such a dismissal—even twenty years later, the Coalition still recalled Evans's remark with bittersweet feelings).[32] Collins set about proving him wrong and soon organized the Idaho Public Land Users Association. With encouragement from Darryl Harris, owner and publisher of *SnoWest* magazine (a national publication for snowmobilers), Collins expanded his horizons to the national level in 1987, renaming his group the BlueRibbon Coalition and inviting all national motorized user groups to join in advocating for ORV freedoms. Within five years, his coalition included seventy different motorized user organizations with a combined membership of over half a million Americans nationwide. His enthusiastic response also included ORV manufacturers, retailers, and buyers, who provided much of the organization's support. The Coalition, based in Pocatello, Idaho, consistently would remain faithful to its industry contributors.[33]

Collins and Harris chose a name that they felt conferred legitimacy upon their members. Collins wrote, "We represent the very best of outdoor recreationists. Our member organizations and individuals truly are BlueRibbon citizens. That is the reason for the name." Calling themselves the "new environmental movement," the group's motto was "Preserving our natural resources FOR the public instead of FROM the public." Accordingly, the Coalition advocated the preservation of ORV opportunities on federal lands and encouraged citizens to become involved in their cause (much like the other coalition). Their members were often motivated to join when federal agencies closed areas that had become favorite family haunts (however, the group usually failed to examine whether those areas were open to ORV travel in the first place). They wanted to preserve places for ORV family outings as well as the chance to enjoy the freedom offered by their machines. While the group may not have initially or knowingly understood the power inherent in those values (family and freedom), they would eventually use them quite effectively in defending snowmobile access to Yellowstone—at times, more effectively than the GYC's use of the sacredness of nature to defend environmental conservation.[34]

During its early years, the BlueRibbon Coalition tapped into a powerful antifederal and antiregulation sentiment in the West but often seemed to be little more than a forum for griping about conservationists and the Wilderness Act. Article after article in the group's early years railed against one or the other while failing to advance an alternative vision of what ORV supporters desired or a fair way of resolving conflicts among the various groups interested in federal land policy-making. Although the GYC sometimes used inflammatory and confrontational tactics in the 1980s and may not have suggested a fair way of resolving conflicts either, its engaging vision made it the more effective of the two coalitions at that time. BlueRibbon did pay some attention to the simmering Yellowstone winter use debate, and it managed to influence some of the region's politicians. But it was not until the late 1990s that it became more politically powerful, in part because it hired a "Legal Action Team" in 1996. Thereafter, it found its power growing in the legislative and legal arenas, developments that will be more fully explored in the next chapter.[35]

For the time being, the two coalitions helped to prime the pump regarding winter use planning in Yellowstone. They highlighted two of the major issues (developments at Canyon and the CDST) and encouraged an increasing number of Americans to become involved in winter use planning. Due in part to their activities, the NPS soon escalated work on the Winter Use Plan and rediscovered the strength of a certain Wyoming politician.

Carrying Capacities, the CDST, and Politics

The CDST proposal highlighted a fact that was more and more evident to managers in both Grand Teton and Yellowstone national parks, that winter use in the two parks was integrally related, just as both parks were central pieces of the Greater Yellowstone Ecosystem. Because Yellowstone's managers had been engaged in winter use planning for several years, it was easy and logical for them to expand the scope of their project to include Grand Teton National Park (all future winter use planning would include both parks). Also, prodding by Wyoming politicians to expeditiously build the CDST accelerated the previously sluggish pace of winter use planning. Consequently, in 1989 the winter use planning effort expanded and picked up steam.[36]

Early that year, personnel from the two parks and the NPS regional office resumed work on the Winter Use Plan. They began by compiling a list of winter use issues along with potential solutions for each. The list included the two hot-button issues (the CDST and new lodging developments) as well as several related concerns and some mundane operational issues beyond the scope of this story (things like park housing and gasoline availability, which greatly concerned park employees and some visitors but do not set national policy precedents). The planners added two other options for the CDST (in addition to the two trail options previously discussed). The third called for CDST travelers to haul their snowmobiles through Grand Teton by trailer, while the fourth was the obligatory "No-action" alternative, which meant that the CDST would not be constructed. (NEPA requires that agencies compare proposed actions to such an alternative, usually continuing the present state or set of policies.)[37]

The other major issue, new park developments (especially at Canyon), had broadened into concern over visitor use levels and what the two parks could sustain—their carrying capacity—as well as the kind of visitor experience the NPS wished to provide. Should the agency emphasize quiet and solitude, or touring freedom? And should it undertake some sort of research to determine the parks' human carrying capacity? More and more, the agency and many conservation groups felt that such a study was necessary and that winter use policies should be adjusted based on its outcome. For that reason, planners identified research as one way to address visitor use levels.[38]

The agency's planners recognized several associated concerns. They discussed different ways to minimize wildlife harassment and disruption. Plowing more park roads was again considered, with Mammoth to Norris being specifically mentioned (of the mid-elevation roads, that one receives the lowest snowfall, especially at the Mammoth end). In response to urging by Cody interests, park managers discussed providing snowcoach service to the East Entrance (its distance from major park attractions, the Sylvan Pass hazards, and lack of demand for such service were all obstacles), as well as finding ways to improve the speed and affordability of such travel. Lodging was a prominent concern, with planners encouraging renovation or replacement of Old Faithful Snowlodge and raising the possibility of opening new lodging at Colter Bay and Signal Mountain in the Tetons in addition to Canyon Village in Yellowstone. Closing the Potholes off-road snowmobile area was an option, along with closing the Teton Park Road to snowmobiles. Finally, snowmobile noise was mentioned, with planners presenting different ways to reduce noise levels (primarily through working with the industry to develop quieter models, using temporal or spatial separation of snowmobilers from nonmotorized users, and using regulations to restrict the noisiest machines from entering Yellowstone).[39]

In September 1989, the planners sought public opinion for the second time on the various means of addressing these issues.[40] Public comment did not greatly differ in content from previous public meetings, though there were substantially more people speaking up (partly because conservation groups encouraged their members to become involved). Comments were fairly evenly split between those promoting snowmobile use and those urging restrictions upon it.[41] The pro-snowmobile forces all supported CDST construction along the backcountry power-line corridor, with many also calling for increased lodging availability in the Yellowstone area. Because Yellowstone was "widely considered to be the premier snowmobiling destination in North America," the International Snowmobile Industry Association added its support to the pro-snowmobile interests. Even Montana Congressman Ron Marlenee wrote to support snowmobiling, stating "National Parks are to be protected for the people not from the people," echoing the BlueRibbon Coalition, which also endorsed increased snowmobiling opportunity.[42]

Conservationists had not changed their position much either, honing their earlier criticism of increased development into a nearly unanimous call for a carrying capacity study. The National Parks and Conservation Association (NPCA) provided particularly helpful details on its Visitor Impact Management program, which it had developed and used to help managers in Arches National Park in Utah determine social carrying capacity for a popular site there (thereby eliminating the need for a larger parking lot).[43] Conservationists also requested that the U.S. Forest Service prepare an Environmental Impact Statement (EIS, a more comprehensive look at the environmental consequences of a federal action) on the CDST to examine its potential impacts (the agency managed most of the lands the trail crossed and was silent on the issue, for the time being). Others worried that the CDST could become a precedent encouraging snowmobile interests to press for a similar trail linking Cooke City to Tower or Mammoth, which would extend snowmobiling opportunities throughout the region, including areas currently closed to the activity.[44]

After analyzing the comments, park planners developed a preferred alternative, that combination of policies, management tools, and changes to the existing program that they would like to see implemented. In so doing, they evidently tried to please all constituent interests. They zoned the parks into backcountry, threshold, and developed zones, hoping to provide opportunities to experience quiet and solitude as well as more social opportunities. Similarly, they proposed

Cross-country skiers at Upper Geyser Basin (Old Faithful), 1970s or 1980s. Cross-country skiing has been a popular activity in Yellowstone since the 1930s, when park managers first began welcoming winter visitors. Although the 1990 Winter Use Plan suggested that the backcountry was the appropriate place for skiers seeking solitude, the high levels of snowmobile use prevalent in the park in the 1990s meant that true silence was not possible to find in many portions of the backcountry, including the Upper Geyser Basin. NPS photo.

to institute a "visitor use management program" to determine social and physical carrying capacities (a program very similar to that developed by the NPCA at Arches). Significantly, they proposed to build the CDST as a linear snow-berm on the road shoulder between Moran and Yellowstone's South Entrance, not in the backcountry (but still constructed). Finally, they would look into new snowmobile noise-abatement technologies and establish a noise-monitoring program.[45]

The proposal answered the question of what uses were appropriate in the parks by stating that all current uses were, and even some new uses like the CDST; any problems could be addressed through management actions (an approach in line with that of Anderson and Townsley, to be sure). The zoning concept also suggested that, while the parks could not be all things to all people, they could be most things to most people, providing a mix of natural and social experiences as they had done for decades. If one wanted a natural experience, the backcountry was the place to go; and if one wanted a social experience, the parks were large enough to provide that as well.

In reality (at least to those concerned with increasing snowmobile use), the planners had taken more of a soft glance than the hard look that winter use merited. To many observers on the conservationist side, the mitigations were poorly defined, without measurable goals or regulatory teeth. Making matters worse was the fact that the proposal skirted the most difficult issue—the very use of snowmobiles in the park—even though a recent survey found that when asked what they most disliked about their visit, more visitors listed snowmobiles than any other component. Yellowstone's managers simply continued the pattern that their predecessors had started, allowing themselves to be guided more by what was already occurring in the park, and by the sociopolitical pressures they confronted, than by the ideas that careful reflection suggested would be appropriate.[46]

This failure to examine winter use more critically was due primarily to the pressure park planners felt to accommodate more use, pressure largely emanating from the consortium of pro-snowmobile interests in Wyoming, including several cities such as Dubois and Cody, several counties, the state, chambers of commerce, and snowmobile advocacy groups throughout the state. As early as 1988, when the CDST was first proposed, managers were feeling pressure to capitulate; they undoubtedly looked to mitigation measures as ways to satisfy that pressure while preserving their park's resources. A year later, most of the trail was complete, having been patched together from existing trails on the national forests. The Grand Teton stretch was all that remained, a situation that was an increasingly sore spot with many Wyoming constituents, including some in Cody (interested in the trail even though it did not approach the town closely) and their senator, Alan Simpson.[47]

In early 1990, the pot of political pressure boiled over, when Simpson became directly involved. The "Son of Cody" took particular interest in Yellowstone affairs, and being Wyoming's senior senator, he carried substantial influence. Though he was generally a friendly man with a good sense of humor, he knew how to get his way when he wanted. Toward those ends, he was not afraid to use four-letter words (especially in the absence of women) or to castigate people publicly in fairly personal terms. Such actions gave him a reputation as a bully. Many of the Park Service staff who had worked with him on the earlier Fishing Bridge issue, in fact, used that very word to describe him, citing his successful bullying tactics as the main reason they went against their own scientists' advice to close some developments there, with unknown consequences for grizzly bears. With that issue now settled and with his constituents asking for his help to complete the CDST through Grand Teton, Simpson redirected his NPS focus accordingly.[48]

Simpson was interested in the issue at least in part because snowmobiling by this time was more and more a multimillion-dollar part of the regional economy. West Yellowstone best exemplified an economy successfully based on snowmobiling, realizing about $12.5 million annually from the activity and associated spending. With only about 1,000 residents, there were an equal number of snow-mobiles available for rent and some 284 jobs attributable to nonresident snow-mobile spending. Given the town's success, it was natural for people living in the Wyoming communities near Yellowstone (most of whose economies were more stagnant in winter), to want to boost their own season—indeed, that was one of the primary motivations behind the CDST—and it was natural for the senator to support his constituents' desires.[49]

Simpson, unaware of the behind-the-scenes progress that park planners were making, felt the agency was stalling on the CDST proposal. In January 1990 he sent NPS Director James Ridenour a letter that was a stunning example of his typical tactics. He began with an accusation: "I believe that Park Service officials have been intentionally dragging their feet in considering routes for this snowmobile trail through Teton National Park. . . . They are pleasant and sincere—but they are stalling and really not doing a damn thing. Many of us are tired of the 'bum's rush' we are getting." Simpson next surmised that this negligence was due to the "many 'purists' in the Park Service who would prefer to see no winter use in the park at all." "Certain Park Service personnel," he wrote, "have attempted to slow down the winter use planning process in an effort to completely derail plans for the Continental Divide Snowmobile Trail." He then concluded with an obvious threat: "If I do not determine that adequate and vigorous progress is being made in the next few weeks, I will introduce and work for legislation requiring the Park Service to allow the snowmobile trail to be completed through Teton National Park. I don't know if I will succeed, but I'll sure give it my best shot."[50]

Strong language and threats are a bully's tools, and Simpson used them successfully. Cowed, Regional Director Mintzmyer sent him an obsequious response three weeks later: "We are certainly distressed over the displeasure you expressed on the progress we are making on this important issue. We are addressing the trail in the context of a joint Grand Teton–Yellowstone Winter Use Plan, and the project is being given top priority with an accelerated schedule to complete the process as expeditiously as we can achieve. We are scrupulously adhering to the schedule." Intimidated, she kowtowed to Simpson, and the project continued to move forward under its tight schedule. There now seemed to be neither sufficient time for a full examination of the issues at hand nor the open atmosphere necessary for an objective look.[51]

Mintzmyer had acquiesced to Simpson's pressure, even knowing that to do so would be the "invitation to potential tragedy" that she feared. But it would not be the last time the NPS compromised its standards to satisfy public officials.[52] Park managers would compromise with demanding politicians time and again. Defending such actions, they consistently stated that to do otherwise was to risk being replaced with staff less committed to park preservation, a budget cut, or undesired legislation, as Simpson had threatened. Even though some such threats are far from ensured of success, managers have felt that they are unacceptable risks. Consequently, they do their best to stay at the decision-making table so that they can influence the outcome in whatever way is politically possible. This strategy has paid off in that the agency as a whole has not been disregarded; it has made substantial progress in the face of great political pressure, at least at times. However, capitulation as a general approach to dealing with political realities also means that compromise can be piled on compromise, an accumulation that can not only weaken resource protections in the parks but also the agency itself as powerful political actors learn that the agency will give in if pushed. The compromises that took place regarding winter use demonstrate the problems with such an approach, for noise, air pollution, and ongoing visitation growth would continue to be troublesome, and the CDST would be crammed down Grand Teton's throat. Being forced to capitulate to Simpson's bullying meant that the tragedy Mintzmyer feared would occur; indeed, the agency has spent much of the past decade attempting to rein in the winter use that soon burgeoned, as the rest of this book will detail. If the agency could have countered this powerful political pressure, it could have avoided such compromises and tragedies. Unfortunately, the agency still does not possess that political strength.[53]

Under these circumstances, Yellowstone and Grand Teton planners moved toward completion of the *Winter Use Plan Environmental Assessment*. Given the plan's history to date, it is not surprising that it was more a Band-Aid than a cure.

A Band-Aid: The 1990 *Winter Use Plan Environmental Assessment*

Feeling pressured to move the plan forward quickly, Yellowstone and Grand Teton staff released the draft *Winter Use Plan Environmental Assessment* for public review in June 1990.[54] Not much had changed from the original preferred alternative, and as time would soon make clear, little would change in public opinion or, unfortunately, in the park's on-the-ground conditions. The plan did little, if anything, to rein in burgeoning snowmobile problems, deferring for the future the more difficult decisions and thereby making them even more difficult. By releasing such a weak plan, the agency would demonstrate that powerful forces promoting continued (or increased) snowmobile use carried substantial influence over its policy-making.

The environmental assessment presented four alternatives for the public to comment upon. One was the obligatory "no-action" alternative, which was, again, continuation of the parks' existing winter use policies. Three other alternatives were presented: one positing increased winter use, one positing decreased use, and a third designated as "The Plan" (the preferred alternative).[55] The Plan differed in only a few substantive ways from the no-action alternative and from the earlier proposal. In Grand Teton, managers would close the Potholes area but would construct the CDST along the road shoulder, subject to congressional funding. Closing the Potholes was justified because its availability as a snowmobile area did not conform with national policy. Additionally, only about 300 snowmobilers used the area annually, and the restrictive conditions necessary for its opening (3 feet of snow on the ground, to protect most plants from snowmobile crushing) had not occurred in several recent winters. Closing it would therefore not affect many snowmobilers. By contrast, opening the CDST put Grand Teton back into murky policy terrain because it would allow for increased snowmobile use during a time when such use was coming under increasing national scrutiny in the parks. As partial mitigation for the questionable policy move, the Plan stipulated that the NPS would begin a carrying-capacity study if and when the trail actually opened.[56]

The carrying-capacity study would be broadened to Yellowstone when a separate threshold was reached (this was another way in which the Plan differed from the no-action situation). When and if combined visitation for the two parks (whether by oversnow vehicles or wheeled vehicles) exceeded that forecasted for the year 2000 (which the planners predicted would be about 143,500), managers would begin the Visitor Use Management process. Based on experience in other national parks, where periods of high visitation growth usually subsided relatively quickly, planners believed that the growth in Yellowstone and Grand Teton's winter visitation would do the same within a couple of years and grow more slowly throughout the 1990s, making the study unnecessary. However, recognizing that visitation predictions were an inexact science, they stipulated that if actual visitation exceeded that forecasted, they would begin the carrying-capacity study.[57]

Yellowstone would diverge from the status quo in only a few other substantive ways. Planners called for replacement or renovation of the Snowlodge at Old Faithful, but not opening the lodge at Canyon. They would seek improvements in snowcoach affordability, but would not provide service to the East Entrance. Finally, they would seek reductions in snowmobile noise levels through the means previously identified.[58]

The Winter Use Plan, then, seemed to have victories for all constituents. Snowmobilers, economy boosters, and politicians got the CDST, while conservationists and park protectors got specific triggers to compel the carrying-capacity study. The NPS may have been trying to satisfy all groups, and to some extent, it succeeded. But in striking this evident compromise, the planners simply put off the day of reckoning. By failing to initiate the carrying-capacity study immediately or to address the core issue—continually growing snowmobile use—the compromise merely allowed the current problems to continue getting worse.

The proposal differed little from the status quo, and public comment differed little from previous rounds—except in quantity (still more people filed comments this time, about 450 total). Most of the towns and counties along the CDST route, many different snowmobile clubs, and several elected or appointed officials in Wyoming endorsed the CDST and the alternative proposing increased visitor use. Not surprisingly, most of them also opposed closing the Potholes area. Similarly, comments from the environmental community differed little from the expected. Many environmental groups and individuals with similar viewpoints wrote in support of the decreased-use alternative or stricter park protections. Most opposed the CDST while supporting the Potholes closure, as well as an immediate start to the carrying-capacity study and as much protection of natural resources as possible.[59]

All told, a majority of commenters supported restrictions on winter use at least as protective or even more so than those proposed by the NPS. NEPA does not require park managers to adhere to majority opinion (what if the majority wanted a strip mall built at Old Faithful?), although it encourages managers to address the concerns of the interested parties. Believing they had done so, park managers chose to go with the plan. Alan Simpson's pressure, combined with that from the CDST's other Wyoming supporters, probably left managers feeling that they had little choice; the plan provided for CDST construction in the least disruptive way possible. Still, it was questionable whether allowing the trail to be built at all addressed the concerns of many. As John Zelazny of the Wyoming Wildlife Federation wrote, "It appears that the NPS has heeded the good senator's urging and is now fully committed to hastily implementing the CDST without regard to resource values, process, NPS regulations, taxpayer cost, or state and federal laws."[60]

A closer examination of the public comments reveals some insights that would come to bear on the issue's future evolution. Roy Muth of the ISIA, for example, downplayed the NPS's concern about snowmobile noise, stating, "Aesthetics are highly subjective; for some individuals any motor noise at all, however limited, is unacceptable. We maintain that with such vast areas of the parks closed to motorized vehicles in winter, any such concerns about noise can be easily accommodated without more restrictions on snowmobiles."[61] Muth's comment, not all that noticeable in his long letter, could have served as a warning to the NPS that its proposed noise-monitoring program was essential for future efforts to curb snowmobile noise (the monitoring program would presumably demonstrate the need for such efforts). Unfortunately, park managers would fail to begin that program in Yellowstone for more than a decade, as noise monitoring is expensive and the Winter Use Plan did not produce the needed funding. More important, Muth's comment suggested that his industry would be less than sympathetic to NPS planners' hopes for a quieter snowmobile; indeed, the industry would not attempt to quiet its machines until it was forced to take action more than a decade later (more on this in the next chapter).

Authorship (or lack thereof) of the letters contained some surprises as well. The BlueRibbon Coalition did not file comments, suggesting that the group was not particularly adept at working within government planning processes at this time. In contrast, all three members of Wyoming's U.S. congressional delegation filed comments in support of the CDST and increased snowmobile use. Certainly, such involvement and unanimity illustrate how park planners were operating under a political microscope.[62]

Also supporting enhanced snowmobile use were the executive directors of the Cody Country Chamber of Commerce and the Wyoming Lodging and Restaurant Association, Paul Hoffman and Lynn Birleffi, respectively. Hoffman went on to become the Department of the Interior's deputy assistant secretary for fish, wildlife, and parks under the George W. Bush administration in 2002, and Birleffi's group became a litigant against the NPS in 2004. Although Chapter 5 will cover these events in more detail, their involvement is noted here to illustrate that some pro-snowmobile actors have long experience with winter use issues in Wyoming's national parks and tortoise-like memories regarding their history. Though the same can be said of some environmental representatives, they generally occupy politically weaker positions in the conservative interior west.[63]

These two pro-snowmobile actors were partly products of Wyoming's unique political geography. As in other interior west states, the prevalence of federal land in Wyoming (49 percent of the state is federally owned) leads to a political disposition favoring state empowerment regarding the management of those lands.[64] Furthermore, Wyoming may be large in size, but it has only about half a million residents, a small pool of candidates from which to draw persons to represent state government and economic interests. With such a small population, but with two U.S. senators and a representative (who has fewer constituents than any other U.S. House member) needing staffers and promoting the state's interests in Washington, it can be easier for Wyomingites to advance in their political careers than it is for the residents of more populous states to do so. Also helping Wyomingites in such an endeavor is the tendency of many presidents to appoint interior secretaries from western states (such as James Watt, from Wyoming). In this manner, Wyoming's political geography encourages long-lived and antifederal political careers, relative ease in getting political attention, and simple statewide political networking, situations that have significantly influenced the Yellowstone snowmobile story.[65]

Some Winter Use Plan comments from the conservationist community are also revealing. GYC's Don Bachman criticized the agency's visitation forecasts as too modest, a criticism shared even by some NPS employees who had worked on the plan.[66] Several conservation groups also called for the NPS to produce a more comprehensive Environmental Impact Statement on winter use in general (in addition to the demands for an EIS on the CDST). To them, the plan was precedent setting and controversial, two attributes that the Council on Environmental Quality (which oversees implementation of NEPA) specifically stipulated should trigger the more exhaustive study. In fact, at least one planner working on the document said she knew the document was generally inadequate.[67]

Political pressure was not the only explanation for the inadequate analysis; insufficient funding was another. As discussed earlier, there as yet had been no winter use crisis, so Yellowstone lacked the funding for an EIS. Such analyses often entail research and modeling, which accrue additional costs. With funding in short supply, managers did as well as they could (or as well as they had to, recognizing the political influence at this time). Some knew that a weak analysis might provoke a lawsuit, presumably from the conservation community. Such a suit might not have been unwelcome, for it would have been the "crisis" necessary for the agency to appropriate the necessary EIS funding.[68] Not until 1997 would that lawsuit arrive (driven more by heavy snowfall and associated wildlife response than by human action). This was later than some in the NPS believed or hoped would happen, and during the time that elapsed, the winter use problems continued to grow, largely unchecked. The delay allowed snowmobile use in the park to become further institutionalized and exacerbated the difficulty of future decision-making.

At least to conservationists, it seemed that the CDST approval merited a lawsuit. Instead of being subjected to an EIS of its own, the CDST became reality, with only a superficial analysis (less than ten pages in the *Winter Use Plan Environmental Assessment*). Upset over the approval, the NPCA devoted more than ten pages of its comments to a listing of federal laws the agencies had violated in approving it, an indication that the group was on the verge of filing suit against the NPS. But neither the NPCA nor any other group sued over either the CDST approval or the Plan more broadly. It seems that the two thresholds for the carrying-capacity analysis (one specific to completion of the CDST) assuaged some concerns, while the Forest Service relieved other worries by agreeing to monitor use of and impacts on the trail. Once the trail fully opened, the long-distance travel that many had feared failed to materialize in any significant volume. Impacts from snowmobilers were minimal, and the conservationists' concerns apparently faded.[69]

To some extent, the NPS can be faulted for its reactive style of park planning. It was obvious to many agency personnel, from the field to the regional office, that winter use in Yellowstone was slipping out of control. The issue demanded attention, and even though employees tackled it as best they could, their effort was inadequate. Defending their actions, agency staff noted that the NPS had always suffered from a lack of sufficient funding and had always had to cobble together its planning and park management on a shoestring budget. With other pressing needs occurring throughout the parks—not to mention the fire policy review that was ongoing—funds and staff time were in short supply. Also, the political context of the era, with Simpson dominating the agenda, made it unlikely that any proposal to seriously limit snowmobiling could have succeeded. So, lacking the means or political climate necessary for a more comprehensive look at the problem, park planners did as well as they had to, treating the symptoms without addressing the underlying (and more comprehensive) illness, which would have been controlling the unbridled snowmobile use. They gave the issue a soft glance, which helped for the moment but allowed the snowball to continue growing. Winter use continued happening *to* Yellowstone (and Grand Teton) without significant forethought and direction. Unlike earlier park managers who could not envision a different winter place, the park managers of the 1980s could. But they were prevented from moving in that direction by strong political pressure, inadequate funding, and their own unwillingness to tackle the difficult issue. As a result, snowmobiling continued to grow, along with its problems.

Finally, few conservationists suggested or demanded that snowmobile use be banned entirely from the two parks. In fact, though most conservationists opposed building the CDST, they said little or nothing against continued snowmobile use in Yellowstone.[70] In less than a decade, their position would transform into direct support for a snowmobile ban in the two parks. At this time, however, the CDST was the focal point in the winter use debate, diverting attention from the more serious issue, the appropriateness of snowmobiles in national parks. Once the CDST was built, it would no longer capture all the attention, and the public would focus upon the more basic question. Helping to sharpen that focus would be the next planning endeavor, the Visitor Use Management process, which would begin in just a few years. For the moment, however, debate over winter use subsided.

Late in 1990, the agency approved the Winter Use Plan with little fanfare. Other than those promoting the CDST, few supported it. Conservationists found it disappointing, but they believed (correctly) that in focusing attention on Yellowstone's winter use, the plan would open the debate to greater possibilities in the future. Legal scholar Joseph Sax, author of *Mountains without Handrails: Reflections on the National Parks,* perhaps summarized conservationist opinion of the plan best when he wrote in a comment letter that it was "junk-talk, . . . so lacking in vision and purpose that it gives me a great sense of unease about the fu-

Snowmobilers along the Madison River, 1970s or 1980s. Enjoying the support of merchants in West Yellowstone (from where these visitors probably entered the park), snowmobiling continued to grow in popularity in the 1980s and early 1990s. Hampered by inadequate funding and strong political support for the activity, the NPS was unable to exert substantial direction or control over the activity, allowing a tragedy of the commons to occur. NPS photo.

ture of our parks."[71] His despair was well-founded, for the issue would fester and grow until it became the single greatest demand on the attention of Yellowstone managers. For now, the agency contented itself with slowing the snowball's growth a little.

Before long, park managers tried another tactic, but again they found the snowball to be too big. In reality, the Visitor Use Management process did little more than delay the inevitable, the need to redirect or stop the growing snowball. That snowball was growing larger and more powerful, and tragedy loomed.

Visitor Use Management Can't Turn Back the Clock

For a little while, the winter use debate settled down, a situation that did not match the actual on-the-ground reality, where snowmobile use continued to climb rapidly. In just two winters, visitation exceeded the carrying-capacity-study threshold specified in the newly completed plan. For the winter of 1992–1993,

Yellowstone alone saw 140,000 visitors, a number that, when combined with Grand Teton's visitation, well exceeded the 143,500 threshold. That same winter, the CDST became operational, with snowmobilers hauling their machines by trailer through Grand Teton to Yellowstone's South Entrance. Two years later, the trailbed through the park was complete, enabling snowmobilers to travel directly from the Togwotee Pass area through Teton Park to Yellowstone without ever leaving a groomed snowmobile trail.[72]

Although visitor use of the CDST did not grow as much as anticipated, the high visitation in the parks confirmed park managers' worst fears: Winter use was not slowing down. In fact, it was evidently increasing so fast that a "tragedy of the commons" was looming. Ecologist Garrett Hardin had first coined this expression in 1968 to describe what he argued would usually occur to an unregulated public resource (the commons): Those who harvested that resource (say, fish in lakes and rivers) would maximize their taking of it for personal gain, without consideration of the public good or an attempt to share the resource equitably. Because all such resources are limited, eventually overharvesting would occur and the resource would drop dramatically in abundance or disappear altogether (the tragedy, along with the human harm that results from the declining resource abundance). Complaints from the public to Yellowstone managers in the early 1990s suggested that a tragedy of the commons was occurring there. In Yellowstone's case, the commons were more experiential than material, consisting of the opportunity to enjoy clean air, nature's quiet, and solitude. But, as evidenced by over 300 unsolicited complaints filed between 1993 and 1996, these opportunities were either harder to find or gone entirely (certainly, my experience at Shoshone Geyser Basin detailed in the Introduction suggested such opportunities had disappeared). Noise and air pollution, wildlife harassment, crowding, and lack of solitude were the most frequent problems mentioned, and the growing numbers of snowmobiles were the cause of the tragedy.[73]

If the high volume of unsolicited letters was not a sufficient call for more attention, the fact that both of the carrying-capacity thresholds specified by the 1990 Winter Use Plan had been met certainly was. In 1993, managers in the two parks began the Visitor Use Management (VUM) process, which segregated each park into various zones of front- or backcountry experience, discerned what conditions park managers and visitors wanted for each zone (perhaps through visitor surveys), and recommended modifications to park management on how to bring the actual situations more into line with the desired conditions.[74]

Not surprisingly, the team of planners recognized that there were many visitor conflicts and that natural-resource protection could be suffering from the rapidly growing use. However, in many cases, they needed more specific information to determine the extent of the problems and to resolve them. For example, they rec-

Snowmobiles parked at Old Faithful Snowlodge, late 1990s. An average of 795 snowmobiles per day entered Yellowstone in the 1990s, with daily peaks at Christmastime and President's Day weekend of 1,500 to 1,800 machines, most with Old Faithful as a destination. All used two-stroke technology, producing high levels of air pollution. In the background is the rebuilt Old Faithful Snowlodge, which opened in 1998. Photo by author.

ognized that snowmobile emissions could be a problem, especially at the West Entrance where hundreds (over 1,000 on the busiest days) of snowmobiles entered daily and where topography produced air inversions that trapped emissions near the ground. To determine the extent of the problem, managers installed an air-quality monitor there to measure the emissions. After a few winters of monitoring, it became clear that there was indeed a problem, especially with carbon monoxide, whose levels came close to violating the Clean Air Act at times. Managers eventually revised fee collection and entry procedures to eliminate the need for snowmobilers to wait in long lines there. With this change, the machines moved faster through the entrance area, and emissions were reduced. Although there were no longer enough emissions to violate federal law, there were still relatively high levels.[75]

Air-quality monitoring became one of several ways that the Visitor Use Management effort distinguished itself from the 1990 Winter Use Plan effort. Managers also initiated plans to replace the Old Faithful Snowlodge, and their efforts reached fruition in 1998, when a comfortable new building opened.[76] They began to examine the impact of winter use on wildlife more seriously, compiling two large annotated bibliographies on the subject,[77] and they commissioned research into typical visitor profiles, travel patterns, and concerns.[78] They visited snowmobile manufacturers to discuss quieting the machines (and cleaning them up) and placed decibel meters at the entrances to begin standardized enforcement of existing noise regulations. Finally, recognizing that the sheer number of snowmobiles was a major component of all the other problems, they began actually discussing methods of resolution. Three preferred solutions were placing daily limits on visitor numbers, restricting visitation to guided tours (both via snowcoach and snowmobile), and/or limiting access to snowcoaches only.[79] By 2003, they would either propose or actually implement all three ideas, generating great effort and controversy along the way (the subject of Chapters 4 and 5). Overall, by beginning these long overdue monitoring and research thrusts, the VUM effort became the state of knowledge for the time. The VUM process therefore became what the 1990 Winter Use Plan was not—more than a glance at winter use—including the first serious discussion of limits or restrictions on snowmobile use—but not, as time would reveal, a hard look.

Funding for the effort was still limited, and some of the studies and monitoring procedures, rather than resolving any problems, confounded them or demonstrated that easy solutions were not to be found. In one instance in the late 1990s, for example, both Yellowstone managers and West Yellowstone businesses began using gasohol and bio-based lubricants in their snowmobiles in an attempt to solve the air pollution problems. Unfortunately, these changes reduced snowmobile air pollution by only a small fraction, when reductions more resembling an order of magnitude were needed, probably through a substantial change in snowmobile technology.[80] Recognizing that need, at least one entrepreneur in West Yellowstone soon unveiled a "four-stroke" snowmobile prototype. Four-stroke machines used technology similar to the typical automobile engine's to combust fuel without burning oil, significantly reducing emissions. The large snowmobile manufacturer Polaris soon unveiled another prototype, but the other three major manufacturers were reluctant to follow suit. As a result, mass-produced, cleaner—and quieter—machines were slow to arrive on the market, prolonging and confounding Yellowstone's air pollution problems.[81] In part for this reason, Yellowstone's managers deferred again any substantive changes in either the modes of winter transportation or the number of vehicles.[82] The VUM effort, like the 1990 Winter Use Plan, became a delaying tactic.

Wildlife studies performed as part of the VUM effort added confusion to the frustration. The bibliographies mentioned earlier illustrated a wide variety of findings from throughout the country, along with associated scientific opinion, on whether snowmobile use harmed or helped wildlife survival and distribution. In Yellowstone, the same difference of opinion seemed to prevail, especially regarding park bison. Since the late 1970s, Yellowstone's bison had used the groomed roadways at times to travel from one pasture to another. Did such travel alter their natural distribution, and if so, was that good, bad, or otherwise? Yellowstone's own bison ecologist Mary Meagher asserted that groomed roads had altered their distribution, which to her meant that grooming the roads had an unnatural and therefore unacceptable influence on the animals. Meagher's findings, however, seemed to conflict with those of Frances Cassirer and Keith Aune, the student researchers on two studies of the 1980s. Looking more at individual displacement than at population movement and migration, they both demonstrated that snowmobile trails were not as much a problem as cross-country skiers, who displaced wildlife more. Although the studies examined different nuances of bison biology and behavior, they seemed to send conflicting messages to park managers. Were snowmobile trails a real problem or not? And what, if anything, should they do about the issue or about cross-country skiing?[83]

By highlighting problems with the cash cow, the VUM effort may have served to polarize the various factions concerned with winter use even more. Snowmobiling supporters reacted in defense of the activity. Paul Hoffman, the Cody Chamber of Commerce director, had recently implemented a marketing campaign to attract winter visitors to the Cody region, and he had made Cody's proximity to Yellowstone the centerpiece of his effort. Fearing that the VUM effort would restrict that accessibility, in 1995 he organized a meeting of local community chamber of commerce representatives to devise a resolution to the underlying problems without the limits. This group, which became the Yellowstone Gateway Coalition, felt that the Park Service should improve traffic flow by building four-lane highways through Yellowstone or even new roads through backcountry areas. Although they preferred to work directly with Yellowstone managers to solve the VUM problems, Coalition members were ready to call upon their "ace in the hole," their congressional delegations. Though Hoffman's group disbanded soon thereafter, when their somewhat secret discussions became known (members of the public were particularly incensed over the road-building proposals), its proposals suggested that VUM discussions might have made the situation worse as much as better. Regardless, the chambers of commerce would continue to watch winter use planning closely.[84]

Another indication of growing polarization came from other snowmobile advocates, who reacted in a surprisingly strong way to a restriction park managers announced just before the VUM effort: that snowmobile drivers in Yellowstone must possess a valid driver's license. According to NPS general regulations, persons between the ages of twelve and fifteen could drive a snowmobile as long as a responsible adult oversaw them. By the late 1980s, however, park managers realized that such young drivers were responsible for a disproportionate share of snowmobile accidents, particularly those requiring medical attention. When they decided to require driver's licenses from all operators in 1993, a variety of snowmobile advocates (ranging from West Yellowstone rental operators to the ISIA in Michigan) registered their opposition to the move, claiming that it would make family snowmobiling more difficult and that a safety certification program would be more responsive. Park managers, however, went ahead with the requirement, hoping it would both address their safety concerns and provide some small measure of control over the seeming free-for-all. Unfortunately, that requirement and the fact that park managers announced it after some families had already made winter reservations further polarized the parties on the two sides of the controversy.[85]

These two examples were indicative of the general approach that snowmobile advocates took toward the VUM effort. Led now by the BlueRibbon Coalition, which more and more understood how to influence federal decision-making, snowmobilers criticized the VUM effort as biased against their activity. They particularly defended the economic stimulus provided by snowmobiling, its value as a family activity, and the fact that it provided access to Yellowstone's winter wonders. Such claims were both accurate and increasingly compelling, and the Coalition was learning to use them for its own ends. Specifically, spending by nonresident snowmobilers in Montana (about 75 percent of whom spent time in or near West Yellowstone, which by now had about 1,500 snowmobiles available for rent) had more than doubled between 1987–1988 and 1993–1994, in constant dollars. Adding this amount to resident expenditures, studies found that snowmobilers dropped about $100 million in Montana every winter and $117 million in Wyoming. The same studies also showed that resident snowmobilers often went snowmobiling as a family. Finally, snowmobilers loved the access their machines provided to Old Faithful, the Lower Falls, and Yellowstone's other sights. Snowmobiling was a powerful part of experiencing Yellowstone in winter, of the region's winter economy, and of the values of some families. These in turn were motivating reasons to defend the activity.[86]

Unfortunately, the coalitions began a disturbing pattern of using misinformation to advance their goals. In response to the NPS concern that high numbers of snowmobiles destroyed the quiet, serene experience desired by many park visitors, Adena Cook of the BlueRibbon Coalition claimed that Yellowstone's size, "200 miles square," provided "plenty of room for solitude." In actuality, Yellowstone is only about 60 miles square, and snowmobile noise permeated much of the backcountry, especially on calm, clear winter days. Cook's error exaggerated the space available for visitors seeking silence and serenity and trivialized the agency's attempt to address this issue. About the same time, a flyer began circulating in the area entitled "An Analysis of Snowmobile Emissions Compared to Auto Emissions." The flyer claimed that "1000 Snowmobiles in Yellowstone are the equivalent of 1,170,000 automobiles in hydro carbon and nitrous oxide emissions and 224,000 automobiles in Carbon Monoxide emissions!" The two-stroke snow-mobiles then in use were indeed highly polluting machines, but the claim that they were three orders of magnitude worse than a typical auto was later shown to be incorrect. Though its authorship was unknown, the flyer's claims were reported in the press, cited by some NPS employees, and used by members of the conservation community. Such uses of misinformation, whether intentional or not, diverted discussions away from the calm and reasoned ones needed to produce proactive and workable solutions and would come to be a recurring problem for all involved.[87]

To some degree, the problems with misinformation suggested the dearth of quality information regarding snowmobile impacts at the time and highlighted the role that good science can play in NPS policy-making. During the same era, the debate over the reintroduction of wolves to Yellowstone was occurring—a debate assisted by accurate scientific knowledge. Responding to a congressional directive and associated funding in the late 1980s, Yellowstone managers had commissioned reams of research (1,400 pages) on the potential effects of reintroducing the large predators. By 1990, the science was complete, and the agency moved forward with a science-based and legally defensible reintroduction effort, completed in 1995. Similarly, the fire policy review that had just taken place was greatly aided by a preexisting and detailed scientific understanding of fire's role in wildland ecosystems like Yellowstone. With such science, the agency was able to again allow natural fires to burn by 1992. In both cases, the NPS and the scientific community had first completed the necessary science and then the agency had made a well-informed decision based in part upon the research findings.[88]

With winter use, the case would be different. As this chapter has often noted, park managers knew for fifteen years that they needed a comprehensive look at winter use, including scientific research into its specifics. Unable to commission that research or policy inquiry, the matter festered until it could not be ignored. Had park managers been able to address these issues more thoroughly, all parties would have been able to debate them and move forward more proactively. Unfortunately, a far different situation would come to prevail as Yellowstone policy-makers attempted to craft policy without either funding or adequate social and natural science research. Other authors have found that such situations (where policy decisions are needed but necessary information is lacking) are fraught with peril because they encourage interested stakeholders to utilize only that information that is consistent with their attitudes and beliefs. Stakeholders are also more likely to distort information to suit their needs and to dispute the factual nature of information that does not suit their needs.[89] All these tendencies would continue to be evident in the Yellowstone winter use story.

As suggested by the erroneous flyer, conservationists were taking more notice of Yellowstone's snowmobile issue. Several groups published articles about the dilemma in the mid-1990s, with an article by journalist Todd Wilkinson—engagingly titled "Snowed Under"—published in NPCA's magazine, being perhaps the most prominent. Generally, these articles highlighted the noise and air pollution issues, expressed concern about bison use of groomed snowmobile routes, and called for the NPS to institute an interim snowmobile limit until the VUM studies were complete. Although the agency would not accede to such a request, this spate of articles publicized Yellowstone's problems widely and focused public attention in particular upon the potential bison impacts of winter use. Soon, an emotional controversy (made worse by the conflicting information regarding snowmobile impacts upon bison) would erupt over the connection between groomed roads and bison habits, a controversy that had great bearing upon the snowmobile story.[90]

Behind the scenes, staffers at the Greater Yellowstone Coalition were agonizing over winter use and wondering what to do about it. They recognized that their group's focus on the Greater Yellowstone area positioned them better than most other conservation groups to take action. By 1995, they began to narrow their focus for the first time, considering a campaign to ban snowmobiles from Yellowstone. Recognizing that snowmobile use had become institutionalized there, the group realized that it could take a decade or more for such a campaign to achieve results. They had little energy or time for such an effort at the time, as they were working intensively to prevent a large gold mine from being built just outside of Yellowstone. However, in 1996, President Bill Clinton announced a buy-out of the New World Mine, giving the GYC its first large-scale and highly visible success. Pumped up with victory and now free to focus attention on other pressing issues, the group turned its attention to an anti-snowmobile campaign. Later in 1996, they began to consider legal action to "take back the park" from its profligate snowmobile use. With its new confidence, the group would soon undertake that very project.[91]

The escalating controversy regarding Yellowstone's winter use became more evident in 1996. That summer, park managers held several public meetings in local communities to inform people of their thinking and gather input on the VUM process. These meetings turned up a surprising number of people, many of them angry. More than 200 people appeared at the meeting in Jackson Hole, many registering bitter, vituperative comments, such as, "What right do you in green have to start taking *anyone's rights away?*" or "WE WANT OUR FAIR SHARE!!" (emphases in original, and those "in green" were the park planners holding the meetings). These constituents believed they had a *right* to use park roads and trails—if not a legal right, an implied right conferred by thirty years of using the parks. That "right" conflicted with the "right" that conservationists perceived to have a quiet, serene experience. Both groups would be motivated—strongly—to defend these perceived rights in the future.[92] All told, the growing discontent with winter use was triggering a polarity and defensiveness that would come to characterize future discussions on the issue while also making proactive decision-making more difficult.

Notwithstanding these strident comments, a majority of commenters at the six meetings agreed that rampant snowmobile use in the two parks was creating many unpleasant problems and that the agency needed to address these substantively.[93] More important, however, is that the majority of *local residents* found the existing situation in Yellowstone unacceptable. Their support for change was unfortunately drowned out by certain shrill snowmobile advocates—not only at these meetings but also in the public discourse on the matter over much of the next decade (with shrill anti-snowmobile advocates soon to make their presence known as well). The ability of a vociferous interest group representing a minority of constituents to dominate discussion like this would come to be another hallmark of the winter use debate, continually frustrating forward movement. Certainly, other western public land issues—including Yellowstone's own recently completed wolf reintroduction effort—have seen the same extreme behavior (the ample science on the wolf issue was one way in which managers quieted the shouting). Finding the silent majority in the middle, the group that Yellowstone authors John Varley and Paul Schullery called the "great many people of lukewarm opinion" that constitute the high middle of the bell-curve of public opinion on a given issue, would become progressively more difficult for the National Park Service.[94]

The final VUM report was published in 1999.[95] Overall, that effort produced little substantive change for at least two major reasons. First, the deck was already stacked against it: Though it seemed more evident that resource protections were compromised (through air pollution, noise pollution, and wildlife harassment) along with the quality of park visits, the political and economic actors were already too entrenched in the snowmobile business and were too strong to permit substantial change. As Superintendent Barbee had said, "we can't turn back the clock. Winter recreation in Yellowstone is here to stay whether we like it or not."[96] Now, the NPS more and more needed a crisis, not only to provide the funding necessary for a hard look at winter use, but also to gain the legal strength necessary to move these powerful, resistant actors toward change.

Second, the crisis arrived before the final report did, in the winter of 1996–1997. As the next chapter will reveal, that winter produced an NPS commitment to write an Environmental Impact Statement on winter use. And that commitment, grounded in a lawsuit settlement, was already underway by the time the VUM report was completed, effectively superseding it.

Fallen through the Ice

Throughout the 1980s and early 1990s, the National Park Service gradually recognized that its winter use snowball was rolling downhill, out of control. Where snowmobile use had originally been welcomed as a way to preserve Yellowstone, it was rapidly transforming into one of the primary perceived threats to the integrity of both Yellowstone and Grand Teton, as Regional Director Mintzmyer had feared. Attempting to deal with the increasing problems as best they could, park managers found that they were unable to deal effectively with creeping change. Had there been a crisis, they could have responded with sufficient funding to address the issues. But in this case, the best they could do was respond fitfully, due to persistent agency funding difficulties and political opposition. So the snowball continued to grow, and it began to roll faster.

Meanwhile, the good old days passed. Though reminders of Yellowstone's magnificence were still present, the park's silence, clean air, and unimpeded wildlife movements were disappearing or gone, especially on the busiest days. In place were hundreds of snowmobiles, along with their seemingly ever-present din, clouds of blue exhaust, and crowds of people. Even though the thrill of exploration remained for some, the hundreds or thousands of other snowmobilers present diminished the sense of discovery. A tragedy of the commons had occurred, and Yellowstone was now a snowmobile racetrack.

Along the way, most of the primary actors for the rest of the story fell into place. At the center of the stage was the National Park Service, charged with protecting Yellowstone and Grand Teton national parks while accommodating visitation, an ever-present tightrope act. Attempting to influence its decisions were the coalitions, each with their strengths and weaknesses. While the GYC tapped into compelling scientific arguments and the public's desire to see national parks preserved as sacred space, the other coalition was beginning to tap into equally compelling family, freedom, and business values, and learning to point out any inconsistencies in the science. The BlueRibbon Coalition had the additional support of sympathetic politicians, especially in Wyoming (but also in Montana and Idaho), some of whom were not afraid to use their power to influence NPS decisions. By the late 1990s, a conflict of values and power politics was brewing. The stage was set for more controversy: All that was needed was a crisis, which nature would soon provide.

4
Crises, Lawsuits, and Politics

We are committed to allowing responsible winter access through cleaner
operating . . . machines, restricting snowmobiles to the same paved roads that
are used by vehicles in the summer months.
Secretary of the Interior Gale Norton, 2004

This is an issue about freedom.
Jackson Hole resident Doyle Vaughn, 1999

No one loses when beauty wins.
National park scholar Al Runte, 2003[1]

Between 1997 and 2004, two different crises presented themselves to Yellowstone's
managers. Nature caused the first, a harsh winter with dire consequences for
many Yellowstone buffalo. Upset over the NPS's response to the crisis and its Winter Use Plan, and the potential effects of both on the bison population, the
wildlife advocacy group Fund for Animals filed suit against the agency, giving it
the long-sought opportunity for crisis funding. By 2000, park managers were
moving toward banning snowmobiles from both Yellowstone and Grand Teton
national parks. This solution to the persistent winter problems seemed radical to
snowmobilers, resulting in another lawsuit, another Environmental Impact Statement, and a very different solution that seemed unfair to conservationists.

The conflicting decisions came to a head in the winter of 2003–2004, when
judges in two different federal courts struck down the two NPS actions for violations of the same two laws. In each case, the litigants were the coalitions and their
allies, who sought out courts they believed would be sympathetic to their cause.
After both decisions were announced, park managers had to alter the rules governing winter operations in mere hours, casting confusion over an issue already
clouded by political meddling. These judicial decisions became the second crisis
facing the agency. Although the litigation enabled the park to receive funding to
address the festering issues comprehensively, the lawsuits also brought a new set
of problems into existence. Controversy, political micromanagement, and a be-
wildering array of legal battles ensued.

Fueling this crisis and controversy were conflicting values and identities that became even more sharply divided. Some stakeholders in the issue wanted Yellowstone to remain a sacred temple of nature while others wished to express American freedom and independence via their snowmobiles. Still others felt the parks should be economic engines or research reserves. Most stakeholders cherry-picked research to support their agendas and sought support from both politicians and the public. Attempting to sort through these values and their appropriateness to Yellowstone, the National Park Service found itself in an extremely difficult predicament, barely retaining control of its policy-making.

A Crisis with Buffalo Leads to the First Hard Look

While Yellowstone is known for extreme winter weather, the winter of 1996–1997 was exceptional. Christmas week brought 3 feet of new snow across most of the park, and January brought rain. Separately, these events would not have made history (both had occurred previously), but the rapid swing from one extreme to another was unusual. The return to normal winter temperatures that soon followed the rain produced a thick layer of ice in the snowpack. Heavy snowfall returned, burying the ice and making that winter one of the three harshest of the twentieth century, with about 150 percent of normal precipitation for the park.[2]

Such conditions made survival that winter especially difficult for Yellowstone's large animals. Many bison, ordinarily well equipped to deal with winter conditions, found the situation impossible. Although they could move snow above the ice layer aside with their large heads (in a sweeping motion powered by strong hump muscles), the ice prevented even large bulls from reaching the grasses below. When conditions like this exist, bison respond by migrating to lower elevations or areas of less snowfall. Soon after the rain froze, the migration began, with bison using their own trails and, to some extent, snowmobile routes to find lower, more snow-free habitat. While some park land near Gardiner was adequately snow-free, the extremely harsh conditions and the large number of bison—4,000 at the time—meant that some left the park entirely in search of still lower or drier conditions.[3]

Outside of the park's embrace, bison are not welcome because about 50 percent of them carry brucellosis. This nonnative disease, first transmitted to bison from cattle kept in the park in the early 1900s to provide tourists with milk and beef, causes spontaneous abortion of fetuses in domestic cattle and, to a lesser extent, bison, along with undulant fever in humans. To reduce or eliminate the human health risk, the Department of Agriculture's Animal and Plant Health Inspection Service (APHIS) began a campaign in 1968 to eliminate the disease in

Bison walking on oversnow vehicle road, 2008. Bison began using such roads for travel in the late 1970s or early 1980s. The habit has caused substantial controversy, with animal rights advocates and some scientists asserting it has allowed the bison herd to alter their distribution in Yellowstone. Some visitors enjoy the habit, which brings the animals into close proximity with people, and other scientists believe bison use of groomed roads has not led to substantial changes in their distribution or population. Photo by author.

all U.S. cattle within seven years. The campaign was successful throughout most of the country, but Yellowstone bison remained (and still remain, along with elk in the region) the country's greatest single reservoir of the disease. Bison can transmit the disease only through females, when one spontaneously aborts a fetus that is then licked or touched by another animal.[4]

In the 1990s, APHIS considered Montana cattle to be brucellosis-free, a zealously guarded status that allowed stock growers there to ship cows out of state without expensive, time-consuming quarantine procedures. Though Yellowstone bison have never given the disease to cattle under wild conditions, such transmission was at least theoretically possible (and had occurred in laboratory tests). Should Montana cattle contract brucellosis, all ranchers in the state would have to resume quarantine procedures. Consequently, the state took a dim view of bison leaving Yellowstone. When bison first began leaving Yellowstone in winter in the 1970s, the National Park Service and the state of Montana agreed to control them at the park boundary. Most winters, that meant that less than two dozen were either herded back into Yellowstone or captured and slaughtered.[5]

By the late 1980s, however, the Yellowstone bison population had surpassed 2,000, and more of them were attempting to leave the park in heavy snow periods. The winter following the 1988 fires saw 569 bison slaughtered at the boundary, many by modern-day hunters licensed in Montana. With twice as many bison inhabiting the park in 1996, the out-migration was even larger, and so was the eventual bison kill. A record number of bison were shot or sent to slaughter that winter—1,084. This was the largest control of bison departing Yellowstone to date (more than 1,700 were killed in the winter of 2007–2008) and one of the largest killings of bison anywhere since they were eliminated from the Great Plains in 1883. Additional bison succumbed to natural causes inside the park during the harsh winter. In all, more than a third of the buffalo living in the park at the start of that winter died by April 1997.[6]

Bison—particularly Yellowstone bison—are widely viewed as totemic creatures. They symbolize the Old West, the wisdom and success of the conservation movement, and wildness itself. Guides today often relate stories about their preservation, explain that Yellowstone's herd of bison is the only one in the country that has ranged continuously in the wild since prehistoric times, and note that Yellowstone bison are some of the few in the United States not possessing cattle genes (most bison in domestic herds have at least a few). The richness of meanings that Yellowstone bison embody is clearly not lost on such guides; Native Americans and others are also well aware of them.[7]

Because of these powerful meanings, it is no surprise that the 1997 bison slaughter provoked strong reactions in some Americans. The Fund for Animals, a national animal rights group, had threatened as early as May 1996 to sue the NPS, arguing that grooming park snowmobile routes altered bison distribution and habits, contributing eventually to their exodus from the park and associated slaughter. The group wanted the agency to cease snowmobile road grooming and examine the environmental impacts of the winter use program. The NPS did not comply with the request. Considering this a "question of law, morality, [and] conscience," and upset over the winter's bison kill, the group filed suit against the NPS in May 1997.[8]

In their suit, the Fund and some coplaintiffs alleged that the agency had violated several laws in developing Yellowstone's winter use program, especially snowmobile trail grooming. In failing to perform environmental analysis on that grooming, the group charged, the NPS had violated the National Environmental Policy Act. The Fund alleged a violation of the Endangered Species Act as well: that grizzly bears and wolves, two species on the federal threatened and endangered species list, were harmed by the lack of winter-killed bison carcasses, since many bison were killed in slaughterhouses. Finally, the group alleged that the agency had failed to prevent snowmobiles and trail grooming from impairing park resources, thereby violating the Yellowstone National Park and National Park Service organic acts. The group was aware that the agency had begun a separate Environmental Impact Statement on brucellosis and bison management in 1990, but was dissatisfied with the lack of progress on that EIS. (The EIS, finally completed in 2000, led to a decision to continue the control of bison leaving the park when their population exceeded 3,000 and plans to eventually eliminate the disease in park bison.)[9]

Overseeing Yellowstone by this time was Superintendent Mike Finley, who had come from Yosemite National Park, where he instituted the first visitation limits to the heavily used Yosemite Valley. He had close to thirty years of NPS experience, including time as a seasonal firefighter in Yellowstone early in his career. Before serving at Yosemite, Finley had made waves in Everglades National Park by suing two Florida state agencies for failing to control farm runoff polluting the park. He was afraid neither of controversy nor of speaking his mind, saying at one point, "I really believe the American people pay me to protect Yellowstone National Park. That means from damage that occurs from within, from our management decisions, and from those actions that could damage Yellowstone from the outside." While at Yellowstone, he was fortunate to work for a secretary of the interior who supported his preservationist efforts, Bruce Babbitt, who distinguished himself and President Clinton as friends of the NPS (Clinton designated numerous national monuments between 1996 and 2001). Finley relished Babbitt's support as he took on the snowmobile issue, but his outspokenness would result in some repercussions for both the snowmobile issue and NPS policy-making in general.[10]

In the lawsuit from the Fund for Animals, Finley saw both merit and an opportunity to get a grip on the winter use snowball. He recognized that it could be the crisis that at last brought the funding needed to review Yellowstone's winter policies in detail. Consequently, the NPS settled the suit in September 1997 by agreeing to write a new winter use plan and an associated Environmental Impact Statement. The hard look at winter use that Bob Barbee had probably desired was about to become reality.[11]

In April 1998, Finley's staff began the EIS process.[12] Based on the previous planning efforts and complaints, they knew that snowmobile air and noise pollution consistently led the list of winter use issues, along with wildlife impacts, crowding, and visitor conflicts. Snowmobiles were still powered by two-cycle engines, which were light and powerful but surprisingly polluting, discharging 25 to 30 percent of their fuel, unburned, out the tailpipe in a toxic mist. They also produced large amounts of carbon monoxide, particulates, and volatile organic compounds such as benzene and toluene.[13] The same engines were loud: Their noise sometimes traveled amazingly far from the roads. Skiers at the time reported hearing them from as far away as 10 miles. Old Faithful visitors could not escape the noise, which occurred throughout daylight hours in that area.[14] All impacts were exacerbated by the numbers of snowmobiles touring Yellowstone at the time. An average day saw 795 machines enter, with about two-thirds of them arriving at the West Entrance. Busy days, like those during the Christmas holidays or President's Day weekend in February, saw 1,500 to 1,800 snowmobiles parkwide. By the end of the winter, 60,000 to almost 80,000 snowmobiles entered Yellowstone, a number exceeding such use in any other national park.[15]

Park planners considered many different proposals, the most distinctive being to plow the 30 miles of road from West Yellowstone to Old Faithful (restricting the remaining road system to snowcoaches and cleaner and quieter snowmobiles by 2008). One of the primary benefits of this idea was that it would substantially reduce costs for both the agency and the public. Visitors would be able to tour the park in their own vehicles rather than renting snowmobiles at over $100 per day (riding double on a snowmobile could halve the per person cost, but few chose to do so) or buying snowcoach tickets, which started at about $60. The plowing idea was not unique to the NPS; at a three-day workshop in October 1998 with other local government agencies interested in Yellowstone's winter use, two different work groups (out of five, total) independently came up with the same idea. With several groups thinking the same way, park planners were confident enough to incorporate the limited plowing proposal into the preferred alternative in the Draft EIS.[16]

The EIS presented a range of alternatives to the plowing idea. Two that came to attract particular attention were Alternatives E and G. The former would have allowed snowmobiling to continue under new noise and air pollution limits, with adaptive management to be utilized to adjust the snowmobile regulations as needed. Four-cycle (or "four-stroke") snowmobiles were still being prototyped; they used more modern technology to burn fuel more completely, thereby lowering emissions dramatically and noise somewhat. Under the provisions of adaptive management, such new technologies would be included when they became commercially available (still an unknown for snowmobiles), and visitor numbers could be adjusted upward or downward when monitoring information indicated the need for such a change. Alternative G would have restricted park traffic to snowcoaches, which were powered by traditional van or automobile engines (and therefore were thought to be cleaner and quieter than snowmobiles).[17]

The NPS released the Draft EIS to the public for comment in fall 1999. As word about the plowing proposal spread to both the snowmobile and environmental communities, the issue became one of the NPS's major national issues, with politicians and interest groups attempting to influence the agency's thinking. Whether through legislation, litigation, public opinion, high-visibility national press, or behind-the-scenes directives, park planners found themselves increasingly in the spotlight of public attention and caught between seemingly irreconcilable American values.[18]

American Values in NPS Decision-Making

Knowing the Fund for Animals wanted to ban snowmobiles from Yellowstone, the BlueRibbon Coalition paid careful attention to the NPS's policy-making actions. Coalition members feared that if the Fund succeeded in banning snowmobiles from Yellowstone, it would turn next to the national forests, where snowmobiling was also popular. They had good reason for the fear, for Jasper Carlton, one of the Fund's coplaintiffs, had been heard stating publicly that "the Forest Service is next. When they refuse, we are going to sue them." Even though the Forest Service's multiple-use mission made a snowmobile ban on its lands less likely, Carlton's remark led the Coalition and other snowmobile advocates to fear that Yellowstone would be the precedent. This is perhaps the single best example of the common perception that Yellowstone, being the first national park, is the trendsetter. Hoping that whatever policy Yellowstone adopted would transfer to other national parks, interest groups (especially the two coalitions) began paying careful attention to the snowmobile issue, elevating its public visibility.[19]

Soon, the BlueRibbon Coalition began moving away from its reactive roots and toward a proactive strategy regarding winter use in Yellowstone. In September 1999, the group took part in discussions with other snowmobile advocates to develop their own winter use EIS alternative. NEPA regulations encouraged citizens to suggest alternative management strategies for federal agencies to consider. Kim Raap, trails coordinator for the state of Wyoming, authored the proposal, which was dubbed "Revised Alternative E" because it was almost identical to the EIS's Alternative E. Raap's alternative would have permitted continued snowmobile use in the parks, but with noise and air pollution limits that would be developed pursuant to further studies. Adaptive management would be used, with new and ongoing research subjected to third-party or National Academy of Sciences review. Although this alternative would have allowed continued snowmobiling, the fact that it involved limits showed that snowmobiling advocates were beginning to recognize that some aspects of their activity needed to change. Alternatively, their proposal could be seen as an attempt to continue the status quo because it included few hard restrictions (the pollution limits, for example, were not specified).[20] Regardless, the BlueRibbon Coalition, the American Council of Snowmobile Associations (ACSA), and most local and regional governments endorsed it.[21]

The Coalition also allied itself with the ACSA and the International Snowmobile Manufacturers Association (ISMA, a powerful industry trade group, and formerly the International Snowmobile Industry Association) to form the Yellowstone Legal Action Task Group. The well-organized lobby had deep pockets: The industry sold 162,000 machines annually in the United States alone (along with more than 100,000 in Scandinavia and Canada), at an average price of $5,800, for an annual sales total of $6 billion. With 2.3 million snowmobilers in North America, the Task Group was easily able to raise more than $50,000 for its legal efforts by early 1998—including $24,000 from merchants in West Yellowstone. With funding secured, the group requested to intervene in the Fund for Animals lawsuit (that is, petitioned the court to join the plaintiffs in the lawsuit to advocate for their interest in that suit) and received such permission from Judge Emmet Sullivan in August 1998. From this point forward, much of the debate over winter use took place in the courts, with the BlueRibbon Coalition's legal group enjoying some successes.[22]

The Coalition had substantial local support as well, particularly in West Yellowstone. Often speaking for the town was Clyde Seely, owner of several properties there, including the largest hotel and snowmobile fleet (with 275 machines available for rent at that time). Snowmobiling was particularly important to him because he had been one of the founders of the West Yellowstone snowmobile industry in the 1960s. Seely was well-connected politically, being on a first-name basis with Montana U.S. Senator Conrad Burns; he dominated the town's pro-snowmobile faction over the next few years.[23]

Many in the pro-snowmobile camp supported Revised Alternative E because it preserved individual access to Yellowstone and the associated personal freedoms. As geographer Yi-Fu Tuan has argued, machines can make one feel free: "Being free has several levels of meaning. Fundamental is the ability to transcend the present condition, and this transcendence is most simply manifest as the elementary power to move." Combine these attributes with the general perception of the West as open and spacious, and one can see how snowmobiles in Yellowstone became powerful symbols of freedom. This meaning is evident in many comments from snowmobile advocates in the Yellowstone debate. Raap, for example, argued that the desire for "personal freedom" motivated the typical visitor to rent a snowmobile instead of a snowcoach seat, while Paul Kruse, representing the five Yellowstone-area county governments, equated snowmobiles with "freedom of movement and expression." Jackson Hole resident Doyle Vaughn said it most simply: "This is an issue about freedom." Such statements left little doubt that snowmobile supporters viewed their activity in Yellowstone as an expression of American freedom and individualism. From this point forward, they would consistently draw upon this powerful value to defend their access.[24]

West Yellowstone, 2008. Advertising itself as the "Snowmobile Capital of the World," by the 1990s many merchants in this small town at Yellowstone's West Entrance depended heavily on income derived from snowmobile rentals. Proposals by Yellowstone National Park managers late in the decade to ban snowmobiles threatened not only that income but also the town's identity, based on the iconography of freedom embedded in the machines and the hard work it took by town residents to develop a prosperous winter economy. Photo by author.

The environmental community also sensed the importance of the snowmobile issue—and, like the snowmobile enthusiasts, disliked the plowing idea (conservationists feared that wildlife could get trapped on plowed roads and that providing for wheeled access to the park's higher and snowier interior would set an unfortunate precedent). Led by the Greater Yellowstone Coalition (ready to take on a long anti-snowmobile campaign now that the New World Mine battle was successfully concluded), an alliance of ten national and regional conservation organizations also developed strategy on the EIS and snowmobile issue.[25] They hammered out another EIS alternative that they felt would address winter use problems while assuring park access.[26] The "Citizens' Solution for Winter Access to Yellowstone" proposed to phase out snowmobile use over the next two years, restricting access to the park's interior to snowcoaches, which were generally quieter and cleaner than two-stroke snowmobiles.[27] The "Citizens' Solution" also addressed two familiar conservationist concerns: the Continental Divide Snowmobile Trail, which it would have closed, and the need for a carrying-capacity study, which it would have required. Further, off-trail backcountry use would have been restricted to protect wintering wildlife, and Sylvan Pass would have been closed. Overall, the option was very similar to option G of the EIS. Revealing their marketing skills, though, conservationists gave it a compelling name that highlighted visitor access, the very theme that snowmobile advocates frequently used.[28]

American conservationists do not generally enjoy the industry support that snowmobile advocates do. Weaker financially (and often politically), the conservation community does, however, often have an advantage with the press. Working with reporters for positive publicity is therefore an important strategy for conservation groups. The Greater Yellowstone Coalition illustrated this tactic with the "Citizens' Solution," unveiling it at a prominent news conference in October 1999. Before the event, GYC organizers sent press releases to the editorial boards of major national newspapers and arranged for Jackie Mathews, a West Yellowstone business owner opposed to continued snowmobile use, to be present. They may also have coordinated a letter to NPS Director Robert Stanton signed by thirty-eight members of Congress. The letter deplored snowmobile air and noise pollution in Yellowstone and called for stricter regulations on such use. These broad-based efforts were successful, with the press devoting extensive coverage to them. The *Los Angeles Times* supported the proposal to ban the "screaming banshees" from Yellowstone, as did other West Coast newspapers, and the *Seattle Post-Intelligencer* said snowmobiles should be banned from the park because they "destroy an intrinsic value of national parks: quiet." As expressed by the editorial board there, Yellowstone in its existing situation was not a national park, but rather "an amusement park."[29]

The significance of the press as a tool for the conservationist movement was again demonstrated in 1999, when the Bluewater Network, a San Francisco–based group dedicated to reducing the pollution from all two-cycle engines, such as jet-skis and snowmobiles (and not to be confused with the BlueRibbon Coalition), formally requested that the NPS ban snowmobiles from all of its parks. The group deplored the impacts of snowmobiles on national park users, wildlife, threatened and endangered species, air quality, and natural silence. The group, representing more than sixty environmental organizations, was aware that the NPS had the authority to implement such a ban. Summing up the Bluewater Network's perspective, its executive director, Russell Long, said that "snowmobiles destroy wilderness."[30] The request was widely publicized and was responsible in part for transforming the Yellowstone snowmobile conflict from a regional debate into a national one. Over fifty media outlets, including such high-profile publications as the *New York Times*, the *Washington Post*, *USA Today*, and the *Salt Lake Tribune*, carried the story, with most giving positive press to the Network. The request also succeeded in stirring significant self-examination in the NPS. Though it would take another five years—and a change in presidential administrations—for the agency to respond, the group's request certainly provided support for those in Yellowstone wanting to ban the machines.[31]

The Bluewater Network's petition indicates that the conservationist perception of snowmobiles was now plainly negative, not uncertain as it had been thirty years ago. Originally developed as a practical way to get out into the natural world in the wintertime, snowmobiles by the 1990s were no longer merely a means of exploration. With the development of more powerful machines, snowmobiling had become a male-dominated activity often centered around driving fast and pushing ever farther into remote terrain. Thrill-based activities such as "high-marking"—that is, competing with others to see who could drive one's snowmobile the highest onto steep mountainsides—had become common. Reflecting the activity's changing nature, industry advertisements usually showed snowmobilers crashing through mounds of snow, the white stuff flying everywhere. Only rarely were snowmobilers shown touring quietly, observing wildlife, or enjoying a scenic view. In Yellowstone, speeding was a common problem, the raw power of the machines too great a temptation for some visitors. For these reasons (along with snowmobile noise and fumes), snowmobiling clashed with the popular conception of wilderness as clean, quiet, and devoid of crowds; they were the antithesis of wilderness. Consequently, the Network and most other conservation groups wanted them out of national parks.[32]

As is evident from the editorials, motivations to support the "Citizens' Solution" centered on protecting the park's air quality, natural silence, and wildlife resources from harm by snowmobiles. Parks were to be protected in an unimpaired state; they were sacred space. Obnoxious vehicles like snowmobiles were akin to the money-changers in the temple. Such thinking was part of a long tradition in American thought, extending back to Henry David Thoreau and other writers, revering nature as sacred and deserving of care and respect. One contemporary author has called this tradition the "American Nature Religion."[33] Conservationists today still commonly advance this view, as evidenced by a fall 1997 Greater Yellowstone Coalition article arguing that Yellowstone had "intangible aesthetic and spiritual values." The Coalition and other conservation groups would often call on this sacredness value in support of a snowmobile ban. Just as freedom became the rallying cry for the BlueRibbon Coalition, faith in sacred nature attracted many to the conservationist cause.[34]

The name of the conservationists' alternative (the "Citizens' Solution for Winter *Access*" [emphasis added]) was revealing in another way. Conservationists incorporated the word "access" into the name not only because they knew it would sell better, but also because access and traveling freedom were important to them, just as they were to snowmobile advocates. Conservationists, however, more commonly enjoy different aspects of freedom, such as the ability to enjoy those qualities that make nature sacred—silence and tranquility—as well as freedom *from* the machine. Snowmobiles are the winter equivalent of the auto, which, for con-

Winter sunshine and frosted trees, 1990s. Conservationists viewed Yellowstone Park as sacred, with snowmobiles equivalent to the machine in the garden. Meanwhile, snowmobilers saw their machines as the winter equivalent to the automobile and the freedom it represents. As the snowmobile controversy escalated in the late 1990s and early 2000s, it substantially devolved into a conflict between these two sets of fundamental American values. Photo by author.

servationists, as many authors have argued, is anathema to wilderness preservation, national park protection, and natural sacredness. Everything about the auto and the snowmobile—their roads, noise, exhaust, and passengers—is contrary to these goals, which have in common the absence of people. Conversely, in the Yellowstone winter situation, snowcoaches seemed to produce less noise and fumes, and because they were multi-passenger, their impacts were lower overall. To conservationists in Yellowstone, therefore, snowmobiles destroyed wilderness values while snowcoaches provided both the freedom to experience Yellowstone's natural sacredness and also freedom from a machine with far more drawbacks, the snowmobile.[35]

As the snowmobile controversy unfolded in the late 1990s and early 2000s, American values, the associated personal or group identities, and the related attitudes toward park management would become some of the strongest influences over park policy-making. The two primary and opposing camps of values at stake in this issue were individualism and freedom and their embodiment in motorized access, on the one hand, and the American Nature Religion and its embodiment in nature protection and quiet, muscle-powered recreation, on the other. Snowmobilers would come to see attempts to curtail snowmobile use as anti-American. Similarly, curtailing or eliminating snowmobile use threatened the family values linked to snowmobile rentals in West Yellowstone and elsewhere, where many of the businesses (like Clyde Seely's) were built from scratch with a lot of hard work. Not only were those businesses expressions of family values, but they also manifested the Protestant work ethic, another powerful American value.[36] Consequently, restrictions on snowmobiling were sometimes also viewed as antifamily and even anti-Christian. Conversely, to conservationists, activities like cross-country skiing, hiking, and wildlife observation were the proper forms of worship in nature temples. Snowmobiles were inappropriate because their emissions, noise, and image threatened or cheapened the inviolability of Yellowstone.[37] Similarly, animal rights advocates such as Fund for Animals members viewed bison as sacred, a broad symbolism that Yellowstone bison, with their many meanings, easily suggested. To these activists, wildlife harassment was wrong not only because it harmed individual animals but also because those animals should be treated with the dignity and respect one would accord anything sacred.

These values were reflected in the language used by the interest groups discussed above as well as in the imagery they used to advance their positions. Conservationists used images of rangers wearing gas masks (discussed later in this chapter) and snowmobilers wearing shiny helmets and full-body snowmobile suits. As a result, the subjects in the photos bore a resemblance to the evil Darth Vader from the *Star Wars* movies. In such a way, they portrayed snowmobiling as an "invention of the devil" inherently out of place in a sacred natural wonder. That the majority of Americans view nature as pristine and untouched by human influence advances the conservationist cause, even though conservationists are well aware that at least portions of the park have been altered by humans. Both conservationists and snowmobilers have attempted to portray their preferred activity—snowcoach travel or snowmobiling, respectively—as family activities, depicting parents with children enjoying the park with the relevant machine(s) nearby. Snowmobile advertisements were quite different from conservationist portrayals of the activity. The ads typically depicted the machines flying through the white landscape with an explosion of snow in their wake, glorious mountain scenery as a backdrop. The sense of freedom and rugged individualism was obvious. The pictures, as the saying goes, were worth a thousand words, bearing witness to the powerful values driving this developing controversy.[38]

The values that came to be in opposition to each other in the controversy are not mutually exclusive, however. Most conservationists value aspects of freedom, and most snowmobile advocates would agree that nature is sacred. Indeed, these two sets of values are widely shared among Americans. Snowmobilers may believe that nature is sacred because it is the venue for experiencing the freedom of their machines; similarly, conservationists may find it sacred because they can hike or ski through it at will. Nature to both groups can represent some kind of freedom or individualism. In this story, though, snowmobile advocates defending their activity have strongly identified with the freedom and independence that their machines represent; they have not suggested that snowmobiles should be retained because nature's sacredness would be diminished without snowmobile access. Similarly, conservationists have frequently demanded snowmobiles be banned to preserve nature's sacredness; only rarely have they suggested that nature's freedoms could be protected or enhanced by banning snowmobiles.[39] Conservationists could easily call upon the freedoms they value in opposing snowmobile use in Yellowstone, just as snowmobilers could call upon nature's sacredness as the reason they wish to retain snowmobile access, but neither side does so. Most often, snowmobilers view nature as a means to the end of experiencing freedom; conservationists see nature as inherently sacred—an end in itself, not the means to something else.

Confirming this interpretation of the snowmobile controversy are several scholars working within two other fields of inquiry. Natural resource social psychologists William T. Borrie, Wayne A. Freimund, and Mae A. Davenport found a breakdown in values between various stakeholders in this debate that is almost identical to that portrayed in this book. In their words, proponents of "recreation and tourism resource values" tend to support continued snowmobiling, while adherents to "natural values" generally want a ban on the activity. Similarly, political scientist Judith Layzer argued that, like many federal land-management controversies, the Yellowstone snowmobiling issue cascades to a conflict between promoters of a cornucopian vision of nature as boundless and those promoting a conservationist worldview emphasizing nature's limitations. The titles and descriptions of the values at conflict in Yellowstone may differ slightly, but there is essential agreement across disciplines that the snowmobile conflict comes down to a fundamental conflict in values and their manifestations in policy.[40]

In choosing which value set to express, the stakeholders are implicitly gambling that their set is—or should be—the more widely accepted one in American society. As Chapter 5 will reveal, both sets have a powerful appeal, for snowmobile use in Yellowstone continues, but with restrictions that eliminate some of the freedom traditionally associated with its use in order to protect Yellowstone's sacredness. The fact that snowmobiling remains in Yellowstone (its restrictions notwithstanding), however, suggests that freedom is the stronger value, that it has more powerful political defenders, or both. To some, it might also suggest that science supports continued snowmobile use. As park managers continued to find, however, the science relevant to this issue is confounding and ambivalent, giving mixed signals, and it is used in different ways by the affected interest groups.

Science and Technology in NPS Decision-Making

Environmental Impact Statements should utilize the latest science and technology available. Yellowstone's planners used what science they could but found that there are many limitations to the use of science in park management. Some findings and technological improvements came too late to assist in their efforts; some had inherent problems; some were more confounding than helpful; and some were limited in their usefulness by conditions beyond park managers' control.

Soundscape findings were perhaps the best example of science that was too late to assist in park decision-making (wildlife findings would soon illustrate the same problem). The soundscapes field in general was brand new at this time, with regular monitoring of Yellowstone's soundscape and the human impacts upon it not to begin for several more years. Park managers were limited to just one study performed by the Greater Yellowstone Coalition. Working in the heavily visited Firehole Valley, which contains Old Faithful at its southern end, on President's Day weekend (the busiest weekend of the winter) in 2000, the group found snowmobile noise to be audible 90 percent of the time at eight of thirteen study sites and 100 percent of the time at Old Faithful. Only one site—Lone Star Geyser, about 2 miles from the nearest road—was quiet the entire time. The study provided the first hard evidence that snowmobiles really did disturb the serenity associated with national parks, but looked only at the busiest weekend, not the entire winter. It would be several more years before the NPS procured funding for winter-long efforts at more sites. So for now, there was little solid information upon which managers could base their decisions.[41]

An air-quality investigation released at about the same time demonstrated other problems with the use of science. NPS scientists Miguel Flores and Tonnie Maniero examined snowmobile emissions, finding that the machines produced extraordinary amounts of air pollution, as suspected by many park employees. Specifically, the two wrote that snowmobiles emitted 100 times as much carbon monoxide and 300 times as much hydrocarbon pollution as the typical auto (significant amounts, but not as much as the earlier broadside had claimed). Such extreme amounts were reflected in air-quality monitoring at Yellowstone's West Entrance in 1997. One carbon-monoxide reading there came dangerously close to violating the Clean Air Act's provisions for national parks (9.0 parts per million [ppm] as averaged over eight hours; the park reading was 8.9 ppm). Particulate monitoring was little better, producing a reading of 122, almost twice the maximum twenty-four-hour reading from the polluted Los Angeles suburb Azusa. Snowmobiles also produced significant amounts of nitrogen oxides, ammonium, sulfate, and hydrocarbons such as benzene and formaldehyde. The authors concluded that persons riding toward the end of a line of snowmobiles and those exposed on a regular basis to their emissions—such as park employees—could suffer significant health risks.[42]

Releasing the air-quality report late in 1999, Superintendent Finley soon found that public scrutiny of it turned up two errors, both of which exaggerated snowmobile air pollution. Specifically, the particulate comparison to Azusa reflected different lengths of time and was therefore inaccurate, and the amount of one toxic pollutant (polycyclicaromatic hydrocarbons) was exaggerated, arising from an error in converting the figure from metric to English units.[43] The errors triggered wide criticism from snowmobile advocates, who already feared that park managers wanted to ban snowmobiles. Finley publicly apologized for the mistakes and requested a revised report as quickly as possible. The corrected report (issued in February 2000) still demonstrated that snowmobiles were very polluting. They emitted 10 to 70 times more carbon monoxide than the typical auto, and 45 to 250 times more hydrocarbons. In Yellowstone, such emissions constituted 35 to 68 percent of all annual carbon-monoxide pollution and 68 to 90 percent of all annual hydrocarbon pollution. These percentages were lower than those in the original report, but still significant given the fact that 16 times as many autos entered in summer as snowmobiles in winter.[44]

Overall, the errors hurt Park Service credibility and added to the increasing polarization among stakeholders. If science is to be used in park policy-making—as it should be, recognizing its limits and other policy referents—the flap over the

Snowmobile air pollution, 1990s. The two-stroke snowmobiles then in use produced prodigious quantities of air pollutants, including carbon monoxide, particulates, and hydrocarbons such as benzene and formaldehyde. Pollution was worst when the vehicles were first started for the day, as shown here, or when temperature inversions produced stable air masses (which allow pollutants to accumulate instead of dispersing), such as at the West Entrance. Photo by author.

errors in the air-quality report suggested that the science must be solid and error-free. Most unfortunately, the errors encouraged the tendency among stakeholders to selectively choose the scientific information that most supported their various causes.[45] Americans tend to believe in the ability of science to settle disputes objectively, but when a preexisting science base does not exist, interest groups often pick and choose the science as it becomes available, seeking legitimacy for the values to which they already adhere. Science, in this way, becomes the cover for existing beliefs rather than a basis for belief formulation.

Perhaps the best illustration of this tendency would come in late 2007 and early 2008, when conservationists claimed that the NPS was continuing to allow more snowmobile use than its own wildlife scientists recommended. Although there was some truth to this claim, the conservationists neglected to mention that the alternative they favored, snowcoaches only, would also allow more winter users than those same biologists recommended. More broadly, they also failed to mention that those same biologists more and more felt that winter use was not harming wildlife populations and that the issue was not so much a biological issue as it was a social one. In making their claim, they used only that portion of the existing knowledge base on wildlife that supported their goal and associated values: reducing or eliminating snowmobile use to preserve Yellowstone's sacredness.[46]

The increasing concerns and publicity over air-quality problems did begin to stir some changes, though nothing that helped substantially in the short term. West Yellowstone merchants began to pump only cleaner-burning ethanol and to use biodegradable lubricating oils in their machines. These efforts reduced emissions slightly, but not enough; changes more resembling a reduction of an order of magnitude were needed, and those would only come through technological advances. Those were on the way, with engineering students and major snowmobile manufacturer Arctic Cat both unveiling snowmobile prototypes in early 2000 that substantially reduced typical carbon-monoxide and hydrocarbon emissions along with snowmobile noise.[47] Despite these efforts, it was not clear that such machines would be commercially available in time to influence the NPS's EIS decision-making. As with research findings, technological improvements are not always available when park managers need them. The major manufacturers were understandably reluctant to expend much effort on the relatively small Yellowstone market, but they did not yet seem to understand the precedent that Yellowstone could set for the country: that if society deemed snowmobiles to be appropriate there, they would be acceptable almost anywhere. Soon, that would become more evident.

Studies involving wildlife illustrated the same disjunct between the time needed for research and the time frames in which park managers must make decisions, compounded by the fact that scientific findings are not always consistent. In the mid- or late 1990s, two Montana State University–Bozeman graduate students were working on master's theses investigating the effects that groomed roads and motorized traffic had on park bison and elk. Such studies take time, however, and results from the two projects were only becoming available in draft form in late 1999; one of the studies was not finalized until November 2001. Such a block of time is more than park managers often have to make a decision. Managers could have avoided this recurring situation by contracting the necessary research earlier or on a recurring basis, but they were unable to acquire the necessary funding or support for such research in the 1980s and early 1990s. Whether their fault or not, managers in the 1990s did not have the necessary research at their disposal and were forced to stumble forward without it.[48]

Additionally, scientists do not always share a uniform opinion. In this case, the two studies did more to add to the contemporary confusion over snowmobile impacts on wildlife than they did to disperse the controversy. Dan Bjornlie, the first of the two students to finish, found that bison primarily traveled off the roads, on their own trails, neither seeking nor avoiding the hard-packed oversnow vehicle roads. In contrast to park researcher Mary Meagher, he concluded that "roads are not the major influence on bison ecology that has been proposed." Amanda Hardy, the other researcher, found that bison became habituated to recreational traffic (including snowmobiles, skiers, and snowshoers) on established trails as winter progressed, but that elk avoided roadsides because snowmobiles stressed them. Snowmobiles stressed elk more than automobiles did, she wrote, but recreationists on skis or snowshoes disturbed both species most of all. Nevertheless, and again contradicting Meagher, she concluded that park "bison and elk return to winter in the same area each year, coexisting with winter recreation without incurring losses at the population level." Neither of the master's theses supported Meagher's assertions or confirmed the perception that machines would displace wildlife more than pedestrians (on skis) did. Like the studies from the 1980s (discussed in Chapter 3), they gave little direction to park managers.[49]

Some of the confusion stemmed from differences in snowmobile impacts upon wildlife *populations* and upon *individual animals.* As both students found, the bison population was doing fine even though individual bison had been harassed. The benign population effects were not always what visitors saw and photographed. Some saw bison on roads being chased back and forth between snowmobilers driving in different directions (such unfortunate bison were akin to a hockey puck being batted back and forth between snowmobilers), chasing them off the roads, and even stampeding them. It was hard for these visitors to accept that populations were not disturbed under these circumstances, since individuals clearly were. To some such observers, the wildlife harassment seemed to violate a provision of the NPS's nationwide snowmobile policies, which required that snowmobile use "not disturb wildlife." Other visitors enjoyed seeing bison stolidly grazing, walking, or sleeping on or near the roads and took the opportunity to snap pictures of the shaggy beasts—perhaps with snowmobiles and family on the side. To these observers, even bison individuals did not appear stressed. Skiers displaced them more, so groomed roads seemed to cause little harm. The confusion over population versus individual effects, and even over whether there were any individual effects at all, sent mixed signals to park managers and continued to exacerbate debate on the issue, even becoming the subject of two lawsuits in 2007. Moreover, almost all visitors witnessed both bison harassment and calmly grazing animals, but which scenes became memorable often depended upon the perspectives of the observers. Conservationists were probably more likely to remember scenes of harassment, whereas snowmobile advocates recalled scenes of bison grazing quietly and peacefully and may have felt the harassment was a rare exception to the rule.[50]

Science and technology are useful mainly when they are timely, available when needed, unified in direction, accurate, and intelligible to the public. The fact that studies rarely meet all of these criteria is one of the reasons why science provides only one basis for NPS decisions. In fact, nowhere is there a requirement that park managers must use science as a decision-making criterion, although it is especially helpful when defending agency decisions in court. Federal law, national park tradition, political feasibility, values, and economic analysis provide other bases for NPS decision-making. This helps to explain why cross-country skiing and snowshoeing have not been banned in Yellowstone even though research suggests they displace wildlife more than snowmobiles do. Managers see the muscle-powered activities as more historical and intrinsically more appropriate in the parks than snowmobiling. They also seem to be more in keeping with the contemplative experiences that managers hope parks provide. Knowing that science was only one of many inputs to park policy-making, park managers were likely to continue allowing the muscle-powered activities.[51]

Consumed by the EIS work, park managers may have been too busy to contemplate the interrelated roles of science and values in their decision-making. Instead, they knew that the sight of snowmobilers chasing bison looked terrible, especially in the park that provided the last American wild shelter for them. It was clear that no matter what kind of transportation was allowed, drivers without experience passing bison on the roads would continue to cause them undue stress, and documentation of such events would continue to inflame the debate. Managers knew that whatever the solution was going to be, it needed to reduce or eliminate the possibility of such harassment. The next step in that direction came from an unexpected source, the Environmental Protection Agency (EPA).

The First EIS Concludes under Public and Political Scrutiny

Besides utilizing the latest science available, federal agencies writing Environmental Impact Statements should also confer with the EPA by asking it to review their Draft EIS. Consequently, Yellowstone planners forwarded the EPA a copy of the Draft EIS in 1999. Late that year, the EPA replied with a letter saying the EIS had a "thorough and substantial" science base, a claim not necessarily reflecting the reality discussed above (like the NPS, the EPA is certainly influenced by the contemporary political climate—see the section entitled "Political Influence in NPS Policy-Making" [page 156]). The EPA felt that the science base "clearly and convincingly" proved that snowmobiles were adversely affecting the park's natural, aesthetic, and scenic values. Therefore, all but one of the EIS alternatives, in the EPA's opinion, failed to meet the provisions of Executive Order 11644. The exception was Alternative G, the snowcoach-only alternative (mirrored by the "Citizens' Solution"), which was also the only alternative that would reduce carbon-monoxide emissions enough to comply with the Clean Air Act. For these two reasons, the EPA felt that the NPS had no choice but to adopt Alternative G and ban snowmobiles entirely.[52]

At the same time, park planners were reviewing the public comments received on the Draft EIS. Citizens seemed to want snowmobiles out, with supporters of the conservationists' "Citizens' Solution" narrowly eclipsing those supporting the snowmobilers' Revised Alternative E. Very few supported the road-plowing idea. The overall response—46,500 commenters—was the largest to date, and even though there was not a substantial majority opinion, many commenters raised probing questions about snowmobile use.[53]

Impressed by the EPA's conclusion, Superintendent Finley publicly released the letter in February 2000, suggesting as he did so that the NPS would open itself up to lawsuits if it did not come up with an option that reduced snowmobile emissions (unsaid was the possibility of other lawsuits if the agency curtailed snowmobile use). The combination of the EPA letter and the public comments questioning snowmobile impacts, continuing problems with wildlife harassment, and the ongoing absence of commercially available four-stroke snowmobiles all began turning the tide against future snowmobile use in the park. Finley, his staff, and his superiors (decisions of this magnitude were discussed by the regional and national NPS directors, and sometimes even the secretary of the interior) began to lean toward a snowmobile ban; by converting to snowcoach-only transportation, they would solve most of these problems. The professional drivers of such vehicles could be trained in how to pass wildlife on or near roadways with as little disturbance as possible. To park planners, this seemed to be the only solution to the persistent problems.[54]

Prodding them to adopt the snowcoach-only alternative was the assistant interior secretary for fish and wildlife and parks, Don Barry. About this time, in a memo to park staff outlining a conversation that he had evidently had with them and expressing his clear support for the snowcoach-only alternative, Barry wrote: "Given the resounding rejection by the majority of public comments of the Draft EIS's preferred alternative, and EPA's negative assessment of all of the other alternatives except Alternative G, a revised Preferred Alternative should adhere closely to the major elements of Alternative G in the Draft EIS." He went on to say that the park should ban snowmobiles by the winter of 2002–2003 and restrict over-snow vehicle travel to snowcoaches only. He took pains to note that this was a shared decision between himself and park staff and that it was not final. Whether the purported conversation was indeed a shared one involving mutual decision-making or a decision from Barry given to park managers is not clear, but managers in Yellowstone now knew what to do.[55]

Finley and his staff announced the idea in March and quickly saw criticism (including some directed at the science used in the decision-making), with snowmobile proponents requesting a reconsideration.[56] Such requests soon seemed pointless, as Barry announced a decision in April to ban snowmobiles from all park units nationwide. He and NPS Deputy Director Denis Galvin said the NPS would be phasing out recreational snowmobile use throughout most of the national park system in response to the Bluewater Network's petition. Barry's opinion was very clear: At the press conference announcing the decision, he said, "Like a messy, noisy house guest that has left a trail of dirty clothes and dishes, recreational snowmobiling has worn out its Park Service welcome, and is not getting its invitation renewed." Snowmobiles, he said, degraded park resources with their air pollution, destroyed park "solitude and serenity" through their noise pollution, and promoted an "image of power, speed and thrills" that was not an "introspective and educational means of interpreting the landscape and wildlife wonders of our national parks." He exempted Yellowstone and Grand Teton national parks from the decision because their EIS was nearly complete (and was going to ban snowmobiles anyway) and Voyageurs National Park in Minnesota and most Alaskan national parks because their charters accepted traditional uses and snowmobiling in those parks predated park creation.[57]

The Finley and Barry decisions produced responses in line with the values held by stakeholders. Conservationists were jubilant, noting that national parks were not created for any and all forms of access. Just as "running a chainsaw in the Sistine Chapel" would be offensive, driving noisy snowmobiles into the sacred space of national parks was not appropriate. "Snowmobiling conflicts with the ideal of unimpaired nature it embodies," the New York Times wrote. Hearkening more to values of sacredness than snowmobilers did, conservationists looked forward to the return of silence to the parks.[58] Snowmobile enthusiasts, meanwhile, complained that their rights were being taken away (presumably the perceived right to enter Yellowstone on a snowmobile) or that their freedoms were being threatened. A few also decried the likely economic effects of a ban on West Yellowstone; snowmobile rental owner Doug Schmier, for example, predicted the proposed ban "will devastate this community."[59]

In addition to their value-laden rhetoric, both groups increased their lobbying activities. Conservationists continued organizing among their members, writing Congress, and testifying at hearings. Such efforts got both press and political attention, with the NPCA designating Yellowstone one of the "Ten Most Endangered" National Parks in 2000 because of its snowmobile problems. Congressmen Bruce Vento and Christopher Shays asked their colleagues to join them in supporting the NPS proposal.[60] The snowmobile industry and lobby decided to attack both the Yellowstone and nationwide snowmobile bans mostly through legislative action but also through lawsuits (one of which would eventually be successful) and public opinion.[61] Executives from the four major snowmobile manufacturers participating in ISMA met at about this time with Senators Craig

Thomas and Michael B. Enzi of Wyoming, Conrad Burns and Max Baucus of Montana, and Larry Craig from Idaho and found sympathetic ears. Thomas took the charge. A friend of the national parks from the Cody area—and, like most politicians, a booster of economic development—he desired a compromise that would protect the parks while allowing snowmobiling to continue. Most likely, that compromise would involve the four-stroke snowmobile, which Arctic Cat was about to produce commercially. Hoping to expedite such development, Thomas hinted to the manufacturers at the meeting that failure to do so could mean that the ban would be implemented. The industry leaders, as a result, began to understand the importance of the Yellowstone issue.[62]

Thomas apparently realized that Yellowstone's proposed snowmobile ban could derail his envisioned compromise. In an attempt to preserve park snowmobile access, he soon sent a letter, cosigned by eleven colleagues (including all of the above, except for Baucus), to the NPS complaining that the proposed snowmobile ban would "reduce access to public lands across the country." This letter was the second of two threatening letters from the congressional delegations; an earlier one had promised "strong opposition" to the Park Service's "unilateral decisions" and predicted (accurately, at that) that they "will not stand." Over the next several months, Thomas and others would go to great lengths to live up to their promises (see Table 4.2 later in this chapter for a summary of their actions).[63]

To that end, upon learning of Yellowstone's decision, local congressional delegations held a show of force on May 25, 2000, in Washington, D.C., via hearings in both the House and Senate. They then introduced various bills attempting to overturn or stall the snowmobile ban.[64] None of the legislation passed, but, like the hearings, the bills demonstrated the political attention and opposition the proposed ban was receiving (Table 4.2 details the legislation). The Senate hearing focused in particular on the potential precedent of such a ban and on Barry's polarizing actions. Senator Thomas chaired that hearing and expressed the concern of many that an NPS ban on snowmobiles would be replicated on Forest Service and Bureau of Land Management (BLM) lands (though, again, the multiple-use mandates of those agencies made complete snowmobile bans less likely) and that other forms of recreation would be next. Thomas and Idaho Senator Larry Craig then grilled Don Barry, trying to get him to admit that he had personally directed Yellowstone managers to ban snowmobiles. Barry refused to confess (his earlier memo to park staff was clear in its intent, but careful to state that the decision was not final or unilateral) and defended the nationwide ban. Overall, the May 25 show of force was a call to arms for many and a warning to park managers that their policy-making was generating high-level political opposition. As long as the political climate remained friendly, they had little to fear—but that situation could and would soon change.[65]

A third hearing—this one held by the House Subcommittee on Tax, Finance, and Exports of the Committee on Small Business two months later in Washington—highlighted the impacts that changes in Yellowstone's winter use could have on West Yellowstone. The ban would indeed hurt some businesses in the small town, though estimates on the extent of such impacts varied. Park planners estimated that it would cost the five-county Greater Yellowstone region $19.2 million, a drop in the bucket of its $5.7 billion annual economic output. However, that loss would be concentrated in Yellowstone's small gateway communities. Clyde Seely, for example, predicted at the hearing that a snowmobile ban would cut his winter revenue alone by 60 to 70 percent, forcing him to lay off many of his 220 employees.[66] Seely's was the majority opinion, but the town had a substantial minority opinion as well. Led by town residents Jackie Mathews and Doug Edgerton, this group saw an opportunity rather than a threat in a snowmobile ban and encouraged their neighbors to see that they could become the exclusive providers of Yellowstone tours (few people own a snowcoach or bus, so visitors would have to tour the park on coaches owned by town merchants). Edgerton even traveled to Washington, D.C., to deliver a petition containing the signatures of 150 town residents advocating the snowmobile ban. With the town's voting population numbering only about 500, the minority opinion was substantial, but still a minority.[67]

Attempts to overturn the proposed snowmobile ban were not immediately successful (though they would continue), and Finley and his staff finalized the EIS on October 10, 2000. Reflecting the level of controversy and analysis that had gone into the issue, the document was 4 inches thick, and its three volumes weighed a total of 11 pounds. The final proposal would allow snowmobile use to continue for two more winters as it currently existed. In the winter of 2002–2003, park managers would cut snowmobile numbers in half, and they would eliminate them completely the following winter from both parks. Sylvan Pass would remain open, but the Continental Divide Snowmobile Trail would be closed. All Yellowstone winter travel would be by snowcoach.[68]

Making major federal decisions like this requires three significant steps. The first step is to complete the Final EIS, which discloses the environmental impacts of the alternatives; the second is to issue a "Record of Decision," which finalizes the agency's decision and explains its rationale; and the last is to publish a Final Rule, which contains the actual regulations implementing the decision, in the *Federal Register*.[69] Finley quickly began the second step, preparing the Record of Decision. He accepted more public comment on the Final EIS, an optional step, taken, in this case, to reassess public opinion. By this time, the battle lines were clear, and the three primary interest groups adhered to their earlier positions. Overall, a 60 percent majority of the 10,880 commenters favored snowmobile elimination (as noted earlier, public comments during the NEPA process are not

Three snowcoaches, 2008. In 2000, the NPS moved to ban snowmobiles and provide all visitor transportation by snowcoach. Completing the proposal in the final hours of the Clinton administration, the agency and its proposal stirred significant opposition among snowmobile advocates, including the incoming secretary of the interior. Photo by author.

votes, and the NPS is not obligated to adhere to majority opinion; it only needs to respond to public comments and should address common concerns).[70]

With the comment analysis complete and her confidence boosted, NPS Intermountain Regional Director Karen Wade signed the Record of Decision on November 22, 2000. The Record not only confirmed the snowmobile ban but also made an important finding: that the NPS had failed its congressional mandate to "leave [park resources] unimpaired for the enjoyment of future generations." Wade declared that snowmobiles in Yellowstone had impaired park resources, specifically park air quality, wildlife, natural soundscapes, and opportunities for visitor enjoyment.[71] In the national parks, impairment of park resources is seen as the worst violation of the NPS Organic Act; indeed, the first park commandment is "Thou shalt not impair." Wade's finding was significant because it was the first time the NPS had ever admitted failing in its mission. That finding would not only have implications for snowmobiles in Yellowstone but would also come to be a point of continued debate, especially in court.

There are indications that the impairment finding may have been politically desired, for the agency had just issued guidance on what constituted impairment.[72] Throughout 2000, the agency had been revising its *Management Policies*, the handbook translating its congressional mission into actual policies to be followed. That revision would not be complete for several more months, making any impairment declaration in Yellowstone difficult to issue. Making such a declaration required the handbook's framework, and the previous version of the handbook lacked the specific impairment guidance. Although conclusive evidence is lacking, it appears that the agency rushed the impairment guidance to approval before the full *Management Policies* handbook was finalized in order to provide Yellowstone managers with the necessary framework for Wade's declaration. If so, Yellowstone managers certainly took advantage of the new guidance, helping their cause. However, because such guidance requires the approval of the Department of the Interior, it is likely that Interior Secretary Babbitt or his appointee(s)— probably Don Barry—helped to publish the guidance ahead of schedule.[73] If so, the guidance and rush to publish it—like Barry's actions and those of the congressional delegations—illustrate that the agency is substantially influenced by both political parties. While that influence can help the agency (as it did in this case), it can just as easily hurt, as it did under the next secretary of the interior (detailed below in the section "Political Influence in NPS Policy-Making").

Wade's impairment declaration was issued after the 2000 presidential election but before the contested election results were resolved. When it became clear that George W. Bush would become the next president, Finley and his staff realized they needed to erect as many firewalls as possible before he took office to preserve the gains they had made. Most time sensitive was the need to publish the Final Rule (the third and last step) in the *Federal Register* by Friday, January 19, the day before Bush would be inaugurated. That would be the last day that support for a snowmobile ban would be likely to exist from the field level in Yellowstone through all NPS and Interior offices up to the presidential level; after that, things would probably be very different.[74]

Time was short. There was barely enough time for the minimum thirty-day comment period that agencies had to provide between publishing the draft and final rules. Working quickly, the NPS published the Draft Rule for public comment on December 18, 2000, leaving just two days between the end of the comment period and the last publication day. Park planners analyzed the comments as they arrived—finding over 80 percent in favor of the ban—and worked on getting a Final Rule text ready. As inauguration day approached, NPS and Interior staff in Washington and Yellowstone seemingly moved heaven and earth to get the Final Rule published. Bruce Babbitt made this publication a high priority, pushing Washington staff to work expeditiously to accomplish that goal (further evidence of the high-level political attention the NPS received). The NPS needed to submit the shortest rule possible to assure its publication, because other last-minute rules were also in the wings. Working on it until 4:00 A.M. some nights, the group produced a concise 39-page rule. They submitted it to the Office of Management and Budget (OMB) three days before inauguration day (OMB must approve all rules being published and had agreed to accept it as late as 1:00 A.M. that night). OMB quickly approved and forwarded it on to the *Federal Register* office—only to see it delayed past Friday the 19th by a different 300-page rule.[75] However, the NPS staff had one extra day they did not expect: Once a rule was in the *Federal Register* "Reading Room," it was as good as published. Yellowstone's snowmobile ban made it there on the last possible day—Friday, January 19, 2001—so it was the last Clinton rule published, and on Monday, January 22, 2001, two days after Bush's inauguration, the actual publication took place. With that, the snowmobile ban became a federal regulation.[76]

Both conservative and liberal legal scholars agreed that the new administration would have a difficult time overturning the ban. A change in policy would now need to be especially well-justified, not simply politically desired, or the administration could be sued (and in this case, would be sued) for being arbitrary and capricious. Recognizing this, the new Bush administration delayed implementation of all recently published Clinton rules for two months in order to study its options. In that period of time, ways to circumvent the snowmobile ban would become clear. So would the realization that a fundamental rule of physics also applied to park policy-making: Finley's strong action in banning snowmobiles would result in an equally strong and opposing reaction. The snowmobile ban, despite Finley's efforts to implement it, would remain a ban on paper only. The massive political pendulum had already reversed direction, and Yellowstone was in its path.[77]

A New President, a New EIS, and a New Decision

With a snowmobile ban now seeming very real, snowmobile proponents increased their attempts to overturn (or stall) it. Even while park staff members were working to finalize the ban, Senator Thomas was working to counter their plans. He introduced three separate bills that autumn in his effort (detailed in Table 4.2). Although none were directly successful (as before), it soon became clear that he could relax.[78]

Back on December 6, the International Snowmobile Manufacturers Association, the BlueRibbon Coalition, and the Wyoming State Snowmobile Association had sued the Department of the Interior and the NPS in Wyoming Federal District Court, alleging that they had violated the Administrative Procedure Act and the National Environmental Policy Act in developing the snowmobile ban. The groups felt the ban was politically motivated and did not adequately consider the cleaner and quieter four-cycle snowmobiles just becoming available. They requested the judge set aside the EIS and snowmobile ban. In a display of growing polarity three months later, the state of Wyoming intervened on behalf of the snowmobile plaintiffs, and the GYC and several other environmental groups intervened on behalf of the NPS. Soon, this lawsuit became the means to overturn the proposed ban.[79]

In spring 2001, rumors began to circulate that the Department of the Interior would not be fighting the suit and was instead seeking an out-of-court settlement (just as the agency had done with the first suit in 1997). Indeed, Department of Justice lawyers (who represent other federal agencies in court) were doing just that and reached a settlement in June wherein the NPS would prepare a Supplemental Environmental Impact Statement focusing on the use of the new four-cycle snowmobiles in Yellowstone and Grand Teton. The agency also committed to an aggressive schedule for the Supplemental EIS, hoping to finish it in two years, before the recently formalized snowmobile ban was to begin. In this way, the agency could reach a new decision—likely allowing snowmobile use to continue in the two parks—that could supplant the snowmobile ban.[80]

In summer 2001, Grand Teton National Park staff took the lead in drafting the Supplemental EIS because they had more staffing than Yellowstone. As before, the planners began by gathering what information they could, including emissions information on the new snowmobiles from ISMA, pursuant to the court settlement. The group provided some information, but park planners found nothing in it to dissuade them from their previous conclusion about four-strokes.[81]

Interest groups resumed their strategizing as well. Snowmobile groups saw this as a chance to overturn what they felt was an unfair decision. The BlueRibbon Coalition continued to encourage its members to involve themselves in the process, and snowmobile manufacturer Polaris encouraged its dealers and snowmobile buyers to become politically active in order to preserve snowmobiling. Claiming "It's all about access," the corporation encouraged its members to comment on the Supplemental EIS for the "national snowmobiling mecca." Their continued focus on access and freedom was evident.[82]

Because the settlement threatened a cherished victory, it goaded conservationists into even greater action than before. GYC staff resolved to win public opinion through regional and national editorials and by motivating more than 100,000 people to comment on the document. They also began working with Earthjustice, a group that pursued legal action on behalf of environmental causes, on a legal strategy should the NPS decide to continue allowing snowmobiles—to them, an expected outcome under the Bush administration. The GYC scored at least two high-visibility actions that summer: a letter signed by 102 House representatives to President Bush contesting the lawsuit settlement and a similar letter to the new secretary of the interior, Gale Norton, from 18 prominent scientists. The latter stated that "snowmobiling results in significant direct, indirect, and cumulative impacts on wildlife, their behavior and environment." Both letters may have been ghost-written by GYC staff members, who did gather signatures by fax. The GYC and its allies used these letters to keep the issue in the public eye, successfully plying their connections with regional and national newspapers for positive press for their argument. For conservationists, such group letters became a recurring means of attracting public attention to the issue, as Table 4.1 demonstrates.[83]

As the Supplemental EIS process unfolded, another winter passed and more problems with snowmobile use became clear. Because ethanol and biodegradable oils had not solved the air pollution problems at the West Entrance, park managers tinkered with other possible solutions, again without success. They began using an express lane and prepurchased park passes, for example, and these measures reduced emissions slightly, but still not enough to end health complaints from employees. Indeed, Occupational Safety and Health Administration (OSHA) tests revealed higher than recommended levels of benzene, formaldehyde, and carbon monoxide. Park managers, desperate to help their employees, finally hit upon a solution that worked, one that was a sad but powerful illustration of the problems with winter use. In February 2002, West Entrance employees began wearing gas masks. As a result, they experienced immediate improvements to their health. Snowmobile proponents derided it as a publicity stunt, particularly since the employees first wore the respirators on the busy President's Day weekend. Nonetheless, park rangers in the world's first national park wearing gas masks to protect themselves from snowmobile fumes epitomized to others the industrial and political manipulation of park policy.[84]

Local newspapers revealed another problem with Yellowstone snowmobile use that winter: illegal snowmobile trespass into the park's backcountry. This problem had existed for years, but that winter it seemed especially severe, perhaps because the NPS had recently stepped up its patrols in the area. Rangers found hundreds or even thousands of trespassing violations, mainly on the Madison Plateau south of West Yellowstone. Some snowmobilers traveled miles into the backcountry, and one even drove a sled over a snow-covered historic backcountry patrol cabin. Park employees speculated that snowmobilers upset with the potential ban were responsible. Given the area's remoteness and size and the issue's volatility, problems were likely to continue despite the patrols. This problem was another illustration of the way the issue had polarized people with different opinions on the matter and different underlying values.[85]

Table 4.1. High-Profile Letters Organized by Conservationists regarding the Snowmobile Issue (sent to NPS director, secretary of interior, and/or the president)

Date	Sender	Subject of Letter
July 1999	Rep. Bruce Vento and 37 other U.S. representatives	Deplored snowmobile air and noise pollution in Yellowstone and called for stricter regulations on their use
September 2001	Rep. Rush Holt and 101 other U.S. representatives	Expressed concern about 2001 lawsuit settlement of ISMA lawsuit
October 2001	18 prominent scientists	Expressed concern about effects of snowmobiling on park wildlife
May 2002	Physicians for Social Responsibility (PSR) and Public Employees for Environmental Responsibility (PEER)	Expressed concerns about health effects of snowmobile use on visitor and employee health and supported snowmobile ban
February 2003	American Cancer Society	Urged the NPS to issue warnings about airborne, snowmobile-derived carcinogens
February 2003	Former NPS Director Roger Kennedy and Deputy Director Denis Galvin	Criticized the Bush administration's retreat from the ban, stating that the "ride isn't what Yellowstone is all about, the park is what Yellowstone is all about"
March 2003	Several physicians	Expressed concerns that serious public health risks would remain with four-cycle snowmobiles
May 2003	Five former NPS directors	Expressed support for snowmobile ban
September 2003	Five former NPS directors	Expressed support for snowmobile ban, stating that "to do otherwise would be a radical departure from the Interior Department's stewardship mission"
August 2003	123 ex-NPS employees	Expressed support for snowmobile ban

Sources (in the order provided in the table): Bruce Vento et al. to Robert Stanton, July 30, 1999, file "Letter from 38 Members of Congress to Director Stanton," Environmental Impact Statement Collection, Management Assistant's Office Files, National Park Service, Mammoth Hot Springs, Yellowstone National Park, Wyoming; Rush Holt et al. to Mr. President, Sept. 26, 2001, file "WU," Greater Yellowstone Coalition files, 13 S. Willson Avenue, Bozeman, Montana (hereafter GYC); David Wilcove et al. to Gale Norton, Oct. 17, 2001, file "Science Letter, 10/01," GYC; Thomas C. Kiernan to Fran Mainella, May 31, 2002, file "WU CEO Letter," GYC; Scott McMillion, "Study Says Emissions Harm Pregnant Women, Elderly," *Bozeman Daily Chronicle*, Feb. 11, 2003; Denis Galvin and Roger Kennedy criticism from Scott McMillion, "Snowmobile Plan Denounced," *Bozeman Daily Chronicle*, Feb. 21, 2003; Mike Stark, "Doctors Fault Yellowstone Snowmobile Proposal," *Billings Gazette*, March 25, 2003; "Former Park Officials Back Snowmobile Ban," *Bozeman Daily Chronicle*, May 21, 2003; George B. Hartzog, Gary Everhardt, Russell Dickenson, and Roger Kennedy to Gale Norton, Sept. 10, 2003, as reprinted in "Snowmobile Industry Backsliding on Promises," *Bozeman Daily Chronicle*, Sept. 20, 2003; and Christopher Lee, "Ex-Park Service Workers Say Bush Reneges on Promises," *Washington Post*, Aug. 25, 2003.

Early in 2002, when the Draft Supplemental EIS was made public, two alternatives proposing continued snowmobile use received the most attention. Both suggested allowing snowmobiles under restricted numbers and conditions: They would need to be the quieter and cleaner four-cycle snowmobiles, and possibly guided.[86] The draft identified no preferred alternative, which is unusual for federal agencies preparing EISs; they generally indicate their preference so the public has an idea which option is most likely to be chosen and where to focus their attention when offering support or mounting an opposition. Park managers opted not to designate a preferred alternative because they were stung by criticism over their choice in the first EIS. Still, most observers suspected that some form of continued snowmobile use was the politically preferred alternative, if not the agency-endorsed one.[87]

As expected, this new information stimulated all sides to action, by now a déjà vu experience. The Idaho State Snowmobile Association sponsored a "2002 Yellowstone Freedom Ride" on four-cycle snowmobiles through the park in January 2002. Touring on the new sleds, the group hoped to demonstrate a sensitivity to the park's noise and emissions concerns and show that environmental stewardship could be reconciled with continued individual access. Members of the BlueRibbon Coalition participated as well, lauding the efforts of such "Access Pioneers."[88] Certainly, the event's name illustrated that, to snowmobile advocates, the machines were to winter as automobiles were to summer. The Coalition also led its own effort to get snowmobilers to submit comments on the Supplemental EIS. Members could call a toll-free number for "Yellowstone Form Letter Kits" to use in writing the NPS with their pro-snowmobile opinions. Interestingly, the group also published a story celebrating the Yellowstone winter scenery and wildlife visible from a snowmobile; this was one of very few instances in which the snowmobile community celebrated the natural resources made accessible by their machines.[89]

Conservationists were even more successful at making this a high-profile national issue. NPCA again named Yellowstone one of the "Ten Most Endangered" national parks, citing the continued snowmobile use as the reason. They announced the designation at the beginning of the public comment period (March 2002) to get publicity and spur conservationists to action.[90] The GYC and the Wilderness Society used the Internet (by now a powerful publicity tool) and assistance from the U.S. Public Interest Research Group (PIRG) Education Fund to motivate others, including the Physicians for Social Responsibility and the Public Employees for Environmental Responsibility, to file comments (see Table 4.1).[91] These publicity efforts were successful, with local, regional, and national papers criticizing the Bush administration's rollback of the snowmobile ban.[92]

With so much publicity and advocacy work, a huge number of comments on the Draft EIS rolled in—a total of 307,592 unduplicated letters, a volume of comment unprecedented for any NPS project anywhere. A large majority—79 percent of those sending form letters and 87 percent of those writing their own—opposed continued snowmobile use, for a total of 244,274 anti-snowmobile commenters (recall the GYC's goal of stimulating 100,000 anti-snowmobile comments). Letters that are not just signed form letters carry more weight with government decision-makers because they often have more detailed and thoughtful analysis. Of these individually written letters, those supporting the snowmobile ban made up the majority in all fifty states. Even among the three Yellowstone area states, between 79 percent and 85 percent of non-form letter writers were opposed to continued snowmobile use. Public opinion, at least among those motivated to write, seemed clear. (Those who are ambivalent about the issue usually do not write with their opinion, so such comment periods are not polls.)[93]

With the public comment period complete, park managers turned to completing the Final Supplemental EIS and its decision. By this time, Mike Finley had retired from government service, and Suzanne Lewis from Glacier National Park had taken his place. In Glacier, Lewis had completed a General Management Plan that most saw as quite protective of park resources. Her record at Yellowstone was more mixed. She worked in a challenging political climate, one that limited her potential for conservation successes and taxed her ability to administer to intrapark affairs. Astute politically, she was able to advance the cause of preservation to some degree (see Chapter 5, for example), but she sometimes failed to communicate effectively with park employees or empathize with their needs and concerns.[94]

In fall 2002, in one of her first actions on the Yellowstone snowmobile issue, Lewis released the details on the upcoming snowmobile decision. In two years, all machines entering Yellowstone would need to utilize Best Available Technology, which reduced hydrocarbon emissions below current averages by at least 90 percent, carbon monoxide by at least 70 percent, and noise by 5 decibels, or about 25 percent. Most, but not all, four-cycle snowmobiles on the market already met these requirements, and future technological improvements could result in even stricter requirements. Also required for 80 percent of park visitors would be commercial guides who were trained to minimize the impact of visitation upon park wildlife and other resources. Finally, no more than 950 snowmobiles per day could enter Yellowstone (550 of those from the West Entrance). An additional 150 would be permitted to enter Grand Teton (these numbers were somewhat above average daily use levels at the time).[95]

Lewis released the Final Supplemental EIS on February 20, 2003, and Regional Director Karen Wade made the decision official when she signed the Record of Decision on March 25 (she was the same person who had signed the previous decision banning snowmobiles and making the impairment finding). The environmentally preferred alternative, that alternative thought to be the one that would

Guided snowmobile group at Madison Warming Hut, 2008. Influenced by Secretary of the Interior Gale Norton, the NPS reversed its decision to ban snowmobiles and in 2003 decided to continue allowing them into Yellowstone, under three conditions: that 80 percent of visitors had to be commercially guided (as shown here), that all machines had to utilize Best Available Technology to reduce air and noise emissions (also as shown here), and that no more than 950 snowmobiles per day could enter Yellowstone. Photo by author.

best protect the natural environment, remained the snowmobile ban from the previous EIS. It is unusual for national park managers to choose against that alternative, as they did in this case. Lewis and her staff explained that they had to consider other elements of the debate, such as socioeconomic impacts and public comments. While that statement is true, how an 80 percent majority in those comments favoring the environmentally preferred alternative could persuade them to choose otherwise was not explained. Hints at the real explanation came from the answer that Lewis and park managers gave to the question of whether they had been directed by higher powers to overturn the ban. Their response lacked a firm yes or no and in fact sounded a lot like the kinds of responses politicians give when dodging difficult questions, but it certainly hinted at the real answer. This did nothing to disperse the cloud of political capitulation that shrouded the entire Supplemental EIS process, a topic that will be explored in the next section of this chapter in more detail.[96]

The public response to the new plan was mixed and ultimately litigious. Snowmobilers generally liked it because it was better than the ban, though some snowmobile boosters wanted to see the limits raised to provide a greater economic base. Conservationists held two rallies in the region to advocate for a snowmobile ban, organized more high-profile letters, and filed more lawsuits requesting a return to the EIS and the ban. Separately, the Fund for Animals also sued, requesting an end to trail grooming.[97] The suits would not be decided until December.

On December 11, 2003, Superintendent Lewis took the last step in formalizing her agency's decision, publishing the Final Rule in the *Federal Register*. Public comment on the rule was overwhelmed by snowmobile opponents, with 91 percent—the highest percentage yet—of the 105,000 comments wanting the machines out. Only about 8,000 persons supported continued snowmobile use, even though the BlueRibbon Coalition had solicited comments from its members.[98] That such a lopsided majority opinion was not more fully followed suggests that other forces were influencing the outcome. With President Bush in office and a snowmobile advocate now in the secretary of the interior's office, other very political forces were indeed at play.

Political Influence in NPS Policy-Making

If park managers had thought they were working under political scrutiny before George W. Bush took office, they were soon to get a new perspective. By 2003, Yellowstone policy-making on the winter use issue was being reviewed in all three branches of the U.S. government. Most obvious was congressional attention, this time from the Democratic side of the aisle, and an intense personal interest in Yellowstone snowmobiling by the new secretary of the interior. Before long, the courts were involved too, ruling on the different lawsuits.

Probably as a delayed response to Senator Thomas's efforts, early in 2001 other U.S. House representatives introduced their own bill to ban snowmobiles in all park units nationwide. Like Thomas's efforts, this bill, promoted by Representative Rush Holt (D-NJ), did not go anywhere; nor did two other bills with the same goal that Holt introduced in the next two years (complemented by a fourth bill in the Senate). As before, these congressional attempts at policy-making for the NPS (summarized in Table 4.2) were more show than substance, illustrating congressional attention to, but not control over, NPS policy-making.[99]

Congress also held two more hearings on the snowmobile issue. The first was held in West Yellowstone on January 26, 2002. Following up on the earlier Small Business Committee hearing in Washington, Montana Representative Denny Rehberg went to locals themselves, finding them to be fairly divided on the issue. Two hundred people attended, with Clyde Seely leading the pro-snowmobile contingent and predicting losses of $6 million to $8 million annually. Jackie Mathews led the anti-snowmobile contingent and submitted letters from thirty-three other West Yellowstone residents supporting the proposed ban. Two months later, Senator Joseph Lieberman (D-CT) held another hearing in Washington on the Bush administration's overall environmental record. Hope Sieck of the GYC testified on the snowmobile issue, stating, "National Parks were not created in order to serve as national playgrounds, available for any and all uses. They were created to preserve 'nature as it exists,' affording Americans . . . the unparalleled opportunity to see, hear and experience these national treasures in as natural a state as possible." Her motivation to see Yellowstone's wilderness values protected and to preserve the public's ability to experience them is clear. Like the bills, though, these hearings were more bark than bite.[100]

Beyond publicizing the controversial nature of NPS winter use policy-making, the congressional bills and hearings had little overt influence on the NPS and its final decision.[101] More influential was the intimidation that park managers may have felt from such efforts, particularly those that would have contravened their own plans, such as Thomas's bills. At least one scholar, William R. Lowry, has argued that Congress and political appointees seem to be increasingly micromanaging the parks. Holding more and more hearings on park management since 1970, they have asserted power over NPS management and engendered a climate of deference to politicians among park managers. In the past, Congress more often deferred to NPS professionals. Also contributing to this trend has been the tendency for NPS directors in the same time period to serve terms coinciding with presidential elections; as soon as a new president takes office, the NPS director resigns the post and a new director takes over.[102]

In part, the NPS attracts this attention because it is the favorite agency of federal politicians who wish to make a statement about the environment. Most Americans are familiar with the NPS and at least its most prominent parks, so when a president or other elected politician wants to illustrate a commitment to responsible environmental stewardship, they frequently use the NPS or one of its parks as an example or as the venue for a pronouncement.[103] Such statements are part of life in American politics, but they have the side effect of making the NPS more subject to political influence than its location in the Department of the Interior would otherwise dictate.

Attempts to influence the NPS politically come from many directions: from interest groups, lobbyists, state and local government sources, members of Congress and congressional committees, and so on. But perhaps the strongest form of political influence the NPS must face is the influence exerted by the Department of the Interior and its political appointees, a point made exquisitely clear to park

Table 4.2. Actions Taken by Elected and Appointed Politicians to Influence NPS Winter Use Policy-Making in Yellowstone

Date	Sponsor/Actor	Action	Desired Effect	Resolution
November 1997	Senator Conrad Burns (R-MT)	Yellowstone National Park Community Participation Act (bill in Senate)	Compel NPS to continue allowing snowmobiling	Did not pass
November 1997	Senators Craig Thomas and Mike Enzi (both R-WY)	Letter to Council on Environmental Quality requesting that counties around Yellowstone be designated "cooperating agencies" on EIS	Empower nearby counties to have input into NPS decision-making and retain snowmobile use	NPS invited five counties and three local states to be cooperating agencies; all eight ultimately defended snowmobiling, but had little effect overall
April 1999	Assistant Secretary for Fish and Wildlife and Parks Don Barry	News conference	Ban snowmobiles nationwide from units	Influenced public and NPS movement toward national and Yellowstone ban
July 1999	Congressman Bruce Vento (D-MN) and GYC	Letter to NPS Director Robert Stanton	Encourage NPS to issue stricter regulations on snowmobile use	NPS proposed to ban snowmobiles (though not directly linking the decision to this letter)
March 2000	Congressmen Bruce Vento (D-MN) and Chris Shays (R-CT)	Letter to House colleagues	Gather support for NPS-proposed snowmobile ban	No direct effects

Date	Actor	Action	Goal	Outcome
March–April 2000	Governors Marc Racicot (R-MT) and Jim Geringer (R-WY)	Letters to EPA contesting its position that a snowmobile ban was needed to protect air and water quality	Preserve snowmobiling access	EPA did not alter its position
[April] 2000	Assistant Secretary for Fish and Wildlife and Parks Don Barry	Letter to Yellowstone managers (and possible efforts to approve impairment guidance later that year)	Ban snowmobiles in Yellowstone and Grand Teton national parks	NPS changed preferred alternative to snowcoach-only and declared that snowmobiles impaired park resources
April and May 2000	Senator Craig Thomas (R-WY) and others	Two letters to Bruce Babbitt contesting snowmobile ban	Overthrow proposed snowmobile ban	NPS did not give in, but in response to a later lawsuit did agree to reconsider the ban
May 25, 2000	Senator Craig Thomas (R-WY) and Congressman James Hansen (R-UT)	Two hearings, one each in House and Senate, on snowmobile ban	Investigate reasoning for ban and its effects	No direct effects
May 25, 2000	Congresswoman Barbara Cubin (R-WY)	Winter Recreation Access to National Parks Act of 2000 (bill in House)	Compel NPS to continue allowing snowmobiling	Did not pass
June 2000	Congressman Rick Hill (R-MT)	Rider on Department of the Interior appropriations bill	Prohibit NPS from spending funds to implement snowmobile ban	Did not pass
July 2000	Senator Craig Thomas (R-WY)	Rider on Department of the Interior appropriations bill	Prohibit NPS from spending funds to implement snowmobile ban	Blocked by Senator Harry Reid (D-NV)

Table 4.2. (Continued)

Date	Sponsor/Actor	Action	Desired Effect	Resolution
July 13, 2000	Congressman Donald A. Manzullo (R-IL)	Congressional hearing in Washington, D.C.: *Impact of Banning Snowmobiles inside National Parks on Small Business*	Highlight impacts of snowmobile ban on small businesses and stall the ban	NPS did not alter its plan, but in response to a later lawsuit agreed to reconsider the ban with the SEIS
October 2000	Senators Craig Thomas (R-WY) and Ted Stevens (R-AK)	Rider on Department of the Interior appropriations bill	Compel NPS to continue allowing snowmobile use in Yellowstone and other parks that had previously allowed it	Withdrawn initially, but passed in late 2000; delayed snowmobile bans till July 31, 2001, but Yellowstone ban not affected
December 2000	Secretary of the Interior Bruce Babbitt	Encourage Washington, D.C., personnel to publish Final Rule quickly	Finalize snowmobile ban before Bush took office	Ban was finalized, but shortly thereafter delayed and overturned
February 2001	Senator Craig Thomas (R-WY)	National Park Service Winter Access Act (bill in Senate)	Compel NPS to continue allowing snowmobile use in Yellowstone and other parks that had previously allowed it	Not brought to a vote because ISMA lawsuit made it moot
Summer 2001	Congressman Rush Holt (D-NJ)	National Park Snowmobile Restrictions Act of 2001 (bill in House)	Compel NPS to ban snowmobiles nationwide	Not brought to a vote
May 15, 2001	Senator Harry Reid (D-NV) and 10 other senators	Letter to President George W. Bush protesting impending lawsuit settlement	Contest lawsuit settlement and institute proposed snowmobile ban	No effect/ignored

September 26, 2001	Congressman Rush Holt (D-NJ) and 101 other representatives	Letter to President George W. Bush expressing concern about lawsuit settlement	Return to proposed snowmobile ban	No effect/ignored
January 26, 2002	Congressman Donald Manzullo (R-IL) and Denny Rehberg (R-MT)	Congressional hearing in West Yellowstone: *Protecting Small Business and National Parks: The Goals Are Not Mutually Exclusive*	Highlight impacts of snowmobile ban on businesses in West Yellowstone and overthrow the proposed ban	No effect/may have increased support for a return to snowmobiling
March 13, 2002	Senator Joseph Lieberman (D-CT)	Congressional hearing in Washington, D.C.: *Hearing regarding Public Health and Natural Resources: A Review of the Implementation of Our Environmental Laws*	Highlight abuses in the Bush administration's approach to environmental laws and their enforcement	No effect
May 29, 2002	EPA Administrator Christie Todd Whitman and Secretary of the Interior Gale Norton	Revised letter to NPS about softening EPA's interpretation of snowmobiling alternatives in SEIS	Promote adoption of an alternative allowing continued snowmobiling	No discernible effect, but NPS did adopt an alternative allowing snowmobiling to continue
June 2002	Congressman Rush Holt (D-NJ) and 121 cosponsors in U.S. House, and Senator Harry Reid (D-NV) and 5 cosponsors in U.S. Senate	Yellowstone Protection Act, in both houses	Compel a snowmobile ban in Yellowstone	Not brought to a vote

Table 4.2. (Continued)

Date	Sponsor/Actor	Action	Desired Effect	Resolution
June 2004	Congressman Rush Holt (D-NJ)	Interior Appropriations Amendment	Compel a snowmobile ban in Yellowstone	Defeated by Congressmen Denny Rehberg (R-MT), Collin Peterson (D-MN), and James Oberstar (D-MN) and Congresswoman Barbara Cubin (R-WY)
Fall 2004 (see Chapter 5)	Deputy Secretary of the Interior Steve Griles	Park authorities seek permission to reduce snowmobile numbers by 10 percent	Preserve park soundscapes better	Griles denied permission
February 2005 (see Chapter 5)	Secretary of the Interior Gale Norton	Personal visit to Yellowstone	Promote snowmobiling	No direct effect, but Norton indicated her strong interest in continued snowmobile access
November 2007 (see Chapter 5)	Various officials in Washington	Review of NPS's Record of Decision (ROD) on 2007 EIS	Compel park managers to increase snowmobile limits and leave Sylvan Pass open	NPS revised ROD to allow snowmobile numbers to increase if adaptive management thresholds were met and to allow Sylvan Pass to remain open, under certain restrictions

Sources: Burn's bill; Scott McMillion, "Burns Has Plan for Park," *Bozeman Daily Chronicle*, Nov. 8, 1997, and Conrad Burns, "Locals Need Say in Park Winter Policy," op-ed piece, *Bozeman Daily Chronicle*, Dec. 9, 1997. Cooperating agency designation: Craig Thomas to Kathleen A. McGinty, Nov. 13, 1997, and McGinty to

Thomas, Environmental Impact Statement (EIS) Collection, Management Assistant's Office Files, National Park Service, Mammoth Hot Springs, Yellowstone National Park, Wyoming (hereafter MAOF); Don Barry to Mike Enzi, file "Letter from Sens. Enzi, Craig, Burns, Thomas, Cubin, Hill, & Simpson to Sec. Babbitt," EIS Collection, MAOF; 40 CFR (Code of Federal Regulations), Sec. 1501.6; John E. Cook to Wyoming Governor Jim Geringer, Dec. 1, 1997, and Idaho Governor Phil Batt, Geringer, and Montana Governor Marc Racicot to Cook, Feb. 10, 1998, EIS Collection, MAOF. Barry's news conference: U.S. Department of the Interior, "National Park Service Puts the Brakes on Escalating Snowmobile Use in the National Park System," press release, April 27, 2000, and Barry to Director, NPS, April 27, 2000, both in file "Materials from Linda Canzanelli," EIS Collection, MAOF; "Remarks by Donald J. Barry, . . . Snowmobile Press Conference, April 27, 2000," EIS Collection, MAOF. Vento letter: Bruce Vento et al. to Robert Stanton, July 30, 1999, file "Letter from 38 Members of Congress to Director Stanton," EIS Collection, MAOF. Vento/Shays letter: the two to colleague, March 8, 2000, loose within Greater Yellowstone Coalition (GYC) files. Racicot-Geringer letters: Geringer to Yellowtail, April 26, 2000, and Acting Regional Administrator William P. Yellowtail, March 7, 2000, Yellowtail to Geringer, March 29, 2000, Geringer to Yellowtail, March 29, 2000, Racicot to Yellowtail, April 26, 2000, and Acting Regional Administrator Rebecca W. Hanmer to Racicot, June 5, 2000, all in EIS Collection, MAOF. Barry's letter: Barry to NPS Director, [April 2000], file "Materials from Linda Canzanelli," EIS Collection, MAOF. Thomas's two letters: Thomas et al. to Bruce Babbitt, May 12, 2000, file "Winter Use '99, '00," GYC, and Thomas et al. to Babbitt, April 11, 2000, file "Snowmobiles/Winter Use," Box A-366, National Archives, Yellowstone National Park, Gardiner, Montana (YNPA). Two May 25, 2000, hearings: Senate Committee on Energy and Natural Resources, Snowmobile Activities in the National Park System, May 25, 2000, 6, 10, 31, 36, 42–48; House Subcommittee on National Parks and Public Lands, Committee on Resources, Oversight Hearing on Snowmobile Recreation in National Parks, Particularly Yellowstone National Park, 106th Cong., 2nd sess., May 25, 2000 (found at http://resourcescommittee.house.gov/parks/. Cubin's bill: H.R. 4560, 106th Cong., 2nd sess., Congressional Record, 146, no. 67, daily ed. (May 25, 2000): H3867. Hill's rider: Scott McMillion, "Hill Hopes to Stall Ban until after Election," Bozeman Daily Chronicle, June 15, 2000, and GYC, "Stop Amendment 39 to the Interior Appropriations Bill Sponsored by Mr. Hill of Montana," undated, file "Rep. Hill/Econ/Correspondence," GYC. Thomas's rider: Congressional Record, 106th Cong., 2nd sess., daily ed. (July 17, 2000), 146, pt. 92: S7014–7024. Manzullo's hearing: House Subcommittee on Tax, Finance, and Exports of the Committee on Small Business, Impact of Banning Snowmobiles inside National Parks on Small Business, 106th Cong., 2nd sess., July 13, 2000. Thomas/Stevens rider: "Thomas Joins Strategy to Thwart Snowmobile Ban," Bozeman Daily Chronicle, Aug. 21, 2000, and "Congress May Not Consider Stopping Snowmobile Ban," Bozeman Daily Chronicle, Oct. 29, 2000. Babbitt's involvement: John Sacklin, personal interview with author, Feb. 13, 2003. Thomas's bill: National Park Service Winter Access Act, 107th Cong., 1st sess., S. 365, Congressional Record, 147, no. 15, daily ed. (Feb. 15, 2001): S1503–1505. Holt's bill: National Park Snowmobile Restrictions Act of 2001, 107th Cong., 1st sess., H.R. 1465. Reid's letter: Harry Reid et al. to Mr. President, May 15, 2001, file "WU Senate Letter," GYC. Holt's letter with 101 others: Rush Holt et al. to Mr. President, Sept. 26, 2001, file "WU," GYC. Manzullo and Rehberg's West Yellowstone hearing: House Committee on Small Business, Protecting Small Business and National Parks: The Goals Are Not Mutually Exclusive, 107th Cong., 2nd sess., Jan. 26, 2002. Lieberman's hearing: Senate Committee on Governmental Affairs, Hearing regarding Public Health and Natural Resources: A Review of the Implementation of Our Environmental Laws, Part II, 107th Cong., 2nd sess., March 13, 2002, http://hsgac.senate.gov/031302witness.htm, accessed Oct. 20, 2008. EPA's revised letter: Robert Roberts to Steve Iobst, May 29, 2002, file "EPA DSEIS Comments," GYC, and "EPA Softens Stance on Park Snowmobiling," Bozeman Daily Chronicle, June 4, 2002. Holt's and Reid's Yellowstone Protection Act: Yellowstone Protection Act (same title for both bills), H.R. 5044 and S. 6259, 107th Cong, 2nd sess. Holt's June 2004 amendment: Ted Monoson, "House Kills Proposal to Ban Sleds in Parks," Billings Gazette, June 18, 2004. Griles's action: John Sacklin to Kevin Schneider, e-mail, Sept. 21, 2004, file "Briefing Phone Call w/Region on Final FONSI," "Talking Points for Deputy Secretary Griles," circa Oct. 14, 2004, file of same name; and Schneider to Chris Turk et al., e-mail, Oct. 22, 2004, file "Final FONSI for Review," all in EA Collection, MAOF. Norton's Yellowstone visit: "Secretary's Day at the Park," Bozeman Daily Chronicle, Feb. 16, 2005; Felicity Barringer, "A 3-Day Yellowstone Tour in Support of Snowmobiles," New York Times, Feb. 17, 2005; and Becky Bohrer, "Norton Checks Yellowstone Snowmobile Plan," LA Times, Feb. 15, 2005. Review of 2007 ROD/FEIS: Jim Drinkard, "White House Reverses Experts on Yellowstone Policy," San Jose [CA] Mercury News, July 24, 2008 (quotes), and "White House Over-

managers after Gale Norton took the secretary's office in spring 2001. Previously, she had worked under James Watt (Ronald Reagan's interior secretary) at the Mountain States Legal Foundation in Colorado, a conservative legal group that defended private property rights in the West. Norton shared many of Watt's beliefs and sympathized with snowmobile proponents wanting to overturn the ban. She was friends with Christine Jourdain, president of the American Council of Snowmobile Associations, and shared her viewpoint on snowmobiling. Not long after Norton took office, she received letters from many who recognized that she would probably approach the issue differently than Don Barry had. Clyde Seely, for example, thanked her "for your department's influence as the 'settlement agreement' was reached through the recent litigation." The Small Business Administration's Advocacy Office suggested to her in April that a compromise involving the cleaner four-cycle snowmobiles would protect nearby small businesses from economic harm better than a complete ban would (a solution also suggested by Montana Governor Marc Racicot). These letter writers would see their efforts pay off, although not immediately.[104]

Two indications that Norton would be sympathetic to snowmobiler concerns came shortly after she took office. As part of the NPS's plan to convert all park traffic to snowcoaches, the agency had set aside funding to develop a new snowcoach, one that would address persistent criticisms of the vehicles. It would be faster, more reliable, and more comfortable, and hopefully more feasible for widespread use in Yellowstone. After Norton's appointment, though, Superintendent Finley found that account in his budget zeroed out. Second, Finley soon found that neither he nor the other defendants in the ISMA lawsuit had been consulted by the Department of Justice in its decision to settle the suit out of court (with the decision to write the Supplemental EIS). This was the first time during his Yellowstone tenure that Finley was not consulted on a legal case involving Yellowstone. Justice broke no laws in failing to consult with the defendants, but such actions were certainly questionable, especially to Finley. More importantly, they were the first indication that park managers were operating in a new political climate, one that would probably retain some form of snowmobile use in the park.[105]

Norton's opinion on winter use—and her influence—were clarified in 2002. In June, after analyzing the comments on their Draft Supplemental EIS, NPS personnel from across the country met in Denver, Colorado, to make a decision on Yellowstone's future winter use. The meeting had differing internal and external objectives, indicating it had an unstated purpose: to come up with a way to sell continued snowmobile use to a skeptical public. Externally (that is, publicly), park personnel were deciding "whether to affirm the previous decision or to make a new one," but internally (that is, within the walls of the meeting room), they were meeting "to determine under what terms and conditions snowmobile use will continue." It was now clear that Interior Secretary Gale Norton was, according to some at the meeting, "personally interested in this issue," did not support the snowmobile ban, and wanted "to be able to come away saying some snowmobiles are allowed." Park managers knew that a 180-degree reversal of a just-made decision was subject to stringent standards of justification and that it would be difficult to get around the impairment finding from the previous decision. But they made that change anyway, feeling distinct pressure from above to allow snowmobile use to continue and fearing political retribution if they stuck to the snowmobile ban.[106]

Secretary Norton's interest in, and influence upon, this policy-making process was evident at another point that spring. In April, EPA Assistant Regional Administrator Max Dodson filed his agency's comments on the Draft Supplemental EIS, indicating (as his agency had before) that a full snowmobile ban would "provide the best available protection to human health, wildlife, air quality, water quality, soundscapes, visitor experiences, and visibility while maintaining motorized and non-motorized winter access to these Parks." He objected to the alternatives that would allow continued snowmobile use and designated the snowmobile ban as the environmentally preferred alternative, as it was in the first EIS. Dodson, though, had failed to run his letter past his boss, EPA Administrator Christine Todd Whitman. At her monthly lunch with Gale Norton in Washington in May, the two found out about Dodson's letter. Norton, who was not Whitman's boss (rather an equal cabinet secretary), bluntly asked Whitman how a letter affirming the Clinton administration snowmobile ban could have been released. Whitman responded by directing her employees to run such high-visibility letters through her office in the future. She also had Dodson send the NPS another letter stating that the EPA was not ordering the NPS to ban snowmobiles (which it could not do anyway) and pointing out the potential for improvements in snowmobile emissions in the near future.[107]

Norton's influence on the process and ultimate decision seems clear. Evidently, she never issued a direct order to NPS staff to retain snowmobile use; indeed, a Freedom of Information Act request that I filed with Norton's office turned up no such written command.[108] More than likely, her influence was less direct. By visibly indicating her interest in continued snowmobile use but never issuing an order to retain it, she made clear her desire to park managers. Picking up on the cues (sometimes subtle, sometimes overt), and fearing that to ignore them would result in undesirable consequences (such as replacement of the park superintendent or regional director with a more complicit person), the managers understood what was to be done and reversed their snowmobile ban.

Secretary Norton was hardly the only political appointee in the Department of the Interior to have had an influence on NPS policy-making, as Don Barry's actions just a few years earlier illustrate. Barry's memo to park managers, along with his highly visible public hearing announcing the nationwide NPS snowmobile ban, had made his intentions as clear to park managers as Norton's actions did. Under both the Clinton and Bush administrations, park managers chose the alternative they knew the secretary or deputy secretary wanted—the snowmobile ban under Barry (and Bruce Babbitt), and continued snowmobile use under Norton.[109] The NPS's position as an agency within the Department of the Interior constrains its ability to differ from the secretary and predisposes it to follow his or her opinion. The direction that Barry had set was more or less welcomed by park managers; the direction that Norton set was not. In both cases, however, the secretary exercised control over the agency's policy-making, turning the agency and its decisions into a venue for whatever point the secretary wished to make. The secretaries do listen to park managers, so their voices are heard (to whatever degree the secretary chooses). But in both of these cases involving Yellowstone, the secretaries influenced, or perhaps made, the ultimate decisions. As long as the agency remains under the secretary's control, it can do little but go along with the secretary's wishes, regardless of whether his or her intentions are supportive of the agency's preservation mission.[110]

Secretaries of the interior are not above the law, however, and Norton's and Barry's actions raise the question of whether they went beyond their authority. Secretaries certainly can direct park managers to reexamine a previous decision, but they cannot violate the National Environmental Policy Act, which directs agency decision-makers to "look before they leap." Through their environmental analyses, agency managers must examine the impacts of a variety of actions *before* making a decision, rather than making a choice and then jumping through the NEPA steps just to satisfy formalities. They do not have to choose the environmentally preferred alternative, but they must do their homework before making a decision and be ready to explain their choice, whatever that may be. Norton's actions seemed to compel park managers to make their choice before doing their homework, according to many, including former superintendent Mike Finley. To him, her early actions on this issue (zeroing out the snowcoach research account and settling the ISMA lawsuit without consulting him) were a sign of her intent and confirmation that the new EIS would be "pre-decided." Whether Barry's actions had a similar effect is less clear, because he sent his memo to the NPS director well after the Draft EIS was complete. Also, park managers ended up choosing the environmentally preferred alternative (the snowcoach-only alternative in the first EIS) when he was in office. Barry's directives, then, seem more legally defensible than those of his successor—a finding that a federal judge would soon reach.[111]

A Crisis with the Courts

Once the NPS published the Final Rule retaining snowmobile use (on December 11, 2003), with six days remaining until the winter season was to start, the GYC and the Fund for Animals pressed Judge Emmet Sullivan for a decision on the lawsuits they had filed. A Reagan appointee, he was the same judge in the Washington, D.C., court who had approved the first lawsuit settlement back in 1997, resulting in the first EIS.[112] As with the agency's efforts to finalize the snowmobile ban before George W. Bush took office, the timing had come down to a matter of days, perhaps even hours. This time, though, a judge was actually ruling on snowmobile use in Yellowstone (thereby bringing review of NPS snowmobile policy-making into the third branch of government), with major potential and immediate consequences for park management. Those six days were suspenseful: His decision could have ranged from one upholding snowmobile use to one closing the parks to all winter visitor use.

With only thirteen hours remaining before the start of the season, Sullivan ruled against the Bush administration, remanding the decision to allow continued snowmobile use back to the NPS. That left the 2001 Clinton administration rule banning snowmobiles in effect. For park managers, this meant that, overnight, they would need to roughly halve the allowable daily number of snowmobiles for the ensuing winter and ban them completely in one year (actual snowmobile numbers were cut from 950 per day in Yellowstone to 493 for that winter).[113]

In his forty-nine-page decision, Sullivan cited multiple NPS violations of the Administrative Procedure Act (APA) and National Environmental Policy Act (NEPA). The APA and its case history direct federal agencies to provide a higher level of explanation when they reverse previous decisions than is needed when making a decision initially. To Sullivan, the agency's "180 degree reversal . . . conspicuously timed with the change in administrations," opened it to examination on this front, as park managers had earlier predicted. Looking for guidance in assessing the merits of the reversal, Sullivan turned to the NPS's *2001 Management Policies*, the booklet detailing the agency's policies. The booklet stated that, "when there is a conflict between conserving resources and values and providing for enjoyment of them, conservation is to be predominant"; in short, it "trumps all other considerations." He then noted the agency's own impairment finding from 2000 (that snowmobile usage impaired the park's resources in several ways). But by 2003, in his courtroom, the agency had changed its mind on snowmobile impairment, repeatedly claiming that the Supplemental EIS's provisions for use of the new cleaner and quieter snowmobiles and mandatory guiding would solve the impairment problem. Sullivan, though, noted that the agency had explicitly examined and rejected such provisions in the first EIS because they would not eliminate impairment. Sullivan's APA ruling, then, contradicted the NPS's decision:

> In light of its clear conservation mandate, and the previous conclusion that snowmobile use amounted to unlawful impairment, the Agency is under an obligation to explain this 180 degree reversal. NPS has not met this obligation. NPS's explanation that technological improvements and mitigation measures justify this change has . . . proven weak at best. . . . An agency decision codifying such an unreasoned change is "quintessentially arbitrary and capricious," and thus cannot stand.[114]

Regarding NEPA, the Fund for Animals argued that the NPS had violated the law's requirement to examine a full range of alternatives, especially an alternative ending road grooming, as the group had requested back in 1997. Sullivan agreed, stating that the agency's failure to consider such an alternative "defies logic." He felt that a closure would provide a good opportunity to study whether groomed roads affected bison numbers and distribution, a topic that the Fund had emphasized. The NPS had claimed that it had reviewed the bison literature, but had found no obvious consensus on that issue, and that it had considered closing a trail but then dismissed the idea. Sullivan felt the bison issue was ripe for more study and that the agency's explanation of why the trail closure was not fully considered was "wholly devoid of analysis" and "flatly inadequate."[115]

Sullivan's decision was reported nationwide, with the sympathetic press and conservationists obviously celebrating. National park scholar Alfred Runte (author of *National Parks: The American Experience*) summarized conservationist opinion of the ruling when he said, "Today's decision confirms what Yellowstone was meant to be. This struggle was not against Americans who like their snowmobiles, but rather against the notion that anything goes in the national parks. The courts have reminded us that we have a different, higher standard for our national parks. Our history proves that no one loses when beauty wins."[116]

The local press printed editorials that were less celebratory, but perhaps more insightful. Some deplored the debate's political nature, with the *Bozeman Daily Chronicle* longing for the days when parks were "run by professionals chosen for their expertise, not their political history." The *Livingston Enterprise* predicted, perhaps accurately, that Congress would ultimately have to decide the issue. And, the *Billings Gazette* argued that the political tug-of-war between politicians and bureaucrats must end—and that conservation must prevail, a fairly strong preservationist stance for a local paper more intimately familiar with the issue and its stakeholders. The *Gazette* and others especially deplored the ruling's timing, which was bound to hurt local communities preparing for the winter season.[117]

Indeed, this was a second crisis, as much for the NPS as for the surrounding communities dependent on Yellowstone tourism. The immediate reaction among the local snowmobile community was "ghastly silence," according to Clyde Seely. Because many snowmobile rental owners had already purchased four-cycle snowmobiles for the upcoming winter, believing (as had Yellowstone's managers) that the decision to continue snowmobiling would be implemented, the timing really did hurt, forcing some nearby businesses to close for the winter.[118]

Sullivan's decision was also a threat to snowmobiler freedoms. This threat (along with the fear of economic harm) motivated snowmobile advocates to appeal the decision. Quickly, the state of Wyoming, ISMA, and the BlueRibbon Coalition did appeal, along with reopening their 2000 lawsuit contesting the snowmobile ban. In both situations, they requested that the court either implement the 2003 pro-snowmobile decision (an unlikely outcome, since it would conflict with Sullivan's decision) or that it overturn the 2000 EIS and snowmobile ban (see Table 5.1 for a listing of the various legal actions on this issue from 1997 to 2008). While the courts considered this request, the groups requested a temporary restraining order or preliminary injunction putting Sullivan's ruling on hold.[119]

They had a sympathetic judge in Cheyenne, Wyoming: Clarence Brimmer, who agreed to reopen the case. On February 10, 2004, he issued a preliminary injunction restraining the NPS from continuing to implement the 2000 snowmobile ban. Because Sullivan's last-minute order halving snowmobile numbers for that winter was harming local residents (even threatening some with bankruptcy), Brimmer felt that suspending the 2000 EIS from implementation was justified until he could determine whether, like its successor, it was illegal. So, with both EISs now in limbo, Brimmer ordered park managers to issue temporary rules for the remainder of the winter season that were "fair and equitable" to all parties concerned.[120] (Brimmer was concerned primarily with the 2000 EIS decision banning snowmobiles, where Judge Sullivan's ruling affected only the 2003 Supplemental EIS decision allowing continued snowmobile use. Because the two courts were ruling on different NPS decisions, their rulings did not technically contradict each other.)

Brimmer's ruling was only a preliminary injunction, not a final ruling. In his February brief, however, he suggested that the snowmobile plaintiffs had a good chance of showing that the NPS, in producing its first EIS, had violated the same two laws (NEPA and APA) that Judge Sullivan had just found the agency had violated with the second EIS. Brimmer pointed to four specific potential NEPA violations, including a failure to fully analyze the snowcoach-only option, a failure to adequately involve surrounding government agencies in the decision-making, a failure to make a decision that was not prejudged, and a failure to fully involve the public. In the agency's proposed snowmobile ban, a 180-degree reversal of nearly forty years of snowmobile access, Brimmer also saw a possible APA violation. Based essentially on this reasoning—so parallel to Sullivan's—Brimmer made his injunction permanent in October, remanding the first EIS to the NPS. The snowmobile ban was now invalidated, just like the supplemental plan to allow continued snowmobile use.[121]

The ruling by Judge Brimmer, similar to Sullivan's but from a different position, made the issue's recent history (especially the legal portion) seem like a farce to some, with conflicting decisions from judges in two different courts both asserting violations of the same laws (see Figure 4.1). Some people (especially park managers) wondered if they would ever be able to craft a durable and effective solution, given the legal difficulties, the strident emotions and values, and the political tampering in the issue. Others decried the seemingly activist leanings of both judges.

The two court cases prompt the question of why the state of Wyoming seemed so upset over this issue, pursuing legal action in two different courts. By contrast, the state of Montana stood to lose much more economically, but it was much less aggressive in suing the NPS. Certainly, Wyoming stood to lose some tax revenue from the loss of snowmobile rentals entering Yellowstone's south or east gates, but these would not have been significant to the state or local counties, especially as compared to snowmobile-related income in Montana's West Yellowstone. Further, sales tax revenues (from snowmobile rentals) at Yellowstone's South Entrance paled in comparison to those from skiers at the Jackson Hole ski resort in the same county.

The state and Judge Brimmer hinted at the underlying reasons in their legal arguments and in a letter from Brimmer to Superintendent Suzanne Lewis. First, in its brief, the state complained about infringements upon its sovereignty: The snowmobile ban would make it difficult to manage its state trails program and its fish populations in Jackson Lake. Though these concerns are really minor worries (the state has no jurisdiction over Yellowstone or Grand Teton trails, and Grand Teton managers had guaranteed the necessary access to Jackson Lake), the state felt its rights were threatened. Antifederalism is prevalent in Wyoming, and any step the federal agencies take that might threaten that autonomy is closely examined.[122]

Judge Brimmer himself suggested the same reason for Wyoming's persistence in a surprising letter he wrote to Superintendent Lewis shortly after issuing his decision. Although such direct communication between a judge and defendants in his own court strains the impartiality that judges should demonstrate, Brimmer wrote Lewis advocating for a solution acceptable to Wyomingites. He had received a number of letters from state residents suffering economic impacts from

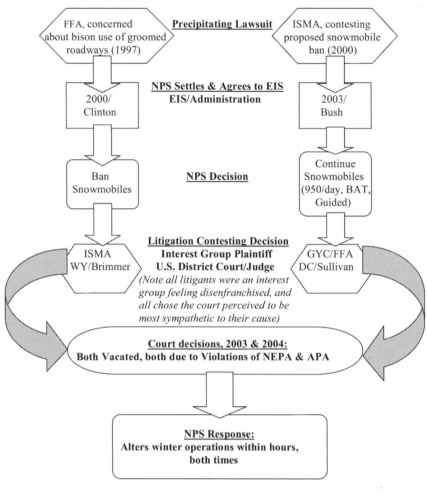

Figure 4.1. Flow chart of two EISs and judicial decisions, illustrating the parallel histories of two EISs completed in a political world. Left column illustrates first EIS; right column illustrates second EIS. Chart and time proceed from top to bottom.

The flow chart contains the following text elements:

FFA, concerned about bison use of groomed roadways (1997)

Precipitating Lawsuit

ISMA, contesting proposed snowmobile ban (2000)

2000/ Clinton

NPS Settles & Agrees to EIS
EIS/Administration

2003/ Bush

Ban Snowmobiles

NPS Decision

Continue Snowmobiles (950/day, BAT, Guided)

ISMA WY/Brimmer

Litigation Contesting Decision
Interest Group Plaintiff
U.S. District Court/Judge
(Note all litigants were an interest group feeling disenfranchised, and all chose the court perceived to be most sympathetic to their cause)

GYC/FFA DC/Sullivan

Court decisions, 2003 & 2004:
Both Vacated, both due to Violations of NEPA & APA

NPS Response:
Alters winter operations within hours,
both times

APA = Administrative Procedure Act
BAT = Best Available Technology
EIS = Environmental Impact Statement
FFA = Fund for Animals

GYC = Greater Yellowstone Coalition
ISMA = International Snowmobile Manufacturer's Association
NEPA = National Environmental Policy Act
SEIS = Supplemental EIS

Sullivan's decision and complaining about the decision to require guides for most visitors. In his letter, Brimmer focused on the guiding requirement:

> Many of these objectors feel that the requirement of a guide ought to be optional and I think that the principal [sic] thought there is that Western people know how to run their machines and don't need a guide to help them start or stop them or set them right in deep snow and that they can be trusted to stay on the marked trails. . . . I think it would be for those reasons that if I were to impose a rule I would not require guides in every instance since that just costs people another $40.00.

Brimmer obviously felt that westerners (especially Wyomingites) were inherently more capable of snowmobile touring on their own than the typical Yellowstone tourist. They did not need Big Brother to watch them as they explored Yellowstone; they should be free to explore independently. The moral for Yellowstone managers was that stakeholders feeling their values threatened—including two federal judges—would go to great lengths to defend them.[123]

Even without his letter, Brimmer's decision became the subject of a critique by legal scholar Jeffrey Bissegger. Examining Yellowstone's winter use legal history, Bissegger found that Brimmer was breaking new ground in ordering park managers to issue rules that were "fair and equitable" to all parties. In making his order, Brimmer seemed to step into the legislative world, ordering park managers to make a decision that treated the snowmobile industry and park preservation "as if they were coequal interests with equivalent claims on NPS's policymaking priorities." Such equal treatment contradicted the NPS Organic Act, which states that the NPS must preserve its natural, historical, and cultural resources. It never mentions economic interests as something the NPS should consider in crafting its policies. Bissegger called this "judicial activism" and concluded that "the preservation of our national parks will likely suffer as a result" of it. Brimmer's decision may have accomplished something that some political interests had been trying to accomplish in Yellowstone for some time: making those economic interests "coequal" with national park preservation.[124]

Yellowstone managers did not have the luxury of time to ponder such thoughts, however, because they had yet another crisis on their hands, having to alter winter rules before dawn the next day (as they had just done following Sullivan's ruling). Many staff members stayed late into the night, attempting to devise rules that would presumably satisfy Judge Brimmer. They ended up increasing the daily snowmobile limit for Yellowstone to 780 (from 493) and to 140 for the Tetons (from 50). The additional snowmobiles would all have to be Best Available Technology (BAT), and all 780 snowmobiles for Yellowstone would have to be guided (Brimmer's comments notwithstanding). The numbers were a compromise between the two EISs, and at a little more than half the difference between them, unlikely to draw opposition from the snowmobile interests or Brimmer.[125]

On the ground in Yellowstone, the new numbers mattered little. The reversals in winter policy, both by the NPS and the courts, along with public confusion as to whether the park would even be open, meant that fewer people were willing to risk a Yellowstone visit. Potential visitors no doubt worried that a last-minute policy change might affect their plans. Hotel and snowmobile reservations were down even before Sullivan's decision, and visitation over the Christmas holidays (ordinarily the busiest time of the winter season) did not reach the approved limit (493 per day) even once. The pending lawsuits only continued the uncertainty, making increased visitation the next winter no more likely. Overall, an average of only 260 snowmobiles per day entered Yellowstone that winter, just over a third of the historical average.[126]

That winter ended quietly, partly because visitation dropped so much and partly because there were no other EISs to strike down. All parties to the issue had time to breathe and reflect on the winter's events. NPS employees and observers contemplated what had gone wrong, where they had succeeded, their relationship with elected and appointed officials, and their relationships with interest groups. Snowmobilers and conservationists reconsidered their positions and rethought their strategies. While everyone looked to the future for redress of grievances, a transformation began to take place in Yellowstone. Before we explore that transformation, some reflections on the seven years of tumult are in order.

Policy Reversals, Values, and Diminishing NPS Autonomy

In permitting snowmobiling to occur for nearly forty years, Yellowstone's managers inadvertently allowed several core American values to become entrenched. Throughout the 1990s and 2000s (as of this writing in mid-2008), stakeholders more and more drew upon those powerful value connections in articulating their perspectives. With their machines and snowmobiling serving as expressions of freedom and rugged individualism, snowmobile advocates viewed attempts to curtail their activity as un-American. Likewise, the owners of snowmobile rentals and other businesses in West Yellowstone viewed those same attempts as anti-family (and perhaps even as anti-Christian, given the Protestant work ethic that commonly motivates small business owners in America). Meanwhile, conservationists and others saw continued snowmobiling as a threat to Yellowstone's sanctity and that of its emblematic bison. Values equate to identities, and NPS attempts to ban snowmobiles threatened West Yellowstone's identity as a self-made town, while continued snowmobiling threatened the park's identity as a cherished natural icon. The strength of those values and the conflict between them would fuel this controversy well beyond 2004; indeed, it has no end in sight.

Helping to fuel the controversy have been science and the conflict between its limitations and society's belief in it. The contradictory findings regarding snowmobiling's impacts on wildlife and the difficulties associated with explaining scientific concepts to general audiences were challenge enough. Making science even less useful for park managers were persistent funding limitations that delayed necessary research until well after it was needed (indeed, some research is still lacking). In the absence of solid research, and given persistent contradictions, interest groups used evolving scientific findings to support their underlying and often conflicting perspectives. In other words, perception of truth is reality, no matter what the science may say.

Especially pervasive during this seven-year period have been efforts to tamper with and influence park policy-making by both elected and appointed politicians. As Table 4.2 suggests, elected politicians have gone to great lengths to influence NPS policies and decision-making. While actions by some appointed officials, such as Gale Norton or Bruce Babbitt, are almost absent from the listing (because they mainly occurred behind closed doors or in verbal, nonrecorded media), their influence was pervasive and stronger than that of elected officials, bordering at times on overt control.

Superintendent Mike Finley understood the political strength of the pro-snowmobiling camp, but he took a strong stand and tried to eliminate snowmobile use from Yellowstone. He knew he would not succeed in that endeavor, but he felt that he had to adopt an extreme position to get industry and other actors in the issue to concede that there were indeed problems in the park in the 1990s.[127] The snowmobile industry (whether it was powerful stakeholders in West Yellowstone or in ISMA) had a lock upon Yellowstone and was reluctant to take the major steps necessary to make positive change possible. In taking his strong but ultimately unsuccessful stand, Finley did succeed in moving the center of debate from whether there were indeed problems to what (perhaps drastic) actions were necessary to solve them. Finley may deserve praise for his action, but the very need for it suggests, again, that certain actors—namely, industry and complicit politicians—have had a disproportionate say in determining the look and feel of Yellowstone in winter.

A strong stand comes with another risk, that of creating polarization. Although Finley transformed the debate, he also alienated some who otherwise might have been willing to work toward positive change. Finley might argue that, given the resistance to change by some in this issue, he had little choice but to adopt a strong stance, but the consequences of that action have been polarization and lingering hostility toward the agency.[128] Overall, Finley probably had to do what he did, but it came with some unfortunate consequences.

Forced into that position, Finley and his successors have had to resort to crisis management. They needed, and perhaps engineered, a crisis to make the point to local stakeholders, the snowmobile industry, regional politicians, and their own Washington office that there really was a problem in Yellowstone in the late 1990s. Their success ultimately came at the cost of significant suffering when last-minute legal judgments of those crisis maneuvers caused personal hardship in nearby communities and in Yellowstone. No one, including park managers, likes crisis management, but in this case, the park managers seemingly had little choice.

Such political and industrial influences do not bode well for NPS autonomy, authority, or effectiveness. Over time, the politics of capitulation and compromise in Yellowstone may lead to a diluted level of protection for park resources. By allowing itself to be prone to compromise, the agency has set a pattern that politicians (whether elected or appointed, Republican or Democrat) have come to expect. The politicians have learned that if pushed, the NPS will roll over and accommodate their wishes. Over time, and especially as they encounter strong-willed politicians, that tendency may lead to a weakened agency no longer fully capable of preserving America's natural resources. The agency has tended to compromise too much, weakening itself over time at the expense of natural resource preservation.

Managers defend themselves by claiming that to admit such influence is occurring or to take strong stands against political pressure risks political retribution, such as replacement by more complicit managers, political tampering with NPS budgets, or congressional legislation compelling policy-making without NPS concurrence (all of which have occurred in NPS history, though not often). A manager who takes a strong stand risks being completely left out of the decision-making, especially in win-or-lose administrations like that of George W. Bush. By being willing to compromise, park managers remain at the table and can at least attempt to make decisions more compatible with park preservation. The approach of the NPS in Yellowstone has not only allowed the agency to retain a voice in that park's decision-making, but due to Yellowstone's prominence, has also allowed the agency to retain a presence in the hundreds of other issues the NPS faces across the nation.

Besides weakening the agency, succumbing to political influence may also have unintended effects upon the NPS and other actors in the controversy as well as the general public. For example, the refusal of park managers to admit that such influence is taking place may lead to a loss of public trust in the agency. In another example, if left to its own devices, the NPS would have given local communities three years to adapt to the original snowmobile ban. But political tampering with policy-making meant that residents of most snowmobile-dependent communities placed their hope in a revised policy instead of preparing for the ban to take effect. Eventually, the political tampering backfired when Judge Sullivan reinstated the snowmobile ban and made the NPS appear the villain when its plan was reinstated with only thirteen hours' notice. In this way, persistent political efforts to circumvent NPS policy-making have not only harmed local communities but also weakened public faith in the agency. Its credibility has suffered along with its autonomy, authority, and effectiveness.

Beyond these reflections, Yellowstone managers were haunted by a twist of fate that had great influence on this history: the 2000 presidential election. How different this history would have been if the United States elected its presidents by majority vote, or if Al Gore had won his own state (Tennessee), or if the U.S. Supreme Court had ruled in favor of him, are mere topics of speculation—but ones that will long plague park policy-making observers. Given the rapidity with which the new George W. Bush administration overturned the snowmobile ban, completed in the waning days of the Clinton administration, future managers would be well-advised to complete policy changes long before a presidential election takes place.

With both of its EISs invalidated, Yellowstone managers realized they had no satisfactory rules under which to operate the park for the next winter. Consequently, as spring turned into summer, they had to move quickly to assure Americans that they could visit Yellowstone in December 2004. The outcome of that realization is the subject of the next chapter and was the impetus behind a partial transformation in winter use.

5
A New Era or More of the Same?

Even with the solid, and publicly shared respect and love for Yellowstone and Grand Teton in the winter, the conditions for good faith negotiations are not in place right now.
[Nedra Chandler]/Cadence, Inc., 2005

The Current Plan is Working: [It] effectively addresses a challenging and almost intractable issue using an old concept: compromise!
NPS, 2006 [1]

After working for seven years to reform the situation in Yellowstone, managers finally had a chance in 2004 to bring about substantial changes—changes that actually held, for at least four years. Through their own political acumen and a back-door stroke of luck, they were able to put restrictions on snowmobiling that restored some of the park's quiet, cleaned the air, protected the wildlife, and improved the visitor's experience. Relative to the previous situation, conditions were delightful (and in some ways reminiscent of the 1950s), with a pristine, spectacular landscape complemented by cold, sharp air and natural tranquility.

Park managers enjoyed these successes despite having to contend with many of the same influences as before. Gale Norton and other politicians continued their efforts to affect the outcome while interest groups maintained their watch over the issue, hoping their values would be the final ones to see fruition in the park. Whether these actors were fatigued by the ongoing debate, increasingly comfortable with the recent changes, or mollified by the compromise park managers proposed, the debate's combativeness settled down a little (certainly not completely, though).

The effort to produce those rules brought some new twists to the conflict. West Yellowstone was adapting to the previous changes and stayed relatively quiet, but Cody felt its identity and associated values threatened by a proposed route closure and reacted defensively, elevating the opposition to political levels higher than had been seen in some time. With the issuance of the new rules distracting attention from other related concerns, park managers closed the Continental Divide Snow-mobile Trail in Grand Teton National Park, thereby demonstrating that quietly re-dressing disagreeable policies can sometimes be a more effective way to achieve long-term park protection than trying to make major policy changes. Throughout, it appeared that some stakeholders had been involved in the issue for so long that they had forgotten the bigger picture behind their immediate goals.

As this book goes to press, new lawsuits have been filed, new judicial decisions have been issued, and more rhetoric issued. Debates over the proper look and feel of Yellowstone in winter, the role and meaning of scientific findings and new technologies, and the proper level of political involvement continue. Fatigue there may be, but the institutionalized values and identities evident in this debate promise to keep it alive for some time to come.

An Unprecedented Opportunity

Contemplating the recent judicial decisions, Yellowstone's managers found them-selves in a difficult predicament in early 2004, caught between dueling courts. While that was perplexing enough, more pressing was the upcoming winter: Could they legally even open Yellowstone for tourism, and if so, under what set of rules would they operate? Both of the EISs they had just finished were invalidated (or soon would be), and the Winter Use Plan of the 1990s (their other potential choice for winter rules) was not an option either because it had resulted in im-pairment of park resources.[2] No rules were usable, but managers knew they would have to open the park to snowmobiles (and snowcoaches) somehow. They had precious little time to craft new rules.

As early as January 2004 (before Judge Brimmer even ruled on the Yellowstone case), park managers had begun considering various responses or potential solu-tions to the brewing dilemma. They had debated whether to even defend the ac-tive suits and appeals, instead initiating yet another EIS process and discarding the two they had just finished. Brimmer's preliminary injunction in February made their search for a solution more urgent, as it was now likely that both EISs would be invalidated (his ruling that October confirmed managers' thinking).[3]

Turning to the National Environmental Policy Act, through which government planning must occur if it affects the natural environment, Yellowstone's managers found little help. They had only eight months before they would have to reopen the park to winter visitation, a period of time too short for another EIS and proba-bly too short for even a less comprehensive Environmental Assessment (EA). An EIS usually took at least three years to complete, and an EA usually took at least a year. Furthermore, EAs by law could result only in a decision to proceed to an EIS (putting managers back into an overly time-consuming response) or a "FONSI"—that is, a "Finding of No Significant Impact." As the legal term implies, an EA resulting in a FONSI cannot incur any significant impacts upon the environment. Even if managers did have time for an EA, a FONSI seemed impossible to achieve under the current administration because it still seemed to want high levels of snowmobile use and because even four-stroke and guided snowmobile use could result in continued significant impacts. Due to both time constraints and the political climate, a solution involving only another EIS or EA seemed impossible.[4]

Park managers then considered court or congressional actions. Their recent court experiences strongly suggested that the various litigants would not be able to agree on a path forward, and under the Bush administration, there was little guarantee that any legislation Congress might be able to pass would either be passed in time for the upcoming winter or successful in forging a proper balance between park preservation and visitation. Realizing that their drawing board had less and less writing room, park managers went back to their attorneys, asking them if they had overlooked any options. By now it was May, with the time before another winter season arrived ticking away. Managers knew that no one with an economic stake in the issue would accept a closure of Yellowstone; likewise, no one with an environmental stake in the issue would accept a return to the 1990 Winter Use Plan.[5]

As they considered their predicament, the managers began to realize that they did have a potential solution, one that might not only retain oversnow visitation but also remedy some of the persistent problems with snowmobiling. The solution was actually an Environmental Assessment, which their attorneys helped them realize could be done in as little as six months (the amount they had remaining by this time) by combining two or three of the steps necessary in the EA process, as other federal agencies routinely did. Like the EIS process, the EA process consists of three steps: the EA itself, the FONSI (instead of the EIS's Record of Decision), and the Draft Rule and Final Rule, both published in the *Federal Register* (though the publication is necessary only if there are substantial new rules coming out of the EA). Rather than waiting to complete the EA and FONSI before publishing the Draft Rule, the NPS could publish all three simultaneously, thereby slicing several months off the EA schedule. The attempt to avert another winter use crisis would be tight, but doable.[6]

Still, the EA would have to result in a FONSI, meaning that no significant impacts from snowmobile use would be allowed. And, that June, Judge Sullivan ordered park authorities to finish their rule-making by November to avoid a repeat of the last-minute orders from the previous winter. A few months earlier, these two requirements seemed impossible. Now that time had elapsed, they became a golden opportunity, for park managers had no other recourse but to produce an

EA with a FONSI. That, in turn, meant they had *no choice but to reduce snowmobile impacts and associated numbers*. Snowmobile use would have to be curtailed and restricted in such a way that the "major" impacts of the past would disappear; while some impacts could remain, those would have to be either "negligible, minor, or moderate," in the language of the NPS's NEPA guidelines. The previous winter had seen substantially reduced snowmobile use, with most visitors guided and using cleaner and quieter machines. The corresponding improvement in conditions illustrated that managers could use those restrictions to improve conditions more permanently. In short, the need to produce a FONSI became a tool to reduce snowmobile impacts substantially. The powers in Washington could (and would) push for more snowmobile use, but the NPS finally had the leverage it needed to push back, with some strength.[7]

Rapidly, park planners began the EA process. They released the draft to the public in August 2004, with the preferred alternative proposing to reduce Yellowstone's daily snowmobile limit to 720 machines. All would have to be BAT, and all (not just 80 percent, as proposed in the Supplemental EIS) would have to be led by commercial guides who knew how to pass bison on the roadways without harassing them and who were proficient in the park's natural and cultural history. These three primary restrictions, managers believed, would reduce the noise and air pollution to acceptable levels, along with the wildlife impacts. If adopted, the rules would be in place for only the next three winters, during which time the staff would produce another EIS with long-term rules for winter use, as well as a comprehensive scholarly assessment of the bison road-use issue. The time restriction, the associated EIS, and the bison study, like the need to avoid major impacts, were crucial elements of a FONSI. Permanent rules would have required an EIS and serious attention to the bison issue (both of which would also take more than six months).[8]

Gathering public comment, park managers found that little had changed: An 84 percent majority wanted snowmobiles out completely, and only 669 commenters out of 95,000 supported the preferred alternative. More than 72,000 commenters questioned the Bush administration's influence; many felt the administration seemed to think itself immune from public accountability.[9] Once again, though, park managers continued to permit snowmobiling, for two reasons. First, the issue was still alive in two different courts, and managers hoped that their proposal would walk a middle line between the two courts' previous rulings. Second, the NPS was still under a political microscope; managers knew that the Bush administration still wanted snowmobiles in Yellowstone in significant numbers. The latter understanding was reemphasized that fall when some of the planners traveled to Washington to present their case for reducing the daily snowmobile allotment by about 10 percent. Meeting with Department of the Interior Deputy Secretary Stephen Griles and Assistant Secretary Craig Manson, the planners argued that reducing the daily limit to 650 would better insure that snowmobile impacts remained at the "moderate" level, not crossing into "major." Particularly with soundscape protection, their modeling suggested that 720 machines would still produce a moderate or even major volume of noise, making the FONSI tenuous. They also argued that the lower number would demonstrate responsiveness to the large public-comment majority favoring snowmobile elimination. Though they assured Manson and Griles that 650 machines would still allow room for growth over the previous winter's low use, the two insisted upon the higher number. Their reasoning is unclear, but their position was consistent with that of their boss, Gale Norton.[10]

Despite the soundscape uncertainty, Yellowstone's managers issued the FONSI on November 4 and the Final Rule implementing those new limits (720 BAT, guided machines) six days later.[11] They could now breathe more easily and enjoy their success. For the first time in forty years, snowmobile use in Yellowstone had some real limits that promised to provide at least partial remedies for the trio of winter problems (noise, air pollution, and wildlife impacts). Through the unplanned opportunity presented by the conflicting judicial decisions and through their own sagacity in recognizing that open door, a transformation in winter use was about to begin.

That winter (2004–2005) did indeed see delightful conditions continuing from the previous winter (at least as compared to the earlier situation).[12] For the first time in over twenty years, nature's sounds, smells, sights, and wildlife activity were not overwhelmed by snowmobile impacts. Gone was the air pollution, thanks to the cleaner BAT machines. Gone too were most wildlife harassment and speeding violations, primarily as a result of the commercial guide restriction. Finally, the noise was reduced somewhat, both because BAT machines were a little quieter and because guided groups confined snowmobile noise to more specific times, rather than being spread out all day as before. Helping to produce all of these improvements was continued low snowmobile use; average daily use once again hovered only around 250 machines, far fewer than the 720 limit and the historical average of 795 machines daily. As Figure 5.1 indicates, visitation has not even approached these numbers since, with the single busiest day since 2004 seeing just 557 snowmobiles. The free-for-all was over; now, visitors toured the park in orderly groups, enjoying more pristine conditions than they had experienced in years and learning about Yellowstone from their guides. Given the long-term effort it took to achieve this change, it was a substantial transformation, one that appeared to be durable (such conditions still prevailed as of the writing of this book).[13]

Conditions may have been refreshing on the ground, but they were hardly different in court, as four lawsuits were filed against the EA (see Table 5.1). Both the

Frosted tree, 1990s. While Yellowstone's amazing scenery was visible to all in the 1990s, snowmobile noise and air pollution frequently distracted visitors from them. Such conditions largely disappeared by the mid-2000s, due to lower snowmobile numbers, guided visitation, and mandatory use of Best Available Technology machines (and snowcoaches). Although some noise problems remain, park managers' persistence finally began to produce positive results. Photo by author.

Fund for Animals and the Greater Yellowstone Coalition sued again in Washington, but Judge Sullivan dismissed both suits as either moot or going beyond the scope of the court. In the Wyoming court, a dark-horse group called Save Our Snowplanes sued to regain snowplane access to Jackson Lake in Grand Teton (the NPS had banned the activity there in 2000 because it impaired the lake's soundscape). Judge William F. Downes ruled against the group in June 2007, upholding the NPS's ban on snowplanes on Jackson Lake because of their noise level.[14]

The most interesting action occurred in the remaining lawsuit filed in the Wyoming court, from the Wyoming Lodging and Restaurant Association (WLRA—the group discussed in Chapter 3), which the state of Wyoming joined as intervener. The two argued that the NPS had committed familiar NEPA and Administrative Procedure Act (APA) violations, that the temporary rules were hampering business in the state, and that the guiding restriction hampered the ability of Wyoming residents to tour Yellowstone.[15] The case was assigned to

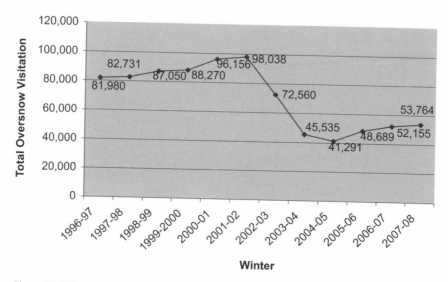

Figure 5.1. Yellowstone Oversnow Visitation, 1996/97–2007/08
Source: NPS, *Winter Use Plans Final Environmental Impact Statement, 2007,* 155–156, and
March 2008 Yellowstone Winter Statistics Report, http://www.nature.nps.gov/stats/park.cfm,
accessed October 20, 2008.

Judge Brimmer, who again demonstrated his distinctive perspective. In a preliminary hearing on the suit, he thanked the WLRA for keeping it in Wyoming (not
Washington's more distant court) and then promised to do his "damndest" to retain jurisdiction over the matter. He felt Judge Sullivan "wouldn't be very fair" if it
were given to him and hoped the Wyoming congressional delegation would be
successful passing legislation retaining jurisdiction of such cases in the West,
where the action occurred (he certainly seemed to ignore the many attempted
congressional and executive branch actions taking place in Washington that
hoped to influence NPS policies; see again Table 4.2, and note that the hoped-for
legislation did not pass). His final decision (rendered in October 2005) actually
went entirely against the WLRA and in favor of the NPS, but he continued to
demonstrate his concern for Wyomingites. He not only retained jurisdiction over
this matter for the future but also reiterated his dislike for the mandatory guide
requirement. He wrote that he could "think of at least half a dozen responsible
Wyoming natives with snowmobiles who observe the rules and . . . therefore need
no guides and would regard the guiding fee as an excessive tax or surcharge." "The
Court," he added, "hopes that the ultimate conclusion reached . . . allows many
visitors to visit the Parks on an unguided basis." Directly ordering park authorities
to eliminate the guide requirement was beyond his authority, but Brimmer made

Table 5.1. Significant Legal Actions on Yellowstone Winter Use Issue, 1997–2005

Date of Action	Litigant and Court	Goal of Action/ Legal Request	Immediate Outcome and Date	Final Outcome(s)
May 1997	Fund for Animals (FFA), Washington, D.C.	Critically examine winter use in Yellowstone National Park (YNP)	National Park Service (NPS) agreed to Environmental Impact Statement (EIS) on winter use in the parks (September 1997)	EIS proposed banning snowmobiles and converting to snowcoaches only (late fall 2000)
December 2000	International Snowmobile Manufacturers Association (ISMA), Wyoming	Overthrow 2000 decision to ban snowmobiles	NPS agreed to Supplemental EIS (SEIS) focusing on new technologies (June 2001). Related action: NPS delayed implementation of snowmobile ban by one year (November 2002)	SEIS proposed allowing up to 950, Best Available Technology (BAT), mostly guided snowmobiles to continue in YNP (2003)
March 2003	FFA and Greater Yellowstone Coalition (GYC) (in separate actions), Washington, D.C.	Overthrow Supplemental Environmental Impact Statement (SEIS) decision to retain snowmobile use; return to snowmobile ban	After consolidating the two cases, the Washington, D.C., District Court (Judge Emmet Sullivan) ruled in favor of plaintiffs, remanding SEIS to NPS for National Environmental Policy Act (NEPA) and Administrative Procedure Act (APA) violations (December 2003)	ISMA, BlueRibbon Coalition (BRC), and State of Wyoming appealed decision in D.C. District Court, but court denied the appeal in February 2005. NPS issued Temporary Winter Use Environmental Assessment (EA) with rules for three winters: up to 720, BAT, all guided snowmobiles in YNP (November 2004). NPS also began Third EIS; see November 2004 actions below.

December 2003	ISMA, Wyoming	Reopen 2000 suit to contest snowmobile ban	Wyoming District Court (Judge Clarence Brimmer) issued preliminary injunction in favor of plaintiffs (February 2004), making the injunction permanent in October 2004 by remanding 2000 EIS to NPS for NEPA and APA violations	NPS responded with Temporary EA (explained above under March 2003 actions)
June 2004	GYC and FFA, D.C.	Consider NPS in contempt of court for not banning snowmobiles	D.C. District Court (Judge Sullivan) ruled against plaintiffs (June 2004)	Court also ordered NPS to finish its rule-making for upcoming winter by thirty days before winter opening (NPS complied)
November 2004	GYC, Washington, D.C.	Make NPS adaptive management thresholds enforceable by law, which would have led to significant reduction in allowable snowmobile numbers	D.C. District Court (Judge Sullivan) ruled against Greater Yellowstone Coalition (GYC) (Fall 2005)	NPS began Third EIS on this issue (see also WLRA case below)
November 2004	Wyoming Lodging and Restaurant Association (WLRA), Wyoming	Contest Temporary EA decision and retain jurisdiction in Wyoming court	Wyoming District Court (Judge Brimmer) ruled against WLRA (Fall 2005) but retained jurisdiction over the matter	NPS began Third EIS on this issue
November 2004	FFA, Washington, D.C.	Contest Temporary EA decision	Suit dismissed as moot because Temporary EA expired (March 2006)	

Table 5.1. (Continued)

Date of Action	Litigant and Court	Goal of Action/ Legal Request	Immediate Outcome and Date	Final Outcome(s)
February 2005	Save Our Snowplanes, Wyoming	Contest SEIS decision to ban snowplane use on Jackson Lake in Grand Teton National Park	Wyoming District Court (Judge William F. Downes) ruled in favor of NPS in June 2007; on appeal to 10th Circuit Court	Snowplane ban on Jackson Lake remained in place
November 2007	National Parks and Conservation Association (NPCA) and GYC, Washington, D.C.	Contest EIS decision to allow continued snowmobile use	On September 15, 2008, the D.C. District Court (Judge Sullivan) vacated and remanded the FEIS to the NPS for violations of the NPS Organic Act, the APA, and NEPA	NPS issued another environmental assessment with winter use rules for three winters (see Postscript, page 220)
November 2007	ISMA and State of Wyoming, Wyoming	Contest EIS decision to allow only guided snowmobile use and cease avalanche control on Sylvan Pass	Pending; oral arguments heard on September 15, 2008	
December 2007	Park County, Wyoming	Contest EIS decision to cease avalanche control on Sylvan Pass	Pending; oral arguments heard on September 15, 2008	

Sources: May 1997 suit: Fund for Animals, Biodiversity Legal Foundation, Predator Project, Ecology Center, [and five individuals] v. Bruce Babbitt, Denis Galvin, Jack Neckels, Michael Finley, and John Rogers, May 20, 1997, Case Number 97–1126 (EGS), U.S. District Court, District of Columbia. EIS Collection, MAOF; and Settlement Agreement, Fund for Animals et al. v. Bruce Babbitt et al., Civil No. 97–1126 (EGS), Sept. 23, 1997, U.S. District Court for the District of Columbia, EIS Collection, MAOF. December 2000 suit: ISMA et al. v. Bruce Babbitt et al., Dec. 6, 2000, Complaint for Declaratory and Injunctive Relief, U.S. District Court, Wyoming; and ISMA and State of Wyoming v. Gale Norton and GYC et al., June 29, 2001, Civil Case 00CV-229B, Stay Order, U.S. District Court for Wyoming in Cheyenne, approved by Judge Clarence Brimmer, file "WU Settlement," GYC. March 2003 suits and decision: Scott McMillion, "Park Snowmobile Policy Finalized, Lawsuit Follows," Bozeman Daily Chronicle, March 26, 2003; Mike Stark, "Pro-Snowmobile Rules Challenged in Court," Billings Gazette, March 26, 2003; and Fund for Animals v. Norton, Dec. 16, 2003, 294 F. Supp. 2d 92 (D.D.C. 2003). December 2003 suit and decision: ISMA et al. and State of Wyoming v. Gale Norton et al. and Greater Yellowstone Coalition et al., Dec. 31, 2003, Civil

Action #00-CV-229-B, Order Reopening Case, EA Collection, MAOF; preliminary injunction from *ISMA et al. and State of Wyoming v. Gale Norton et al. and Greater Yellowstone Coalition et al.*, Feb. 10, 2004, Civil Action #00-CV-229-B, Order on Plaintiff-Intervenor's Motion for Temporary Restraining Order and for Preliminary Injunction and Plaintiff ISMA's Motion for Preliminary Injunction, 304 F. Supp. 2d 1278, 1293 (D. WY 2004); and permanent injunction, *ISMA et al. and State of Wyoming v. Gale Norton et al. and Greater Yellowstone Coalition et al.*, Oct. 14, 2004, Civil Action #00-CV-229-B, Order, 304 F. Supp. 2d 1278, 1293 (D. WY 2004). June 2004 suit and decision: *Fund for Animals et al. v. Gale Norton et al. [and] Greater Yellowstone Coalition et al. v. Gale Norton et al.*, Memorandum Opinion and Order, June 30, 2004, Civil Action No. 02-2367, MAOF. November 2004 GYC and Fund for Animals suits and decisions: Mike Stark, "Sled Plan Faces New Lawsuit," *Billings Gazette*, Nov. 10, 2004; "Snowmobile Plan Draws 2 More Challenges," *Billings Gazette*, Nov. 13, 2004; Lauren Fischer to Jason Waanders, e-mail, March 16, 2006, Third EIS Collection, MAOF; *Fund for Animals v. Norton*, 390 F. Supp. 2d 12 (D.D.C. 2005); and Emmet Sullivan, Memorandum Opinion and Order, Sept. 28, 2005, Third EIS Collection, MAOF. November 2004 WLRA suit and decision: Bill Luckett, "Tourism Group Sues over Sled Ban," *Casper Star Tribune*, Nov. 12, 2004; Whitney Royster, "Snowplaners Use for Park Access," *Casper Star Tribune*, March 31, 2005; and *Wyoming Lodging and Restaurant Association v. U.S. Dept. of Interior*, 398 F. Supp. 2d 1197 (D. WY 2005). November 2004 FFA suit and decision: "Enviros Sue over Parks Groomed Trails," *BDC*, Nov. 10, 2004, and *The Fund for Animals et al. v. Norton et al.*, Minute Order, March 15, 2006, Third EIS Collection, MAOF. February 2005 suit and decision: "Snowmobile Plan Draws 2 More Challenges," *Billings Gazette*, Nov. 13, 2004, and "Order Upholding Agency Action," June 27, 2007, Third EIS Collection, MAOF. November/December 2007 lawsuits: *National Parks Conservation Association v. U.S. Dept. of Interior–National Park Service*, Petition for Review of Agency Action, Nov. 21, 2007; *Greater Yellowstone Coalition, The Wilderness Society, Natural Resources Defense Council, Winter Wildlands Alliance, and Sierra Club v. Dirk Kempthorne, Mary Bomar, and Mike Snyder*, Complaint for Declaratory and Injunctive Relief, Nov. 21, 2007; *State of Wyoming v. U.S. Dept. of Interior, The National Park Service, Dirk Kempthorne, Mary Bomar, and Michael Snyder*, Petition for Review of Final Agency Action, Dec. 13, 2007; and *Bucky Hall, Tim A. French, Jill Shockley Siggins, Bill Brewer, and Marie Fontaine v. U.S. Dept. of Interior, Dirk Kempthorne, Mary Bomar, and Michael Snyder*, Petition for Review of Agency Action, Dec. 31, 2007, all in MAOF. Sept. 2008 decision: *Greater Yellowstone Coalition, et al., v. Dirk Kempthorne, et al., [and] National Parks Conservation Association v. United States Department of Interior; National Park Service*, Memorandum Opinion, Sept. 15, 2008, Civil Action # 2007-2112, https://ecf.dcd.uscourts.gov/cgi_bin/opinions.pl?2008, accessed October 27, 2008.

clear his opinion on jurisdiction, guiding, and (again) the role of economic considerations in park management (as equal in importance to resource preservation).[16]

Reflecting upon Brimmer's actions, some in Yellowstone probably agreed with law scholar Jeffrey Bissegger, who argued that Brimmer sat on "the traditionally conservative side of the dispute, that decries judges who legislate from the bench, [but] has resorted to judicial activism to accomplish [their] policy goals." Although Brimmer's two actual winter use decisions to date illustrated a more mixed record of such advocacy, his language certainly seconded the political pressure that Yellowstone's managers were already feeling to continue allowing snowmobile use and associated economic activity. Activist or not, he sent a message to Yellowstone managers that any decision banning snowmobiles would likely not stand, at least in his court.[17]

With this cloud of uncertainty hanging over their otherwise partly sunny situation, Yellowstone managers turned their attention to the future. They had only three years to write a third EIS, and they hoped that somehow, this one would result in a lasting solution. Given the track record of their two previous EISs, they knew they needed to calm the waters, so this one would probably have to reach some kind of compromise. But they faced difficult odds, given the polarized factions, strong value attachments, and political and legal scrutiny. Even with the shrewdness and luck that had produced such remarkable change, they did not know whether they would be able to find that compromise, and if they did, how they could make it stick, or whether it would be enough to protect park resources.

Challenges to Collaborative Solutions

Once the dust over the EA settled and the winter of 2004–2005 was underway, park managers considered their options. Jumping into a new EIS without engaging their stakeholders more fully would make another judicial or congressional upset likely; if park managers did not at least try to involve them more, they would probably see the EIS tossed out again. Yet some stakeholders were currently suing the agency, making it legally difficult to get them involved in significant ways. And with the NPS still operating in a challenging political climate, any real involvement of conservation and animal rights groups was likely to exist more on paper than in reality. Despite these potential limitations, park planners decided to consider a collaborative policy-making effort for this EIS.[18] To do so, it hired the services of Cadence, Inc., a Helena, Montana–based neutral facilitator and public-engagement firm.[19]

The first step in involving a neutral facilitator is for the facilitator (in this case, Nedra Chandler, principal of Cadence) to assess the situation in which he or she is becoming involved. Such assessments involve interviewing the controversy's primary stakeholders to determine what public-involvement success the federal agency is likely to experience, given the issue's history and sensitivities. Chandler quickly went about this task, talking with more than sixty governmental, conservationist, animal rights, and pro-snowmobile representatives. Her report, submitted to the NPS in July 2005, summarized the challenges that she and the agency would face as they tried to produce a more durable solution and/or compromise.[20]

Six major themes emerged from Chandler's interviews, many of which were not a surprise to park managers. First, stakeholders wondered how the agency should weight the opinions of people who lived far from Yellowstone against those who lived closer and felt they were more familiar with the park and its winter use issue. Many reported similar uncertainty over science and its use—or disuse—in the decision-making process. To some stakeholders in all major camps, the previous NPS decisions seemed to ignore the relevant science and were therefore not trustworthy.[21] To varying degrees, these are two recurrent themes in most federal land disputes (and certainly in this issue); Chandler offered no solution for them, but the science theme certainly suggested the tendency among many stakeholders to believe only that science that agrees with their perspective (as discussed in Chapters 3 and 4).

The third and fourth themes involved the ongoing litigation and the issue's complex recent history. Stakeholders wondered how the litigation would affect the agency's work, as well as their involvement; many felt that a significant investment of their time in another EIS was futile because a court decision was likely to override it. Others felt that their involvement was pointless because the agency had twice contradicted overwhelming public opinion in its recent decisions allowing continued snowmobile use (perhaps forgetting that NEPA public-comment periods are not votes). If the agency did not listen to the public in the past, why would it behave any differently this time around?[22]

The final two themes were perhaps the most pervasive. Almost ten years of debating these issues had resulted in significant participant fatigue. Tired of arguing about winter use in Yellowstone, few looked forward to another drawn-out battle, and most wished there was a different way to resolve the problem. Finally, many by now distrusted the process, focusing in particular upon Gale Norton and her involvement. If she was so clearly in favor of continued snowmobile use, then was the decision not already made? How could the NPS come up with anything different from continued snowmobile use?[23]

Norton's involvement in the issue was particularly vexing to many stakeholders because she had just visited Yellowstone in winter. With Superintendent Lewis and some of her staff, she had snowmobiled more than 100 miles throughout the park, taking a snowcoach for only a 5-mile side trip. In several press conferences and informal interviews, she made no secret of her view that snowmobiling was a "great way to be able to see the landscape." Snowcoaches were a "much more ordinary kind of experience, . . . not as special as a snowmobile" (hers, in fact, "purr[ed] a little bit"). Given that she had toured the park with her friend Christine Jourdain, executive director of the American Council of Snowmobile Associations, and that she had recently published letters to the editor in both the *New York Times* and the *Minneapolis Star-Tribune* promoting snowmobiling in Yellowstone, her visit left little doubt where she stood on the issue. Regarding the next EIS, it was hard for anyone to believe that she would not influence the NPS to retain snowmobile use.[24]

In fact, just a month after Chandler released her situation assessment, word leaked to the press that one of Norton's deputy assistant secretaries, Paul Hoffman, former director of the Cody Country Chamber of Commerce, had apparently taken it upon himself to rewrite the National Park Service's *Management Policies*, the 2001 version completed just after the impairment guidance was issued in late 2000. Hoffman's changes would have dramatically shifted the NPS emphasis away from preservation and in favor of recreation. They would have gutted the policy calling for protection of natural soundscapes, thereby allowing additional forms and elevated usages of motorized vehicles in the parks.[25] Had his changes become policy, Hoffman would have succeeded in extending Norton's Yellowstone perspective to all parks, well past the end of her tenure as interior secretary in early 2009. However, the effort soon backfired, mainly as a result of public outcry over his seemingly covert attempt to gut the NPS's policies.[26] Hoffman was soon transferred to a different division, and after Norton unexpectedly resigned in March 2006, the NPS actually strengthened the *Management Policies*, with a renewed emphasis on preservation over recreation.[27] Those outcomes, though, were far from clear in 2005 when Yellowstone managers were debating their long-term options. At that time, Hoffman's efforts only seemed to highlight Norton's influence over the process—and the implications for winter use in Yellowstone were clear.

The long-term implications of Norton and Hoffman's involvement in winter use have yet to be seen. At least one informed observer of the debate fears that those six years of intimidation and intense political scrutiny will have a recurring effect: The agency will continue to be weakened in its political ability to preserve its resources, becoming less and less able to withstand political or industry attempts to gut resource protection. I agree with this assessment. Only the future will tell, of course, but as of this writing, Norton and Hoffman may have succeeded in their evident mission in a durable way, helping to transform the NPS into an agency unable to take the strong stand sometimes necessary to assure resource protection for all time, changes in the *NPS Management Policies* notwithstanding.[28]

Contradicting those who decried Norton's involvement, other people interviewed by Chandler were not surprised at secretarial involvement in NPS affairs. They knew that other secretaries of the interior had involved themselves directly

Secretary of the Interior Gale Norton touring Yellowstone in winter, 2005. Several secretaries of the interior have visited the park in winter, most recently Gale Norton. She made no secret of her preference for snowmobiling as a mode of winter transportation for the park, frustrating many of the issue's stakeholders and illustrating political influence on NPS policy-making. NPS photo by Jim Peaco.

in Yellowstone policy-making. After all, Norton's predecessor, Bruce Babbitt, had promoted the reintroduction of wolves to Yellowstone, and Babbitt's assistant Don Barry had used his influence to oppose snowmobile use. However, Norton's influence seemed excessive to some observers. Some felt that her well-publicized personal visit to Yellowstone in wintertime made her influence seem more tangible (perhaps forgetting or unaware that previous interior secretaries had done the same). Judge Sullivan's 2003 decision seemed to confirm that she had compelled the NPS to violate the "look before you leap" provision of NEPA in allowing snowmobile use to continue. Her actions went against NPS opinion and the "environmentally preferred alternative," both of which would have banned snowmobiles. Finally, her actions belied her own statements promoting stakeholder involvement in federal land decision-making (her mantra was "communication, consultation and cooperation, all in the service of conservation"[29]). For many reasons, then, Norton's involvement cast a cloud of distrust over the entire issue, even though some observers felt that such involvement was not inappropriate.

Chandler's report hinted at other challenges confronting park managers. Perhaps the greatest one was the obvious polarization among the interests. The ongoing litigation from three stakeholder groups (conservationists, animal rights advocates, and pro-snowmobile forces) was perhaps the most obvious sign of this division. Further, during the EA process, all groups stuck with their traditional positions; no chinks in their armor were evident. Snowmobilers continued to desire high levels of snowmobile use, and after the implications of the mandatory guiding restriction became evident (mainly, that it infringed upon their touring freedom), they began calling for its relaxation.[30] Similarly, conservationists were still stuck on snowcoach-only transportation, prodding their members to visit Yellowstone in such manner to demonstrate its feasibility, and animal rights groups still wanted to close the park to all winter human use.[31] Though wilderness enthusiasts and snowmobile advocates had reached some successful compromises on U.S. Forest Service land-management policies nearby in Montana, there were no such attempts in Yellowstone. In part, Yellowstone's prominence explains this intransigence; all groups believed that institutionalization of their preferred policy in the mother park would lead to the adoption of similar policies in other parks. Collaboration, by contrast, would likely mean eventual compromise elsewhere. Furthermore, all primary stakeholders had found traction in some court. This made them uncomfortable with collaboration because it could compromise their legal power over the issue. Consequently, Chandler recommended against making any strong attempt to collaboratively resolve the issue.[32]

This polarization was reinforced by some unfortunate events in early 2006. In one instance, when Yellowstone's management assistant, John Sacklin, forwarded an e-mail joke about the snowmobile issue to some of his colleagues, he got an unexpected response. The joke was a three-page satire of the snowmobile situation authored by Jay F. Kirkpatrick of Billings, Montana, and had been forwarded via e-mail to park planners by some friends. In the satire, Kirkpatrick facetiously suggested holding a snowmobile hunt in Yellowstone. Poking fun at all the issue's actors and drawing upon Montana's rural hunting heritage, he wrote,

> This hunt must have some semblance of the "fair chase" or a plethora of ACLU freaks and enviro weirdos will protest and draw the eastern liberal media to photograph the slaughtering of helpless, human-habituated snowmobiles, thereby damaging the image of Montana as an enlightened highly intellectual center of critical thought. Thus, the regulations for the hunt must be strict. . . . Machines sitting in front of bars, bordellos, casinos, poker parlors, or adult book stores may not be taken. . . .
>
> All shots must be fired from the front seat of a Chevy or Ford pickup truck. . . . Shooting at snowmobile drivers is discouraged, unless they are non-residents or NPS employees. . . .

Only legal "bull snowmobiles" may be taken. These can be identified by 7,000 decibel noise, large clouds of blue oil–laden smoke (for novices, these will appear much like a crop duster, but traveling on the ground instead of the air; often there is a long line of gasping snowmobile drivers behind a bull), and NASCAR and Havoline Oil stickers on the body parts. Usually these bull machines will be traveling at approximately mach 3. Some of the really big ones will have decals of nude women on the hood. Conversely, the "cows," which it is illegal to take, are puny small machines, sometimes with powerless 4-cylce [sic] non-polluting engines. Normally they will be traveling under 50 mph, usually by some whimp with poofy looking hair and a Calvin Klein snowmobile suit at the helm.

. . . The National Park Service shall have no regulating authority in the conduct of the hunt, based on the seldom read Constitutional mandate that Yellowstone was created primarily for the enjoyment and economic benefit of those living within seven miles of the border.[33]

Enjoying a moment of levity, Sacklin shared the joke with three snowmobile advocates whom he knew through his work. He quickly realized that his action was unwise and apologized for it. Evidently, one of the three did not appreciate the humor, or the apology, and forwarded the joke to Kim Raap, who had been the state of Wyoming's representative on this issue. Raap evidently deleted Kirkpatrick's name from the e-mail (twice, at that) and issued a press release stating that Sacklin himself had suggested the hunt, using a government computer and staff time to draft the satire and distribute it. Failing to investigate the matter fully, many snowmobilers took Raap's comments at face value and believed that Sacklin had acted as accused. They joined the *Bozeman Daily Chronicle* (in a display of especially poor journalism for a local paper previously covering this issue with insight and sensitivity) in calling for Sacklin's removal from direct work on the snowmobile issue. Raap never apologized, and his obfuscating actions, rather than resulting in Sacklin's transfer as he had wished, did more to stoke the feelings of distrust permeating the issue.[34]

Another cause of polarization was continued snowmobiler trespass over the park's western boundary. In 2004, some drove as far as 45 miles into the park's backcountry, over frozen waterfalls and across remote and pristine meadows. The activity continued in 2005, with park rangers citing seventeen people for such violations—one of them twice, for trespass in the same, well-marked area.[35] Such activity made any collaboration or compromise all the more difficult. Obviously, not all snowmobilers could be trusted to obey the laws. Why should conservationists bother to spend their time working out a solution knowing that some snowmobilers might intentionally violate its potential provisions?

As well, the snowmobile industry was reluctant to produce even cleaner and quieter machines unless it was compelled to do so. Although the BAT snowmobiles used in Yellowstone were indeed better on both counts than two-stroke machines, they still lacked catalytic converters and emitted fair amounts of noise at high throttle volumes. Consequently, their air emissions were still substantially more than the typical automobile's, and the park was still fairly noisy at times. For these reasons, park managers considered making the BAT requirements even stricter, an idea they eventually discarded, probably because it would have been difficult to accomplish.[36] Though the industry's resistance to more improvement was somewhat understandable, given the small market share that Yellowstone represented (most customers demanded stronger and faster machines), it made any potential solution involving continued snowmobile use in Yellowstone that much less acceptable to conservationists.[37]

Meanwhile, Yellowstone continued to gentrify, a concern recognized by few of the issue's stakeholders. For some twenty years, Yellowstone in winter had been the province of the wealthy, or at least moderately wealthy (upper middle class). With the implementation of mandatory guiding, snowmobiling became even more expensive than it had been previously, and snowcoaches were not much less expensive. Making matters worse, since the new Old Faithful Snowlodge had opened in 1999 (replacing the former aging and inadequate structure), room rates had more than doubled. By 2006–2007, an overnight stay there cost most people $171, with a few rooms priced at $123, still at the high end of most middle-class budgets and about twice the cost of the former Snowlodge. Concerned about the increasing cost, park planners wanted to make visiting the geyser more accessible to more people.[38]

Weighing these challenges and concerns, park managers began to draft the EIS—the third one on this issue in ten years. They had no choice but to do so, given their legal situation and the impending expiration of the Temporary EA (spring 2007). Under these circumstances, park managers moved toward completing the EIS late 2007.

Compromise, Incrementalism, and Tunnel Vision in the Third EIS

In 2005, the NPS began the EIS process anew. As it did, some local and regional residents called for compromise. Aware that a compromise stood a better chance of court approval than the previous polarizing decisions had, park managers began moving toward a solution that was, in some ways, a compromise among the various camps of stakeholders.[39]

Late the next year, the initial thinking of the park managers became public when they released the Draft EIS. Knowing that most visitors were relatively satisfied with the new but temporary rules, managers proposed sticking with them more permanently, with some changes. As noted earlier, the 720 daily snowmobile limit was about 10 percent below the historical average, but only about half of the historical maximum daily visitation, which usually fell between 1,500 and 1,800 machines. The current limit, then, seemed to be a compromise taking divergent viewpoints into account, especially since it might only be reached rarely (average daily use continued to hover between 250 and 300 machines, peaking around 500 machines on the busiest days). Meanwhile, snowcoach use was on the increase, making up about 40 percent of the park's oversnow visitors by 2006 (up from only 10 percent three years earlier). Certainly, such numbers—if they continued—would seem like a compromise to some, but even if the trend away from snowmobile visitation diminished or reversed, the 720 cap would be a moderate improvement over historical conditions. Though this compromise met with disapproval among conservationists, many local residents and editorialists were pleased with it.[40]

For conservationists, any move to retain snowmobile use represented a continued defeat. They repeated their opposition to snowmobile use in the parks, focusing in particular on the machines' noise. To them, even at 250 machines daily, the park continued to see some periods of objectionable vehicle noise.[41] Park managers, knowing the sound issue was problematic, proposed addressing it in part by making snowcoaches both quieter and cleaner. With all snowmobiles now using Best Available Technology, some snowcoaches had become the noisiest and dirtiest vehicles used in the park (over 80 percent of the loudest events during the winter of 2006–2007 were snowcoaches). Some even emitted levels of noise and air pollution rivaling that of two-stroke snowmobiles when computed on a per capita basis (levels of emissions per passenger). The snowcoaches could be much cleaner and quieter if the operators upgraded their machines. Some already had: A retrofitted Bombardier used by West Yellowstone's Alpen Guides, for example, was the cleanest oversnow vehicle in use in the park (again on a per capita basis), and it was also very quiet.[42] To prod all snowcoach operators to clean up their vehicles and make them less noisy, park managers proposed a snowcoach BAT requirement. This proposal was widely accepted, in part because many critics saw the agency applying the same requirements toward snowcoaches as it already had applied to snowmobiles.[43]

Still, this requirement offered no guarantee that winter vehicle noise would drop enough to be satisfactory for all (especially conservationists), because there was another kind of sound measurement still being violated: the percent of the day in which oversnow vehicle noise was audible. In roadside areas, park managers wanted oversnow vehicles to be audible for 50 percent or less of daylight hours; in developed areas, 75 percent. Even with the BAT noise restrictions for snowmobiles and the lower overall numbers of them in recent years, these thresholds were exceeded regularly at Madison Junction (a roadside area, averaging 59 percent of the day) and about a quarter of the time at Old Faithful (a developed area, averaging 68 percent). Although administrative use of snowmobiles by park employees contributed to the audibility, visitor snowmobiles and snowcoaches still constituted the lion's share of the noise. In short, the park was still not as quiet as park managers or conservationists wanted it to be. The new snowcoach BAT restriction would help matters somewhat but might not solve the noise problem completely. Hundreds of snowmobiles, after all, were still touring the park.[44]

Recognizing the need to take stronger steps to protect park soundscapes, and feeling that a lower limit for the number of snowmobiles would be a better compromise among the various stakeholders, park planners modified their preferred alternative in the Final EIS, which was released in September 2007. Examining their soundscapes-monitoring information closely, they found that oversnow vehicle audibility on the busiest days was somewhat correlated to the number of machines touring the park. Therefore, in the Final EIS, they dropped the daily snowmobile limit from 720 machines to 540 daily, a number that approximated the busiest days. The numerical reduction would do a better job of preventing snowmobile noise from dominating the park's soundscapes throughout the day. If the 540 limit did not protect park soundscapes adequately, managers could utilize yet another component of their final plan, an adaptive management program calling for further reductions in snowmobile numbers if various thresholds, including one for noise, were exceeded.[45] Although untested as of this writing, these appeared to be additional incremental steps toward better protection of park soundscapes.

Another component of the final decision was to close the Continental Divide Snowmobile Trail in the Tetons. Since the agency had restricted snowmobile use on the CDST to BAT machines, use had plummeted to only about 15 snowmobiles *per winter*. Most of the trail's users had been Wyomingites who owned private two-stroke snowmobiles and did not care to rent BAT machines to enter the park. Grand Teton managers felt that the $100,000 they were spending to maintain the trail was not a wise government expenditure, and had never liked the trail to begin with. They planned to close it in 2008.[46] They met with surprisingly little opposition, perhaps because Wyomingites were focused on another provision of the final plan, the closure of Yellowstone's East Entrance Road (discussed in detail in the next section of this chapter). With public attention elsewhere, Grand Teton's managers were at long last able to eliminate the trail that Alan Simpson had forced upon them (he had since retired). This is perhaps the best illustration that, although they sometimes accept political influence and associated policies that compromise park protection, dedicated park employees can outlast politicians and are sometimes (but not always) able to reverse those compromises.

Throughout this EIS process, park managers tried to involve the public in more meaningful ways than they had previously, an effort that helped to temper the debate somewhat but brought no unqualified successes. In her stakeholder assessment, Nedra Chandler had suggested this approach, making specific recommendations. For example, she said, they could share evolving information (such as monitoring reports) more expeditiously with the public. They could actively listen to stakeholders and let them know where they did or did not use the public input. These steps managers took, prominently advertising their commitment to them at the public meetings they held on the EIS throughout 2006 and 2007. Park personnel also held many small group meetings with interested stakeholders to advise them of the current EIS status. Participants appreciated the personal effort those staff members made to keep them informed, even if they did not agree with the agency's thinking and even though they may have desired more inclusive, collaborative decision-making. Moreover, putting a face on the otherwise faceless NPS bureaucracy probably helped keep the rhetoric more civil.[47]

Another indication that the storm was calming a little was that locals began to adapt to the new situation. Editorials began promoting compromise, and some entrepreneurs began encouraging modes of visitation that took advantage of the new rules. For example, some tour operators began actively promoting snowcoach tours, developing faster, more comfortable, and more reliable coaches that in part accounted for the rise in snowcoach visitation seen at this time (the NPS was also proceeding in its own efforts, for which it found other funding). Some in West Yellowstone tried to recast their town as something other than the "Snowmobile Capital of the World," advertising a broad-based winter playground that included dogsledding, cross-country skiing, and snowmobiling, all with a sprinkling of local history (an attribute popular with tourists). Not everyone there welcomed the move away from abundant snowmobile use, but the emphasis on diversity and heritage became more dominant. And, in 2007 and 2008, winter tourism in the town began to rebound from the lows experienced a few years earlier.[48]

In addition, park managers took some steps to reach a fuller understanding of some of the issue's key drivers. Perhaps the most significant was the assessment of the state of knowledge regarding the groomed roads and how they affected the bison population. The NPS contracted with Dr. Cormack Gates of the University of Calgary, a bison expert who had never done research in Yellowstone before (and was therefore as dispassionate an investigator as could be found). He was to examine all relevant research, interview about twenty key bison informants (such as Mary Meagher and other bison researchers), and perform extensive modeling of Yellowstone bison movements, using varying assumptions as provided by the experts. He released a 300-page report early in 2005. That report advanced the state of bison knowledge, as hoped, but left at least one fundamental question unanswered. Gates found that Yellowstone's bison population was released from artificial control (the NPS limited their numbers as late as 1966) at roughly the same time that snowmobile use began in the park. Bison are fecund creatures and their population immediately began to grow. As this happened, the animals needed more range, so they expanded it using primarily their own network of trails. In most cases, these followed river valleys and strings of thermal areas—the same routes traversed by some Yellowstone roads. Bison would have expanded their range in the absence of groomed roadways, but with the roads present, they occasionally used them to connect their own pathways. In this way, groomed roads may have helped facilitate a population increase and range expansion that would have occurred anyway, in the absence of road grooming. A possible exception to this natural range expansion, Gates noted, was the road from Madison to Norris, which traversed a rugged canyon, one that bison might not have learned to use on their own (another exception may have been the road from Norris to Mammoth). Gates could not discern whether bison would have utilized the Madison-Norris route in the absence of road grooming, so he suggested a management experiment to address this knowledge gap.[49]

To design that research, Yellowstone managers invited Gates's group of bison stakeholders to a workshop in January 2006. Over two days, participants discussed their varying viewpoints, generally agreeing that closing the Gibbon Canyon route (from Madison to Norris) and observing the response among park bison would be the best way to address the question. They did not have time to devise actual research protocols and procedures, so the agency contracted with Dr. Robert Garrott of Montana State University–Bozeman a year later for that job. Garrott, working with NPS ungulate biologist P. J. White, suggested a tiered research approach that could shed some light on the issue, with the closure of that road being the ultimate action. *Some* light is probably all that would be possible, the two argued, for the fundamental question of whether winter road grooming led to alteration in bison movements and distribution could never be fully answered. Baseline data had not been gathered in the era before road grooming, and it was impossible to erase the bison herd's knowledge of winter foraging areas and the routes connecting them (some of which included the oversnow routes). As of this writing, managers planned to implement the research, although the road closure experiment may never be carried out because baseline data is lacking and because the closure would disrupt the popular Lower Loop tour route. As in other matters, such as efforts to reduce noise levels and temper the rhetoric of the debate, the agency's progress on this front has been incremental and so far incomplete.[50]

Park managers commissioned two other research projects at this time, both regarding sociocultural facets of the winter visitor's experience in Yellowstone. One study would examine another angle of the long-running bison debate: how visitors perceived their interactions with bison, and what to them constituted bison harassment and disturbance. In many ways, this project responded to some NPS biologists' conclusions that the bison harassment issue was more a social issue than an ecological one (most biologists agreed with Gates that interactions with park visitors and the use of groomed roadways were not harmful to bison on a population level). Even if harassment (whether inadvertent or otherwise) did not harm bison, it still looked terrible and was one of the issue's main drivers. Consequently, this research project proposed to examine public perceptions of bison harassment and why those events seemed so emotional to many. Similarly, snowmobile noise was still a primary driver of the issue, so a third study would investigate the visitor's perception of that noise. Was it an issue that visitors cared about? Were they still bothered by snowmobile noise, and/or was it only an issue in the minds of some conservationists? Managers certainly hoped that these studies would help them better understand what drove the winter use issue and enable them to craft a more enduring winter use policy. These research efforts are still in progress.[51]

Certainly, managers have not given up, and their persistent efforts have paid off with the recent transformation of the Yellowstone winter visit. Much of that transformation took place with implementation of the 2004 Temporary EA, but park managers continue to try to make improvements. If they are successful with the most recent EIS, for example, winter soundscapes will be quieter and visitation will remain orderly and enjoyable. These improvements confirm the assertions of some political scientists that agencies can be more effective pursuing a course of incrementalism than they can by attempting to fix problems in one radical, all-encompassing action.[52] Given the human tendency to accept change in small portions more readily than in large chunks, incrementalism may well be the path Yellowstone finds most successful in the future. If they combine this incrementalist approach with continued efforts to include stakeholders in NPS decision-making (thereby respecting their diverse values), park managers may be more able to fully realize their long-term goals of improving the winter experience and protecting park resources. However, such an effort will have to be viewed as a long-term process, not something to be accomplished within the three years typically needed to produce an Environmental Impact Statement. With seventy-five years of ongoing discussions about winter use already behind us, it is naive to believe this issue will go away in the near future.

The long tenure of some involved stakeholders also suggests that this issue will continue to draw attention and sometimes controversy, as Paul Hoffman's recent actions indicate. Other stakeholder actions provide similar evidence; some people have been involved so long that they have difficulty accepting compromises or solutions different from the ones they have always advocated, even if these solutions would achieve their own ultimate goals. For example, the Final EIS provided figures on visitor fuel consumption under each alternative—figures that did not make snowcoaches look environmentally benign. Using average fuel-efficiency and vehicle-ridership figures from Yellowstone, the EIS demonstrated that snowcoach transportation consumed 10 percent more fuel than snowmobile transportation. In fact, compared to buses (on wheels, not tracks like snowcoaches), they gobbled gas—2.5 times the fuel that buses would consume to transport the same number of people over the same distance. Buses would be more environmentally benign in other ways as well, according to the EIS, which featured an alternative that would have plowed the park's west-side roads for commercial bus or van tours (with snowmobile and snowcoach use continuing elsewhere in the park). As explained in the analysis of that alternative (which was not chosen for final implementation), buses would protect the park's soundscapes much more than either snowmobiles or snowcoaches, they would have about the same effects on wildlife (all vehicles would be driven by trained guides), and their air-quality effects would be similar to those of modern snowcoaches (although road sanding for bus transportation could produce more particulate emissions due to airborne dust, the NPS could minimize this problem with conservative sanding practices). Bus tour tickets would also cost only about half the typical snowcoach fare and about a third of the typical snowmobile rental.[53]

Despite these benefits, conservationists adhered to the snowcoach-only option throughout this third EIS process, even criticizing the plowing alternative at times.[54] They made no mention of the fuel consumption information in their formal communications. When asked why they supported the most energy-intensive option for the park, they struggled to present convincing reasons why snowcoaches were still better than buses. Some said that snowcoaches should be used as a long-term transition to buses because people were not yet ready for bus use in Yellowstone, while others felt that the snowcoach experience was a key part of visiting Yellowstone in winter and should be retained despite its high fuel consumption.[55] However, given that buses are used throughout America (indeed, in many national parks, where conservationists celebrate them), that snowcoach use would continue on the park's eastern and southern roads if the west-side roads were plowed for buses, and that the primary reason visitors come to Yellowstone is not to take a snowcoach ride but to experience the park in winter, these justifications seemed shallow. Conservationists had been fighting the winter battle so long that they had acquired tunnel vision. A different solution that would accomplish their own ends in more desirable ways

Snowcoaches at Madison, 2008. In the last ten years, conservationists have remained consistent in their support for snowcoach-only transportation in Yellowstone in the winter, with such visitation increasing substantially in the same time period. New information indicating that snowcoaches are the most fuel-intensive mode of winter transportation has not altered their unwavering support for them over snowmobile or bus transportation. Similarly, snowmobile advocates remain consistent in their support for snowmobiling, despite the lack of legal mandate for their use in national parks. Photo by author.

would threaten the credibility that they, and their interest groups, had achieved in advocating a consistent position for the better part of a decade.

These conservationists were hardly the only ones with tunnel vision. Snowmobile advocates still cannot envision a transportation mode other than their machines, even something like buses that would be considerably more affordable to many persons with values similar to their own. Animal rights groups still want to close the park, even sending the park a 210-page "letter" (more a dissertation, for it was as long as this book) late in 2007 advocating that position, but they still failed to recognize the human attraction to Yellowstone in winter, an attraction that has been welcomed and made accessible for decades.[56] Indeed, the major camps of interest groups can all be likened to people speaking different dialects of the same language. They sound different to each other, so they refuse to listen or attempt to understand one another, when merely listening closely would confer comprehension and empathy. All are bound to the dialects they speak, unable to understand that the language is more important than the dialects. It is preserving

Yellowstone and the ability to experience it in winter that is important, not the mode of transportation, whether snowcoach or snowmobile.

Tunnel vision seemed to be particularly evident in a new aspect of the controversy that flared up in 2006: arguments over whether to close Sylvan Pass on the East Entrance Road due to avalanche danger. As park managers would come to find, defenders of Buffalo Bill and all that he represents to Cody, Wyoming, seemingly could not envision a way to preserve their town's identity while changing routes of access to Yellowstone.

Buffalo Bill, Avalanches, and Politics

The Final EIS contained another modification to the temporary rules from the previous three winters, a change more than incremental and drawing substantial opposition: closing Sylvan Pass on the East Entrance Road to oversnow vehicle travel.[57] In the last three years, Yellowstone staff had taken a more critical look at the avalanche-control operation there. The road traversed about twenty avalanche paths on the steep slopes of Hoyt Peak. Rangers had been releasing avalanches since the early 1970s, using a 75 mm recoilless rifle until 1996, when they began using a 105 mm howitzer. The gun was stationed right at the pass in the only location from which its projectiles could target all avalanche paths that crossed the road. The program had several serious safety hazards. To reach the howitzer, park employees had no choice but to travel through up to ten (depending on the exact route they took to the gun mount, which was a short distance off the main road) uncontrolled avalanche run-out zones. The mount was also at the base of a cliff from which rocks and cornices regularly fell. Once employees discharged avalanches, natural slides could still occur. These were difficult to predict and had occurred previously, nearly burying employees a few times. Duds, especially from the 75 mm recoilless rifle, were a common occurrence, and searching for them in springtime presented obvious safety hazards (in fact, in 1995, a visitor had brought one to a nearby visitor center, not knowing what it was or that it could have detonated at any time, probably killing all who would have been in its proximity). Duds could also leach toxic chemicals into the environment.[58] In short, there were many grave dangers to park personnel involved in avalanche risk reduction at the pass, along with some environmental damage from the duds and the explosions.

Park managers had already taken many steps to mitigate the human hazards, but serious risks remained, most of which were exacerbated by the area's distance from medical facilities and rescue personnel. Managers had built a berm behind the howitzer to protect against rock or cornice falls and had installed a radio re-

Snowmobilers traveling through the avalanche zone at Sylvan Pass, 2007. In 2006, park managers proposed closing the East Entrance due to safety concerns about avalanches at Sylvan Pass, along with low visitation through the remote entrance. Upset over the possibility of being shut out of Yellowstone in winter, some Cody-area residents went to great lengths to oppose, and eventually overturn, the closure. NPS photo.

peater in the area to improve communication (and thereby emergency response). In 2004, they began using a helicopter to drop explosives onto the avalanche slopes. The helicopter offered greater precision and the hope that the howitzer and its dangers could be eliminated. Their experience over the next three winters, however, demonstrated that these hopes were false. The pass's frequently poor flying weather meant either that they would continue to need the howitzer to keep the pass open to ensure predictable tourist travel (using the howitzer as a backup when the helicopter could not fly) or that they would have to close the pass for up to a week after major snowfalls while they waited for suitable flying weather. Moreover, helicopter use carried its own set of risks equal in gravity to those of using the howitzer, such as the potential for a crash caused by changing weather. Neither howitzers nor helicopters seemed acceptable.[59]

Other solutions were possible, but all of them came with other problems. Snowsheds (linear sheds allowing avalanches to pass over a roadway without harming traffic) might have been the best solution, but they were expensive, estimated now to cost $150 million or more (recall that they had been discussed in the 1950s—and think of the irony of building snowsheds to shelter vehicles that required snow for safe steering: Managers might have to place snow in the sheds!). Stationary explosive devices called "Avalhex" or "Gazex" structures could be built in the avalanche start zones; both of them used explosions of gases to trigger avalanches in a controlled situation (when closed to visitors and safe for park staff). Such new permanent structures came with hefty price tags of their own—$2 to $3 million—and associated visual impacts. A third solution would be to eliminate the control program altogether, allowing access only when detailed avalanche forecasting indicated that natural slide events were unlikely. Because of the inherent uncertainty of such forecasts, the pass would be closed much of the winter season, depending on weather severity and avalanche danger. Commercial snowmobile and snowcoach operators would be unable to reliably plan park trips through the East Entrance.[60]

Avalanche danger was not the only reason park managers wanted to close the pass; a second reason was its low traffic volume and high per capita cost to maintain. Visitation to this entrance had plummeted in recent years, averaging only 13 people per day for the winter of 2006–2007. Winter visitation there had never been significant, always staying below 5,000 for the season, less than 5 percent of all park winter visitation. All travel, furthermore, over the pass was discretionary recreational travel, not the interstate commerce that justified avalanche control on other slide-prone routes in the West. For perspective on Sylvan Pass's light use, consider that even U.S. 550 in Colorado, the avalanche-controlled highway with the next lowest traffic volume in the United States, still saw an average of around 400 vehicles per day or more. Also, more people would enter Yellowstone's East Entrance on just one busy summer day than during an entire winter. Nevertheless, Yellowstone managers spent about $200,000 per winter keeping Sylvan Pass open, or more than $200 per visitor by 2007. Continued pass maintenance therefore seemed to park managers an unjustified, unreasonable expense.[61]

Coincidentally, a separate and unrelated highway project was nearing completion at the same time, offering a potential solution. The Federal Highway Administration was improving U.S. 212 over Cooke Pass, just east of Cooke City and Yellowstone's Northeast Entrance. That 8-mile stretch of highway was locally known as "the plug" because it was the only stretch of highway from Mammoth Hot Springs to Cody through Sunlight Basin that was not plowed. Authorities had not previously plowed it because it was too narrow and winding, with little room for snow storage (the area received 300–400 inches of snow per winter).[62] Knowing the rebuilt road would offer ample snow storage, some local residents and Yellowstone managers saw a quid-pro-quo possibility: opening Cooke Pass to automobile travel while closing Sylvan Pass. Cody would still have a Yellowstone entrance (a year-round one, at that), and park managers would be able to eliminate the dangers and expenses at Sylvan Pass (Cooke Pass had only two less dangerous avalanche zones). As they might never again have as golden an opportunity to close the dangerous route, the park managers proposed closing it, stopping short, though, of openly discussing Cooke Pass.[63] They were quiet about this possibility partly because the pass was outside the park on U.S. Forest Service lands, so they believed that the decision about whether to plow it was not theirs to make. As well, they feared that to discuss it openly could backfire, resulting in the worst possible outcome: Yellowstone would become responsible for keeping both passes open all year (park managers suspected that Cody interests would defend access through Sylvan Pass), perhaps without the possibility of examining the environmental effects of opening Cooke Pass to year-round travel.[64]

The proposed closure quickly touched off a blizzard of activity. Not only Cody residents but many snowmobile stakeholders in Wyoming and the region rose to defend Sylvan Pass access. Calls to keep the pass open emanated from Wyoming's congressional delegation, Wyoming Governor Dave Freudenthal, the City of Cody, and its county representatives. A citizens group called "Shut Out of Yellowstone" formed in the Cody area to oppose the proposed closure; it consistently raised public consciousness of the issue. All argued that the pass was key to Cody's economic well-being. They questioned the park managers' reasoning, pointing out that they had a thirty-year record of safe avalanche control on the pass, and claimed the agency was really only trying to reduce spending. Park staff found themselves performing shuttle diplomacy, traveling to Cody almost every month for a while to explain their rationale: Safety was the primary concern—there was no guarantee they would continue to enjoy their thirty-year string of luck, for example. They also listened to concerned stakeholders and staffed a hearing at which over 500 upset persons were present.[65]

Economic stimulation was really just a cover for something more important, for the small amount of visitation currently or previously going through the entrance stimulated little economic activity. The more likely reason stakeholders objected was because the proposed closure threatened an important identity for the town and Wyoming. As historian Liza J. Nicholas argued in *Becoming Western: Stories of Culture and Identity in the Cowboy State*, Wyoming's creation myth is that it is the country's greatest reservoir of American freedom and independence. Those incredibly important American values are embodied in the West's most powerful symbol, the cowboy, that person who confronted the Wild West with masculine strength and rugged individualism. Wyoming has long sustained this mythology, as is evidenced by its two mottoes—it is the Equality State and the Cowboy State—and it has a bucking bronco on every license plate. The personification of Wyoming freedom is Buffalo Bill, that cowboy turned showman who helped found the town of Cody. Today, visitors to Cody often tour a museum memorializing him (the Buffalo Bill Historical Center) and then travel to Yellowstone, where they discover the same West, along with the freedom and individualism that Cody himself enjoyed. When Yellowstone managers proposed closing Sylvan Pass, they threatened to take away the ability of modern tourists on their "snowmobile broncs" to experience Yellowstone. Tourists would not be able to experience the freedoms so important to Cody and its progenitor, so the town's identity would suffer, just as West Yellowstone's was threatened by the earlier proposal to ban snowmobiles. (Cody residents did not embrace the idea of plowing the plug on Cooke Pass, because Buffalo Bill never apparently went there, whereas he founded Pahaska Tepee, just outside the East Entrance).[66]

Some Wyomingites found this identity so important that they (perhaps unknowingly) created history to support it. Cody's representative to the State House in Cheyenne, Alan Simpson's son Colin, wrote the following in a letter to NPS Management Assistant John Sacklin:

> Buffalo Bill Cody started the East Gate, established the route up Sylvan, obtained authorization for the East entrance and put up $50,000 of his own money for the road. He built Pahaska Teepe [sic], the Irma Hotel and another hotel near Wapiti that helped bring the railroad to Cody and greatly enhanced the ability of tourists to visit YNP through the Ease [sic] entrance. . . . Year round motorized travel over Sylvan Pass is a cultural resource to YNP that will be impaired by the preferred alternative.

Nothing in the first sentence about Buffalo Bill constructing the East Entrance or its route is true; U.S. Army Engineer Hyram Chittenden and a Cody mayor of the early 1900s, George Beck, pioneered the route to and over Sylvan Pass (Buffalo Bill did build the hotels mentioned). Simpson's historical gaffe—not unimportant, as he represented the town politically—bears witness to what Wyoming's U.S. Representative Barbara Cubin wrote more succinctly at the same time, "The closure of the East Entrance to snowmobile use is an attack on Wyoming's way of life." In short, creation myths are more powerful than history or safety—and the arrival of a third generation of the Simpson family on the political scene did not go unnoticed by park managers.[67]

Park managers responded initially by sticking to their guns (figuratively, not literally) and quietly prodding the town's residents to see the benefits of travel through Sunlight Basin. Their efforts were in vain. Sunlight Basin might be wild, remote, and beautiful—arguably more so than the North Fork area leading to the East Entrance—but representatives of the town were unable to envision a new entrance to Yellowstone, one at which Buffalo Bill would feel at home even today (and despite the fact that the county had supported plowing the Sunlight Basin

Buffalo Bill statue, Cody, Wyoming, 2008. Buffalo Bill founded the town of Cody, which today takes great pride in his legacy. Yellowstone's proposed Sylvan Pass closure threatened the town's identity as a wellspring of the freedom and rugged individualism embodied in the showman. Photo by Kevin Franken; used with permission.

route thirty years earlier).Pursuing their cause, Cody representatives eventually succeeded in elevating the issue well above the heads of the NPS staff. Although the historical record is not entirely conclusive yet, it appears as though they got the attention of high-level politicians in Washington, including even the president and/or vice president or their staffs (recall that Dick Cheney is from Wyoming), who then evidently prevailed upon park managers to keep the pass open. This much is known: Park managers altered their decision between the Final EIS and the Record of Decision to allow the pass to remain open under "full forecasting" (as explained above, relying only upon avalanche forecasting to open the pass, not avalanche control). There would indeed be frequent closures, but the pass would be technically open for motorized visitor travel. They also agreed to further meetings with Cody area representatives to determine if a way could be found to keep the pass open more regularly. Park managers communicated with several Washington staff persons about these changes, including policy advisers for both President George W. Bush and Vice President Dick Cheney. They also met several times with Colin Simpson, who later said that the Cody community applied "whatever political pressure we could bring to bear. . . . There was knowledge at high levels of the issue." When asked whether Vice President Cheney was involved, Simpson said, "I'm sure he was aware of it." Wyoming and Cody pulled out their big guns and intimidated the NPS into a compromise—the latest in a long line in this issue.[68]

Throughout the winter of 2007–2008, park staff met several times with Cody area representatives regarding the future management of the pass. The NPS hired another neutral facilitator to moderate discussions between the parties, which by now consisted of Cody representatives and those who sided with them, on the one hand, who felt that the NPS had been disingenuous in presenting its reasons for closure, and NPS personnel, on the other, who felt that Cody representatives were being dismissive of their very real concerns. With the help of the facilitator, in June 2008 the "Sylvan Pass Study Group" announced its compromise: The NPS would continue to keep the pass open using explosives, while the state and county governments would agree to a slightly shorter season, seek funding for additional emergency vehicles, and assume responsibility for the howitzer. These stipulations would allow the NPS to hire additional staffpersons to assist in avalanche management. Fundamentally, the pass would remain open for predictable tourist travel. Employees working in the area would be safer, but they would still be vulnerable to avalanches as they traveled to the site and operated the howitzer. Given the powerful political interests in Cody and Wyoming and their desire to preserve their myth and identity, it is no surprise that the NPS agreed to continue more active means of keeping the pass open.[69]

To some observers, it seemed like a recurrence of the Fishing Bridge controversy from the 1980s (discussed in Chapter 3): Powerful Wyoming politicians had forced Yellowstone managers into a compromise that did not fully address their concerns. Both proposed closures (that of the Fishing Bridge developed area and of Sylvan Pass) threatened a form of access between Cody and the park, whether summer or snowmobile tourist traffic (and no matter whether such access was real or perceived). Both proposals threatened the town's identity as a gateway to Yellowstone, along with the values implied in that identity. Both confronted a skewed balance of political power, with Wyoming unexpectedly possessing more power regarding Yellowstone's management than the NPS itself.[70] And finally, in both cases, perception was stronger than reality and the NPS compromised to suit politicians with more power.[71]

Progress and Stagnation

And here the story ends, in mid-2008. More chapters in the story will undoubtedly come, because stakeholders with widely divergent sets of values cannot agree on which of those should be expressed in Yellowstone. In their efforts to see their values displayed, interest groups will continue to position themselves for maximum influence over park policy-making—no matter the cost or consequences, at least at times. Snowmobilers will continue to advocate for the freedom to use their machines in the park, failing to recognize that Yellowstone was not set aside for recreational vehicle driving but to preserve its resources; other means of touring may well be more appropriate. So, they file their litigation in the state of Wyoming's conservative court, hoping the cowboy judge will aid their cause.

Similarly, conservationists will continue to advocate for the snowcoach-only alternative, failing to celebrate the improvements that have occurred in the park, as well as failing to admit that snowcoaches consume much more fuel and are twice the cost of buses. They file their litigation in the District of Columbia, hoping the liberal judge will aid their cause. To do otherwise—to celebrate success and move on or to change their position to support plowing—would be to risk losing control of the issue and the perceived ability to emplace their values in Yellowstone. By claiming that snowmobiles continue to devastate park resources, conservationists portray the issue dichotomously, painting themselves as Yellowstone's savior in white with the correct solution (and associated values). The position, no matter its omissions, succeeds in enabling conservationists to claim that the public is on their side. It is a position that offers them some sort of control over the issue and that justifies their pursuit to see their values institutionalized in Yellowstone.

And so the game of snowmobile power politics in Yellowstone goes on. Watching and participating in the politicking is the National Park Service. Dealt a hand of cards that firmly includes interest-group and associated political influence upon its policy-making, agency staff have been forced to become politically astute. Thanks in part to that acumen, Yellowstone's managers have taken a situation that was largely out of control and turned it around. The park is quieter now, its air much cleaner, its wildlife less harassed, and many of its visitors happier. In some ways, the agency attempted to calm the waters and relieve the polarization in the issue by seeking a middle-of-the-road solution, one that would pass muster in two very different courts. Agency staff deserve credit for their persistence over the past twenty years in navigating the twisting political course needed to improve Yellowstone's winter conditions, even while they have had to make some compromises. With a little luck and more hard work, they may be able to enact further improvements to the park's resources, especially its soundscapes.

Still, the compromises the agency has made in recent years attest to another premise of this book: that the agency was partly forced to make them because it is not always the strongest actor in the winter use story. Through their actions regarding Sylvan Pass (and Fishing Bridge), residents of the Equality State remind us that not all is equal between politicians and NPS policy-makers; the NPS is frequently the underdog, so Sylvan Pass will remain open. With another Simpson arriving in the political world, and the Wyoming political landscape unlikely to change in upcoming elections, the park's political situation is not likely to change much either, no matter the outcome of future national elections. Another strong actor is industry. Surely, a society that routinely sends people into outer space has the technological capacity—if not the will—to design a snowmobile as clean and quiet as a modern automobile. That the agency has so far been unable to compel the industry to do so suggests that it is the weaker of the two.

The values and related identities driving this controversy will do more to keep the debate alive than any environmentalist rhetoric, industry position, politician hyperbole, court decision, or congressional directive. Ultimately, values and identities are what drive both industry and politicians, as well as the other stakeholders in this issue. Understanding this, we are left with questions as we look to the future. Will the various stakeholders realize that the conflict here comes down to a core difference of values among Americans, all of whom care deeply about Yellowstone? Will they realize that they share many of the same values, with only some differences in interpretation? Will they realize that, if those values and identities are respected and discussed openly, more durable and protective solutions may be possible?

Conclusion

Yellowstone's Wonderland, Alice's Wonderland

Wonderland is not only a historical nickname for Yellowstone, but was also the creation of Lewis Carroll. Alice might feel at home in the Yellowstone Wonderland, for the park is fascinating, strange, and unpredictable, and things are sometimes not as they would seem—especially when it comes to elements of the winter use debate. For instance, conservationists fighting the good fight for snowcoaches in Yellowstone now find themselves perversely advocating for the most energy-intensive transportation mode of them all. With the best of intentions, they have remained consistent in their support for these vehicles so long that it seems they have lost sight of their larger goal: instituting an environmentally benign and affordable mode of transportation in Yellowstone.

Alice might feel comfortable in a park manager's shoes as well, at least in one way. She would no doubt find a familiar sense of irony in the plowing debate. Plowing would be easier for park managers than their current program of nightly road grooming, but public opinion—so in favor of plowing forty years ago—seems set against it now, even though plowing is common outside the park. Still, many park managers would welcome plows in exchange for grooming machines; many expect that climate change will soon negotiate that exchange regardless of popular opinion. Though they are concerned about the impacts of global warming on the park they should protect, managers may privately and perversely find themselves hoping that it happens quickly, rendering the whole winter issue moot and negating the need for grooming machines.

Alice might also relate to an experience I had early in 2006, when I returned to Shoshone Geyser Basin. Once again, I enjoyed a spectacular day of solitude and sunshine and a world of frost, steam, vibrant green vegetation, and open water. In the twelve years since I had first heard snowmobiles there, park managers had succeeded in converting all visitor snowmobiles to Best Available Technology machines, and their overall numbers had dropped substantially. Consequently, I enjoyed a quiet morning, hearing nothing other than the sounds of nature and my skis. But when I turned to ski home, I was again surprised to hear the sound of oversnow vehicles. Although the noise was very faint—almost below the threshold of human hearing—it was distinctly present. This was not supposed to be the

Ghost trees and warm ground, Shoshone Geyser Basin, 1990s. Visitors will continue to be amazed by Yellowstone's always fascinating wonders. While problems remain with winter use in Yellowstone, park managers are committed to preserving the park's resources. However, the value conflicts and political influence on the NPS promise to keep the winter use controversy alive for the foreseeable future. Photo by author.

case, for the BAT snowmobiles were quieter than the two-stroke machines of the past; they should have fixed this problem. But, again, things are not always as they seem. In one of the many ironies surrounding this issue, four-stroke snowmobiles may be quieter overall, but their noise—like that of many snowcoaches—is a lower frequency that travels even farther than the high-frequencies of two-stroke machines, particularly when the air is cold and dense like it was that day.[1] Also, Bombardier snowcoaches, previously thought to be more environmentally benign than snowmobiles, were now known to be the loudest vehicles on the road. Once again, my memories are dominated not by the geyser basin but by the intrusion of unwelcome noise.

Why these paradoxes? Why does the Yellowstone Wonderland seem so much like Alice's? Mostly, because the various stakeholders and the NPS cannot agree within and among themselves whether and how snowmobiles are appropriate in Yellowstone. Fascinated by Yellowstone's weird and unpredictable wonders, stakeholders have long promoted opposing policies for the winter wonderland—policies that draw upon the conflicting values and identities they treasure, the confounding science on the issue, and their differing political connections. These divergent visions confuse the public and, sometimes, the stakeholders themselves. Caught in the middle is the NPS, an agency that was never strong politically and that lacked its own strong vision of what Yellowstone's winter geography should be like—two shortcomings that mean the agency is increasingly compromised politically and unable to preserve nature as it desires. Alice would find that the agency charged with protecting the park does not always have the final say in its management; that stakeholders and political representatives often play a game of smoke and mirrors to effect their desired ends; and that science and technology (so revered in America) are more chimeras than definitive aids to policy-making.

Reflecting upon the real-world situation in Yellowstone, we see that the park in winter is both cherished and contested because of the values people find expressed there. Members of society have been arguing for almost eighty years about Yellowstone's winter use policies, with the NPS often participating in such discussions. Yet we are far from agreement. As the *Billings Gazette* wrote after the plowing debate of the 1950s, "Obviously, the final shot hasn't been heard yet." We as a society will be arguing about the policies that determine the Yellowstone winter experience for many years to come.[2] In so doing, we are not so much trying to determine what mode of winter transportation is most appropriate there as we are seeking answers to more fundamental questions: Is it more important to embrace nature's sacredness or personal liberties? Which should prevail in Yellowstone, or can we as a society find a happy (or at least tolerable) marriage of the two? And what about science, economic stimulation, and family values? Our society has no easy way to answer these questions—indeed, the answers depend on the person answering. The debate over winter policies and place creation in Yellowstone will continue through times of both quiet discussion and angry shouting.[3]

Politicians, both powerful and less so, both red and blue, have been frequent participants in the debate. Yellowstone's winter use policy-making is a stage upon which they attempt to realize their larger political ambitions. The continuing snowmobile use today is a direct result of the political climate of the early 2000s, just as the proposal to ban snowmobiles was the result of late 1990s politics. The NPS, partly because it is an agency within the Department of the Interior, continues to succumb to political pressure, caught in a dance between getting its way in the world in which it must live and inviting public officials to move from influence to control over park policy-making. Over time, persistent compromises, dominant personalities, treasured community identities, and changing and divergent political administrations make it more likely that public officials will control the agency more than influence it. These difficulties take their toll on both the agency and the resources it is charged to protect.

Also influencing this debate has been science. Partly because the NPS had to begin its effort to transform Yellowstone with a crisis, science was inadequate and conflicting from the start. Scholars have found elsewhere that tardy science inflames an existing policy debate more than settling it. Science is sometimes only a tool for reinforcing our values: Although we proclaim our faith in it, we generally use it only when it agrees with the values we already hold dear. For park managers, science is generally useful only when it is timely, presents a uniform opinion, and is bulletproof. Understandings that evolve over time are more often harmful than helpful.

Weak though it may be in certain situations, the agency has nevertheless been successful at transforming Yellowstone's winter landscape back into something resembling that which the earliest motorized winter explorers found. It is a "windshield wilderness," a large, wild, natural landscape with maintained oversnow roads coursing through it and two hotels sheltering visitors.[4] While problems certainly remain, snowmobiles no longer dominate the experience. It is a credit to NPS personnel that they have worked with whatever cards they have been dealt to protect Yellowstone for—and from—society. Although the agency has been navigating the political card game as best it can (occasionally as the dealer), the fact that it must sit at the table with more powerful players (those possessing the jokers) means that it must fold now and then.

The polarized discourse about winter policies is the way Americans create place in Yellowstone; it is how we lay our values upon the land. Conversations about land use in America are not always pleasant, and often some voices are excluded, but they always result in a landscape reflecting the dominant values of society.[5] Yellowstone reflects the values of a society wise enough to create national parks and their administering agency to begin with, bright enough to develop modes of transport capable of traversing it in winter, fascinated enough to always find pleasure in it, and spiritual enough to see sacred value there. Segments of the same society resort to power plays in attempts to impose preferred values over others. Overall, the Yellowstone conversations have produced a park dominated by nature's awesome forces and scenery. It is made accessible by varying kinds of oversnow vehicles, some that hurt one's ears, others that guzzle gas, all of which are expensive. It is sought out by tens of thousands of people each winter, people who are thrilled by the park's magic but predominantly from the upper or upper-middle classes. And it is a place where most visitors find inspiration despite the continued snowmobile presence, the high cost of visiting it, and/or the restrictions imposed upon such a visit. Cherished and contested, the landscape is Yellowstone: truly American in both its beauty and its shortcomings.

In sum, the forces and influences explored in this book have helped preserve Yellowstone as a place that charms and fascinates, mystifies and befuddles. Interest groups and individuals promote different visions of reality in Yellowstone—or preferred reality, since it is really their values and identities made manifest. Science confounds the debate, lending support to conflicting interests, depending on which values they embrace. Evolving technologies throw curve balls at park managers and interest groups, making consistent positions not always possible. Shifting political influence and strident personalities mean that personal, financial, or political aggrandizement are more often goals than are resource protection or open-minded evaluation of new technologies. The growing economic importance of snowmobiling has clouded the vision of some. Throughout the history of the issue, withering NPS autonomy has led to an agency increasingly struggling to protect Yellowstone. Society and the NPS cannot agree, either from within or with each other, about the policies that should govern Yellowstone in winter or whether snowmobiles are appropriate there. Their alternative visions, influenced by so many factors, conflict, confound, and confuse, transforming Yellowstone's Wonderland into one where things are "curiouser and curiouser."[6]

We as a society have created a National Park Service that sits firmly in the world of politics; we must expect it to be influenced by that world. The influence is obvious: Politicians are elected, many senior agency personnel (in both the Department of the Interior and the NPS) are appointed by the president, and agency organizational structures are created by those same people. We cannot deplore this influence unless we are willing to take the steps necessary to rectify it.

Alternative structures that could reduce political influence while ensuring better resource protection are possible; in fact, good examples already exist in the United States. Former NPS Chief Historian Dwight Pitcaithley, for example, has argued that the NPS should be removed from the Department of the Interior and made into an independent agency similar to the National Archives and Records Administration, which would mean it was no longer controlled by a department whose leader was politically appointed. He suggested, additionally, that the NPS director be appointed for a term of fifteen years so that the agency could work toward long-term goals in accordance with a carefully considered vision for the national parks, rather than shifting from one extreme to the other depending on which party manages to win the White House every four years. Directors would be appointed based not on their political affiliations or outlook but rather on their experience and excellence in the NPS's three core functions: preservation, research, and education. These two basic changes, Pitcaithley suggested, would enable the agency to focus more effectively on its mission.[7]

The structure of the Smithsonian Institution is another possible model. The Smithsonian is overseen by a chancellor and sixteen additional members of a board of regents.[8] A similar board for the NPS could include one or two of each of the following: NPS career employees, educators, historians, research scientists (such as ecologists, geologists, archeologists, botanists, geographers, and so on), policy experts and lawyers, conservationists, visitor advocacy representatives, wildlife advocates, gateway community representatives, and national politicians.

Political scientist William R. Lowry suggested that all federal agencies with a preservation mission could be given a new institutional home. He specifically proposed that the U.S. Fish and Wildlife Service be included, since its mission is primarily preservation of nature as well. If the concept of one institutional home for all federal preservationist agencies were expanded to include those committed to preserving the nation's cultural and historical sites and treasures, then the National Archives and Smithsonian would be logical additions as well. The idea of such an umbrella agency has merit, although it probably should not be a Cabinet-level department, for the agency would then be subject to the same level of political interference that the NPS experiences currently. Modeling the umbrella agency's structure after the National Archives and/or the Smithsonian is probably a better way to go.[9]

Whichever of the three possible models was chosen, several more changes would further assist the NPS in its long-term mission. Many of these have been suggested by other scholars, but they are worth repeating here. As Lowry suggested, Congress should give the NPS's recreational areas, such as Amistad National Recreation Area in Texas, to a different agency because these areas place recreation over preservation in importance. Including them in the NPS system tells the agency, the public, and some politicians that recreation is or can be co-equal with preservation, when the agency's own congressional mandate stipulates otherwise. Similarly, Congress should provide a strengthened mission statement to the NPS that reemphasizes the priority of preservation over recreation. Commissioning the agency to produce its own stronger mission statement would be an excellent way to accomplish this goal, for its likelihood of internal acceptance would then be greater. The agency's 2006 *Management Policies* may already meet that need, but Congress would need to make those policies enforceable by law (they are not currently). Using the *Management Policies* would also send a powerful message to NPS employees, the public, and involved politicians that preservation trumps recreation in the U.S. national parks, even in administrations like that of George W. Bush. Again, as Lowry argued, the National Park Service should create or be given its own comprehensive plan specifying the kinds of natural and cultural sites acceptable for inclusion in the national park system. Currently lacking such guidance, the agency simply adds a site whenever a local congressperson pushes hard enough for his or her cause. In this way, undesirable sites like Steamtown National Historic Site (created as a pork-barrel project for the state of Pennsylvania and lacking historical significance) would no longer be included, and the agency's mission no longer diminished or strained. Representative ecosystems and nationally significant historic sites currently missing from the park system would be more likely to be included. Such a comprehensive plan would sharpen the agency's focus on an inclusive mission, further enabling it to defuse contrary political desires.

Pitcaithley provides two other worthy suggestions. First, Congress should provide more consistent and increased funding; the agency simply cannot be expected to excel on the shoestring budget it currently receives. The agency has responded by raising funds from private donors, a move encouraged by some NPS observers. However, failing to invest adequate public funds in the NPS abrogates the public trust that is the very reason for its existence. In failing to put its money where its mouth is, Congress effectively says that the NPS mission is not worthy of American time and support. And second, Pitcaithley's suggestions about the appointment and term of the director should absolutely be implemented, although a ten-year term might be more realistic than his idea of a fifteen-year term in the current career climate where professionals regularly change jobs. Preference for the director should be given to existing NPS employees, rather than persons working outside of the agency, to further instill employee trust in their leadership.

A stronger commitment to research and education would assist in the agency's preservation goal as well. Specifically, the agency needs to redouble its commitment to research, both within its own workforce and from partner institutions such as universities. Such research should include studies by political and social scientists as well as by ecologists, historians, anthropologists, geologists, and other scholars and scientists. In Yellowstone, social science is desperately needed; the park's natural resources have attracted the bulk of research interest (such as ecological and geological investigations), but comparatively little social science research has been done.[10] Continuing and strengthening the NPS's commitment to public communication and education regarding its policy-making and preservation activities would also be helpful. Being more candid with the public about the nature of political influence upon the NPS, for example, would strengthen the agency's credibility along with its employee morale and would help to subject such influence to public scrutiny. Finally, the NPS needs to recommit itself to both academic and agency-specific training. Through hiring and promotion practices, the agency should demand the most qualified employees, for only with such staff is it likely to succeed in its ever more complex mission of preservation. In these ways, the agency would both become better prepared for controversies when they erupted and further excel in its efforts to communicate its raison d'être to the public. Improved public and political support would be the natural outcomes.

Such alternative structures and associated changes, if instituted without alterations to retain partisan influence, would strengthen the NPS's autonomy. Complete elimination of political influence is neither possible nor desirable, for

Congress funds federal agencies and through the power of appropriation can affect their policies, and Congress should have the authority to remove persons who act unacceptably (a clear code of ethics would help to prevent the latter problem from developing). Nonetheless, these other structures could reduce the political pressures the agency must face, enabling it to more effectively manage the parks for preservation and appropriate recreation.

Unfortunately, neither Republican nor Democratic elected officials are likely to undertake a reformation that would reduce their own influence. In the meantime, all Americans will lose as national park preservation continues to suffer from excessive political intervention. We can only hope that a bipartisan coalition will acknowledge the problem and have the courage to undertake NPS structural reform.

The question that underlies this entire debate remains: Do snowmobiles belong in Yellowstone? Are they appropriate there? It seems they are not, at least in their current form, for several reasons. National park observers generally agree that motorized transportation is acceptable in the parks, but only in the most environmentally benign and affordable forms. In Yellowstone's case, while snowmobiles and snowcoaches are indeed modes of winter transportation, they are neither the only forms possible, the most affordable, nor as clean or quiet as they could be. There are better options.

Also, for some, snowmobiles project an image of speed and a rush of adrenaline that seems out of place in Yellowstone. Decorated with racing stripes and bold colors (even the four-stroke models), they are almost always depicted in popular media in aggressive postures, such as making sharp turns or jumps, usually with snow flying everywhere. These macho images are jarring for those who treasure a contrasting but long-established image of parks as contemplative retreats, natural places of tranquility and clean air. The media and advertisers do not have to depict them this way, but they do, and the image, whether created by the media or simply reflected in them, sticks: They appear to be playthings rather than means of transportation.

These problems—noise and air emissions, speed and image, and cost and exclusivity—challenge the ability of some people to experience nature, which is the fundamental purpose of national parks. The late T. H. Watkins, writing about snowmobiles in Yellowstone, perhaps best articulated the problem they present: "A man ripping across the landscape on a snowmobile," he said, does not "experience the true character of a Yellowstone winter. . . . By experiencing the wilderness only from the other side of a great wall of human-made noise, [snowmobilers] are shutting themselves off from earthly conversations—and when the voice of the Earth is stifled, so is the hope of understanding our place in it."[11] We as a society have set Yellowstone aside to have those conversations. We have also determined that public access is essential to allow those conversations to occur. But when a form of access snuffs out the possibility of such conversations, it is time to search for other answers.

Snowcoaches are little better. While their image may harmonize better with that of national parks for some, they consume more fuel and therefore produce more greenhouse gases than any other form of practical winter transportation. With the reality of global warming and the human contribution thereto now proven and commonly accepted, it would be irresponsible for the NPS to convert to a snow-coach-only transportation system when more fuel-efficient options, such as public buses and vans (on wheels, not tracks and skis), are readily available.

In addition to contributing less to global warming, buses and vans would affect park resources less than oversnow vehicles do; furthermore, because they have fewer moving parts and have been regulated for years, buses are quieter than oversnow vehicles. Emissions for wheeled vehicles and oversnow vehicles are similar. Their effects on wildlife would be similar as well; since today's commercial snowmobile guides and snowcoach drivers would be the professional bus drivers of tomorrow, their familiarity with the park would encourage them to use caution in wildlife habitat. Plow operators could contribute by cutting escape holes in the snow berms on road margins to allow wildlife to exit the roadways; they could also spread traction gravel conservatively, minimizing the possibility of airborne particulates. Using buses and vans would cause parkwide fuel use to decline because visitor travel would consume less fuel and the NPS would not need to plow roads in spring (the overall fuel and labor used to plow roads in winter would be similar to the amounts currently used to groom them, but the lack of spring plowing would save large amounts of fuel and reduce labor costs).

In addition to being beneficial to the park, public buses could provide an enjoyable visitor experience. Familiar to most Americans, bus travel would help the visitor focus on Yellowstone instead of being distracted by the novelty of oversnow vehicles. More affordable than snowcoach tickets or snowmobile rentals, buses would enable more Americans to visit Old Faithful. With their taller profiles, buses would allow passengers to see out over the snow berms. Finally, by restricting travel exclusively to public vehicles, buses and vans would prevent park roads from becoming thoroughfares or speedways (note that, during the winter, Sylvan Pass should be closed to all vehicle use).

In short, public transportation and associated plowing would better protect visitor pocketbooks, park resources, global climate, and Yellowstone's retreat-like nature than either snowcoaches or snowmobiles. In comparison, oversnow vehicles consume substantially more fuel, are louder, and are much more expensive than wheeled vehicles.

For now, oversnow vehicle use continues, Sylvan Pass remains open, problems remain with winter use in Yellowstone, and stakeholder lawsuits persist. Until we as a society empower the National Park Service to fulfill its mission of preservation unfettered, parks will continue to face an uncertain future. Without such fundamental change, Yellowstone's winter majesty will continue to be both cherished and highly contested, and in the end, compromised by political and industrial influences. Earthly conversations will be more difficult, as will our search for meaning through the national park experience.

Postscript

In fall 2008, both Judges Sullivan and Brimmer had another say on Yellowstone's winter use. Sullivan ruled first, remanding and vacating the 2007 EIS back to the NPS. The conservationists' judge wrote that the plan elevated visitor use over park preservation, thereby violating the NPS Organic Act. Sullivan also wrote that the NPS had explained neither the source of the daily limit of 540 snowmobiles nor why that limit would prevent impairment, thereby violating the Administrative Procedure Act and NEPA.

Two months later, Judge Brimmer ruled. He could not issue a ruling contrary to Sullivan's. So, after chastising a judge sitting 2,000 miles away from the actual subject of the litigation for failing to cede jurisdiction to him, Brimmer stated that he would have upheld the EIS. He then ordered the NPS to reinstate the 2004 rule allowing 720 snowmobiles per day into the park, so that visitors and businesses would have some certainty while the NPS attempted again to find an acceptable resolution.

As this book goes to press, American voters had just elected Barack Obama to be their next president, and he was preparing his new cabinet. After more than two decades of close political attention, park managers knew that Yellowstone's winter use was likely to attract the new interior secretary's interest and that the secretary might push a snowcoach-only agenda. No matter what the new secretary's perspective is, however, the strong value attachments of the different stakeholders mean that they are not likely to reach resolution; they will not stop defending their machine of choice. As well, the agency's lack of confidence in its ability to articulate and promote its own vision for winter use will continue to hamstring its protective efforts. For these reasons, we can expect to be arguing about winter use for many years to come; horns will remain locked for the foreseeable future.

Notes

ABBREVIATIONS

AHC   American Heritage Center, University of Wyoming, Laramie

BGZ   *Billings Gazette*, Billings, Montana

BDC   *Bozeman Daily Chronicle*, Bozeman, Montana

BRM   *BlueRibbon Magazine* (the BlueRibbon Coalition's periodical, available at the Denver Public Library)

CEP   *Cody Enterprise*, Cody, Wyoming

CFR   Code of Federal Regulations

CST   *Casper Star Tribune*, Casper, Wyoming

DPL   Conservation Collection, Denver Public Library, Denver, Colorado

FEIS   National Park Service, *Winter Use Plans Final Environmental Impact Statement*

. GMP   Gale McGee Papers, Accession #9800, American Heritage Center, University of Wyoming, Laramie

GYC   Greater Yellowstone Coalition files, 13 South Willson Avenue, Bozeman, Montana

GYR   *Greater Yellowstone Report*, newsletter of the GYC

HCN   *High Country News* (periodical from Paonia, Colorado)

JHNG   *Jackson Hole News and Guide*, Jackson, Wyoming

LVE   *Livingston Enterprise*, Livingston, Montana

MAOF   Management Assistant's Office Files, National Park Service, Mammoth Hot Springs, Yellowstone National Park, Wyoming. Note that this office has a Winter Use Environmental Impact Statement Collection ("EIS Collection"), a Supplemental EIS Collection ("SEIS Collection"), a Temporary Environmental Assessment Collection ("EA Collection"), a Third EIS Collection (for the EIS begun in 2005, "Third EIS Collection"), a 2008 Environmental Assessment collection, and a collection of winter use research ("Research Collection"). In all these collections, the file name often nearly matches the document contained within. To save space and avoid redundancy in the extensive endnotes, I have not included the names for such files, only the collection in which the document can be obtained (for example, "EIS Collection, MAOF"), unless the file name is not obvious, in which case it is included. Future researchers can easily use the Management Assistant Office's database along with the description of the document I include to find the document themselves.

NACP	National Archives, College Park, Maryland
NYT	*New York Times*
PCN	*Park County News,* Livingston, Montana
RG	Record Group
SAR(s)	Superintendent's Annual Report(s), found in YNPL
SMR(s)	Superintendent's Monthly Report(s), found in YNPL
2000 FEIS	*Winter Use Plans Final Environmental Impact Statement,* Oct. 2000
2007 FEIS	*Winter Use Plans Final Environmental Impact Statement,* 2007
2003 Final SEIS	*Winter Use Plans Final Supplemental Environmental Impact Statement,* Feb. 2003
TWS	The Wilderness Society Collection (CONS 130), Conservation Collection, Denver Public Library, Denver
YNPA	National Archives, Yellowstone National Park, Gardiner, Montana
YNPL	Yellowstone National Park Research Library, Gardiner, Montana
YNPV	Vertical Files, Yellowstone National Park Research Library, Gardiner, Montana

INTRODUCTION: MACHINES IN THE WINTER WONDERLAND

1. Parts of this book are substantially derived from my master's thesis, "The Development of Snowmobile Policy in Yellowstone National Park" (University of Montana, 1998), and Chapter 4 of my Ph.D. dissertation, "Compromising Yellowstone: The Interest Group–National Park Service Relationship in Modern Policy-Making" (University of Wisconsin–Madison, 2004). Paul Schullery, in *Yellowstone's Ski Pioneers: Peril and Heroism on the Winter Trail* (Worland, WY: High Plains, 1995), provides a comprehensive history of early winter exploration by U.S. Army Scouts, National Park Service (NPS) rangers, and early visitors.

2. NPS employee Marc Hanna had the same experience at Shoshone at about this time (personal communication with the author, Feb. 7, 2008).

3. Indeed, some have wondered why I am writing this book before the controversy is resolved. Not only might it be many years before the controversy is fully resolved (producing a waiting game that may never end), but a comprehensive history of the issue is needed now, in part because its availability may help people to understand the issue.

4. See Hal K. Rothman, *Devil's Bargains: Tourism in the Twentieth-Century American West* (Lawrence: University Press of Kansas, 1998), and Annie Gilbert Coleman, *Ski Style: Sport and Culture in the Rockies* (Lawrence: University Press of Kansas, 2004) for histories of the ski industry in the West, including some references to national park winter recreation. Hal Clifford, in *Downhill Slide: Why the Corporate Ski Industry Is Bad for Skiing, Ski Towns, and the Environment* (San Francisco: Sierra Club Books, 2002), provides a more comprehensive, if critical, history of skiing in America.

5. A partial listing of such authors is: Alfred Runte, *National Parks: The American Experience* (Lincoln: University of Nebraska Press, 1979); Ronald A. Foresta, *America's National Parks and Their Keepers* (Washington, DC: Resources for the Future, 1984); Richard West Sellars, *Preserving Nature in the National Parks: A History* (New Haven, CT: Yale University Press, 1997); Richard A. Bartlett, *Yellowstone: A Wilderness Besieged* (Tucson: University of Arizona Press, 1985); C. W. Buchholtz, *Rocky Mountain National Park: A History* (Niwot: University Press of Colorado, 1983); Lary M. Dilsaver and William C. Tweed, *Challenge of the Big Trees: A Resource History of Sequoia and Kings Canyon National Parks* (Three Rivers, CA: Sequoia Natural History Association, 1990); Lary M. Dilsaver, *Cumberland Island National Seashore: A History of Conservation Conflict* (Charlottesville: University of Virginia Press, 2004); Aubrey L. Haines, *The Yellowstone Story: A History of Our First National Park*, rev. ed., vols. 1 and 2 (Yellowstone National Park, WY: Yellowstone Association for Natural Science, History & Education, in cooperation with the University Press of Colorado, 1996); Alfred Runte, *Yosemite: The Embattled Wilderness* (Lincoln: University of Nebraska Press, 1990); and Thomas and Geraldine Vale, *Walking with Muir across Yosemite* (Madison: University of Wisconsin Press, 1998).

6. The NPS Organic Act is "An Act to Establish a National Park Service, and for Other Purposes," 39 Stat. 535, approved Aug. 25, 1916, as found in Lary M. Dilsaver, *America's National Park System: The Critical Documents* (Lanham, MD: Rowman & Littlefield, 1994), 46–47.

7. Two scholars provide a comprehensive overview of science's role in park management: James A. Pritchard, *Preserving Yellowstone's Natural Conditions: Science and the Perception of Nature* (Lincoln: University of Nebraska Press, 1999), and Sellars, *Preserving Nature in the National Parks.* Authors providing an alternative viewpoint are Alston Chase, *Playing God in Yellowstone* (New York: Harcourt Brace Jovanovich, 1986), and Karl Hess, Jr., *Rocky Times in Rocky Mountain National Park: An Unnatural History* (Niwot: University Press of Colorado, 1993). Chase in particular has seen extensive rebuttals by other scholars. See Paul Schullery, *Searching for Yellowstone: Ecology and Wonder in the Last Wilderness* (Boston: Houghton Mifflin, 1997), 44–45, 225, 278, and Holmes Rolston, "Biology and Philosophy in Yellowstone," *Biology and Philosophy* 5 (1990): 241–258.

8. Two good discussions of evolving park meanings are found in Barbara J. Morehouse, *A Place Called Grand Canyon: Contested Geographies* (Tucson: University of Arizona Press, 1996), and Schullery, *Searching for Yellowstone.* Scholars have examined the influence of several different kinds of interest groups on park management. Susan R. Schrepfer examines the role played by various kinds of conservation groups (*The Fight to Save the Redwoods: A History of Environmental Reform, 1917–1978* [Madison: University of Wisconsin Press, 1983]), as does Chase (note again the rebuttals of his work cited above). Chris J. Magoc writes about industry influence in the earliest days of Yellowstone's existence (*Yellowstone: The Creation and Selling of an American Landscape* [Albuquerque: University of New Mexico Press, 1999]), as does Don Hummel in more recent national park history (*Stealing the National Parks: The Destruction of Concessions and Park Access* [Bellevue, WA: Free Enterprise Press, 1987]).

9. Authors examining Native American influence include Mark David Spence, *Dispossessing the Wilderness: Indian Removal and the Making of the National Parks* (New York: Oxford University Press, 1999); Karl Jacoby, *Crimes against Nature: Squatters, Poachers, Thieves, and the Hidden History of American Conservation* (Berkeley: University of California Press, 2001); and Peter Nabokov, *Restoring a Presence: American Indians and Yellowstone National Park* (Norman: University of Oklahoma Press, 2004). Yi-Fu Tuan presents the classic discussion of place creation in *Space and Place: The Perspective of Experience* (Minneapolis: University of Minnesota Press, 1977). At least one geographer, Judith L. Meyer, has explored the creation of place in Yellowstone in her book *The Spirit of Yellowstone* (Lanham, MD: Rowman & Littlefield, 2003). Meyer, in fact, argues that Yellowstone has a distinct spirit of its own, a spirit of place. Although she touches upon winter visitation, she does not chronicle the issue's history.

10. Schullery, in *Searching for Yellowstone,* discusses the creation of place in Yellowstone and the ever-present changes therein, but spends little time on the creation of a winter place, which is very different from the summer park.

11. As such, I hope that this book is one of the environmental histories called for by Mark Harvey in "Managing the Wild," *Environmental History* 10 (2005): 700–701. In this case, the wilderness whose ecological change and human impacts I chronicle is Yellowstone's winter wilderness landscape.

12. Scholars asserting that the NPS is politicized include William R. Lowry, *The Capacity for Wonder: Preserving National Parks* (Washington, DC: Brookings Institution, 1994), and *Preserving Public Lands for the Future: The Politics of Intergenerational Goods* (Washington, DC: Georgetown University Press, 1998); Daniel L. Dustin and Ingrid E. Schneider, "The Science of Politics/The Politics of Science: Examining the Snowmobile Controversy in Yellowstone National Park," *Environmental Management* 34 (2005): 761–767; Schullery, *Searching for Yellowstone*; Pritchard, *Preserving Yellowstone's Natural Conditions*; and Sellars, *Preserving Nature in the National Parks.* Several ex–NPS directors also assert that the agency is significantly influenced by elected and appointed politicians: William C. Everhart, *The National Park Service* (Boulder, CO: Westview Press, 1983); George B. Hartzog, Jr., *Battling for the National Parks* (Mt. Kisco, NY: Moyer Bell, 1988); and James M. Ridenour, *The National Parks Compromised: Pork Barrel Politics and America's Treasures* (Merrillville, IN: ICS Books, 1994).

13. A wide variety of scholars have noted the superintendent influence. See, for example, the various works by Pritchard, Haines, Bartlett, Runte, and Schullery.

14. It is, again, Chase that provides the clearest call for park management to be scientifically based. He has many followers, however, including Charles Kay in "Aboriginal Overkill: The Role of Native Americans in Structuring Western Ecosystems," *Human Nature* 5 (1994): 359–398, and "Are Ecosystems Structured from the Top-Down or Bottom-Up? A New Look at an Old Debate," *Wildlife Society Bulletin* 26 (1998): 484–498; Hess, *Rocky Times in Rocky Mountain National Park*; and Micah Morrison, *Fire in Paradise: The Yellowstone Fires and the Politics of Environmentalism* (New York: HarperCollins, 1993). Re-

garding Kay, see my rebuttal, "Aboriginal Overkill Overstated: Errors in Charles Kay's Hypothesis," *Human Nature* 12 (2001): 141–167.

15. Daniel Sarewitz, "How Science Makes Environmental Controversies Worse," *Environmental Science & Policy* 7 (2004): 385–403; Robert Meadow, Richard P. Reading, Mike Phillips, Mark Mehringer, and Brian J. Miller, "The Influence of Persuasive Arguments on Public Attitudes toward a Proposed Wolf Restoration in the Southern Rockies," *Wildlife Society Bulletin* 33 (2005): 154–163; and Dustin and Schneider, "The Science of Politics/The Politics of Science."

16. Because the term "environmentalist" has acquired pejorative connotations, I have chosen in this book to use the term "conservationist" to refer to those members of society who advocate for the preservation of Yellowstone's resources.

CHAPTER ONE. THE PUBLIC WANTS IN

1. Frank H. Anderson to the Superintendent, memo, Jan. 31, 1949, loose within Box N-158, Yellowstone National Park Archives, Gardiner, Montana, a depository of the National Archives (hereafter YNPA).

2. Roger's Pass reading from Superintendent's Monthly Report (hereafter SMR), Feb. 1954, 1, Yellowstone Park Library, Gardiner, Montana (hereafter YNPL). Other temperatures in Jan. 1933 from Paul Schullery, *Yellowstone's Ski Pioneers: Peril and Heroism on the Winter Trail* (Worland, WY: High Plains, 1995), 8.

3. Schullery, *Yellowstone's Ski Pioneers.*

4. Ibid., 98–116, and "Winter Instructions to Rangers," Oct. 1, 1918, SMR, Oct. 1918 (quote).

5. Schullery, *Yellowstone's Ski Pioneers,* 98–116, and Mary Ann Franke, *To Save the Wild Bison: Life on the Edge in Yellowstone* (Norman: University of Oklahoma Press, 2005), 49–99.

6. Curtis K. Skinner, "Winter Wallowing in Yellowstone Park's Cold Loose Snow Prior to the 1950's," in John Jay and Curtis K. Skinner, "Transcripts of Interviews with Jay and Skinner," Manuscript Collection, Rare Book Room, YNPL, 1933, 2, and Frank W. Childs, "The Winter Job of Yellowstone Park Forest Ranger," *Union Pacific Magazine,* Feb. 1931, 13–15. Most remote point from Eric Compas, former GIS technician for Yellowstone, personal communication with the author, Dec. 5, 2006.

7. Snow depths from SMRs throughout the winter months of the 1920s and 1930s; 130 inches from SMR, Feb. 1925, 2, and March 1925, 2. Description of life at Thorofare and quote from Skinner, "Thoroughfare," in Jay and Skinner, "Transcripts of Interviews," YNPL, 4.

8. Peter Holte (Scout) to Major John Pitcher, May 21, 1902, Document #4851, Item 20, Letter Box 10, YNPA.

9. Harry V. Reynolds, Jr., to Chief Ranger, April 16, 1956, file "Thorofare Patrol Cabin, YELL #HS-0291, LCS # 51027," Yellowstone Center for Resources National Register files, NPS, Mammoth Hot Springs, Wyoming; and Jay Interview, Sept. 20, 1962, in Jay and Skin-

ner, "Transcripts of Interviews," YNPL. The order was also called the "Amalgamated Order of Mountain Men" by Skinner when he was interviewed by Herb Evison on Sept. 16, 1972, in Moose, Wyoming, in Jay and Skinner, "Transcripts of Interviews," YNPL. Schullery relates some other stories in *Yellowstone Ski Pioneers*, from which I also drew some of the general description of winter life in Yellowstone.

10. Information for this paragraph is drawn from the SMRs at YNPL for the following months: Dec. 1921, Feb. 1922, March 1922, April 1923, Dec. 1923, Jan. 1924, Feb. 1924, and March 1924.

11. SMRs for the following months: Dec. 1921, April 1930, Jan. 1932, Feb. 1932, April 1932, May 1932, June 1932, Jan. 1933, March 1937, and April 1937.

12. Trip of 1925 from SMR, Dec. 1925, 9. Visitation in 1926–1927 from SMR, March 1927, 14, and Schullery, *Yellowstone's Ski Pioneers*, 139 and 158 n.14.

13. Circa 1949 trips from Edmund Rogers to: Jim Sykes, Feb. 17, 1949; C. W. Egbert, Dec. 22, 1949; Carroll Wheeler, Nov. 28, 1950; Herbert A. Richert, Dec. 12, 1950; and Henry Buchtel, March 30, 1951, all in file "857-10 Winter Visitors to Park Interior," Box A-247, YNPA; SMR, Dec. 1949, 4. Further evidence of such confusion comes from Schullery, who discusses evidence of park representatives promoting the beauty and healthfulness of a Yellowstone winter visit in the late 1800s. That boosterism certainly seems to conflict with the quote at the beginning of the chapter directing rangers to view winter visitors with suspicion.

14. John A. Jakle, *The Tourist: Travel in Twentieth-Century North America* (Lincoln: University of Nebraska Press, 1985), 107–110, discusses the condition of pre–World War I roads; and Aubrey L. Haines, in *The Yellowstone Story: A History of Our First National Park*, rev. ed., vol. 2 (Yellowstone National Park, WY: Yellowstone Association for Natural Science, History & Education, in cooperation with the University Press of Colorado, 1996), 265–271, records the first automobile experiences in the park.

15. Jakle, *Tourist*, 101–116, and Warren James Belasco, *Americans on the Road: From Autocamp to Motel, 1910–1945* (Cambridge, MA: MIT Press, 1979), 27–36.

16. Jakle, *Tourist*, 121–131; Belasco, *Americans on the Road*, 138; and Harold A. Meeks, *On the Road to Yellowstone: The Yellowstone Trail and American Highways, 1900–1930* (Missoula, MT: Pictorial Histories Publishing, 2000), 65.

17. Hal K. Rothman, *Devil's Bargains: Tourism in the Twentieth-Century American West* (Lawrence: University Press of Kansas, 1998), 148–151; Belasco, *Americans on the Road*, 93; and Jeannie Cook, Lynn Johnson Houze, Bob Edgar, and Paul Fees, *Buffalo Bill's Town in the Rockies: A Pictorial History of Cody, Wyoming* (Virginia Beach, VA: Donning, 1996), 91. See also Meeks, *On the Road to Yellowstone*.

18. Bruce Blevins, *Park County, Wyoming: Facts and Maps through Time* (n.p.: WIM Marketing, 1999), 27; Ester Johansson Murray, *A History of the North Fork of the Shoshone River* (Cody, WY: Lone Eagle MultiMedia, 1996), 133–134; Lee Whiteley, *The Yellowstone Highway: Denver to the Park, Past and Present* (Boulder, CO: Johnson Printing, 2001), iii; and W. Hudson Kensel, *Pahaska Tepee: Buffalo Bill's Old Hunting Lodge and Hotel, A History, 1901–1946* (Cody, WY: Buffalo Bill Historical Center, 1987), 70–71.

19. Details on changes in Cody from Agnes Chamberlin, *The Cody Club: A History of Cody Country Chamber of Commerce* (1940), eds. Jeannie Cook and Joanita Monteith (Cody, WY: Yellowstone Printing & Design, 1999), 113; W. Hudson Kensel, *Pahaska Tepee,* 70; and Cook et al., *Buffalo Bill's Town in the Rockies,* 89, 94. See also Belasco, *Americans on the Road,* 41–134; Jakle, *Tourist,* 146–168; and Rothman, *Devil's Bargains,* 144–148. Louis S. Warren has written one of the best biographies of Buffalo Bill: *Buffalo Bill's America: William Cody and the Wild West Show* (New York: Alfred A. Knopf, 2005). For more discussion of the importance of Buffalo Bill to Cody, see Liza J. Nicholas, *Becoming Western: Stories of Culture and Identity in the Cowboy State* (Lincoln: University of Nebraska Press, 2006), 33–65.

20. Idaho efforts and complaints from SMR, Jan. 1931, 1–2. History of western skiing from Rothman, *Devil's Bargains,* 178–179. Skiing in Yellowstone from Schullery, *Yellowstone's Ski Pioneers* (see especially pp. 128–143).

21. The exact year that Wyoming began to plow varied, but 1929 seems to be the safest date for statewide systematic plowing, as gathered from "Minutes of the Meeting of the State Highway Commission," Sept. 20, 1929, Wyoming State Archives, Cheyenne, Wyoming; State Highway Commission, *Seventh Biennial Report of the State Highway Commission of the State of Wyoming* ([Cheyenne], WY: Wyoming Labor Journal, 1930), 29–30; Agnes B. Chamberlin, Secretary of the Cody Club, to Senator Reed Smoot, Feb. 3, 1932, file "630-02.2, Part 1: Yellowstone Lands, Buildings, Roads & Trails—Roads (General) Snow Removal," Box 72, Central Classified Files, 1907–1949, 1907–1932, Record Group 79 (hereafter RG 79), NACP; and Glen Shrum, photograph P97-75-191-C, "Up North Fork," taken in 1930, Park County Historical Society, Cody, Wyoming. In general, plowing began about the same time that roads were paved or hard-surfaced; in Cody, paving began in 1930 (Cook et al., *Buffalo Bill's Town in the Rockies,* 111); in the West generally, in the 1930s (Meeks, *On the Road to Yellowstone,* 13). Cody residents had actually been driving toward the East Entrance opportunistically earlier, getting to within 8 miles in Feb. 1924 (SMR, Feb. 1924, 1).

22. Murray, *A History of the North Fork,* 137, and Kensel, *Pahaska Tepee,* 83.

23. Dedication from Lee Whiteley and Jane Whiteley, *The Playground Trail, The National Park-to-Park Highway: To and Through the National Parks of the West in 1920* (Boulder, CO: Johnson Printing, 2003), 40–41. Calls for plowed roads from Chamberlin, *The Cody Club,* 26–27; "Winter Road thru Park Is Suggested," *Lovell [WY] Chronicle,* Jan. 21, 1932; "Plan Is Urged by Cody Club," *Casper [WY] Tribune-Herald,* Jan. 24, 1932; Chamberlin to Smoot, Feb. 3, 1932, file "630-02.2, Part 1: Yellowstone Lands, Buildings, Roads & Trails—Roads (General) Snow Removal," Box 72, Central Classified Files, 1907–1949, 1907–1932, RG 79, NACP; and Chamberlin to W. M. Nichols, Dec. 26, 1931, and Acting Yellowstone Superintendent Guy D. Edwards to the Director, March 16, 1932, both in file "630-02.2, Part 1: Yellowstone Lands, Buildings, Roads & Trails—Roads (General) Snow Removal," Box 472, Central Classified Files, 1907–1949, 1907–1932, RG 79, NACP.

24. Chamberlin, *The Cody Club,* 26–27; Chamberlin to Smoot, Feb. 3, 1932, file "630-02.2, Part 1: Yellowstone Lands, Buildings, Roads & Trails—Roads (General) Snow Re-

moval," Box 72, Central Classified Files, 1907–1949, 1907–1932, RG 79, NACP; SMR, Jan. 1932, 23; President of the Bighorn Basin Development Association H. S. Looper to Horace Albright, March 1, 1932, and R. C. Trueblood to Automobile Club of Northern California, March 31, 1932, both in file "630-02.2, Part 1: Yellowstone Lands, Buildings, Roads & Trails—Roads (General) Snow Removal," Box 472, Central Classified Files, 1907–1949, 1907–1932, RG 79, NACP; "Enrolled Joint Memorial No. 2, House of Representatives, 22nd Legislature of the State of Wyoming," Feb. 16, 1933, file "630-002.2, Snow Removal Part 1," Box 1739, Central Classified Files, 1933–1949, RG 79, NACP; and many of the letters within file "630-02.2, Snow Removal (Road Conditions) (Snow Depths, Etc.) F.Y. 1930–1931 & 1932," YNPA.

25. Although summer travelers would not observe the slides themselves, the naked slopes and battered trees would be clear evidence of winter avalanche activity.

26. Chamberlain to Smoot, Feb. 3, 1932, file "630-02.2, Part 1: Yellowstone Lands, Buildings, Roads & Trails—Roads (General) Snow Removal," Box 72, Central Classified Files, 1907–1949, 1907–1932, RG 79, NACP.

27. Albright to Superintendent, Feb. 12, 1932, file "630-02.2, Snow Removal (Road Conditions) (Snow Depths, Etc.) F.Y. 1930–1931 & 1932," YNPA; Albright to Larry Larom, March 8, 1932, and Albright to the Superintendent, June 10, 1932 (quote against plowing), both in file "630-02.2, Part 1: Yellowstone Lands, Buildings, Roads & Trails—Roads (General) Snow Removal," Box 472, Central Classified Files, 1907–1949, 1907–1932, RG 79, NACP. Plowing in other national parks from Rick Harmon, *Crater Lake National Park: A History* (Corvallis, OR: Oregon State University Press, 2002), 119, and Alfred Runte, *Yosemite: The Embattled Wilderness* (Lincoln: University of Nebraska Press, 1990), 152–153.

28. Albright to the Superintendent, June 10, 1932, file "630-02:2, Part 1: Yellowstone Lands, Buildings, Roads & Trails—Roads (General) Snow Removal," Box 472, Central Classified Files, 1907–1949, 1907–1932, RG 79, NACP.

29. Hal Clifford, *Downhill Slide: Why the Corporate Ski Industry Is Bad for Skiing, Ski Towns, and the Environment* (San Francisco: Sierra Club Books, 2002), 11–15; Rothman, *Devil's Bargains,* 188–226; and Peter Shelton, *Climb to Conquer: The Untold Story of World War II's 10th Mountain Division Ski Troops* (New York: Scribner, 2003), 16.

30. SMR, Dec. 1938, 1, and Jan. 1939, 5.

31. SMR, Jan. 1938, 2 (first quote), and Feb. 1938, 2 (second quote).

32. Although the park's animals (*Bison bison*), are only distantly related to the buffalo of Europe and Asia, the two common names "buffalo" and "bison" have come to be used interchangeably in the region, as I will do in this book.

33. The ranching policies ceased in the mid-1960s, when the agency adopted its current natural regulation (or natural process management) policy, which essentially allows natural forces to regulate wildlife numbers. James A. Pritchard provides the best overview of the evolving wildlife management policies in Yellowstone in his book *Preserving Yellowstone's Natural Conditions: Science and the Perception of Nature* (Lincoln: University of Nebraska Press, 1999). Franke more specifically examines the history of bison management there in her book *To Save the Wild Bison.* For a broader look at science and its application in na-

tional park management, see Richard West Sellars, *Preserving Nature in the National Parks: A History* (New Haven, CT: Yale University Press, 1997).

34. SMR, Jan. 1939, n.p.; Feb. 1939, 1 (quote), and press releases included therein; Jan. 1940, 1–2; Feb. 1940, 1, and pictures, n.p.; Feb. 1941, 1; Feb. 1942, 2; and Feb. 1943, 2; and telephone interview by the author with Fred Staudeher, Bradenton, Florida, Aug. 4, 2005 (an attendee of the celebration in his childhood).

35. SMRs: April 1938, 13 (quote), 16–17, and pictures, n.p.; March 1939, 1; Feb. 1941, 1; March 1941, 1; April 1947, 3; March 1948, 3; March 1949, 6; and April 1950, 3. Rogers to the Regional Director, May 17, 1946, file "868-Winter Sports," Box L-46, YNPA; William A. Wright to R. M. Thompson of Metropolitan Life, Feb. 27, 1943, file "Correspondence (1943–1950)," Box MSC-65, YNPA; and John Whitman (?), "Undine Ski Hill, Yellowstone National Park, Jan. 19, 1994," unpublished report, file "Misc.," Box MSC-65, YNPA. In most reports, the agency only gives the Mount Washburn ski field location by mileage from Tower, but in the March 1940 SMR (p. 1), the "hairpin turn" was specifically mentioned— "Mae West Curve," as it is known to park staff.

36. Bob Barbee, telephone interview by author, March 20, 2006. See the various documents in file "Undine Ski Hill," Box A-403, YNPA. Skiing in other national parks from Thomas R. Vale, *The American Wilderness: Reflections on Nature Protection in the United States* (Charlottesville: University of Virginia Press, 2005), 115, and Shelton, *Climb to Conquer*, 30.

37. Arno Cammerer to Senator Harry H. Schwartz, April 1, 1938, file "630-002.2, Snow Removal Part 1," Box 1739, Central Classified Files, 1933–1949, RG 79, NACP; Acting NPS Director A. E. Demaray to Representative Francis Case, May 3, 1939, and Acting Superintendent J. W. Emmert to the Director, Jan. 6, 1940, both in file "630-02, Road Maintenance, vol. 1, Aug. 1938 to Dec. 31, 1947, 2 of 2," Box D-223, YNPA.

38. Winter plowing from SMR, Jan. 1940, 1, and Feb. 1940, 1. Park managers had actually plowed the road to Old Faithful in February 1935, although the reason for this action is unclear (see SMR, March 1935, showing pictures of park managers driving automobiles to Old Faithful). Cost estimates from Acting Superintendent Emmert to the Director, Jan. 6, 1940; Cammerer to Senator Joseph C. O'Mahoney, Jan. 16, 1940; and Demaray to Case, Jan. 26, 1940, all in file "630-02, Road Maintenance, vol. 1, Aug. 1938 to Dec. 31, 1947, 2 of 2," Box D-223, YNPA.

39. Emmert to the Director, Feb. 19, 1940, file "630-002.2, Snow Removal Part 1," Box 1739, Central Classified Files, 1933–1949, RG 79, NACP; and Cammerer to Representative Frank O. Horton, March 6, 1940, file "630-02.2, Snow Removal and Road Conditions Part 3, Jan. 1, 1940 to Dec. 31, 1943," Box D-181, YNPA.

40. Emmert to the Director, Feb. 19, 1940, file "630-002.2, Snow Removal Part 1," Box 1739, Central Classified Files, 1933–1949, RG 79, NACP, and SMR, Feb. 1940, 2.

41. Ibid.

42. Ibid., and Cammerer to Horton, March 6, 1940, file "630-02.2, Snow Removal and Road Conditions Part 3, Jan. 1, 1940 to Dec. 31, 1943," Box D-181, YNPA.

43. Early openings from SMRs, March 1940, 1; March 1941, 1; and March 1942, 1.

44. Acting Superintendent Joseph Joffe to the Director, March 8, 1940, file "630-02, Road Maintenance, vol. 1 Aug. 1938 to Dec. 31, 1947, 2 of 2," Box D-223, YNPA (*Cody Enterprise* quote), and "Winter Playground," *Helena [MT] Independent,* May 8, 1940.

45. Beverly Kurtz, "History of Skiing—Cody," March 1980, manuscript in vertical files at Park County Historical Society, Cody, Wyoming.

46. Demaray to John J. McIntyre, April 22, 1941, file "630-002.2, Snow Removal Part 1," Box 1739, Central Classified Files, 1933–1949, RG 79, NACP. See the many other letters in that same file for evidence of continued political pressure on the agency to plow its roads.

47. John Sullivan, "Wintry Weather Recalls Snowy Park Rescue Saga," *Livingston (MT) Enterprise* (hereafter *LVE*), Jan. 28, 1972, and SMR, March 1937, 2–3.

48. L. Allister Ingham, *As the Snow Flies: A History of Snowmobile Development in North America* (Lanigan, Saskatchewan, Canada: Snowmobile Research Publishing, 2000), 58–69; Leonard S. Reich, "Ski-Dogs, Pol-Cats, and the Mechanization of Winter: The Development of Recreational Snowmobiling in North America," *Technology and Culture* 40, no. 3 (1999): 484–516 (Reich notes that the Canadian provinces waited until the late 1940s to begin regularly plowing their roads); James J. Tuite, *Snowmobiles and Snowmobiling* (New York: Cowles, 1969), 4–6; Shelton, *Climb to Conquer,* 95; and "Your Next Winter Sport: Snowmobiling," *Popular Gardening & Living Outdoors,* Fall 1968, 14–17.

49. Ingham, *As the Snow Flies,* 58–69, and Reich, "Ski-Dogs, Pol-Cats," 484–516.

50. Roger Lacasse, *Joseph-Armand Bombardier: An Inventor's Dream Come True* (n.p.: Libre Expression, 1988), photos between pp. 48 and 49; Reich, "Ski-Dogs, Pol-Cats"; "Your Next Winter Sport: Snowmobiling"; Ingham, *As the Snow Flies,* 120–125, 269–309; and Dwight Harriman, "Long before Snowmobiles and Snowcoaches, There Were . . . Snowplanes," *LVE,* Dec. 12, 1997.

51. SMRs, Jan. 1939, 1–2, and March 1942, 2.

52. Rental from Jackson Hole resident Fred Abercrombie, recorded in SMR, March 1943, 4. Purchase from SMR, Jan. 1944, 1, and Roger J. Siglin to Brenda Black, Nov. 15, 1977, file "Land and Water Use 75, 76, 77," Box L-35, YNPA.

53. Thomas information from Shelton, *Climb to Conquer,* 52. NPS uses from SMRs, Feb. 1947, 1–2; Dec. 1948, 4; March 1952, 5; and Jan. 1953, 4. Fred Abercrombie assisted the *Look* magazine reporters and, along with others in the Jackson area, had begun using snowplanes on the frozen surface of Jackson Lake in the 1930s, primarily for ice fishing. At the time, such use was outside the purview of the NPS, which would not assume management of Jackson Lake until 1950, when Grand Teton National Park was created (Rick Guerrieri, personal communication with the author, e-mail, Nov. 28, 2005).

54. SMRs, Feb. 1949, 4; Dec. 1949, 4; and Jan. 1950, 5.

55. John S. McLaughlin to the Superintendent of Yellowstone, Dec. 17, 1947, file "857-10: Winter Visitors to Park Interior," Box A-247, YNPA. McLaughlin knew that local residents friendly to the NPS were important allies to keep, because there was significant hostility at that time to the enlargement of Grand Teton Park that would come in 1950. See Robert W. Righter, *Crucible for Conservation: The Struggle for Grand Teton National Park* ([Boulder]: Colorado Associated University Press, 1982).

56. Fred Johnston to Regional Director, Dec. 24, 1947, file "857-10: Winter Visitors to Park Interior," Box A-247, YNPA.

57. Lawrence Merriam to Superintendent, Yellowstone, Dec. 30, 1947, and Johnston to Chief Ranger [Francis] LaNoue, Jan. 2, 1948, both in file "857-10: Winter Visitors to Park Interior," Box A-247, YNPA.

58. National guidance from Newton B. Drury, Director, Memorandum for the Director's Office and All Field Offices, March 21, 1946, file "Winter Use, Winter Sports Policy," Box 24, Record Group 79, NACP.

59. Jackson proposal failure from Johnston to Superintendent, Grand Teton, Jan. 2, 1948, file "857-10: Winter Visitors to Park Interior," Box A-247, YNPA. Snowplane trips from SMRs, Jan. 1949, 5 (quote); Feb. 1949, 4; March 1949, 7; and monthly reports for Dec., Jan., Feb., and March throughout the first half of the 1950s. The winter of 1950–1951 was mild and dry, so very few entered that year, but most years saw between 75 and 150 snowplane visitors. South Entrance trips from SMR, March 1954, 6.

60. Winter description from personal experience; repeat trips from SMR, March 1952, 2–3; hints at the snowplane tour experience from Harriman, "Long before Snowmobiles."

61. Harriman, "Long before Snowmobiles." This is the only record I have found of oversnow vehicles being used on Yellowstone Lake. In recent decades such use has been confined to snow-covered roads.

62. Kurtz, "History of Skiing—Cody"; "200 Gather to Inaugurate Cody's Winter Sports Area," *Cody Enterprise* (hereafter *CEP*), Feb. 8, 1939; and the Park County Story Committee, *The Park County Story* (Dallas: Taylor, 1980), 51.

63. Wartime call for plowing from Kurtz, "History of Skiing—Cody." History of 87th and 10th Mountain Division from Shelton, *Climb to Conquer,* 29–38. The military did continue to use other national parks as sites for recuperative camps for soldiers, but this use did not provide the plowing incentive desired by the Club (John C. Miles, *Guardians of the Parks* [Washington: Taylor & Francis, in cooperation with the National Parks & Conservation Association, 1995], 133–142). See also Carsten Lien, *Olympic Battleground: The Power Politics of Timber Preservation* (San Francisco: Sierra Club Books, 1991), 213–231, for an account of timber interest in logging Olympic National Park during the war.

64. Belasco, *Americans on the Road,* 170; Shelton, *Climb to Conquer,* 229–239; and Kurtz, "History of Skiing—Cody." Skier visits from SMRs, Feb. 1949, 4; April 1949, 7; Feb. 1950, 6; and Jan. 1952, 8.

65. Secretary of the Greybull Club W. A. Simpson to NPS, April 6, 1946, and Acting Director Hillory A. Tolson to Simpson, April 17, 1946, both in file "630-02.2—Snow Removal and Road Conditions, Part 4, Jan. 1, 1944 to Dec. 31, 1947," Box D-181, YNPA; Merriam to Superintendent, Jan. 14, 1947, and D. Chew to Senator James E. Murray, Feb. 3, 1947, both in file "630-002.2, Snow Removal," Box 1739, Central Classified Files, 1933–1949, RG 79, NACP (this file also contains resolutions and letters to the NPS advocating plowing from chambers of commerce and other interested organizations in Pocatello and Idaho Falls, Idaho, and Miles City and Great Falls, Montana).

66. Acting Superintendent Fred T. Johnson to Regional Director, Jan. 30, 1947, file

"630-002.2, Snow Removal," Box 1739, Central Classified Files, 1933–1949, RG 79, NACP. That the west side roads were more feasible to plow was again illustrated in March 1948, when park managers plowed out the roads from Mammoth to Old Faithful and Norris to Canyon to enable the Yellowstone Park Company to install sprinkler systems in hotels there (SMR, March 1948, 3).

67. Johnson to Regional Director, Jan. 30, 1947, file "630-002.2, Snow Removal," Box 1739, Central Classified Files, 1933–1949, RG 79, NACP; Merriam to Superintendent, Feb. 26, 1947, file "630-02.2—Snow Removal and Road Conditions, Part 4, Jan. 1, 1944, to Dec. 31, 1947," Box D-181, YNPA; and Merriam to Superintendent, Nov. 5, 1948, and Drury to Regional Director, Nov. 10, 1948, both in file "630-02.2, Snow Removal and Road Conditions, Jan. 1, 1948, to Dec. 31, 1953," Box D-181, YNPA. Gates of hell quote from Kurtz, "History of Skiing—Cody."

68. The basin is variously called Big Horn or Bighorn, but according to the U.S. Board on Geographic Names, the name is one word (as found at the board's website, http://geo names.usgs.gov/, on March 22, 2007). Because the Club used the two-word variation, I repeat their usage in the text.

69. Big Horn Basin Club's move from SMR, March 1949, and "Seek Year-Round Opening of Yellowstone Hiways," CEP, March 17, 1948. Cody Club division from A. F. Leggett to Rodgers [sic], March 31, 1949, and Rogers to Leggett, April 11, 1949, both in file "630-02.2, Snow Removal and Road Conditions, Jan. 1, 1948, to Dec. 31, 1953," Box D-181, YNPA. Moran's position exemplified by "Let's Have Reasons—Not Excuses," CEP, March 23, 1949; "Charge Park Service Costs 'Padded,'" CEP, March 16, 1949; and Breck Moran to Rogers, June 25, 1959, file "630-02.2, Snow Removal and Road Conditions, Jan. 1, 1948, to Dec. 31, 1953," Box D-181, YNPA.

70. Big Horn Basin Club advocacy from March 8, 1949, resolution, file "Newspaper articles, Jan. 1, 1949, to Dec. 31, 1950," Box A-196, YNPA. Estimates for 1940 from Tolson to Senator Murray, Feb. 18, 1947, file "630-02.2—Snow Removal and Road Conditions, Part 4, Jan. 1, 1944, to Dec. 31, 1947," Box D-181, YNPA. Drury to PRA Commissioner Thos. H. MacDonald, Jan. 24, 1949, file "630-02.2, Snow Removal and Road Conditions, Jan. 1, 1948, to Dec. 31, 1953," Box D-181, YNPA.

71. PRA Division Engineer B. W. Matteson to Rogers, Feb. 9, 1949, file "630-02.2, Snow Removal and Road Conditions, Jan. 1, 1948, to Dec. 31, 1953," Box D-181, YNPA. Park managers may have sent him Fred T. Johnson's report, "An Analysis of the Practicability of Keeping Yellowstone National Park Open for Year-Around Travel," Jan. 11, 1949, file "630-02.2, Snow Removal and Road Conditions," Box D-181, YNPA, which, although prepared before Matteson's request, answered his questions.

72. Clyde E. Learned and D. C. Harrington, "Report on Winter Snow Removal to Provide Year-Round Travel in Yellowstone National Park, Wyoming," March 24, 1949, file "630-02.2, Report on Proposed Snow Removal," Box D-217, YNPA.

73. MacDonald to Drury on July 11, 1949, and Harrington, "Report on Winter Snow Removal to Provide Year-Round Travel in Yellowstone National Park, Wyoming," March

24, 1949 (administrative problem quote), both in file "630-02.2, Report on Proposed Snow Removal," Box D-217, YNPA.

74. Drury to Secretary of the Interior, memo, July 29, 1949, and Acting Director Demaray to Senator Joseph O'Mahoney and several other congressional representatives, Aug. 16, 1949, all in file "630 Roads, vol. 4, July 1, 1949, thru," Box D-221, YNPA. The Gardiner Lions Club issued one more call for plowing, which was firmly dismissed by the NPS in Joffe to President of Bozeman Chamber of Commerce R. H. Elliott, Dec. 22, 1949, file "630-02.2, Snow Removal," Box D-217, YNPA.

75. Jackson's actions from Archie Pendergraft to Drury, April 14, 1949, file "630-02.2, Snow Removal and Road Conditions, Jan. 1, 1948, to Dec. 31, 1953," Box D-181, YNPA. Other chambers also distanced themselves from the plowing proposal; see President of the Bozeman Chamber of Commerce to Joffe, Dec. 30, 1949, and Johnston to Regional Director, Jan. 3, 1950, both in file "630-02, Road Maintenance Jan. 1, 1949, to, 2 of 2," Box D-223, YNPA. Other chamber season extension requests and NPS response from Drury to Pendergraft, April 25, 1959, "630-02.2, Snow Removal and Road Conditions, Jan. 1, 1948, to Dec. 31, 1953," Box D-181, YNPA; and Drury to Senator Lester C. Hunt, Jan. 31, 1951; Drury to Cy Tjomsland, Feb. 21, 1951; Rogers to Charles R. Stark, Aug. 27, 1952; and Jerry W. Housel to Hunt, July 7, 1952, all in file "630-02.2, Snow Removal," Box D-217, YNPA. New rotary plow from SMR, April 1951, 4.

76. See the SMRs from the early 1950s for monthly listings of snowplane visitors. Snowplane use from South Entrance in SMR, Jan. 1952, 7. For correspondent visits, see SMRs, Feb. 1950, 3; Feb. 1952, 2 (*Life*'s photographer Ralph Crane also published some of his photos in *Illustrated,* according to this SMR); Dec. 1953, 2; March 1954, 6; and Feb. 1955, 7. Published articles include "The Yellowstone Tourists Never See," *Collier's,* May 20, 1950, 34–35; "Winter in Yellowstone: Only Animals and Rangers Are Left Behind to Witness Its Spectacular Snow-Covered Beauty," *Life,* Feb. 5, 1951, 66–72; and George D. Marler, "Snowbound in Yellowstone," *Natural History,* Dec. 1953, 440–445.

77. Robert S. Halliday, "Yellowstone in Winter," *Parade,* March 13, 1955, 11.

78. Lacasse, *Joseph Armand-Bombardier,* 33, 60, 96; Halliday, "Yellowstone in Winter," 11; Leslie Quinn, "The Snowcoaches of Yellowstone," *Commentary Newsletter,* Jan. 2000 (a newsletter published internally by Xanterra Parks & Resorts' Transportation Division in Yellowstone and available from the author or at YNPA); and Ingham, *As the Snow Flies,* 131–142. See also Reich, "Ski-Dogs, Pol-Cats," 488. Bombardier also designed a "snowbus," similar to the B12 model still used in Yellowstone but capable of carrying up to eighteen passengers (called the C18). Yellowstone Park Company and NPS officials took a snowbus to Old Faithful from Mammoth on Feb. 14, 1967, to determine its feasibility for use in the park, but evidently decided in favor of the smaller B12s (SMR, Feb. 1967, 9).

79. Halliday, "Yellowstone in Winter," 11; and Quinn, "Snowcoaches of Yellowstone." National winter use guidelines from Drury to the Director's Office and the Regional Directors, memo, Aug. 13, 1945, file "868—Winter Sports," Box L-46, YNPA.

80. SMR, Jan. 1955, 3; "New Innovation Brings Many Winter Visitors to the West Gate

Area," *West Gate Guide*, YELL 50797, YNP Museum Collection, and Halliday, "Yellowstone in Winter," 11. Snowmobile breakdown from SMR, March 1956, 2.

81. Agency refusals: Joffe to Egbert, Dec. 22, 1949 (with the noted contradiction), Johnston to Herbert A. Rickert, Dec. 12, 1950, and Rogers to Buchtel, March 30, 1951, all in file "857-10, Winter Visitors to Park Interior," Box A-247, YNPA. Scout trip, including permission thereof, from Chief Ranger Curtis K. Skinner to the Files, memo, Dec. 28, 1949; Donald L. Peters to Chief Ranger, Nov. 8, 1951; Rogers to Peters, Nov. 15, 1951; Paul V. Wybert and Anderson, "Explorer Scout Winter Trip, 1951–1952," Jan. 4, 1952; Peters to Superintendent, Sept. 18, 1952; Rogers to Peters, Oct. 14, 1952; and Peters to Rogers, Dec. 18, 1952, all in file same file and box as refusals; SMR, Dec. 1951, 2; and "Explorer Scouts Complete Snowshoe Trek into Yellowstone Nat'l. Park," *Bozeman (MT) Courier,* Jan. 8, 1953.

82. First winter's total from SMR, March 1955, 8. Package tours from SMR, Nov. 1964, 3. Conversion to Yellowstone Park Company in 1966 from SMRs, Nov. 1966, 9, and Dec. 1966, 2. *Parade* article: Halliday, "Yellowstone in Winter," 11. Visitor totals from SMRs for late 1950s and early 1960s. New Snowmobile purchases from SMR, Feb. 1964, 1, and SMR, Jan. 1966, 1. Note that within the NPS lexicon, the word is not "concessionaire" but "concessioner."

83. Weasel and SnoCat purchases from Siglin to Black, Nov. 15, 1977, file "L: Land & Water Use '75, '76, '77," Box L-35, YNPA. The NPS sold its last Weasels in 1970 (Superintendent Anderson to Fred Gaffen, Oct. 29, 1973, file "Motor Driven or Propelled Equipment, 1973," Box S-5, YNPA). Increasing need for patrol from SMRs: Jan. 1956, 4 (and SnoCat purchase again); Feb. 1956, 4; March 1956, 2; and Feb. 1960, 2. Weasel trips from SMR, Feb. 1954, 7. Winter keeper information from Robert N. Perkins, Jr., "Winter at Old Faithful," attached to Perkins to Suzanne Lewis [n.d.], Third EIS Collection, Management Assistant's Office Files, Yellowstone National Park (hereafter MAOF).

84. Several authors argue that the agency emphasized preservation over visitor accommodation at this time, such as Ronald A. Foresta, *America's National Parks and Their Keepers* (Washington, DC: Resources for the Future, 1984), 104–111; Alfred Runte, *National Parks: The American Experience* (Lincoln: University of Nebraska Press, 1979), 197–208; and especially Alston Chase, *Playing God in Yellowstone* (New York: Harcourt Brace Jovanovich, 1986), though Chase seems to argue that the NPS always placed preservation over visitor accommodation. Sellars, in *Preserving Nature in the National Parks,* 276–280, feels the agency still does not adequately put preservation over visitor accommodation.

85. SMRs: April 1954, 3; April 1955, 5; April 1957, 10; and March 1967, 14. Wood chip information from Michael J. Yochim, "The Development of Snowmobile Policy in Yellowstone National Park" (Master's thesis, University of Montana, 1998), 29.

86. Rogers to Regional Director, June 12, 1956, memo, file "D30 Book #1, Snow Removal, Oct. 1952 thru June 1957," Box D-216, YNPA. A fifth and sixth plow were added to clear West Thumb to Old Faithful, and then Dunraven Pass. The last assignment for the plows was the Beartooth Highway, which is still the case today.

87. "Wyoming Scores Delay in Opening of Park," *Denver Post,* May 31, 1956; "Simpson

Urges National Park Gates Be Opened Simultaneously," *Billings (MT) Gazette* (hereafter *BGZ*), May 31, 1956; and Simpson to Connie Wirth, May 24, 1956, file "D30 Book #1, Snow Removal, Oct. 1952 thru June 1957," Box D-216, YNPA.

88. Biographical information on Simpson from "Milward Simpson," *Daily Telegraph*, Port Deposit, Maryland, http://www.portdeposit.com/History/MilwardSimpson.htm, accessed Oct. 25, 2005, and "Simpson, Milward Lee (1897–1993)," http://bioguide.congress .gov/scripts/biodisplay.pl?index_S000434, Oct. 25, 2005. His Grand Teton involvement from Righter, *Crucible for Conservation*, 96–97. Quotes from Simpson to Frank A. Barrett, May 27, 1956, folder 6, Box 173, Accession #26, Milward Simpson papers, American Heritage Center, University of Wyoming, Laramie, (hereafter AHC). See also "Simpson Urges National Park Gates Be Opened Simultaneously," *BGZ*, May 31, 1956.

89. Responses to Simpson: Wirth to Simpson, June 5, 1956, and Rogers to Regional Director, June 12, 1956, memo, both in file "D30 Book #1, Snow Removal, Oct. 1952 thru June 1957," Box D-216, YNPA. Other Wyoming pressure from Keith Thomson to Wirth, June 12, 1956, and Barrett to Wirth, June 27, 1956, both in same file and box; and "Wyoming Urges All Entrances to Park Open Simultaneously," *Great Falls (MT) Tribune*, March 12, 1957. Montana interests from Mike Mansfield to Wirth, June 14, 1956, same file and box. NPS defenses from Wirth to Simpson, Feb. 26, 1957, and March 12, 1957, both in same file and box.

90. Simpson to Wirth, Feb. 11, 1957; Wirth to Simpson, Feb. 26, 1957; Simpson to Wirth, n.d., telegram; and Wirth to Simpson, March 12, 1957, all in file "D30 Book #1, Snow Removal, Oct. 1952 thru June 1957," Box D-216, YNPA.

91. Lon Garrison to Regional Director, March 29, 1957, memo, file "D30 Book #1, Snow Removal, Oct. 1952 thru June 1957," Box D-216, YNPA.

92. Change in focus to year-round plowing from E. W. Mass to Simpson, March 6, 1957, folder 8, Box 173, Milward Simpson Papers, Accession #26, AHC; and Fred Houchens to Senator Joseph C. O'Mahoney, Feb. 2, 1957, and Thomson to Wirth, March 27, 1957, both in file "D30 Book #1, Snow Removal, Oct. 1952 thru June 1957," Box D-216, YNPA. Montana pressure from Murray, Mansfield, Metcalf, and Anderson to Wirth, May 15, 1957, same file and box.

93. Garrison to Huntley Child, Feb. 25, 1957, file "NPS—1957," Box YPC-91, YNPA, and "Extended Visitor Season for Yellowstone Allows Public to See Park in Autumn Glory," *Jackson Hole Courier*, Sept. 5, 1957.

94. Overview of Mission 66 and Garrison's role from Sellars, *Preserving Nature in the National Parks*, 180–191; Haines, *Yellowstone Story*, 2: 373–383; Schullery, *Searching for Yellowstone: Ecology and Wonder in the Last Wilderness* (Boston: Houghton Mifflin, 1997), 183–185; and Foresta, *America's National Parks and Their Keepers*, 53–54. Longer seasons from NPS, "Mission 66: To Provide Adequate Protection and Development of the National Park System for Human Use, Jan. 1956," 15, and W. G. Carnes, "A Look Back to Look Ahead," talk given at Mission 66 Frontiers Conference, April 24, 1961, both in file "NPS—1956—General Correspondence," Box YPC-91, YNPA.

95. Tolson to Thomson, June 28, 1957, file "D30 Book #1, Snow Removal, Oct. 1952 thru June 1957," Box D-216, YNPA, and Acting Superintendent Warren F. Hamilton to Yellowstone Park Company President John Q. Nichols, July 9, 1957, file "NPS—1957," Box YPC-91, YNPA.

96. Creation of committee from NPS, "Outline for Snow Removal Study," attached to Hamilton to Nichols, July 9, 1957, file "NPS—1957," Box YPC-91, YNPA, and Tolson to Thomson, June 28, 1957, file "D30 Book #1, Snow Removal, Oct. 1952 thru June 1957," Box D-216, YNPA. Complaints about exclusion from Jackson Hole Chamber of Commerce to Barrett, June 19, 1957, same file and box; and Thomson to Wirth, Aug. 17, 1957, and Mansfield to Wirth, Sept. 23, 1957, both in file "D30 Book #2, Snow Removal, July 1957 thru March 1958 closed (2 of 2)," Box D-216, YNPA.

97. Garrison to Regional Director, Oct. 11, 1957, memo, and George F. Baggley to Regional Director, Oct. 17, 1957, memo, both in file "D30 Book #2, Snow Removal, July 1957 thru March 1958 closed (2 of 2)," Box D-216, YNPA; NPS, "Information for the Snow Survey Committee Concerning Possibilities of Keeping Park Open for General Public Use the Year Round," March 1958, file "Snow Removal (Roads), 1932–1959," Box D-42, YNPA; Child to Hamilton, April 1, 1958, file "D30 Book #3, Snow Removal, April 1958 thru Dec. 1960," Box D-217, YNPA; and Warren F. Hamilton, "Report on Snow Survey Committee Meeting, March 1 to 6, 1958," and Baggley to Regional Director, March 25, 1958, both in file "D30 Book #2, Snow Removal, July 1957 thru March 1958 closed (1 of 2)," Box D-216, YNPA.

98. Spring trip from Baggley to Regional Director, May 16, 1958, memo, file "D30 Book #3, Snow Removal, April 1958 thru Dec. 1960," Box D-217, YNPA. Report is NPS, "Report of the Snow Survey Committee, Yellowstone National Park, May 1958," file "A4055, Conferences & Meetings—1969 Tri-State Comm. & Master Planners," Box A-165, YNPA (quote p. 7). Extension idea from Roger Ernst to Governor, Aug. 4, 1958, folder 10, Box 173, Milward Simpson Papers, Accession #26, AHC.

99. Simpson to Secretary of the Interior Fred Seaton, Feb. 18, 1958, file "D30 Book #2, Snow Removal, July 1957 thru March 1958 closed (1 of 2)," Box D-216, YNPA, and "Park Service Gets Challenge," *BGZ*, Oct. 23, 1958. Earlier opening from Garrison to Regional Director, June 6, 1959, memo, and "Snow Survey Committee Recommendations for Extended Yellowstone National Park Travel Season Approved," press release, Aug. 4, 1958, both in file "D30 Book #3, Snow Removal, April 1958 thru Dec. 1960," Box D-217, YNPA; and "Yellowstone Park Roads Will Stay Open Longer," *Great Falls Tribune*, Aug. 5, 1958.

100. "Who Runs Yellowstone Park: Wyoming or U.S.?" *LVE*, Aug. 14, 1958; and LeRoy Anderson to Seaton, Aug. 18, 1958, and Seaton to Anderson, n.d., both in file "D30 Book #3, Snow Removal, April 1958 thru Dec. 1960," Box D-217, YNPA.

101. Garrison to Regional Director, May 19, 1958, memo, file "D30 Book #3, Snow Removal, April 1958 thru Dec. 1960," Box D-217, YNPA.

102. Howard Baker to the Director, May 29, 1958, and Ernst to Simpson, Aug. 1, 1958, both in file "D30 Book #3, Snow Removal, April 1958 thru Dec. 1960," Box D-217, YNPA.

1. Assistant Director to Regional Directors, April 7, 1966, file "L3427, Recreation Activities—Winter Sports, Oversnow Vehicles, 1966," Box L-40, YNPA; George Hartzog, as quoted in Senate Committee on Appropriations, *Winter Operation of Roads in Yellowstone National Park,* 90th Cong., 2nd sess., 1968, 64 (hereafter Committee on Appropriations, *Winter Operation Hearing,* 1968); and Adolph Murie to Stewart Brandborg, Feb. 25, 1967, file "States/Wyoming: Yellowstone National Park, 1964–1971," Box 7:195, Wilderness Society Collection (CONS 130), DPL.

2. To avoid confusion with the small snowmobile about to arrive on the scene, hereafter I shall refer to Bombardier's large-capacity machines, previously known as "Snowmobiles," by the more modern term "snowcoaches."

3. Roger Lacasse, *Joseph-Armand Bombardier: An Inventor's Dream Come True* (n.p.: Libre Expression, 1988), 148–151; and Leonard S. Reich, "Ski-Dogs, Pol-Cats, and the Mechanization of Winter: The Development of Recreational Snowmobiling in North America," *Technology and Culture* 40, no. 3 (1999): 489–497.

4. Lacasse, *Joseph-Armand Bombardier,* 12–17, 29–30, 99–144; Reich, "Ski-Dogs, Pol-Cats," 487–490; and James J. Tuite, *Snowmobiles and Snowmobiling* (New York: Cowles, 1969), 6.

5. Lacasse, *Joseph-Armand Bombardier,* 143–161; Reich, "Ski-Dogs, Pol-Cats," 487–490; and Howard & The Ranch Crew [from the Stage Coach Corporation, West Yellowstone, Montana] to "Folks," Dec. 1965, file "West Yellowstone, MT—Description—1960," Vertical Files, Montana Historical Society, Helena, Montana.

6. SMR, Jan. 1963, 2.

7. SMR, Jan. 1964, 1. Quote from Assistant Director to Regional Directors, April 7, 1966, file "L3427, Recreation Activities—Winter Sports, Oversnow Vehicles, 1966," Box L-40, YNPA.

8. J. M. Carpenter to Monte Wight, Feb. 18, 1965, file "L3427, Recreation Activities 1965—Winter Sports/Oversnow Vehicles," Box L-49, YNPA; SMR, March 1965, 1; SAR, 1965, 22–23; and Jerry Schmier, personal interview with the author, May 25, 2007, West Yellowstone, Montana. See also Steve Janes, "West Yellowstone Visitors Expand Horizons on Snow," *Snowmobile West,* Oct. 1985.

9. SAR, 1965, 22–23, YNPL. Superintendent information from "John S. McLaughlin, New Y. P. Superintendent, Due to Take Over His Duties on March 20," *Park County (MT) News* (hereafter *PCN*), March 1964, as found in file "Interior Dept. & NPS 1964—Jan. thru June," Box YPC-94, YNPA. McLaughlin was previously superintendent of Grand Teton National Park.

10. Alice Erdmann, "Snowriders Challenge Park," *LVE,* Jan. 24, 1967; "Snowmobilers Seek Record," *LVE,* Feb. 2, 1968; and SMRs, Feb. 1965, photos; Jan. 1966, 2; Feb. 1966, 2; Nov. 1966, 11; Dec. 1966, 2; Jan. 1967, 2; and Feb. 1967, 2.

11. "Blankenship Takes Top Trophy at First Snowmobile Rally," *LVE,* Jan. 17, 1966, reporting on a snowmobile rally in Livingston, Montana, and Russ Wells, "Jardine's Funland

in Full Swing," *LVE,* Jan. 17, 1971, reporting on a winter carnival in Jardine, Montana, near Gardiner. West Yellowstone festivals: George Remington, "West Yellowstone Plans Projects to Make Area Big Winter Resort," *LVE,* Feb. 3, 1966; "Third Annual Snowmobile Roundup," promotional brochure, file "Snowmobiles," Vertical files, Montana Historical Society, Helena, Montana; and SMRs, March 1966, 4, and March 1967, 2. Later in 1966, Young and Nicholls lost their special use permit for snowcoach tours of Yellowstone to the Yellowstone Park Company, which probably furthered their interest in promoting snowmobiling.

12. Steve Moore, "Snowmobiles Bring New Life to West Yellowstone," *Helena (MT) Independent Record,* Jan. 25, 1970. West Yellowstone is not the only community claiming such capital rights; Rhinelander, Wisconsin, also does (billboard outside the town, personal observation, Sept. 1999), as does Valcourt, Quebec, Canada (Lacasse, *Joseph-Armand Bombardier,* 48). Usually such designations are nothing more than booster attempts to stimulate tourism, but Valcourt's claim, given that the Bombardier corporation makes its home there, seems more significant.

13. SMR, March 1967, 2; "Third Annual Snowmobile Roundup," promotional brochure, file "Snowmobiles," Vertical files, Montana Historical Society, Helena, Montana.

14. SMRs, March 1966, 4; Jan. 1965, 3; and Feb. 1965, 10; Moore, "Snowmobiles Bring New Life"; Marlin Perkins, "Winter Comes to Yellowstone," *Wild Kingdom,* March 14, 1965, available at YNPL; Michael J. Yochim, "The Development of Snowmobile Policy in Yellowstone National Park" (Master's thesis, University of Montana, 1998), 35, 99; and "Third Interagency Meeting, Committee for Recreation and Travel," minutes, April 19, 1967, file "A4055, Conferences & Meetings—1969, Tri-State Comm. & Master Planners," Box A-165, YNPA.

15. Sidehilling and Bechler tracks from SMRs, March 1966, 9; Nov. 1966, 2; and Feb. 1967, 7. Dogsleds and skiers from SMRs, March 1961, 1; Dec. 1964, 1; and Dec. 1966, 2. Skiers may have begun avoiding Yellowstone in response to the snowmobile use there, as suggested by McLaughlin, who in 1967 wrote, "While ski or snowshoe touring has been encouraged in the Park, it is rarely done and since the advent of the oversnow vehicle it has practically ceased so far as the public is concerned" (McLaughlin to Director, July 6, 1967, file "D30, Roads & Trails: Winter Travel in Yellowstone, 1967," Box D-166, YNPA).

16. Proposal to open hotels from Ronald R. Beaumont to McLaughlin, April 5, 1966, file "C-38, Concessionaires Contracts & Permits, Yellowstone Park Company 1966–1967," Box C-4, YNPA. Mammoth Motor Inn opening from SMRs, Nov. 1966, photos, and Dec. 1966, 11. Its closure from John D. Amerman to Frank H. Anderson, Aug. 19, 1970, file "Concessions Bldgs," Box C-24, YNPA.

17. NPS, "Yellowstone Master Plan Final Draft, April 1964," p. 100, Box D-67, YNPA. Mission 66 policy from W. G. Carnes, "A Look Back to Look Ahead," talk given at Mission 66 Frontiers Conference, April 24, 1961, file "NPS—1956—General Correspondence," Box YPC-91, YNPA; and NPS, "Mission 66: A Look Ahead," p. 73, file "1956: Final Mission 66 Report for Yellowstone," Box D-20, YNPA. Concerns by staff in Staff Minutes, March 11, 1965, file "A40—Yellowstone Staff Meeting Minutes," Box A-172, YNPA. Lack of regulation

from McLaughlin to Regional Director, March 31, 1966, file "A88: Oversnow Vehicle Travel," Box A-32, YNPA.

18. Election information on all three candidates from http://bioguide.congress.gov/scripts/biodisplay, accessed Nov. 18, 2005. Regional controversy from SMRs, Jan. 1964, 8, and Feb. 1964, 5; Grand Teton Superintendent Fred Fagergren to Regional Director, Feb. 19, 1964, file "D30, Winter Travel in Yellowstone, 1962–64," Box D-173, YNPA; Luis Gastellum to Director, Feb. 14, 1964, file "D30, Roads & Trails—Winter Travel—1965," Box D-126, YNPA; "Why Not Open Park for Winter Activity for All the People?" *PCN*, Feb. 6, 1964; and "Briefing Statement—Year-Round Road Opening, Aug. 10, 1966," folder 6, Box 686, Gale W. McGee Collection, Accession #9800 (hereafter GMP), AHC.

19. "Statement Regarding Possibility of Keeping Roads Open Year-Round in Yellowstone National Park, June 3, 1966," file "A4055: Conferences & Meetings, 1969—Tri State Comm. & Master Planners," Box A-165, YNPA; "Projected Costs (1964) for Winter Snow Operations," statement found in "Snowmobile Briefing Book, Vol. 1," YNPL; Assistant Secretary of the Interior John A. Carver, Jr., to Senator Bourke Hickenlooper, Feb. 25, 1964, file "D30, Winter Travel in Yellowstone, 1962–64," Box D-173, YNPA; and McLaughlin to Regional Director, Sept. 10, 1965, file "D30, Roads & Trails—1965," Box D-126, YNPA.

20. SMR, June 1966, 19; Fred Martin to Mike Mansfield, Lee Metcalf, James Battin, and Arnold Olsen, May 26, 1966, reprinted in *PCN*, May 26, 1966; "Metcalf, Babcock Favor Y. P. Winter Travel Proposal," *PCN*, June 2, 1966; and Idaho Governor Robert E. Smylie to Martin, June 15, 1966, and Martin to Mansfield and Metcalf, June 24, 1966, all in folder 6, Box 665, Gale W. McGee Papers, GMP, AHC.

21. NPS Director George Hartzog to Governors Cliff Hansen, Milward Simpson, and Tim Babcock, Aug. 19, 1966, and H. L. Bill to Director, Sept. 1, 1966, and meeting minutes for the committee's meetings dated Sept. 10, 1966; April 19, 1967; June 2, 1967; and Aug. 14, 1967, all in file "A4055, Conferences & Meetings, 1969—Tri-State Comm. & Master Planners," Box A-165, YNPA; and Carl Lehrkind and Martin to Babcock, April 24, 1967, reprinted in *PCN*, April 27, 1967.

22. Minutes for the committee's meetings, dated Sept. 10, 1966; April 19, 1967; June 2, 1967; and Aug. 14, 1967, all in file "A4055, Conferences & Meetings, 1969—Tri-State Comm. & Master Planners," Box A-165, YNPA; Assistant State Maintenance Engineer to Deputy State Highway Engineer W. E. Sutton, June 2, 1966, Hansen to Hartzog, July 28, 1966, and Superintendent to Regional Director, Aug. 4, 1966, all in file "D30, Roads & Trails, Winter Travel, 1966," Box D-133, YNPA; and telegrams from Hansen, Wyoming Governor Stan Hathaway, and Congressman Henry Harrison to McLaughlin and Sutton, June 1 or 2, 1967, all in file "D30, Roads & Trails: Winter Travel in Yellowstone, 1967," Box D-166, YNPA.

23. Letter campaign from letters dated that February from chambers of commerce in Wyoming to Gale W. McGee in folder 6, Box 686, GMP, AHC. Resolution information from Jackson E. Price to Legislative Counsel, Feb. 10, 1964, file "D30, Winter Travel in Yellowstone, 1962–64," Box D-173, YNPA, and July 11, [1966], folder 6, Box 665, GMP, AHC.

Decision to hold hearing from "Hearing to Be Held on Winter Opening of Y. S. Park Highways," *Jackson Hole News and Guide* (hereafter *JHNG*), March 9, 1967.

24. "Harrison Urges Year Round Park Opening," *JHNG*, March 16, 1967; President of the Jackson Hole Chamber of Commerce Grant Larson to McGee, May 22, 1967, folder 6, Box 686, GMP, AHC; *Congressional Record,* 90th Cong., 1st sess., Feb. 16, 1967, S2081; and Lehrkind and Martin to Babcock, April 24, 1967, reprinted in *PCN,* April 27, 1967.

25. McLaughlin to Director, March 24, 1967, draft, file "A4055, Conferences & Meetings, 1969—Tri-State Comm. & Master Planners," Box A-165, YNPA; McLaughlin to Director, July 6, 1967, file "D30, Roads & Trails: Winter Travel in Yellowstone, 1967," Box D-166, YNPA; and "Disadvantages to Winter Road Opening—Yellowstone," "Oversnow Visitation," and "Road Standards," white papers in file "D30, Roads & Trails 1967—Winter Travel in Yell./Snow Removal," Box D-164, YNPA.

26. Vincent J. Schaefer to Martin, May 12, 1967; Glen F. Cole to Superintendent, Aug. 16, 1967; and William J. Barmore to Superintendent, Sept. 20, 1967, all in file "D30, Roads & Trails: Winter Travel in Yellowstone, 1967," Box D-166, YNPA.

27. Spring and fall traffic from McLaughlin to Director, July 6, 1967, file "D30, Roads & Trails: Winter Travel in Yellowstone, 1967," Box D-166, YNPA. Potential for thoroughfare from Committee on Appropriations, *Winter Operation Hearing,* 1968, 10–11. Although the roads were already open to interstate travel in summer, all commercial through-traffic was banned, and Yellowstone's size and remoteness meant that it remained a destination for most tourists, not a stop en route to a different destination.

28. Raymond T. O'Dell, "Report on Oversnow Vehicles," June 1968, file "L3427, Recreation Activities—Winter Sports, Oversnow Vehicles Use, 1968," Box L-37, YNPA; and Don Hummel to All Regional Directors, May 26, 1967, file "L3427, Recreation Activities 1967—Winter Sports, Oversnow Vehicles," Box H-41, YNPA.

29. McLaughlin to Director, July 6, 1967, file "D30, Roads & Trails: Winter Travel in Yellowstone, 1967," Box D-166, YNPA; "Chamber of Commerce Opposes Winter Opening of Y. P. Roads," *PCN,* Aug. 10, 1967; and Stan Regele to McGee, Aug. 9, 1967, and Art Bazata to McGee, Aug. 18, 1967, both in file "D30, Roads & Trails, Winter Travel in Yellowstone, 1967," Box D-166, YNPA. Manager sympathy from "Disadvantages to Winter Road Opening—Yellowstone," and "Oversnow Visitation," two white papers in file "D30, Roads & Trails 1967—Winter Travel in Yell./Snow Removal," Box D-164, YNPA.

30. "Oversnow Visitation," file "D30, Roads & Trails 1967—Winter Travel in Yell./Snow Removal," Box D-164, YNPA; and McLaughlin to Regional Director, June 14, 1967, file "A88: Oversnow Vehicle Travel," Box A-32, YNPA.

31. The NPS first offered to plow from Cooke City to the Wyoming-Montana state line in Gastellum to Director, Feb. 14, 1964, file "D30, Roads & Trails—Winter Travel—1965," Box D-126, YNPA. The agency already plowed the 4 miles from its Northeast Entrance to Cooke City, so plowing the additional 4 or so miles over Cooke Pass to the state line was not a significant additional burden. Because such plowing would likely reduce or eliminate the long-standing demands that managers plow park roads, they were probably willing to

accept the additional cost. See also U.S. Department of Transportation, Federal Highway Administration, and Wyoming Highway Department, *Final Environmental Impact Statement: Wyoming Highway Project FLH 18-4, Clarks Fork Canyon Road, Park County, Wyoming,* 1973.

32. Committee on Appropriations, *Winter Operation Hearing,* 1968, 3–15; Hartzog's quote from p. 64.

33. Ibid., in its entirety.

34. Ibid., 59–60 (Kelsey quote), 80, 91–92. Kelsey's numbers do not add up in his original quote; no explanation is given for the discrepancy.

35. Ibid., 86–96. Note that both the Wyoming and the national Izaak Walton League offices filed comments, but only the national office specifically endorsed snowmobiling.

36. Clifton R. Merritt to Theodor R. Swem, Oct. 2, 1967, and Murie to Brandborg, Feb. 25, 1967, both in file "States/Wyoming: Yellowstone National Park, 1964–1971," Box 7: 195, Wilderness Society Collection (CONS 130), DPL. Merritt had encouraged local conservationists to attend the hearing, but by the time he did, many already had prior commitments. Machine in the garden idea from Leo Marx, *The Machine in the Garden: Technology and the Pastoral Ideal in America* (New York: Oxford University Press, 1964).

37. "Summary of Issues Discussed at the Three Public Meetings of the Yellowstone–Grand Teton Master Plan Study Team," file "YNP—Master Plan Studies, 1967," Vertical files, YNPL. See also "Proposed Snowmobile Regulations," *Outdoor America,* Jan. 1968, and Malcolm F. Baldwin, "The Snowmobile and Environmental Quality," *Living Wilderness* (Winter 1968–1969): 14–17.

38. Biographical information from Aubrey L. Haines, *The Yellowstone Story: A History of Our First National Park,* rev. ed., vol. 2 (Yellowstone National Park, WY: Yellowstone Association for Natural Science, History & Education, in cooperation with the University Press of Colorado, 1996), 463. Sign over the desk from Richard Ludewig, interview by author, Mammoth Hot Springs, July 2, 2005. James A. Pritchard (*Preserving Yellowstone's Natural Conditions: Science and the Perception of Nature* [Lincoln: University of Nebraska Press, 1999], 201–250), Paul Schullery (*Searching for Yellowstone: Ecology and Wonder in the Last Wilderness* [Boston: Houghton Mifflin, 1997], 148–173, 193–216), and Richard West Sellars (*Preserving Nature in the National Parks: A History* [New Haven, CT: Yale University Press, 1997], 204–266) all discuss the fire- and bear-management controversies. Frank C. Craighead, in *Track of the Grizzly* (San Francisco: Sierra Club Books, 1979), provides his perspective on the grizzly bear controversy; Alice Wondrak Biel has written the most recent history of bear management in Yellowstone in *Do (Not) Feed the Bears: The Fitful History of Wildlife and Tourists in Yellowstone* (Lawrence: University Press of Kansas, 2006). Rocky Barker, in *Scorched Earth: How the Fires of Yellowstone Changed America* (Washington, DC: Island Press, 2005), provides a good, if somewhat journalistic, history of the evolution of fire policy, while Mary Ann Franke summarizes much of the knowledge gained about fires since 1988 in *Yellowstone in the Afterglow: Lessons from the Fires* (Mammoth Hot Springs, WY: National Park Service, 2000).

39. McLaughlin to Director, Sept. 18, 1967, and Harthon L. Bill to Superintendent, Oct. 12, 1967, both in file "D30, Roads & Trails 1967—Winter Travel in Yellowstone," Box D-166, YNPA.

40. Anderson to Jerry D. Atwood, July 1, 1968, file "D30, Roads & Trails: Winter Travel in Yell.—Snow Removal, 1968," Box D-164, YNPA; and "Winter Oversnow Vehicle Operations," minutes of March 18, 1968, meeting, file "L3427, Recreation Activities 1969—Winter Sports (Oversnow Vehicle Use)," Box L-42, YNPA. The date may have been March 17, 1969; see Robert J. Murphy to Chief, Division of Resources Management & Visitor Protection, March 28, 1968, same file and box as meeting minutes.

41. Jack Anderson, "Interview with Jack Anderson, former Park Superintendent," interview conducted by Bob Haraden and Al Mebane, June 12, 1975, Tape 75-3, Drawer 3, YNPA. Note that the idea of a gradual policy evolution differs from the understanding that the March meeting crisply produced the snowmobile policy, as articulated in my master's thesis ("Development of Snowmobile Policy").

42. Anderson to Atwood, July 1, 1968 (quote), file "D30, Roads & Trails: Winter Travel in Yell.—Snow Removal, 1968," Box D-164, YNPA; J. Leonard Volz to Director, Nov. 1971 (exact date indiscernible), file "S5831, Motor-Driven or Propelled Equipment, 1971," Box S-5, YNPA; Monte Later, interview by Lee Whittlesey, e-mail to author, July 11, 2002; and Jack Anderson, "Transcript of Conversation," interview by Jack Crandall, April 1, 1977, in "Snowmobile Briefing Book, Vol. 1," YNPL.

43. Yochim, "Development of Snowmobile Policy," 48–50; and James E. Fox to West District Ranger, May 3, 1970, file "L34, Recreation Activities—1970," Box A-36, YNPA.

44. Harold Estey to Superintendent, June 2, 1969, file "A88: Oversnow Vehicle Travel," Box A-32; and Estey to Superintendent, Feb. 16, 1970, file "A40, Conferences & Meetings, 1970," Box A-35, both in YNPA.

45. Anderson to George F. Baggley, Feb. 26, 1970, file "D30, Roads & Trails 1970," Box A-36; "Approved Equipment Inventory," June 10, 1970, file "S5831, Motor-Driven or Propelled Equipment, 1971," Box S-5; Minutes of staff meeting, Feb. 2, 1971, file "A40, Conferences & Meetings, 1971," Box A-37; Gary Everhardt to Midwest Regional Director, Nov. 8, 1971, and Estey to Acting Superintendent, Nov. 2, 1971, both in file "A6423, Park Mgt. 1971, Park Activity Standards," Box A-47; and Sellers to Gene Bryan, Dec. 20, 1971, file "L3427, Recreation Activities: Winter Sports," Box L-36, all at YNPA.

46. Minutes of March 18, 1968, meeting, file "L3427, Winter Sports—Oversnow Vehicle Use," Box N-115, YNPA; Huntley Child, Jr., to Warren Hamilton, April 1, 1958, file "NPS—1958 (General Correspondence)," Box YPC-92, YNPA; and Ludewig, interview by author, Mammoth Hot Springs, Wyoming, July 2, 2005.

47. "Yellowstone Snowtime Adventures," promotional brochure in executive secretary's office, Xanterra Parks & Resorts, Mammoth Hot Springs, Wyoming (quote); "Yellowstone Full Up for Holiday Season," *LVE*, Dec. 22, 1971; and "Annual Prospectus of Winter Use and Facilities (Winter 1971–72)," "File 2," Box L-59, YNPA. The winter operation was so successful that in 1973 the company permanently renamed the building "Old Faithful

Snowlodge," having previously reverted to its "Campers' Cabins" designation in summer ("Winter Info., 1977," vertical files, YNPL). New Snowlodge from Scott McMillion, "A Winter Visit to Yellowstone Doesn't Mean You'll Be Roughin' It," *Bozeman Daily Chronicle* (hereafter *BDC*), Feb. 22, 2000, and Ruth A. Quinn, "Introducing the Old Faithful Snow Lodge," *Commentary Newsletter,* Sept. 1999, 5–7.

48. Anderson to Martin, Dec. 29, 1969, file "A3815, Public Relations 1969 (Federal, State & Local Agencies)," Box A-158; "Yellowstone Keeps Pace with Rising Winter Use," press release, Nov. 22, 1971, file "K34, Press Releases, Yellowstone National Park," Box K-22; and Earl Young to Anderson, July 20, 1968, file "D30, Roads & Trails: Winter Travel in Yell.—Snow Removal, 1968," Box D-164, all in YNPA.

49. Anderson interview by Haraden and Mebane, June 12, 1975; "Lowell Thomas Visits I. F. Enroute to Park," *Idaho Falls (ID) Post-Register,* Feb. 26, 1969; Hack Miller, "The Joke of Yellowstone," March 6, 1969, and Miller, "And the Big Elk Grinned!" March 7, 1969, both in *(Salt Lake City) Deseret News.* Those assisting Anderson were Art Bazata of the Yellowstone Park Company, who knew Thomas from his time as a war correspondent in World War II; Monte Wight, the snowmobile dealer in Pinedale; and Harold Young, the snowcoach operator (now snowmobile rental owner) from West Yellowstone (Wight and Young were both connected to other individuals who knew Thomas).

50. Hansen to Hartzog, Jan. 9, 1969, file "D30, Roads & Trails: Winter Travel in Yellowstone/Snow Removal, 1969," Box D-168, YNPA; and Hathaway to Hartzog, March 4, 1970, McGee to Hartzog, March 18, 1970, and Harthon Bill to McGee, April 23, 1970, all in folder 11, Box 235, GMP, AHC. Lest the NPS believe that this would completely mollify Wyoming, Governor Hathaway reiterated his request for north-south and east-west plowed routes through or around Yellowstone (Hathaway to Bill, June 25, 1970, same file and box). See also Sellers to Gene Bryan, Dec. 14, 1971 (file "L3427: Recreation Activities/Winter Sports," Box L-36, YNPA), in which Yellowstone agreed to give Wyoming regular updates on snowmobiling conditions, further evidence that the state had come to accept the park's solution. No further efforts to open year-round east-west or north-south routes were undertaken by either the NPS or regional political representatives.

51. Yochim, "Development of Snowmobile Policy," 99, and Fox to West District Ranger, May 3, 1970, file "L34, Recreation Activities, 1970," Box A-36, YNPA.

52. Sound is measured in decibels (abbreviated dB) on a logarithmic scale. This means that every increase of 10 dB is equivalent to a doubling in sound intensity. The "A-weighted" scale is used to mimic human hearing, which is poorest at the high and low ends of the audible spectrum. Finally, snowmobiles are usually measured at 50 feet away to allow for sound attenuation.

53. Douglas J. Riley to West Sub-District Ranger, March 17, 1969, file "L3427: Winter Sports, Oversnow Vehicle Use," Box N-115; Pete Thompson to Chief Park Ranger, March 21, 1967, file "A88, Oversnow Vehicle Travel," Box A-32; Anderson to Regional Director, May 9, 1969, file "S5831, Motor Driven or Propelled Equipment, 1969," Box S-5; and Fox to West District Ranger, May 3, 1970, file "L34, Recreation Activities—1970," Box A-36 (air

pollution quote), all at YNPA. Note that Riley suggested that all snowmobilers travel with a certified guide, a policy that would not be fully adopted until 2004.

54. Anderson to Bud Reed, April 19, 1972, file "Correspondence 1969–1982," Box N-118; Bartley J. D'Alfonso to Anderson, Jan. 22, 1972, file "Complaints 1972, Service & Personnel," Box A-312; Anderson to Scott M. Bailey, Oct. 30, 1973, file "A3615, Complaints 1973," Box A-93; Anderson to Harvard K. Becker, Oct. 27, 1972, file "A3615, Jan. 1972 to Dec. 1972," Box W-101; Acting Superintendent Robert C. Haraden to Henry F. Shovic, Dec. 9, 1975, file "L—Land & Water Use," Box L-35; and Haraden to Lee Wood, March 31, 1972, Anderson to Wells B. Lange, Feb. 19, 1972, and Anderson to D. G. Carpenter, March 27, 1973, all in file "Historical Backcountry Correspondence," Box N-118; all at YNPA.

55. 34 *Federal Register* 11, Jan. 16, 1969; Anderson to Harold Young, Jan. 14, 1971, file "L3427, Rec. Activities: Winter Sports," Box L-36; Estey to Superintendent, Aug. 14, 1970, file "L34, Recreation Activities, 1970," Box A-36; Anderson to Regional Director, Dec. 8, 1970, with attached "Regulations Governing Winter Activities" and "Yellowstone National Park Snowmobile Regulations," file "L34, Recreation Activities," Box L-33, all at YNPA. Visitor center opening from Robert L. Schultz, "Winter Operations Brief," file "Oversnow Activities—Winter of 1969–1970," Box K-93, YNPA.

56. Richard T. Danforth to Superintendent through Chief Park Ranger and West District Ranger, Aug. 12, 1974, file "L3427, Winter Sports/Oversnow Vehicle Use," Box N-115, YNPA. See also Edmund J. Bucknall to Chief Park Ranger, March 16, 1970, file "L34, Recreation Activities, 1970," Box A-36, YNPA.

57. "Funmobile" from Peter Harnik, "Funmobile Folly," *National Parks & Conservation Magazine* (hereafter *National Parks*), Jan. 1972, 29–33. In places where snowmobiles were used primarily for utilitarian purposes (such as hunting in Alaska), an emphasis on their utility, more than their fun factor, would be expected. Mintzmyer's thoughts from Lorraine Denning (her surname in later life) to Suzanne Lewis, May 26, 2007, Third EIS Collection, MAOF.

58. Harnik, "Funmobile Folly." See also Baldwin, "Snowmobile and Environmental Quality."

59. Harnik, "Funmobile Folly"; Gary A. Soucie (of the Sierra Club) to Fran Belcher et al., March 4, 1969, file "Correspondence/Subjects: Snowmobiles, 1967–1969," Box 4:407, TWS; "Snowmobiles: Random Regulations," *National Parks,* June 1976, 23, 25; Les Line and James D. Perry, "Snowmobiles: Love 'em or Hate 'em," *National Wildlife,* Dec.-Jan. 1972, 21–23; Brandborg to Hartzog, Feb. 3, 1970, and Hummel to Wilderness Society, March 20, 1970, both in file "Correspondence/Subjects: Snowmobiles, 1970–1972," Box 4:407, TWS. The NPS's basic regulations were published in 35 *Federal Register* 19: 11553, July 18, 1970. The agency revised the policy on Dec. 12, 1970, to allow snowmobile races, but only in recreation areas (35 *Federal Register* 241: 18915). Glacier snowmobile ban from Michael J. Yochim, "Snow Machines in the Gardens: The History of Snowmobiles in Glacier and Yellowstone National Parks," *Montana: The Magazine of Western History* 53 (Autumn 2003): 2–15.

60. Harnik, "Funmobile Folly"; and Baldwin, "Snowmobile and Environmental Quality." Noise regulations from C. L. Hanner to Director, Midwest Region, June 14, 1972, file "Historical Backcountry Correspondence," Box N-118, YNPA. The noise regulation still stands (36 Code of Federal Regulations [CFR] Chapter 1, § 2.18 [d][1]).

61. United States Congress, Senate Committee on Interior and Insular Affairs, Subcommittee on Parks and Recreation, *Snowmobiles and Other Off-Road Vehicles: A Study of the Effects of the Rapidly Expanding Use of All Terrain Vehicles on the Public Lands,* 92nd Cong., 1st sess., May 21, 1971. Morton's task force from "Interior Organizes Study Group for Off-Road Recreational Vehicles," press release, April 14, 1971, file "S5831, Motor-Driven or Propelled Equipment, 1971," Box S5; his visit from Estey to Robert B. Ranck, Dec. 20, 1974, file "W42, Special Regulations, 1973–75," Box W-129; and EPA hearings from Superintendent, Rocky Mountain Group, to Assistant Superintendent, Operations, Oct. 7, 1971, file "N36: Pollution, General," Box N-116, all at YNPA.

62. Executive Order 11644, Feb. 8, 1972, 42 U.S.C.A. § 4321, and *Conservation Law Foundation of New England v. Clark,* 590 F. Supp. 1467 (1984), 1467–1490.

63. 39 *Federal Register* 63: 11882–11883, April 1, 1974, and 44 *Federal Register* 157: 47412–47414, Aug. 13, 1979. The NPS clarified and strengthened its snowmobile policy in 1983, adding safety considerations and park management objectives to the list of factors to be considered in admitting snowmobiles (48 *Federal Register* 127: 30258, June 30, 1983). The 1983 regulations still guide snowmobile use in the national parks, although most parks have either banned the activity since 1974 or have special regulations directing such use therein. History of NEPA from Zygmunt J. B. Plater, Robert H. Abrams, and William Goldfarb, *Environmental Law and Policy: A Coursebook on Nature, Law, and Society* (St. Paul: West Publishing, 1992), 599–603.

64. 39 *Federal Register* 89: 16151, May 7, 1974; and Acting Regional Director to Superintendents, Rocky Mountain Region, June 21, 1974, in "Snowmobile EA" Box, Glacier National Park Archives, West Glacier, Montana. Because I have been unable to find this memo in Yellowstone's archives, it is not entirely certain that Anderson was aware of it or Bean's directive to examine the environmental impact of snowmobiles.

65. "Snowmobilers' Guide to Rules of the National Parks," *Snow Travel,* Dec. 1966, 18–19.

66. "Acreages—Snowmobile Area," in "Snowmobile Briefing Book," YNPL; "Watt Gets Snowmobiles into Lassen Volcanic," *National Parks,* March/April 1982, 34; Yochim, "Snow Machines in the Gardens"; Acting Regional Director, Western Region, to Director, Sept. 13, 1985, Lassen National Park files, Mineral, California; and Gene Rose, "Court Decision Expected in Yosemite Snowmobiling Case," *Fresno (CA) Bee,* Nov. 9, 1975.

67. Dan Hughes, "Crashing through the Snow," *National Park Newsletter,* Jan. 1977, 1–2 (found in "Articles" file, YNPV); Department of the Interior, "Environmental Assessment: Alternatives for Management of Oversnow Vehicle Use, Grand Teton National Park," loose within "Winter Use Plan EA" Box, MAOF; Theodore Catton, "Wonderland: An Administrative History of Mount Rainier National Park," May 1996, Mount Rainier National Park

files, Ashford, Washington; and "Snowmobile Summit, Feb. 23–24, 2000," file "Materials from NPS Snowmobile Summit . . . , 2/22/00," EIS Collection, MAOF. The listing reflects only national parks; several national recreation areas, lakeshores, monuments, and other NPS sites continued to allow snowmobiling as well.

68. Jack Anderson, "Transcript of Conversation," interview by Derrick Crandall, April 1, 1977, YNPL.

69. Quotes from Anderson, interview by Derrick Crandall, April 1, 1977. Award of Merit from Michael Frome, *Regreening the National Parks* (Tucson: University of Arizona Press, 1992), 197–198. The quote is taken directly from the award, held in the museum collection at the Yellowstone Heritage and Research Center, Gardiner, Montana.

70. Michael J. Yochim, "A Water Wilderness: Battles over Values and Motorboats on Yellowstone Lake," *Historical Geography* 35 (2007): 185–213, and "Compromising Yellowstone: The Interest Group–National Park Service Relationship in Modern Policy-Making" (Ph.D. dissertation, University of Wisconsin–Madison, 2004), 32–93.

71. Biographical info from "Yellowstone Park Chief Dies of Cancer," *BDC*, Sept. 21, 1982. General Host removal from Schullery, *Searching for Yellowstone*, 180, and Ludewig interview, July 2, 2005. Townsley's management character from author's personal interviews with Joe Halladay, May 29, 1997, Belgrade, Montana; Mary Meagher, Nov. 3, 1997, telephone interview; Dale Nuss, Bridger Canyon, Montana, Nov. 11, 1997; and Jerry Mernin, Bozeman, Montana, Nov. 11, 1997.

72. Grooming in the evening from Lynn H. Thompson to Hubert H. Humphrey, April 8, 1976, draft, file "D30—Roads & Trails," Box D-78, YNPA. Sylvan Pass grooming from Peter J. McNiff to Jack Anderson, Jan. 7, 1975, and Russell Dupuis to Anderson, Feb. 21, 1975, both in file "Correspondence, Memoranda, and Reports, 1972–1975," Box D-199, YNPA; Jim Miller, "Are There Snowmobiles in Cody's Economic Future?" *CEP*, Feb. 4, 1976; and Miller, "Sylvan Stays Open for Snowmobiles," *CEP*, Sept. 29, 1976. The following year the NPS stationed the new grooming machine at Lake, where it could serve the East Entrance Road and also groom other roads in the Lake area.

73. Warming huts: SARs, 1977, 11, and 1983, 13. Driver's license change from Robert E. Sellers to W. C. Shields, May 30, 1975, file "W42—Special Regulations, 1973–75," Box W-129, YNPA.

74. Ben Clary to H. L. Ritchie, Aug. 25, 1982, file "Winter Concessions Reports," Box "Winter Use Plan EA," MAOF, and SAR, 1984, 6. The hotel's name was changed between 1970 and 1980 from the Mammoth Motor Inn to the Mammoth Hot Springs Hotel.

75. Approach to complaints from "Position Statement" and "Grooming/Winter Preparations Cost," both in "Snowmobile Briefing Book," vol. 1, YNPL. Quote from Townsley to Rosemary Johnston, Feb. 18, 1977, file "Conference & Mtgs—1977 General," Box A-189, YNPA. Request to jump snowmobile from Jerry R. Phillips to William M. Kirkpatrick, Jr., Attorney at Law, from Butte, Montana, Jan. 24, 1977, file "W46—General Regulations '75, '76, '77," Box W-129, YNPA. Kirkpatrick's client may have been well-known stuntsman Evel Knievel, who was from Butte and had a long-term interest both in Yellowstone issues

and in jumping his motorcycle over the Grand Canyon in Arizona (http://www.evelknievel
.com/bio.html, accessed May 31, 2006).

76. Executive Order 11989, May 24, 1977, 42 U.S.C.A. § 4321. Unlike Executive Order 11644, Carter's order has been interpreted by the courts as lacking regulatory teeth (*Sierra Club v. Clark,* 756 F. 2d 1276). NPS committee from SAR, 1977, 37. National policy and quote from 44 *Federal Register* 157: 47412–47414, Aug. 13, 1979. Conservationist concern from Destry Jarvis, "Snowmobiles: Intruders into Peaceful Winter Parklands," *ORV Monitor,* Jan. 1979 (published by the Sierra Club and found in file "Winter Activities," Box K-57, YNPA); and "NPS Proposes to Open Parks to More Snowmobiling," *National Parks,* April 1979, 26–30. Lack of conservationist alternative to snowmobiling also evident in Verne Huser, "The Winter Wonderland of Yellowstone," *National Parks,* Jan. 1981, 4–9. (Huser gave directions on how to book travel on a snowcoach, but he did not present them as a solution to the snowmobile problems that he also discussed.)

77. Minutes of Town Council meetings on Nov. 16, 1966; Nov. 14, 1967; Jan. 4, 1968; Oct. 8, 1968; and Dec. 20, 1973; and Town of West Yellowstone Resolutions 38 (Dec. 1968) and 62 (Dec. 20, 1973), all at the Yellowstone Historic Center archives, West Yellowstone, Montana; and Paul Shea, archivist, Yellowstone Historic Center, personal communication with author, e-mail, July 15, 2005.

78. Jean Arthur Sellegren, "Blue Haze: Multi-Use Issues Come to a Head in the Land of the Buffalo," *Backcountry,* Jan. 1996, 52–54.

79. Advertising and package tour from Darcy L. Fawcett, "Colonial Status: The Search for Independence in West Yellowstone, Montana" (professional paper, Montana State University, 1993), 21–27. Bar information from John Miller, "West Yellowstone: Montana's Biggest Little Town," *BDC,* Feb. 28, 1999. Big Sky opening from Phyllis Smith, *Bozeman and the Gallatin Valley: A History* (Helena, MT: Two Dot Press, an imprint of Falcon Press, 1996), 290–292. "Having fun" is still a primary component of snowmobiling; see James T. Sylvester and Marlene Nesary, "Snowmobiling in Montana: An Update," *Montana Business Quarterly* (Winter 1994), 3–8 (quote p. 7).

80. Fawcett, "Colonial Status," 21, 27; Calvin W. Dunbar, "Testimony before the Subcommittee on Public Lands and National Parks," [May 1983], loose within "Winter Use Plan EA" Box, MAOF; and Darryl Harris, "Winter Season Extension Needed at Yellowstone," *Snowmobile West,* Sept. 1985, 63–64.

81. James A. Jurale, "History of Winter Use in Yellowstone National Park," (Master's thesis, University of Wyoming, 1986), 135. See also Randy Roberson, "Data Supports Continued Use of Snowmobiles in Park," *BDC,* Nov. 5, 1999. See Chapter 5 for a discussion of how Cody, drawing upon similar meanings for itself, was motivated to oppose a 2006 proposal to close Sylvan Pass entirely in winter.

82. Visitation from Yochim, "Development of Snowmobile Policy," 117. Form letter from Townsley to concerned individuals, undated, file "Correspondence to & from John Townsley," Box A-1, YNPA; protest letters; and "Winter Opening Scheduled for Yellowstone National Park," press release, Aug. 18, 1981, all in file "A36: Protest Letters Re: Winter Closing of

1981," Box A-112, YNPA. According to former Montana U.S. Congressman Pat Williams (personal interview by author, Missoula, Montana, April 22, 1997), Watt's actual motive was to close Yellowstone in winter, and the congressional representatives arranged his visit to convince him to keep the park open. All other sources, though, indicate that Watt visited in order to promote snowmobile use in Yellowstone and other national parks. Indeed, closing the park would have seemed out of character for him (see the various clippings and press releases in file "History—YNP—Special Events [Watt]," YNPV). Watt went on to reopen Lassen Volcanic National Park to snowmobiles a year later ("Watt Gets Snowmobiles into Lassen Volcanic," 34), but he was not successful in promoting the activity in other national parks. Lassen closed its doors to snowmobiles a few years later owing to lack of snowmobiler interest in touring the park ("Finding of No Significant Impact, Snowmobile Use, Lassen Volcanic National Park," Sept. 30, 1985, Lassen National Park files, Mineral, California).

83. 48 *Federal Register* 127: 30258, June 30, 1983; Dick Randall, "Snowmobilers Return to Wyoming's Potholes," *Defenders*, Dec. 1979, 404; and Jack E. Stark to William Edwards, Feb. 11, 1981, file "L3427, Recreation Activities—Winter Sports 1981," Box L-73, YNPA. *Defenders* was motivated to become involved in the controversy because snowmobilers had killed two coyotes in the area in March 1979 (Dick Randall, "Snowmobiles Kill Coyotes in Wyoming National Park," *Defenders*, June 1979, 180).

84. "International Snowmobile Industry Association Citation," May 3, 1981, and "National Park Service Official Receives International Award," press release, May 3, [1981], both in file "Correspondence to & from John Townsley," Box A-1, YNPA; and "Townsley Called 'Great Tribute' to Park Service," *(Cheyenne) Wyoming State Tribune*, Sept. 21, 1982.

85. Nancy Langston, in *Forest Dreams, Forest Nightmares: The Paradox of Old Growth in the Inland West* (Seattle: University of Washington Press, 1995), chronicles a similar effort by U.S. Forest Service managers to prevent a state of existence for their lands that, over time, they inadvertently created.

86. Danforth to Superintendent through Chief Park Ranger and West District Ranger, Aug. 12, 1974, file "L3427, Winter Sports/Oversnow Vehicle Use," Box N-115, YNPA.

CHAPTER THREE. SKATING ON A VERY THIN EDGE

1. Gerald Mernin to Superintendent, March 1, 1984, file "Meetings & Comments, WUSE [evidently an abbreviation for 'Winter Use']," Box "Winter Use Plan EA" (hereafter "WUPEA Box #1"), and [Lorraine Mintzmyer] to Director, n.d., file "Evaluation Report and Input Material," Box "Winter Use Plan EA 1989/90" (hereafter "WUPEA Box #2"), both in MAOF; and Bob Barbee, as quoted in Todd Wilkinson, "Winter Paradox: Yellowstone Struggles to Retain Its Tranquility amid Growing Demands for Winter Tourism," *National Parks*, Nov./Dec. 1990, 32.

2. See the various works by Pritchard, Haines, Bartlett, Runte, and Schullery cited in the Introduction; Barbee himself also made a comment to this end in my personal interview with him in Bozeman, Montana, April 8, 2003.

3. Michael J. Yochim, "Compromising Yellowstone: The Interest Group–National Park

Service Relationship in Modern Policy-Making" (Ph.D. dissertation, University of Wisconsin–Madison, 2004), 100; Rocky Barker, *Scorched Earth: How the Fires of Yellowstone Changed America* (Washington, DC: Island Press, 2005), 172–173; Barbee quote from Jon Jarvis, compiler and editor, "Bob Barbeeisms: Quips, Snappy Comebacks, and Throw-Away Lines for a Successful Career in the National Park Service," Aug. 2000 (a collection of his more memorable lines assembled to commemorate his NPS career as he retired), author's personal collection.

4. John Hamer, in "Geysers and Ice," *Seattle Post-Intelligencer,* Oct. 26, 1986, provides a glimpse into the typical visitor's experience. In describing the Yellowstone "place," I draw upon Yi-Fu Tuan's *Space and Place: The Perspective of Experience* (Minneapolis: University of Minnesota Press, 1977), 54.

5. Barbee to Marge Wanner and Pat Williams, both on Nov. 8, 1985, file "A38—Public Relations," Box W-169, YNPA; Barbee to Ray [*sic*—should be Roy] Muth, Dec. 17, 1987, file "N615, Social & Economic Sciences 1987, Visitor Use Surveys & Statistics," Box N-122, YNPA; and Thomas J. Knudson, "Yellowstone and Its Staff Strained as Ranks of Winter Visitors Swell," *New York Times* (hereafter *NYT*), March 24, 1987.

6. Michael J. Yochim, "The Development of Snowmobile Policy in Yellowstone National Park" (Master's thesis, University of Montana, 1998), 117, 123; Barbee, personal interview by author, Bozeman, Montana, March 24, 2003; and "Statement for Management, Yellowstone National Park," Aug. 1986, 16, 36, MAOF.

7. "Summary, Winter Use Plan, Jan. 28, 1986," file "Winter Use Plan," WUPEA Box #1, MAOF, and "1989 Compendium: 36 CFR 1.7(b)," file "W34—Law Enforcement," Box W-203, YNPA.

8. Barbee to Patricia M. Moon, March 7, 1986, file "L3427, Recreation Activities 1986—Winter Sports," Box L-48, and Kurt Westenbarger to Barbee, Jan. 6, 1990, author's personal collection. See also Barbee to David Bates, March 16, 1987, file "A36, Complaints," Box W-173, and numerous complaints in file "L3427, Recreation Activities—Winter Sports 1990," Box L-73, all at YNPA.

9. Robert Ekey, "Park Plans for Winter Population Boom," *BGZ,* March 20, 1985; Keith E. Aune, "Impacts of Winter Recreationists on Wildlife in a Portion of Yellowstone National Park, Wyoming" (Master's thesis, Montana State University, 1981); and E. Frances Cassirer, David J. Freddy, and Ernest D. Ables, "Elk Responses to Disturbance by Cross-Country Skiers in Yellowstone National Park," *Wildlife Society Bulletin* 20 (1992): 375–381 (most of the latter's research was performed in the late 1980s and was available to park managers at that time—see Barbee to Director, Aug. 12, 1988, file "L3427, Recreation Activities—Winter Sports 1988," Box L-73, YNPA).

10. Quote from Mernin to Superintendent, March 1, 1984, file "Meetings & Comments, WUSE," Box "Winter Use Plan EA"; Barbee, personal interview by author, Bozeman, Montana, March 24, 2003, and telephone interview by author, March 20, 2006; Steve Iobst, personal interview by author, Mammoth Hot Springs, April 4, 2003; Minutes of 1984 Spring Meeting between NPS and Yellowstone Concessioners, file "A40—Conferences and Meetings," Box

W-169, YNPA; Barbee to Sherry Funke, March 20, 1985, file "A3615, Complaints (NPS)," Box W-169, YNPA; and H. L. Ritchie to Barbee, Feb. 1, 1984, loose within WUPEA Box #1, MAOF.

11. SAR, 1983, 56; Barbee to Division Chiefs, District Rangers, Area Rangers, District Naturalists, and Maintenance Area Foreman, Feb. 6, 1984, file "N4615, Soc. & Econ. Sciences, 1984," Box N-150, YNPA; Barbee telephone interview, March 20, 2006; and John Lounsbury to Superintendent's Office, Feb. 8, 1984, Mernin to Superintendent, March 1, 1984, and Douglas A. Barnard to Landscape Architect, March 1, 1984, all in file "Meetings & Comments, WUSE," WUPEA Box #1, MAOF.

12. "Winter Use Plan Environmental Assessment," Working Draft—Third Edition, June 18, 1984, file "WUSE—Purpose and Need & Objectives," WUPEA Box #2, MAOF, and Steve Martin to Chief of Research, Oct. 25, 1984, file "D—Development & Mtnce.," Box W-170, YNPA.

13. SAR, 1985, 36 (quote); Dan Sholly to Iobst, Feb. 17, 1986, and "Issues for Management Decision—Winter Use Plan, June 1986," both in file "Winter Use Plan," WUPEA Box #1, MAOF; and Iobst to Winter Use Planning Team, April 15, 1986, file "Visitor Use Management—Winter Use Plan—1987 and Before," Box N-366, YNPA.

14. Delays from SAR, 1986, 37; and Iobst to All Park Supervisors, July 7, 1988 (quote), file "Spawners," WUPEA Box #2, MAOF. More detailed examinations of the Fishing Bridge controversy can be found in Yochim, "Compromising Yellowstone," 94–152, and Sue Consolo Murphy and Beth Kaeding, "Fishing Bridge: 25 Years of Controversy Regarding Grizzly Bear Management in Yellowstone National Park," *Ursus* 10 (1998): 385–393.

15. Yochim, "Compromising Yellowstone," 153–236; and Barker, *Scorched Earth*.

16. Regional Director to Director, n.d., attached to Regional Director to Superintendent, April 6, 1987, file "Evaluation Report and Input Material," WUPEA Box #2, MAOF. The Winter Use Plan was called a "Development Concept Plan," which was the term used for an area-specific master plan, a common type of plan with the agency during this era.

17. "Congressional Visit to Yellowtone [*sic*] to Review Winter Operations," press release, Feb. 6, 1988, and "Congressional Response to Winter Trip in Yellowstone," press release, Feb. 9, 1988, both in file "[Untitled]," Box K-108; J. Bennett Johnston, James M. McClure, and Malcolm Wallop to Robert C. Byrd, June 8, 1988, file "Winter—General $ Cost," WUPEA Box #2, MAOF; Elizabeth Laden, "Yellowstone National Park Wants More Money for Winter Season," *BDC*, Feb. 17, 1988; and Knudson, "Yellowstone and Its Staff Strained." Allocation of $1.4 million from Tim A. Hudson to Fiscal, Aug. 30, 1989, file "Winter VSP," WUPEA Box #2, MAOF.

18. "Existing Winter Use Management Guidelines, Inventory, and Needs, Yellowstone National Park," March 1989, MAOF, and Tom Howard, "Park Planners Return to Winter-Use Study," *BGZ*, Jan. 8, 1988.

19. Rick Reese, *Greater Yellowstone: The National Park & Adjacent Wildlands* (Helena, MT: American & World Geographic Publishing, 1991), 7–8; see also Frank C. Craighead, *Track of the Grizzly* (San Francisco: Sierra Club Books, 1979) (the "Yellowstone Ecosystem" is specifically mentioned on page 4). Clearcuts from http://www.wildrockiesalliance.org/news/2004/11_12_targheehalt.html, accessed Feb. 27, 2006.

20. Reese, *Greater Yellowstone*, 7–8.

21. Ibid., 8; "1983: The Founding Year," *Greater Yellowstone Report* (hereafter *GYR*), Spring 1984 (quote); and "Coalition Goes Public," *GYR*, Fall 1984. (The *Greater Yellowstone Report* is the group's quarterly magazine; I found this issue in file "1500—External Relations—Greater Yellowstone Coalition—File 1," Box A-392, YNPA. The Bozeman-based group is likely to have all previous issues as well.) See also Michael P. Cohen, *The History of the Sierra Club* (San Francisco: Sierra Club Books, 1988). Though the actors did not use the phrase "conservation biology," their emphasis on the ecosystem theme and their subsequent success match the wider national preservationist emphasis on biodiversity protection that began during this era, as discussed and critiqued (but also supported) by Thomas R. Vale, *The American Wilderness: Reflections on Nature Protection in the United States* (Charlottesville: University of Virginia Press, 2005), 203–221.

22. As summarized and quoted in Reese, *Greater Yellowstone*, 10–11. See also "Yellowstone Unbound," *National Parks*, Nov./Dec. 1985, 10–11, written by Bob Anderson, executive director of the GYC at the time; as well as Charles E. Little, "The Challenge of Greater Yellowstone: A Report on the 'Crown Jewel' of the Nation's Ecosystems," *Wilderness*, Winter 1987, 18–50.

23. "Coalition Goes Public," *GYR*, Fall 1984; Marjane Ambler, "Yellowstone Coalition Is Confronted by Its Ex-Head," *High Country News* (hereafter *HCN*), June 23, 1986; Reese, *Greater Yellowstone*, 11; and Charles E. Little, "Yellowstone and the Holistic Imperative," *Wilderness*, Winter 1987, 51. See Lewis to GYC Board Executive Committee, June 23, 1993, memo, and Gretchen Long Glickman to GYC Executive Committee, June 23, 1993, both in file "Noranda Memos," GYC Noranda Collection, for examples in which GYC employees argued in favor of opposing a large gold mine proposed near Yellowstone because such an action would provide an opportunity to argue for coordinated ecosystem management.

24. "1983: The Founding Year," *GYR*, Spring 1984; Ed Lewis and Michael Scott to Mintzmyer, May 2, 1988 (quote); Terri Martin to Barbee, April 19, 1988; and Mintzmyer to Lewis and Scott (separately, for Scott was with the Wilderness Society at the time; in about 1999, he became the GYC's executive director), June 9, 1988, all in file "WUP Public Input Report," WUPEA Box #1, MAOF; and Paul Richards, "Yellowstone Winter Proposal Draws Fire," *HCN*, March 18, 1988, 7.

25. Benton J. Clary to Division Chiefs, All Supervisors, March 20, 1989, file "Visitor Use Management—Winter Use Plan—1988–1992," Box N-366, YNPA; "Joint Winter Use Planning Process Begins," April 13, 1989, press release, loose within WUPEA Box #1, MAOF; and SAR, 1989, 55–56.

26. Don Bachman to Rick Alesch, May 5, 1989, and "Public Input Report, Winter Use Plan Issues, Yellowstone and Grand Teton National Parks," May 1989, file "2300—Recreation Management," Box A-394, YNPA. See also Susan Dejmal to Friend of Greater Yellowstone, April 19, 1989 (a letter encouraging members to file comments), file "Winter Use Correspondence," Greater Yellowstone Coalition files (hereafter GYC), in which Dejmal states, "In national parks like Yellowstone and Grand Teton, . . . [t]he aesthetic is remarkably pastoral, and the visitor can find true serenity."

27. Bachman to Alesch, May 5, 1989, and "Public Input Report, Winter Use Plan Issues, Yellowstone and Grand Teton National Parks," May 1989, file "2300—Recreation Management," both in Box A-394, YNPA; and Lewis and Scott to Mintzmyer, May 2, 1988, file "Mailing List," Box "Winter Use Plan EA," MAOF.

28. Wyoming Recreation Commission and the Wyoming Continental Divide Snowmobile Trail Association, "Proposal for the Wyoming Continental Divide Snowmobile Trail," June 1988, file of same name, Research Collection, MAOF.

29. Malcolm Wallop to Jack Stark, June 30, 1988, and Dick Cheney to Mintzmyer, Oct. 26, 1988, both in file "Winter Use Correspondence," GYC; Mary Odde to Mintzmyer, Dec. 16, 1988, file "L3427, Recreation Activities—Winter Sports 1989," Box L-73, YNPA; and "Public Input Report," file "2300—Recreation Management," Box A-394, YNPA (this file and box contains letters from the groups mentioned in the text promoting their viewpoints).

30. Adena Cook to Winter Use Plan Project Manager, May 11, 1989, file "2300—Recreation Management," Box A-394, YNPA.

31. Robert Gottlieb, *Forcing the Spring: The Transformation of the American Environmental Movement* (Washington, DC: Island Press, 1993), 316–317; Daniel Kemmis, *This Sovereign Land: A New Vision for Governing the West* (Washington, DC: Island Press, 2001), 12, 59; and Michael Frome, *Regreening the National Parks* (Tucson: University of Arizona Press, 1992), 1992, 39–45.

32. Elizabeth Manning, "Motorheads: The New, Noisy, Organized Force in the West," *HCN*, Dec. 9, 1996, 1, 10–13; Clark Collins, "10 Years: A Milestone for BlueRibbon," *BlueRibbon Magazine* (hereafter *BRM*), May 1997, 3; and Collins, "How a Bill Became a Law," *BRM*, Jan. 1992, 10. Don Amador, in an edition of *BlueRibbon Magazine* celebrating the group's twentieth anniversary, wrote, "Do some of our detractors in legislative halls or conference centers still consider OHV recreation advocates politically insignificant? I would say that number has dwindled significantly in the last two decades" ("The Evolution of Recreation Advocacy," *BRM*, May 2007, 22).

33. Clark Collins, "BlueRibbon Promotes Recreation," *BRM*, June/July 1989, B5; "The BlueRibbon Coalition: An Overview," *BRM*, July 1992, 12; Collins, "How a Bill Became a Law," 10; and Darryl Harris, "BlueRibbon Origins: Telling the Tale," *BRM*, April 1997, 18. Example of funding from "Blue Ribbon Support," *BRM*, Dec. 1990, 20; see also "Earth Day and Mining," *BRM*, April/May 1990, 16.

34. Motto from Darryl W. Harris, "Blue Ribbon's Premier Issue in Your Hands," *BRM*, May 1987, A6. Second quote from Clark Collins, "Join the 'New Environmental Movement,'" *BRM*, May 1987, A7. Name logic from Clark Collins, "BlueRibbon Means Quality," *BRM*, Sept. 1991, 3 (not long after the first article, the group started combining the two words "Blue" and "Ribbon"; the reason for this action is unclear). See Manning, "Motorheads," for more on this and the family and freedom themes. Advocacy from Willy Marshall, "So They Just Threw Up a Gate across Your Trail," *BRM*, Jan. 1990, 5.

35. Examples of such articles include Kay Lloyd and Ron Hadford, "Wilderness Legisla-

tion Violated Civil Rights of Americans," *BRM,* May 1988, 8; Cyndi Likes, "Wilderness Threatens Recreational Opportunities," *BRM,* Dec. 1987, A4; "Eco-War Strategy of the Antis!" (one of several labels the group has applied to conservationists), *BRM,* Sept. 1993, 13; and Alston Chase, "Go Where the Money Is: Become an Environmentalist," *BRM,* Feb. 1995, 12. Hiring legal team in Collins, "10 Years," 3.

36. John W. Bright to Regional Director, April 20, 1989, loose within WUPEA Box #1, MAOF; and Cheney to Mintzmyer, Oct. 26, 1988, and Mike Sullivan to Mintzmyer, Dec. 22, 1988, both in file "Winter Use Correspondence," GYC. Note that the plan also included the John D. Rockefeller, Jr., Memorial Parkway, a small NPS unit between Yellowstone and Grand Teton. Because the parkway is administered by Grand Teton, generally shares the same policies as that park, and is relatively unknown in comparison with its two larger neighbors, the reader should assume that all references to winter use planning involving Grand Teton National Park also include the parkway.

37. Christopher C. Marvel to Chief, Division of Planning and Compliance, Rocky Mountain Region, June 22, 1989, and Alesch to Winter Use Planning Team, July 10, 1989, both in file "Winter Use—Current File," WUPEA Box #2, MAOF. Planners also investigated snowmobile use in Rocky Mountain National Park, finding that snowmobiles and autos shared a 10-mile stretch of road, with travel restricted to 25 mph. Perhaps because the CDST through Grand Teton would be much longer, they did not adopt this possibility for the trail there, although the exact reason is unknown (Alesch and Bill Conrod, "Special Park Snowmobile Regulations: Exceptions to NPS Management Policies," July 1989, file "Winter Use: Current File," and Alesch to Manager, Central Team, Denver Service Center, file "Memos," both in WUPEA Box #2, MAOF.

38. Alesch to Winter Use Planning Team, July 10, 1989, file "Winter Use—Current File," WUPEA Box #2, MAOF.

39. Ibid. Note that the plowing proposal was significantly reduced from that proposed by some employees and members of the public (their specific ideas were not documented, but most likely involved plowing the west side mid-elevation roads or more), and that snowmobiling on Yellowstone Lake's frozen surface (among the original ideas) was also discarded.

40. "Newsletter for the Joint Winter Use Plan," Sept. 1989, file "Winter Use Plan," WUPEA Box #1, MAOF; and Janet H. Ellis to Alesch, Oct. 31, 1989, file "Winter Use," Box A-362, YNPA.

41. Call for comments from Bachman to Bozeman area activists, Nov. 2, 1989; "Yellowstone and Winter Use: The Resource Must Come First!" (informational flyer from the Wilderness Society); and Terri Martin to GYE [Greater Yellowstone Ecosystem] Activists, Nov. 22, 1989, all in file "Winter Use Correspondence," GYC. Comment summary from Denver Service Center, "Public Input Report, Winter Use Plan Alternatives, Yellowstone and Grand Teton National Parks," Nov. 1989, file "Winter Use," Box A-362, YNPA.

42. Denver Service Center, "Public Input Report," Nov. 1989, file "Winter Use," Box A-362, YNPA; "Written Responses from Employees," Nov. 1989, file "WUP Comments," WU-

PEA Box #2, MAOF; and Ron Marlenee to Alesch, Nov. 1, 1989 (quote), and Roy Muth of the ISIA to Alesch, Nov. 9, 1989, both in file "Winter Use," Box A-362, YNPA.

43. Terri Martin to Alesch, Nov. 16, 1989, and Denver Service Center, "Public Input Report," Nov. 1989, both in file "Winter Use," Box A-362, YNPA. See also Todd Wilkinson, "Yellowstone in Winter: Is There Room for Everyone?" *HCN*, March 26, 1990, 1, 8–9.

44. Terri Martin to Alesch, Nov. 16, 1989, and Ellis to Alesch, Oct. 31, 1989, both in file "Winter Use," Box A-362, YNPA. Not all commenters fell tidily into one group or the other. For example, TW Services, Yellowstone's primary concessioner by this time, endorsed the CDST but objected to increasing lodging within Yellowstone. Both positions made sense for the company—the existing lodging barely turned a profit, so opening more was financially questionable, but stimulating business vis-à-vis the CDST would help remedy that situation (S. W. Tedder, winter use plan comments, Oct. 31, 1989, file "Winter Use," Box A-362, YNPA).

45. "Planning Team Recommendation: Proposal for the Winter Use Plan," Dec. 26, 1989, file "Winter VSP," and Alesch to Manager, Central Team, Denver Service Center, Feb. 27, 1990, file "Memos," both in WUPEA Box #2, MAOF.

46. U.S. Department of the Interior/NPS, "Winter Use Survey," Jan. 1990, file of same name, Research Collection, MAOF.

47. Informal, interoffice memo between GYC staffers Todd and Ed, Louisa, Don, and Dennis [last names not given], May 25, 1989, and "Notes on the Meeting between Kevin Brant of the Planning Office, Yellowstone National Park Service, Michael Scott, Larry Mehlhaff, Louisa Willcox, [and] Don Bachman on Sept. 13, 1989," both in file "Winter Use Correspondence," GYC. Cody support from Bob Coe to Barbee, March 30, 1990, file "Letter from Cody Chamber," Box "Misc. Files 1990 WUP" (hereafter "WUPEA Box #3"), MAOF. See also the many letters from Wyoming snowmobile boosters to the NPS (often specifically Ric Alesch) in file "Winter Use," Box A-362, YNPA.

48. Yochim, "Compromising Yellowstone," 94–152 (see especially p. 119). Other residents in and near Cody were inclined to view NPS winter use planning suspiciously because of their experiences with Fishing Bridge, as illustrated in James Hayes to Alesch, Nov. 17, 1989, file "WUP Comments," WUPEA Box #2, MAOF.

49. Paul E. Polzin and Tat P. Fong, "Snowmobiling in Montana: An Economic Study," *Montana Business Quarterly*, Winter 1988, 3–10; Judy S. Clayton, "Continental Divide Snowmobile Trail to Open," *BRM*, Jan. 1995, 6; and "Riding the Peaks and Ridges," *BRM*, Jan. 1989, 1. Rental machines from National Park Service, *Winter Use Plan Environmental Assessment*, Nov. 1990 (hereafter "NPS, *WUPEA*"), 21.

50. Alan Simpson to James Ridenour, Jan. 21, 1990, file "Correspondence—WUP," WUPEA Box #1, MAOF. See also "Plans for Future of Yellowstone Released," *National Parks*, Sept./Oct. 1990, 9–10.

51. Mintzmyer to Simpson, Feb. 13, 1990, file "Correspondence—WUP," WUPEA Box #1, MAOF.

52. [Mintzmyer] to Director, n.d., file "Evaluation Report and Input Material," Box "Winter Use Plan EA 1989/90," MAOF.

53. Simpson was successful in another such effort at about the same time, derailing efforts by the Greater Yellowstone Coordinating Committee (GYCC, composed of the national forest supervisors and national park superintendents in the Yellowstone area) to develop a framework for coordinated management in the Yellowstone area. Fearing that the protective management of the NPS would spread to the surrounding national forests, Senator Simpson, along with the rest of the Wyoming congressional delegation and Representative Marlenee of Montana, not only ordered the GYCC's "Vision for the Future" document to be gutted from 60 pages of progressive management coordination to 10 pages of toothless proclamations, but also succeeded in transferring Lorraine Mintzmyer, cochair of the GYCC at the time, away from Yellowstone to Pennsylvania. See Michael Milstein, "Politics May Destroy Parks," *HCN,* June 15, 1992, and Milstein, "Conspiracy Destroyed Vison [*sic*] for Yellowstone," *HCN,* Jan. 25, 1993.

54. Elizabeth Laden, "Parks' Winter Improvements May Cost Millions," *BDC,* June 10, 1990; and Todd Wilkinson, "Parks' Use Plan Rekindles Controversy," *Denver Post,* June 17, 1990.

55. NPS, *WUPEA,* 53–60.

56. Ibid., 30, 34, 42–45.

57. Ibid., 34, and Alesch to Winter Use Planning Team, June 21, 1990, file "Visitor Use Management—Winter Use Plan—1988–1992," Box N-366, YNPA.

58. NPS, *WUPEA,* 47–49.

59. See the many letters in file "Copies of Public Comments on Draft WUP," WUPEA Box #3, MAOF. See also National Parks and Conservation Association (NPCA), "Yellowstone's Protection in Winter Jeopardized," July 1, 1990, file "WUP Comments," WUPEA Box #2, and GYC, "Flawed Winter Use Plan Released," July 6, 1990, file "GYC Winter Use Comments," GYC, both flyers mailed to group members soliciting their comments on the plan.

60. NPS, *WUPEA,* 85–86; Yochim, "Development of Snowmobile Policy," 142–144; Chris Turk, personal interview by author, Aug. 8, 2002, Moab, Utah; and John Zelazny to Stark and Barbee, Aug. 9, 1990 (quote), file "Copies of Public Comments on Draft WUP," WUPEA Box #3, MAOF.

61. Muth to Stark, July 24, 1990, file "Copies of Public Comments on Draft WUP," WUPEA Box #3, MAOF.

62. Malcolm Wallop to Mintzmyer, Aug. 16, 1990, and Craig Thomas to Barbee, Aug. 13, 1990 (note that Thomas expressed no opinion about the Potholes area and did not expressly support increased visitor use), both in file "Copies of Public Comments on Draft WUP," WUPEA Box #3, MAOF; and Simpson to Ridenour, Aug. 5, 1990, file "Correspondence—WUP," WUPEA Box #1, MAOF.

63. Paul Hoffman to Barbee, July 27, 1990, and Lynn Birleffi to Barbee, Aug. 3, 1990, both in file "Copies of Public Comments on Draft WUP," WUPEA Box #3, MAOF.

64. John Fitzgerald, "Cody Candidate for Interior Post Draws Fire," *BGZ,* Jan. 5, 2002; Roy Jordan, "Wyoming: A New Centennial Reflection," *Annals of Wyoming* 62 (1990): 114–130; and Samuel Western, *Pushed Off the Mountain—Sold Down the River* (Moose, WY: Homestead, 2002), 47, 88.

65. "Census Data Show Who Represents the Extremes," *USA Today,* Oct. 17, 2006, 10A. Wyoming's unique political geography was driven home to me personally by an event in 2004. Traveling through Wyoming, I stopped at Rose's Lariat Café in Rawlins for supper. The café is in a converted railroad boxcar, so most seating is at a counter, making it likely that one will sit next to a stranger. Waiting for my dinner, the woman (a Wyoming resident) next to me struck up a conversation. When she found out that I worked for the NPS with the winter use issue, she laughed and said, "You'll never guess who my brother is." Knowing the answer would be rich, I took the bait, and asked who he was. She answered, "He's the lawyer representing the state against the NPS on the winter use issue." Our conversation then took a different direction, as have the two government agencies regarding this issue. Although something like this could happen in any state, the incident illustrated that Wyoming's vast geography does not mean its political interconnections are strained. Indeed, they are tightly interwoven, making it easy for persons with the dominant antifederal disposition both to be well-represented politically and to advance in political circles.

66. Bachman, "Greater Yellowstone Coalition Comments on Joint Winter Use Plan," Aug. 3, 1990, file "2300, Recreation Management," Box A-394, YNPA, and Bachman to Files and Program Staff, June 11, 1990, file "Winter Use Correspondence," GYC. Park employee concerns from Dan R. Sholly to Management Assistant, March 26, 1990, and Management Assistant to Resource Management and Visitor Protection Division, March 15, 1990, both in file "A18, Advisory Boards," Box W-197, YNPA.

67. EIS requests from Zelazny to Stark and Barbee, Aug. 9, 1990; Ellis to Barbee, Aug. 10, 1990; Scott to Barbee, Aug. 7, 1990; and Dawn Amato to Barbee, Aug. 2, 1990, all in file "Copies of Public Comments on Draft WUP," WUPEA Box #3, MAOF. Planner comments from Chris Turk, personal interview by author, Aug. 8, 2002, Moab, Utah.

68. Personal interviews by author with Steve Iobst, April 4, 2003, Mammoth Hot Springs, Wyoming; Bob Ekey, April 9, 2003, Bozeman, Montana; Chris Turk, Aug. 8, 2002, Moab, Utah; and John Sacklin, April 11, 2003, Mammoth Hot Springs, Wyoming.

69. Terri Martin to Barbee and Stark, Aug. 9, 1990, file "Copies of Public Comments on Draft WUP," WUPEA Box #3, MAOF, and Bob Rossman and Susan Marsh (both Forest Service employees at the time), personal communication with the author, e-mails, both on Jan. 18, 2006.

70. See the many comment letters in file "Copies of Public Comments on Draft WUP," WUPEA Box #3, MAOF, including one from Mardy Murie to Barbee on July 12, 1990.

71. Release of final plan from "Final Winter Use Plan and Environmental Assessment Now Available," press release, Jan. 4, 1991, file "[Untitled]," Box K-108, YNPA, and "Finding of No Significant Impact: Winter Use Plan," signed Nov. 9, 1990, file "Memos," WUPEA Box #2, MAOF. Conservationist reaction from Don Bachman, "Disappointing Winter Use Plan Released," *GYR*, Spring 1991, 15, and Joseph Sax to Stark and Barbee, Aug. 14, 1990 (quote), file "Copies of Public Comments on Draft WUP," WUPEA Box #3, MAOF. See also Joseph Sax, *Mountains without Handrails: Reflections on the National Parks* (Ann Arbor: University of Michigan Press, 1980).

72. "Winter Visitor Use Management Work Plan," loose within WUPEA Box #3, MAOF. Interestingly, such visitation numbers made up less than 5 percent of annual visitation at the time, which approached 3 million in Yellowstone alone. Winter visitors, though, had a greater impact on park wildlife than summer visitors did and used a disproportionate share of the limited park budget. Also, with the CDST opened, Grand Teton authorities were able to proceed with closing the Potholes off-road snowmobile area, finally implementing the closure in 2002, although the last year it was actually open for snowmobiling was 1992 (Gary Pollock, personal communication with the author, e-mail, Feb. 14, 2006).

73. Garrett Hardin, "The Tragedy of the Commons," *Science* 162 (1968): 1243–1248; visitor complaints from Greater Yellowstone Winter Visitor Use Management Working Group, *Winter Visitor Use Management: A Multi-Agency Assessment,* March 1999 (hereafter G. Yell. WVUM Working Group, *Winter Visitor Use Management*).

74. "Winter Visitor Use Management Overview," unpublished paper, Jan. 1995, "VUM Speech" file, MAOF; "Winter Visitor Use Management Work Plan," loose within WUPEA Box #3, MAOF; John A. Sacklin (Yellowstone's lead planner involved with winter use from this point forward) to Superintendent et al., Feb. 18, 1993, file "Visitor Use Management—Winter Use Plan—1993–95," Box N-366, YNPA; and G. Yell. WVUM Working Group, *Winter Visitor Use Management.* See also Robert E. Manning, David W. Lime, Marilyn Hof, and Wayne A. Freimund, "The Visitor Experience and Resource Protection (VERP) Process: The Application of Carrying Capacity to Arches National Park," *George Wright Forum* 12 (1995): 45–54.

75. Start of monitoring from Scott McMillion, "Yellowstone in Winter," *BDC,* Jan. 9, 1994, and "Winter Visitor Use Management Accomplishments," file "VUM Speech," VUM Collection, MAOF. Monitoring results from "Ambient Air Quality Study Results, West Entrance Station, Yellowstone National Park, Winter 1995," and "Winter 1996 Carbon Monoxide Monitoring, West Entrance and West Entrance Road, Yellowstone National Park," both in author's personal collection. To expedite visitor entry, managers allowed visitors to purchase entrance passes in advance and instituted an express lane for them (Brett French, "Park Tests New Snowmobile Rules," *BGZ,* Jan. 24, 2002, and Scott McMillion, "New Rule, Old Gripes," *BDC,* Dec. 20, 2001). Soundscape monitoring also began in Grand Teton at about this time (John Sacklin, personal interview with the author, June 1, 2007, Mammoth Hot Springs, Wyoming).

76. SAR, 1993, 5, and Ruth Quinn, *Weaver of Dreams: The Life and Architecture of Robert C. Reamer* (Gardiner, MT: Leslie & Ruth Quinn, 2004), 175–176.

77. Larry E. Bennett, "A Review of Potential Effects of Winter Recreation on Wildlife in Grand Teton and Yellowstone National Parks: A Bibliographic Data Base," 1995, and James W. Caslick, "Impacts of Winter Recreation on Wildlife in Yellowstone National Park: A Literature Review and Recommendations," March 20, 1997, both in Research Collection, MAOF.

78. Wayne A. Freimund, "Examining Indicators of Quality Winter Use in Yellowstone National Park," report submitted to John Sacklin, Yellowstone, March 18, 1996, EIS Collection, MAOF, and William Borrie, Wayne Freimund, Robert Manning, and Ben Wang, "So-

cial Conditions for Winter Use in Yellowstone National Park," report also submitted to Sacklin, Dec. 31, 1997, Research Collection, MAOF.

79. Sacklin to Superintendent, Sept. 19, 1995, file "Yellowstone Alternatives," VUM Collection, MAOF (note that plowing the road from West Yellowstone to Old Faithful was another option being considered); "Winter Visitor Use Management Work Plan," loose within WUPEA Box #3, MAOF; and "Winter Visitor Use Management Accomplishments," file "VUM Speech," VUM Collection, MAOF.

80. Limited funding from McMillion, "Yellowstone in Winter." Alternative fuels and lubricants from Howard Haines to Jeanne-Marie Souvigney, Nov. 20, 1995, file "Air Quality/Snowmobiles," GYC; "Marketing Gasohol in West Y. a Savvy Move," *BDC,* Dec. 11, 1997; and "Park Service Uses Ethanol to Reduce Emissions," *BDC,* March 31, 1998.

81. Four-stroke machines from Scott McMillion, "Clean Machines: West Yellowstone Man Devises a Quieter, Low-Emission Snowmobile," *BDC,* March 1, 1996, and McMillion, "Lean, Mean and Green Machine," *BDC,* March 20, 1996. Interestingly, the machine mentioned in the first article (hand-built by West Yellowstone resident Ron Gatheridge) had a catalytic converter on it to reduce emissions. Even today, with many different four-stroke models in production by all four major snowmobile manufacturers, not one has a catalytic converter, which could reduce emissions to about the same levels as modern automobiles. Manufacturer reluctance from Muth to Kayle Jackson, March 20, 1992; Alfred Marc Hanna to Muth, May 5, 1992; and Muth to Hanna, May 21, 1992, all in Research Collection, MAOF.

82. Deferring change from G. Yell. WVUM Working Group, *Winter Visitor Use Management,* 50. At the same time, the Environmental Protection Agency (EPA) began working on nationwide emissions regulations for snowmobiles. However, it would be ten years before the EPA implemented any such regulations, a delay that further exacerbated the problems and delayed resolution in Yellowstone (Dee North to Mary Hektner, Feb. 24, 1995, file "Snowmobile Licensing," Box W-214, YNPA; http://www.epa.gov/otaq/recveh.htm, accessed Feb. 25, 2006; 67 *Federal Register* 217: 68242–68447, Nov. 8, 2002; and 70 *Federal Register* 133: 40420–40612, July 13, 2005).

83. Wildlife discussions in Mary Meagher to Superintendent, Dec. 31, 1991, file "Bison—1991," Box N-346, YNPA; Meagher, "Winter Recreation-Induced Changes in Bison Numbers and Distribution in Yellowstone National Park," unpublished paper, [1993], YNPV; Cassirer et al., "Elk Responses to Disturbance"; and Aune, "Impacts of Winter Recreationists."

84. Marketing campaign from Hoffman to Barbee, Feb. 11, 1994, file "Chambers of Commerce," Box A-404, YNPA. Hoffman's actions from Meeting Minutes, Yellowstone Gateway Coalition, July 28, 1995; Hoffman to Superintendent Michael V. Finley (new in 1994, and to be introduced in Chapter 4), Aug. 8, 1995; and Hoffman to Finley, Oct. 5, 1995, all in author's personal collection; and Todd Wilkinson, "Bush Appointee's Assault on Parks Has Deep Roots," www.billingsnews.com/printStory?storyid=18210, accessed Feb. 14, 2006.

85. "Snowmobile MVA Statistics for 1987–1993"; Ken Nelson to Superintendent, n.d.;

and ISIA Chairman Muth to Barbee, Oct. 18, 1993, all in file "Snowmobile Licensing," Box W-214; Muth to Barbee, Aug. 1993, and Barbee to Thomas, Dec. 14, 1993, both in file "L3427, Recreation Activities—Winter Sports 1993," Box L-73; F. W. Howell and Clyde G. Seely to Barbee, Sept. 1, 1993, file "Bison—1992–94," Box N-347; Barbee to Howell and Seely, Oct. 1, 1993, file "W48, Law & Legal Matters, Policy Procedures," Box W-184; and "Yellowstone National Park to Require Driver's License for Snowmobile Operators," press release, Nov. 9, 1993, file "L3427, Winter Sports 1992," Box W-182, all at YNPA.

86. James T. Sylvester and Marlene Nesary, "Snowmobiling in Montana: An Update," *Montana Business Quarterly,* Winter 1994, 3–8; Lynne Bama, "Yellowstone Snowmobile Crowd May Hit Limit," *HCN,* March 6, 1995, 4; [R. Joseph], "Yellowstone in Winter: The Rest of the Story," *BRM,* Feb. 1992, 7; Jack Welch, "Yellowstone Resolutions," *BRM,* Aug. 1996, 3; and Adena Cook, "Winter Visitor Use Assessment Released: Emphasizes Negatives in Snowmobiling for Greater Yellowstone Area," *BRM,* Aug. 1997, 18. See also "Profile of Snowmobile Owners," *BRM,* Jan. 1996, 11.

87. Adena Cook, "Winter Use Meetings Frustrate Public" and "Winter Visitor Use Issues" sidebar, *BRM,* April 1996, 4. Snowmobile noise heard in backcountry from Yochim, "Development of Snowmobile Policy," 140. Flyer in author's personal collection. Its claims repeated by NPS West District Ranger Robert R. Seibert to Superintendent, Jan. 26, 1994, Research Collection, MAOF; Scott McMillion, "Industry Acknowledges Snowmobile Pollution," *BDC,* Jan. 10, 1994; Bama, "Yellowstone Snowmobile Crowd May Hit Limit," 4; and Todd Wilkinson, "Snowed Under," *National Parks,* Jan./Feb. 1995, 32–37. See also "Overstated Snowmobile Emissions in Yellowstone Park," *BRM,* March 1997, 12.

88. John D. Varley and Paul Schullery, "Reaching the Real Public in the Public Involvement Process: Practical Lessons in Ecosystem Management," *George Wright Forum* 13 (1996): 68–75; Yellowstone National Park, U.S. Fish and Wildlife Service, University of Wyoming, University of Idaho, Interagency Grizzly Bear Study Team, and University of Minnesota Cooperative Park Studies Unit, "Wolves for Yellowstone? A Report to the United States Congress," May 1990; Yochim, "Compromising Yellowstone," 153–236; and John Varley, personal interview by author, Dec. 18, 2002, Mammoth Hot Springs, Wyoming.

89. Robert Meadow, Richard P. Reading, Mike Phillips, Mark Mehringer, and Brian J. Miller, "The Influence of Persuasive Arguments on Public Attitudes toward a Proposed Wolf Restoration in the Southern Rockies," *Wildlife Society Bulletin* 33 (2005): 154–163.

90. Wilkinson, "Snowed Under," 32–37; Richard Manning, "Disturbing the Peace," *Audubon,* Jan.-Feb. 1995, 14, 16; Bama, "Yellowstone Snowmobile Crowd May Hit Limit," 4; and Dan Egan, "Yellowstone: Geysers, Grizzlies and the Country's Worst Smog," *HCN,* April 1, 1996, 4.

91. Strategizing on winter from Mike to Jeanne-Marie, Louisa, and Bob [last names again not given], Jan. 31, 1995, file "YNP: Winter Use," GYC; "Guiding Principles for GYC's Position on Winter Use in the GYE," March 1996, file "Winter Use EIS," GYC; and Bachman to Ekey, Aug. 20, 1997 (quote), file "Winter Road Closure EA," GYC. New World Mine campaign from Yochim, "Compromising Yellowstone," 1–5; Tom Turner, *Justice on Earth:*

Earthjustice and the People It Has Served (White River Junction, VT: Chelsea Green, 2002), 22–47; and Amy Irvine, *Making a Difference: Stories of How Our Outdoor Industry and Individuals Are Working to Preserve America's Natural Places* (Guilford, CT: Falcon Press, 2001), 127–148.

92. First quote and public meeting summary from untitled summary of meeting comments, Aug. 28, 1996, and "Winter Visitor Use Management Open House Meeting, Jackson, WY, March 4, 1996"; and second quote from Terri Willsen to Deborah Austin, n.d., all in author's personal collection.

93. Complaint information from Yochim, "Development of Snowmobile Policy," 159; and "Summary of Comments, February through May 1996," Fall 1996 newsletter, and untitled summary of meeting comments, Aug. 28, 1996, both in author's personal collection.

94. Varley and Schullery, "Reaching the Real Public."

95. G. Yell. WVUM Working Group, *Winter Visitor Use Management.*

96. Barbee, as quoted in Wilkinson, "Winter Paradox," 32.

CHAPTER FOUR. CRISES, LAWSUITS, AND POLITICS

1. Gale Norton, as quoted in "Federal Judge Strikes Down Snowmobile Ban," *BDC,* Oct. 16, 2004. See also Norton, "Snowmobiles and Cars," *NYT,* Sept. 3, 2004, letter to editor. Vaughn quote from "County Mulls Response to Flawed Report," *LVE,* Oct. 29, 1999. Runte quote from U.S. Newswire, "Yellowstone Court Decision Draws Swift Approval," Dec. 16, 2003, http://releases.usnewswire.com/printing.asp?id=142–12162003.

2. Winter climate from Mary Meagher, "Winter Recreation-Induced Changes in Bison Numbers and Distribution in Yellowstone National Park," unpublished paper [1993], 53, YNPV; that winter's weather events from Doug Peacock, "The Yellowstone Massacre," *Audubon* 99 (May/June 1997): 42–49.

3. Mary Meagher, *The Bison of Yellowstone National Park,* National Park Service Scientific Monograph No. 1 (Washington, DC: U.S. Government Printing Office, 1973), and Peacock, "Yellowstone Massacre."

4. Mary Meagher, "Evaluation of Boundary Control for Bison of Yellowstone National Park," *Wildlife Society Bulletin* 17 (1989): 15–19, and "Yellowstone's Bison: A Unique Wild Heritage," *National Parks and Conservation Magazine* 48 (May 1974): 9–14; Lee H. Whittlesey, "Cows All Over the Place," *Wyoming Annals* 66 (Winter 1994–1995): 42–57; Henry G. DeYoung, "The Bison Is Beleaguered Again," *Natural History* 82 (May 1973): 48–55; and Yellowstone National Park, "Yellowstone Bison," flyer produced for public dissemination by the NPS, 1968, YNPV.

5. Meagher, "Evaluation of Boundary Control," 15–19; Whittlesey, "Cows All Over the Place," 42–57; and Peacock, "Yellowstone Massacre." Interestingly, neighboring state Wyoming lost its class-free status in early 2004 when brucellosis was identified in two different cattle herds—and it was probably elk that gave them the disease ("Feds Deny Wyoming Brucellosis-Free Status," *BDC,* Feb. 18, 2004, and Mike Stark, "Elk Feeding Eyed as Source of Brucellosis," *BGZ,* Jan. 28, 2004).

6. Peacock, "Yellowstone Massacre." Montana suspended the hunt amid great controversy a year later. More recent kill from Matthew Brown, "Bison Slaughter Moratorium Sought," *BDC*, April 11, 2008.

7. Paul Schullery, *Yellowstone's Ski Pioneers: Peril and Heroism on the Winter Trail* (Worland, WY: High Plains, 1995), 98–127; Aubrey L. Haines, *The Yellowstone Story: A History of Our First National Park,* rev. ed., vol. 2 (Yellowstone National Park, WY: Yellowstone Association for Natural Science, History & Education, in cooperation with the University Press of Colorado, 1996), 54–99; Richard A. Bartlett, *Yellowstone: A Wilderness Besieged* (Tucson: University of Arizona Press, 1985), 319–321; Andrew C. Isenberg, *The Destruction of the Bison: An Environmental History* (New York: Cambridge University Press, 2000), 191; Frances Backhouse, "Pure Bison Make a Comeback," *HCN,* May 1, 2006; and Scott McMillion, "Substantial Portion of Remaining 'Pure' Bison in Yellowstone," *BDC,* April 24, 2002. See also Dan Flores, *The Natural West: Environmental History in the Great Plains and Rocky Mountains* (Norman: University of Oklahoma Press, 2001).

8. D. C. "Jasper" Carlton to Mike Finley, May 10, 1996, file "Correspondence on Winter Use from Others," GYC; Howard B. Crystal and Eric R. Glitzenstein to Bruce Babbitt, Roger Kennedy, Jack Neckels, Michael Finley, and John Rogers, Jan. 24, 1997, EIS Collection, MAOF; and Michael Milstein, "Environmentalists Want Snowmobiles Barred from Park," *BGZ,* May 11, 1996. Joining the Fund for Animals was the Biodiversity Legal Foundation (BLF), a Boulder, Colorado, environmental group that primarily used litigation to compel federal agencies to protect wildlife. The BLF lost interest in the Yellowstone issue fairly quickly, so this story will focus only on the Fund for Animals actions.

9. *Fund for Animals, Biodiversity Legal Foundation, Predator Project, Ecology Center, [and five individuals] v. Bruce Babbitt, Denis Galvin, Jack Neckels, Michael Finley, and John Rogers,* May 20, 1997, Case Number 97-1126 (EGS), U.S. District Court, District of Columbia, EIS Collection, MAOF. Information on the bison management plan from NPS, *Bison Management for the State of Montana and Yellowstone National Park, Executive Summary,* Aug. 2000, 21–23.

10. Cody Beers, "Michael Finley on Yellowstone," *Wyoming Wildlife,* Aug. 1997, 16–21 (Finley quote on p. 17), and Ted Kerasote, "It Comes with the Territory," *Audubon,* July-August 1997, 68–69.

11. Settlement Agreement, *Fund for Animals et al. v. Bruce Babbitt et al.,* Civil No. 97-1126 (EGS), Sept. 23, 1997, U.S. District Court for the District of Columbia, EIS Collection, MAOF. The agency also agreed to consider temporarily closing a 14-mile stretch of snowmobile trail to evaluate the effects of road grooming on bison. From here forward, this story will focus only on the snowmobile issue; see Mary Ann Franke's book *To Save the Wild Bison: Life on the Edge in Yellowstone* (Norman: University of Oklahoma Press, 2005), for more detail on the bison issue.

12. Occupying their time in fall 1997 was the assessment of whether to close the 14-mile road temporarily. Because park managers did not have sufficient baseline data, they decided instead to study the matter and reevaluate the need for such a closure in the future

(NPS, *Environmental Assessment: Temporary Closure of a Winter Road,* Nov. 1997, and Yellowstone National Park, "Finding of No Significant Impact: Temporary Closure of a Winter Road," file "Winter Road Closure EA," EIS Collection, MAOF, Nov. 1997).

13. Visitor concerns from G. Yell. WVUM Working Group, *Winter Visitor Use Management,* 21–23. Two-cycle machines and air pollution information from Tim Radtke, "Industrial Hygiene Consultation Report," June 1997, "West Entrance Air Quality Summary, Winter Season 1997," and Lori Marie Snook Fussell, "Exposure of Snowmobile Riders to Carbon Monoxide," *Park Science* (an NPS publication available at MAOF and elsewhere), July 1997, 1, 8–10, all in Research Collection, MAOF.

14. G. Yell. WVUM Working Group, *Winter Visitor Use Management,* 12, 23–24; Bluewater Network, "Petition to Prohibit Snowmobiling and Road Grooming in National Parks," Jan. 21, 1999, 4, 7, 35, EIS Collection, MAOF; Michael J. Yochim, "The Development of Snowmobile Policy in Yellowstone National Park" (Master's thesis, University of Montana, 1998), 139–141; and Greater Yellowstone Coalition, "Yellowstone National Park Sound Survey," President's Day Weekend, 2000, file "Greater Yellowstone Coalition," Research Collection, MAOF.

15. Bluewater Network, "Petition to Prohibit Snowmobiling and Road Grooming in National Parks," Jan. 21, 1999, 58, EIS Collection, MAOF, and Yochim, "Development of Snowmobile Policy," 98.

16. Developing ideas from NPS, "Winter Use Plan and Environmental Impact Statement Underway," press release, April 15, 1998, and NPS, "Additional Locations Announced for Open House Scoping Meetings on Winter Use Planning for Yellowstone . . . ," press release, June 15, 1998, both in EIS Collection, MAOF; and "Participation of the Cooperating Agencies," June 23, 1999, file "Drafts of CA Summary of Participation, May 1999," EIS Collection, MAOF. October meeting from Finley to Conrad Burns, May 18, 1999, file "Letter from Sens. Burns, Craig, Enzi, & Crapo to Dir. Stanton," EIS Collection, MAOF; John Cook to Paul Kruse, June 17, 1999, file "Responses to CA's 5/99 Comments," EIS Collection, MAOF; and Cook to Jim Geringer, Jan. 31, 2001 (*sic*—should be 2000), file "E-mail from Alice Wondrak to Denis Galvin," EIS Collection, MAOF.

17. An excellent chronology of the generation of alternatives is in "Participation of the Cooperating Agencies," June 23, 1999, file "Drafts of CA Summary of Participation, May 1999," EIS Collection, MAOF. See also Finley to Kruse, contractor for the five local counties, undated (but sometime in July 1999); Sarah Creachbaum to Tim Hudson et al., e-mail, Nov. 6, 1998; "Draft Preliminary Winter Use Alternatives," Jan. 7, 1999 (listing the alternatives considered at a Jan. 1999 meeting of park planners); Kristin Legg to Rick Obernesser with attached "Quick Reference for Yellowstone Winter Use Plan Alternatives," e-mail, May 4, 1999; and Cook to Director, April 2, 1999, all in EIS Collection, MAOF; and "New Winter-Use Plan Dumps Snowcoaches," *BGZ,* April 24, 1999, and NPS, *Winter Use Plan Draft Environmental Impact Statement,* July 1999, 21–78.

18. Release of draft to public in 64 *Federal Register* 188: 52520, Sept. 29, 1999.

19. Jack Welch, "Fund for Animals Sets Snowmobiling in National Forests as Their Next

Target," *BRM,* Nov. 1998, 3; "Portion of Yellowstone Park to Be Closed to Snowmobiles?" *BRM,* Dec. 1997, 11; "You Can Protect Snowmobiling in Yellowstone," *BRM,* Nov. 1997, 7; "Help Save Snowmobiling on Our Public Lands," *BRM,* July 1998, 14; and BlueRibbon Coalition Executive Director to Fellow Snowmobiler, undated letter of solicitation, file "Winter Use EIS," GYC. Carlton quote from James Brooke, "A Move to Rid Parks of Snowmobiles," *NYT,* Feb. 7, 1999.

20. Development of Revised Alternative E from "State, County Officials to Meet on Park's Winter-Use Plan," *BGZ,* Sept. 11, 1999; Joe Kolman, "Officials Work on Park Plan for Winter Use," *BGZ,* Sept. 16, 1999; Will Rizzo, "Counties Agree on Yellowstone Winter Use Plan," *LVE,* Sept. 17, 1999; and Scott McMillion, "Counties Team Up on Park Plan," *BDC,* Sept. 17, 1999. Recognition that snowmobiles needed to be cleaner from Lynn Keillor, "The Anatomy of a DEIS," *Snowmobile,* Jan. 2000, 16–17, and Kim Raap, "The Next Big Target for Environmentalists," *SnoWest Magazine,* Oct. 1999, 50.

21. "Wyoming Backs Winter-Use Alternative," *BDC,* Sept. 30, 1999; Wyoming Governor Geringer to Clifford Hawkes (the winter-planning team captain responsible for collecting public opinion letters), Nov. 29, 1999; Dirk Kempthorne to Hawkes, Dec. 15, 1999; Paul Kruse to Hawkes, Dec. 1, 1999, and Montana Governor Marc Racicot to Hawkes, Nov. 30, 1999, all in file "Coded Copies of CA Comments on DEIS," EIS Collection, MAOF; Jack Welch, "Comments Needed on Future of Snowmobiling in Yellowstone," *BRM,* Nov. 1999, 2; Viki Eggers, "Recreationists Draw a Line in the Snow," *BRM,* Nov. 1999, 8; and BlueRibbon Coalition and ACSA, "You Can Protect Snowmobiling in Yellowstone," undated flyer, File "Blue Ribbon Coalition," EIS Collection, MAOF.

22. C. J. Ramstad, "Snowmobiling Gearing Up to Face Major Challenge in Yellowstone National Park," *BRM,* Oct. 1997, 6, and Adena Cook, "Intervention Denied in Yellowstone Suit; Settlement EA Goes Forward," *BRM,* Dec. 1997, 4. Snowmobile industry and fundraising information from Brooke, "A Move to Rid Parks of Snowmobiles"; Chris Twomey, president and CEO of Arctic Cat snowmobiles, testimony, Senate Committee on Energy and Natural Resources, *Snowmobile Activities in the National Park System and Miscellaneous National Heritage Bills,* 106th Cong., 2nd sess., 2000, 55; and Jack Welch, "International Snowmobile Congress Takes Strong Stand on Access in Yellowstone," *BRM,* Aug. 1998, 3. Intervenor status from Jack Welch to Snowmobile Leader, Feb. 24, 1999, file "BlueRibbon Coalition," EIS Collection, MAOF; and Jack Welch, "Comments Needed on Future of Snowmobiling," 2. Note that West Yellowstone's Chamber of Commerce directors considered joining the BlueRibbon Coalition as an intervenor but decided against it because not all town residents were in favor of continued snowmobiling ("Board of Directors Meeting, June 9, 1997, West Yellowstone Conference Hotel," file "Snowmobile Lawsuit," GYC).

23. Scott McMillion, "Snowmobiles Remain an Issue," *HCN,* Oct. 27, 1997 (see also "Fund for Animals Fails in Latest Attempt to Close Yellowstone to Snowmobiling," *BRM,* May 1999, 19). Clyde Seely and West Yellowstone information from Ray Ring, "Move Over!" *HCN,* April 1, 2002, 10; John Miller, "West Yellowstone: Montana's Biggest Little

Town," *BDC*, Feb. 28, 1999; Scott McMillion, "West Yellowstone Packs 'em in for the . . . Snowmobile Expo," *BDC*, March 18, 2000; and Darryl Harris, "Winter Season Extension Needed at Yellowstone," *Snowmobile West*, Sept. 1985, 63–64. First-name basis from "Clyde" and "Bill" Howell (his business associate and friend) to Burns, Aug. 7, 2001, file "Yellowstone SEIS," GYC.

24. Yi-Fu Tuan, *Space and Place: The Perspective of Experience* (Minneapolis: University of Minnesota Press, 1977), 52–53. Raap quote from Raap to the Editor, undated, file "Revised E," GYC; Kruse information from "State, County Officials to Meet on Park's Winter-Use Plan," *BGZ*, Sept. 11, 1999; his quote from Kruse, "Clear the Air on Revised Alternative E," *Casper (WY) Star-Tribune* (hereafter *CST*), Jan. 8, 2000; and Vaughn quote from "County Mulls Response to Flawed Report," *LVE*, Oct. 29, 1999.

25. The groups included the Bluewater Network, the Montana Wilderness Association, the National Parks and Conservation Association (NPCA), the Natural Resources Defense Council (NRDC), the Sierra Club, the Wilderness Society, and several other regional groups. Meetings and participants from Hope Sieck, "Blueprint for Change," *GYR*, Winter 1999, 4–5. Criticism of plowing from "The Park Service Proposal," *GYR*, Winter 1999, 11, and Jeanne-Marie Souvigney to Yellowstone Winter Use Working Group, Aug. 10, 1999, file "Winter Use Planning, Summer, 1999," GYC.

26. The Fund for Animals distanced itself from the new alternative because it would have meant continued road grooming. The Fund instead developed still another proposal, the "Natural Regulation Alternative," which would have banned road grooming, snowmobile use, and snowcoach use park-wide. To provide visitor access, the NPS would build an elevated monorail system that would run year-round. Because the Fund was the only group supporting this alternative and because it included the relatively radical and expensive monorail idea (it was estimated in 1994 that building just a 16-mile monorail through Yellowstone's Hayden Valley would cost $880 million; see NPS, "Alternative Transportation Modes Feasibility Study," prepared by BRW, Inc., in association with Dames & Moore [Denver: Denver Service Center, 1994]), it was not widely publicized and received little support (Fund for Animals, "The Natural Regulation Alternative," Nov. 1999, EIS Collection, MAOF, and Andy Cole to Creachbaum, April 21, 2000, fax, file "DEIS Comment Summary," EIS Collection, MAOF). Bison biologist Mary Meagher advanced a solution similar to the Fund's alternative (Meagher to NPS, Nov. 17, 1999, file "Winter Use Public Comments," GYC).

27. Not until 2004 and 2005 would there be research into snowcoach air and noise emissions. Although some were indeed quieter and cleaner than snowmobiles, the historic Bombardier snowcoaches (and others using carbureted engines) were not (Gary A. Bishop, Daniel A. Burgard, Thomas R. Dalton, and Donald H. Stedman, "In-Use Emission Measurements of Snowmobiles and Snowcoaches in Yellowstone National Park," Nov. 2005, Third EIS Collection, MAOF, and Christopher W. Menge and Jason C. Ross, "Draft Supplemental Technical Report on Noise," Oct. 2002, in NPS, *Winter Use Plans Final Supplemental Environmental Impact Statement*, Feb. 2003 [hereafter NPS, *2003 Final SEIS*, Feb. 2003], vol. 1, Appendix B).

28. "The Citizens' Solution," *GYR*, Winter 1999, 12–13; GYC representative Souvigney to Yellowstone Winter Use Working Group, Aug. 10, 1999, and Michael Scott and Schuber tas@aol.com (e-mail address of D. J. Schubert of the Fund for Animals) to Hope Sieck, e-mail, Sept. 8, 1999, both in file "Winter Use Planning, Summer 1999," GYC; "Proposed Agenda," [Sept. 13, 1999], file "Winter Use Mtg/Call, Agendas & Notes," GYC; and Ron Tschida, "Enviros Offer Plan to Limit Yellowstone Snowmobiles," *BDC*, Oct. 13, 1999.

29. Sieck to Scott et al., e-mail, Sept. 26, 1999, and "Winter Use Conference Call," Oct. 8, 1999, both in file "Winter Use Call/Draft Notes," GYC; Tschida, "Enviros Offer Plan," *BDC*, Oct. 13, 1999; "Ban Banshees in Yellowstone," *Los Angeles Times* (hereafter *LA Times*), Nov. 3, 1999; "Snowmobiles Threaten Yellowstone's Wonderland," *San Francisco Chronicle*, Nov. 14, 1999; "Fuel from Snowmobiles Polluting Yellowstone," *Seattle Post-Intelligencer*, Nov. 2, 1999; and Bruce Vento et al. to Robert Stanton, July 30, 1999, File "Letter from 38 Members of Congress to Director Stanton," EIS Collection, MAOF. Mathews was not the only West Yellowstone resident opposed to snowmobile use; so was Mayor Doug Edgerton (Edgerton, "Snowplowing Plan Could Actually Benefit West Y.," letter to the editor, *BDC*, Sept. 14, 1999). He supported plowing because he believed it would increase the number of people who could visit the park; the number of snowmobilers would always be limited by the fact that after a few hundred snowmobiles traveled a given road, it would often become too moguled to travel comfortably, especially on warm days.

30. Russell Long to Babbitt, Jan. 21, 1999; Sean Smith to Finley, Jan. 27, 1999; and Bluewater Network, "Petition to Prohibit Snowmobiling and Road Grooming in National Parks," Jan. 21, 1999, all in EIS Collection, MAOF; and Brooke, "A Move to Rid Parks of Snowmobiles." Information on Bluewater Network from its website, http://bluewaternetwork.org/aboutus.shtml, Jan. 18, 2004.

31. Brooke, "A Move to Rid Parks of Snowmobiles," and Bluewater Network, "Snowmobile Letter-Writing Campaign," July 26, 1999, EIS Collection, MAOF. See also U.S. Department of the Interior, "National Park Service Puts the Brakes on Escalating Snowmobile Use in the National Park System," press release, April 27, 2000, EIS Collection, MAOF.

32. Male statistic in NPS, *Winter Use Plan Final Environmental Impact Statement*, [2000], 1:91. Examples of snowmobile ads or pictures in these *BDC* issues: Nov. 20, 1997; Jan. 11, 1998; March 11, 1998; and March 18, 2000. Drinking in bars and male camaraderie were other activities that enhanced the popular conception of snowmobiling. See McMillion, "West Yellowstone Packs 'em In"; Miller, "West Yellowstone"; and James T. Sylvester and Marlene Nesary, "Snowmobiling in Montana: An Update," *Montana Business Quarterly* (Winter 1994): 3–8.

33. Authors writing about the tradition of viewing nature as sacred include Stephen Fox, *The American Conservation Movement: John Muir and His Legacy* (Madison: University of Wisconsin Press, 1981); Catherine L. Albanese, *Nature Religion in America: From the Algonkian Indians to the New Age* (Chicago: University of Chicago Press, 1990) (source of expression); Linda Graber, *Wilderness as Sacred Space* (Washington, DC: American Association of Geographers, 1976); Thomas R. Dunlap, *Faith in Nature: Environmentalism as Re-*

ligious Quest (Seattle: University of Washington Press, 2004); and Sandra Nykerk, "Pilgrims and Rituals in Yellowstone National Park: Touristic Encounters with the Sacred" (Directed Interdisciplinary Studies bachelor's honors thesis, Montana State University–Bozeman, 2000).

34. NPS, "Executive Summary" [of public comments on the Draft EIS], undated, EIS Collection, MAOF. GYC quote from David Cowan, "Yellowstone Park: Speedway or Sanctuary," *GYR*, Fall 1997, 1.

35. Two good discussions of the conservationist view of automobiles and wilderness are Leo Marx, *The Machine in the Garden: Technology and the Pastoral Ideal in America* (New York: Oxford University Press, 1964), and David Louter, *Windshield Wilderness: Cars, Roads, and Nature in Washington's National Parks* (Seattle: University of Washington Press, 2006).

36. Robert J. Duffy discusses the Protestant work ethic and how it motivates some to defend economic enhancement activities in *The Green Agenda in American Politics: New Strategies for the Twenty-First Century* (Lawrence: University Press of Kansas, 2003), 41.

37. Albanese, *Nature Religion in America;* Graber, *Wilderness as Sacred Space;* Dunlap, *Faith in Nature;* and Nykerk, "Pilgrims and Rituals."

38. Imagery ideas from John Sacklin and Bob Barbee (personal interviews on April 11, 2003, Mammoth, and April 9, 2003, Bozeman, respectively), and Jean E. Lavigne, "Constructing Yellowstone: Nature and Environmental Politics in the Rocky Mountain West" (Ph.D. dissertation, University of Kentucky, 2003), 211–290. Along with some park visitors, some managers still had difficulty understanding that the new, more widely shared perception of snowmobiles was not the benign one of a basic form of winter transportation used in Yellowstone for over thirty years (see Mae Davenport and William T. Borrie, "The Appropriateness of Snowmobiling in National Parks: An Investigation of the Meanings of Snowmobiling Experiences in Yellowstone National Park," *Environmental Management* 35 [2005]: 151–160). This difference in perceptions would persist, confounding the debate to some degree in the years ahead.

39. An August 2005 broadside entitled "Yellowstone's Visitor-Led Recovery," issued by the GYC, the Sierra Club, the Wilderness Society, and the Winter Wildlands Alliance (in the author's personal collection) opened with the statement, "A fundamental freedom is returning within Yellowstone National Park. It's the freedom of winter visitors to breathe clean air, view Yellowstone's wonders in razor detail, and hear clearly the subtle sounds of geysers and mud pots." The emphasis on freedom is obvious, but it's not the freedom to travel throughout the park at will (whether by snowmobile, ski, or snowshoe), but rather to experience nature's clean air, silence, and sacredness.

40. William T. Borrie, Wayne A. Freimund, and Mae A. Davenport, "Winter Visitors to Yellowstone National Park: Their Value Orientations and Support for Management Actions," *Human Ecology Review* 9 (2002): 41–48; Davenport and Borrie, "Appropriateness of Snowmobiling in National Parks"; and Judith Layzer, *The Environmental Case: Translating Values into Policy* (Washington, DC: CQ Press, 2006), 1–25, 223–250. Note that these scholars were unaware of each other's work at the time the works were in progress (I was also

unaware of their work when I wrote my Ph.D. dissertation, "Compromising Yellowstone: The Interest Group–National Park Service Relationship in Modern Policy-Making" [University of Wisconsin–Madison, 2004]). See also Mark K. McBeth, Elizabeth A. Shanahan, and Michael D. Jones, "The Science of Storytelling: Measuring Policy Beliefs in Greater Yellowstone," *Society and Natural Resources* 18 (2005): 413–429, and Mark K. McBeth and Elizabeth A. Shanahan, "Public Opinion for Sale: The Role of Policy Marketers in Greater Yellowstone Policy Conflict," *Policy Sciences* 37 (2004): 319–339.

41. GYC, "Yellowstone National Park Sound Survey," President's Day Weekend, 2000, and GYC, "Yellowstone's Visitors Unable to Escape Snowmobile Noise," press release, March 9, 2000, both in file "Greater Yellowstone Coalition," Research Collection, MAOF; Scott McMillion, "Noise Police," *BDC,* March 10, 2000; and Will Rizzo, "Survey: You Can't Escape Noise in Park," *LVE,* March 10, 2000. Serenity mentioned in Brett French, "Debate about What's Quiet in Yellowstone Grows Louder," *BGZ,* Feb. 13, 2000.

42. Miguel Flores and Tonnie Maniero, "Air Quality Concerns Related to Snowmobile Usage," Oct. 1, 1999, file "Snowmobile/Winter Use," Box A-366, YNPA; NPS, "Air Quality Study Results for Yellowstone National Park Available," press release, Oct. 19, 1999, file "E-mail from YNP Public Affairs Office . . . ," Research Collection, MAOF; Karen Mockler, "Dirty Air in the Deep of Winter," *HCN,* Nov. 22, 1999, http://www.hcn.org/servlets/hcn .BulletinBoard?issue_id=167#Dirty; Rebecca Huntington, "Air Quality Study Fingers 'Bilers,'" *JHNG,* Oct. 27, 1999; and Scott McMillion, "Park Pollution Can Rival L.A.'s Smog," *BDC,* Oct. 20, 1999.

43. Mockler, "Dirty Air in the Deep of Winter," *HCN,* Nov. 22, 1999; Scott McMillion, "Pollution Overstated," *BDC,* Oct. 26, 1999; Deb Johnson, "Errors Plague Emissions Study," *West Yellowstone News,* Oct. 28, 1999; and "County Mulls Response to Flawed Report," *LVE,* Oct. 29, 1999.

44. "Teton Official Incensed about Flawed Park Report," *CST,* Oct. 30, 1999; "Emissions Study Leads to Call for Resignations," *BDC,* Oct. 30, 1999; Finley to Mike Soukup and Christine Shaver, Nov. 5, 1999, file "Snowmobiles/Winter Use," Box A-366, YNPA; Scott McMillion, "Yellowstone Air Pollution Drops," *BDC,* March 16, 2000; U.S. Department of the Interior (USDI) and NPS, "Air Quality Concerns Related to Snowmobile Usage in National Parks," Feb. 2000, EIS Collection, MAOF; and "Yellowstone Pollution Estimates Reduced," *BDC,* March 18, 2000.

45. Robert Meadow, Richard P. Reading, Mike Phillips, Mark Mehringer, and Brian J. Miller, "The Influence of Persuasive Arguments on Public Attitudes toward a Proposed Wolf Restoration in the Southern Rockies," *Wildlife Society Bulletin* 33 (2005): 154–163.

46. Conservationist claim from *GYC et al. v. Kempthorne and Snyder,* "First Amended and Supplemented Complaint for Declaratory and Injunctive Relief," Jan. 11, 2008, and *NPCA v. U.S. Dept. of the Interior and NPS,* "First Amended Petition for Review of Agency Action," Dec. 18, 2007, both in U.S. District Court for the District of Columbia and found in MAOF. Wildlife monitoring report: P. J. White, Troy Davis, John Borkowski, Robert Garrott, Dan Reinhart, and Craig McClure, "Behavioral Responses of Wildlife to Snowmobiles

and Coaches in Yellowstone," Oct. 17, 2006, Third EIS Collection, MAOF. Social versus biological issue in P. J. White, Troy Davis, and John Borkowski, "Wildlife Responses to Motorized Winter Recreation in Yellowstone," July 15, 2005, Third EIS Collection, MAOF.

47. Lori M. Fussell, Gary Bishop, and John Daily, "The SAE [Society of Automotive Engineers] Clean Snowmobile Challenge 2000—Summary and Results," Sept. 2000, Research Collection, MAOF (the NPS was one of the sponsors of this college student contest; see Sacklin, personal communication with author, March 29, 2004); "Buffalo U. Captures Clean Snowmobile Contest," *BDC*, April 1, 2000; Anne Eisenberg, "Designing a Cleaner, Quieter Snowmobile," *NYT*, April 13, 2000; Scott McMillion, "Cleaner, Quieter Snow Machines Arrive in Park," *BDC*, Jan. 14, 2000; "Yellowstone Will Test Improved Snowmobiles," *BGZ*, Jan. 15, 2000; Brett French, "Clean Machines?" *BGZ*, Feb. 15, 2000; Scott McMillion, "In Search of a Clean Machine," *BDC*, Feb. 25, 2000; "Clean Machines Headed to Yellowstone Park," *BDC*, Dec. 13, 2000; and Scott McMillion, "Four-Stroke Machines the Future of Sport," *BDC*, Dec. 21, 2000.

48. Amanda Hardy, "Bison and Elk Responses to Winter Recreation in Yellowstone National Park" (Master's thesis, Montana State University–Bozeman, Nov. 2001), and Daniel Bjornlie, "Ecological Effects of Winter Road Grooming on Bison in Yellowstone National Park" (Master's thesis, Montana State University–Bozeman, May 2000).

49. Hardy, "Bison and Elk Responses"; Bjornlie, "Ecological Effects of Winter Road Grooming"; and "Researcher Studies Stress on Animals in Yellowstone Park," *BDC*, March 12, 2000. See also Scott Creel et al., "Snowmobile Activity and Glucocorticoid Stress Responses in Wolves and Elk," n.d., file of same name, Research Collection, MAOF.

50. Prohibition against wildlife disturbance from 36 CFR § 2.18 (c). Disturbance discussions in NPS, *Winter Use Plans Final Environmental Impact Statement*, 2007 (*2007 FEIS*), 111–129. Lawsuits: *NPCA v. U.S. Dept. of the Interior and NPS*, Nov. 21, 2007, and *GYC et al. v. Dirk Kempthorne, Mary Bomar, and Mike Snyder*, n.d., both filed in U.S. District Court for the District of Columbia and both found in 2008 Environmental Assessment Collection, MAOF.

51. Suzanne Lewis, "The Role of Science in National Park Service Decision-Making," *George Wright Forum* 24 (2007): 36–40; Joseph L. Sax, *Mountains without Handrails: Reflections on the National Parks* (Ann Arbor: University of Michigan Press, 1980), 18–37; and Edward Abbey, *Desert Solitaire: A Season in the Wilderness* (New York: Ballantine Books, 1968), 60.

52. Cynthia G. Cody to Hawkes, Dec. 15, 1999, file "Snowmobiles/Winter Use," Box A-366, YNPA.

53. "Park's Winter-Use Plan Draws Sharp Dissent," *BDC*, Oct. 16, 1999; Scott McMillion, "Opponents Bury Park Plan," *BDC*, Oct. 22, 1999; NPS, "First Public Meeting to Begin for Draft Winter Use Plan/Environmental Impact Statement for Yellowstone and Grand Teton National Parks," press release, Oct. 13, 1999, file "Press Releases—WUPEIS, 1998–99, 2000," EIS Collection, MAOF; and NPS, "Executive Summary" [of public comments], undated, EIS Collection, MAOF.

54. Scott McMillion, "Winter Use Plan: EPA Gives Cold Shoulder to All Options but

Snowmobile Ban," *BDC*, Feb. 24, 2000; Will Rizzo, "EPA Says Ban Snowmobiles," *LVE*, Feb. 24, 2000; and "Finley: Park Winter Plans Must Change," *BDC*, March 3, 2000. Significance of EPA letter from Mike Finley, telephone interview by author, June 24, 2003, and Steve Iobst, personal interview by author, April 4, 2003, Mammoth Hot Springs.

55. Don Barry to NPS Director, [April 2000], file "Materials from Linda Canzanelli," EIS Collection, MAOF.

56. Announcement of tentative snowmobile ban from "Cooperating Agency Meeting, Winter Use Plan/Environmental Impact Statement," meeting notes, March 13, 2000, in file "E-mail from Bob Rossman to Rebecca Aus . . . ," EIS Collection, MAOF; Barry to Director, NPS, [April 27, 2000], file "Materials from Linda Canzanelli," EIS Collection, MAOF; Scott McMillion, "Snowmobiles in Yellowstone May Well Become a Vanishing Breed," *BDC*, March 14, 2000; and Rachel Odell, "Parks Rev Up to Ban Snowmobiles," *HCN*, March 27, 2000, 4. Criticism came from Kempthorne, Racicot, and Geringer to Barry, March 22, 2000, and Mike Enzi et al. to Karen Wade, March 30, 2000, both in EIS Collection, MAOF; Commissioners from five counties to Barry, April 4, 2000, file "Snowmobiles/Winter Use," Box A-366, YNPA; and "NPS Favors Snowmobile Ban in Yellowstone," *BRM*, May 2000, 20.

57. U.S. Department of the Interior, "National Park Service Puts the Brakes on Escalating Snowmobile Use in the National Park System," press release, April 27, 2000, and Barry to Director, NPS, [April 2000], both in file "Materials from Linda Canzanelli," EIS Collection, MAOF; "Remarks by Donald J. Barry, . . . Snowmobile Press Conference, April 27, 2000," EIS Collection, MAOF (quotes); Douglas Jehl, "National Parks Will Ban Recreation Snowmobiling," *NYT*, April 27, 2000; Scott McMillion, "Parks Ban Snowmobiles," *BDC*, April 28, 2000; and Joe Kolman, "Snowmobiles Banned in Many Parks," *BGZ*, April 28, 2000. Note that Barry would fail to make the system-wide ban final.

58. Celebratory editorials: "Ousting Snowmobiles from Yellowstone," *NYT*, April 16, 2000 (unimpaired nature quote); "A Broad Ban on Snowmobiles," *NYT*, April 29, 2000; "Restore Yellowstone Quiet," *Denver Post*, March 19, 2000; "Don't Be Snowed by Lobbyists," *LA Times*, May 7, 2000; "Curbing Snowmobiles in Parks," *Christian Science Monitor*, May 4, 2000; Elaine Robbins, "Snow Job in Yellowstone," *Amicus Journal*, Spring 2000, 44–45 (Sistine Chapel quote); and Todd Wilkinson, "Politicians Play Fast and Loose with the Law," *BDC*, March 28, 2000.

59. Infringement on rights and freedom from Josef Hebert, "Just Saying No to Snowmobiles," [*Madison,*] *Wisconsin State Journal*, April 28, 2000 (Schmier's comment) and "Snowmobilers to Ask Congress to Preserve Park Access," *BRM*, July 2000, 17.

60. Continued lobbying efforts from Robbins, "Snow Job in Yellowstone," 44–45; Todd Wilkinson, "Loud, Dirty and Destructive," *Wilderness*, 2000, 27–31; "Park Service to Issue Rules on Off-Road Vehicles," *National Parks*, May/June 2000, 12–13; "Conference Call—May 5, 2000: YNP and System-Wide Snowmobile Strategy: Goals, Needs, and Ongoing Work," file "WU Strategy Spring/Summer," GYC files; Hope Sieck to Senator, June 22, 2000 (a generic letter sent to many different senators), file "Winter Use—Congressional Strategy," GYC; and Thomas Kiernan to Mary Hektner, Sept. 5, 2000, file "NPCA Mailing," EIS Collection, MAOF. Ten Most Endangered designation from "Yellowstone Remains on 'Im-

periled' Parks Roster," *BDC*, April 6, 2000, and Erin P. Billings, "Group Lists Yellowstone among Imperiled Parks," *BGZ*, April 5, 2000. Bruce Vento/Christopher Shays letter from the two to Colleague, March 8, 2000, loose within GYC files. Note that although the Fund for Animals was happy to see that snowmobiles would be banned, the group continued to promote an end to road grooming and snowcoach use in Yellowstone (Schubert to Babbitt, Barry, Stanton, Finley, and Neckels, May 25, 2000, EIS Collection, MAOF).

61. International Snowmobile Manufacturers Association (ISMA), "Snowmobile Manufacturers and Snowmobilers Unite to Fight Proposed Parks Ban," press release, May 12, 2000, file "Winter Use '99, '00," GYC, and ISMA, "U.S. Senators from Wyoming, Montana, Idaho Unite in Opposing Yellowstone Park Snowmobile Ban," press release, April 24, 2000, file "WU," GYC.

62. Gary Pollock, personal communication with author, Feb. 14, 2006.

63. Congressional letters from Craig Thomas et al. to Bruce Babbitt, May 12, 2000, file "Winter Use '99, '00," GYC (access quote), and Thomas et al. to Babbitt, April 11, 2000, file "Snowmobiles/Winter Use," Box A-366 (other three quotes), YNPA. See also Scott McMillion, "Senators: Park Ban 'Will Not Stand,'" *BGZ*, April 13, 2000, and Jason Marsden, "Thomas Expands Senate Sled Caucus," *CST*, May 13, 2000.

64. Wyoming's U.S. House Representative Barbara Cubin introduced the "Winter Recreation Access to National Parks Act of 2000," H.R. 4560, 106th Cong., 2nd sess., *Congressional Record* 146, no. 67, daily ed. (May 25, 2000): H3867; Montana's U.S. House Representative Rick Hill introduced a rider as well (Scott McMillion, "Hill Hopes to Stall Ban Until After Election," *BDC*, June 15, 2000; see also GYC, "Stop Amendment 39 to the Interior Appropriations Bill Sponsored by Mr. Hill of Montana," undated, file "Rep. Hill/Econ/Correspondence," GYC); and Senator Thomas introduced an amendment to the Interior Appropriations bill (*Congressional Record*, 106th Cong., 2nd sess., daily ed. [July 17, 2000], 146, pt. 92: S7014–7024).

65. Senate Committee on Energy and Natural Resources, *Snowmobile Activities in the National Park System*, May 25, 2000, 6, 10, 31, 36, 42–48. House Subcommittee on National Parks and Public Lands, Committee on Resources, *Oversight Hearing on Snowmobile Recreation in National Parks, Particularly Yellowstone National Park*, 106th Cong., 2nd sess., May 25, 2000 (see http://resourcescommittee.house.gov/parks/; see also Committee on Resources, "Department of Interior Strongly Criticized for Snowmobile Ban Proposal," press release, May 25, 2000, http://www.grovetontrailblazers.com/news/yellowstone10.htm, both accessed Jan. 31, 2004. Barry's memo: Barry to NPS Director, [April 27, 2000], file "Materials from Linda Canzanelli," EIS Collection, MAOF.

66. NPS estimate from USDI/NPS, *Winter Use Plans Final Environmental Impact Statement* (*2000 FEIS*), [Oct. 2000], 1: 405. Hearing testimony from House Subcommittee on Tax, Finance, and Exports of the Committee on Small Business, *Impact of Banning Snowmobiles Inside National Parks on Small Business*, 106th Cong., 2nd sess., July 13, 2000 (Seely testimony pp. 17–18).

67. Ron Tschida, "Enviros Offer Plan to Limit Yellowstone Snowmobiles," *BDC*, Oct. 13, 1999; President of "West Yellowstone Citizens for a Healthy Park," Jackie Mathews, to Sena-

tor Burns, undated, File "Winter Use—Congressional Strategy," GYC; Edgerton to Barry, June 4, 2000, EIS Collection, MAOF. Petition information in Hope Sieck, "West Yellowstone Business Owners Go to Washington, D.C.," *GYR* 17 (Summer 2000): 22. See also the various letters from West Yellowstone townspeople to members of Congress in file "Letters and Statements from West Yellowstone Business Owners to Congressionals," EIS Collection, MAOF, many of which were opposed to continued snowmobile use.

68. Release of Final EIS from NPS, "Final Winter Use Plan/Environmental Impact Statement for Yellowstone and Grand Teton National Parks Released to the Public," press release, Oct. 10, 2000, file "Press Releases—WUPEIS, 1998–99, 2000," EIS Collection, MAOF; "Snowmobile Phaseout [*sic*] Supported," *BDC*, Oct. 11, 2000; and Jason Marsden, "Snowmobile Ban Finalized," *CST*, Oct. 11, 2000. Proposed changes from USDI/NPS, *2000 FEIS*, xii–xix. Snowplanes were banned from the frozen surface of Jackson Lake as well. While this move was consistent with the snowmobile ban because they were very loud and Jackson Lake was off-road, it ended traditional use of the oldest oversnow vehicles in the area. See Yochim, "Development of Snowmobile Policy", and my article of the same title in *Yellowstone Science* 7 (Spring 1999): 2–10; USDI/NPS, *2000 FEIS*, xii–xix; and Rebecca Huntington, "Government Proposes Ban on Historic Hobby," *CST*, April 10, 2000.

69. Additional, secondary steps include the following: an optional public comment period about the completion of the Final EIS; a mandatory thirty-day waiting period after the Record of Decision is signed; publication of the Draft Rule in the *Federal Register*, along with a thirty- to sixty-day comment period before publication of the Final Rule; and a thirty-day waiting period after the Final Rule is finally published before its provisions take effect.

70. Comment summary from USDI/NPS (Intermountain Regional Director Karen Wade), "Record of Decision: Winter Use Plans for the Yellowstone and Grand Teton National Parks and John D. Rockefeller, Jr., Memorial Parkway," Nov. 22, 2000, pp. B1-B2, EIS Collection, MAOF, and Grand Teton National Park, "Winter Use FEIS Comment Summaries for Individual Letters Prepared for the Intermountain Regional Director," [undated], EIS Collection, MAOF.

71. USDI/NPS (Intermountain Regional Director Karen Wade), "Record of Decision: Winter Use Plans for the Yellowstone and Grand Teton National Parks and John D. Rockefeller, Jr., Memorial Parkway," Nov. 22, 2000, 11–15, EIS Collection, MAOF; NPS, "Winter Use Decision for Yellowstone and Grand Teton National Parks Is Announced," press release, Nov. 22, 2002, file "Press Releases—WUPEIS, 1998–99, 2000," EIS Collection, MAOF; and Stephen Saunders to Finley, Jan. 18, 2001, file "Snowmobiles/Winter Use," Box A-366, YNPA. Organic Act quote from "An Act to Establish a National Park Service, and for Other Purposes," 39 Stat. 535, approved Aug. 25, 1916.

72. "Director's Order #55: Interpreting the National Park Service Organic Act," approved by Director Robert Stanton on Sept. 8, 2000, www.nps.gov/refdesk/DOrders/DORder55.html, accessed Feb. 27, 2001. The timing of this publication, just two months before Wade's impairment declaration, could have been mere coincidence, but it seems unlikely, given the high visibility this issue had attained by that summer and fall.

73. See again Barry's memo to the Director, NPS, [April 2000], in file "Materials from

Linda Canzanelli," EIS Collection, MAOF; and Barry to Superintendent Lewis, [undated, but in 2007], Third EIS Collection, MAOF.

74. That Bush's approach to this issue would be different is evident in "Snowmobile Policy Shift Hoped for under Bush," *BDC*, Dec. 6, 2000; "Bush Presidency Would Face Pressure on Snowmobile Ban," *LVE*, Dec. 6, 2000; and Adena Cook, "The Dawning of a New Day—2001," *BRM*, Feb. 2001, 4.

75. Draft Rule publication in 65 *Federal Register* 243: 79024–79034, Dec. 18, 2000. Effort to get Final Rule published from Creachbaum to Saunders, e-mail, Jan. 10, 2001; Saunders to Saunders (himself) et al., e-mail, Jan. 10, 2001, and again Jan. 11, 2001; David Hayes to Saunders, e-mail, Jan. 12, 2001; and Saunders to Saunders, e-mail, Jan. 16, 2001, all in EIS Collection, MAOF; USDI Departmental Federal Register Liaison Officer to Raymond A. Mosley, Jan. 17, 2001, file "Copy of Signed Final Rule, Jan. 18, 2001, EIS Collection, MAOF; Saunders to Stanton et al., e-mail, Jan. 19, 2001, file "Release of Final Rule and Communication with the Press from S. Saunders, Jan. 19, 2001," EIS Collection, MAOF; and Sacklin, personal interview with author, Feb. 13, 2003.

76. Final Rule in 66 *Federal Register* 14: 7260–7268, Jan. 22, 2001, and announced in NPS, "Final Snowmobile Regulations for Yellowstone and Grand Teton National Parks Published in Federal Register," press release, Jan. 23, 2001, file "Press Releases—WUPEIS, 1998–99, 2000," EIS Collection, MAOF; Scott McMillion, "Park Snomobile [*sic*] Ban Goes into the Rule Book," *BDC*, Jan. 24, 2001; and Sacklin, personal interview with author, Feb. 13, 2003.

77. Legal opinion in "Snowmobile Ban Will Be Tough to Reverse," *BDC*, Jan. 29, 2001. Bush administration delay in 66 *Federal Register* 21: 8366–8367, Jan. 31, 2001.

78. First bill from "Thomas Joins Strategy to Thwart Snowmobile Ban," *BDC*, Aug. 21, 2000; "Congress May Not Consider Stopping Snowmobile Ban," *BDC*, Oct. 29, 2000; and Ryan Thomas to Multiple Use Fax List, memo, Oct. 10, 2000, EIS Collection, MAOF. Second bill from "Congress Approves Delay on Snowmobile Ban," *BDC*, Dec. 16, 2000; "Feds Say Congress' Rule Won't Stall Snowmobile Phaseout [*sic*]," *BDC*, Dec. 20, 2000; Jeff Tollefson, "Congress' Rule Won't Affect Park," *BGZ*, Dec. 19, 2000; and Rachel Odell, "Thomas Fights for Snowmobiles," *JHNG*, Dec. 27, 2000. Third bill from *National Park Service Winter Access Act*, 107th Cong., 1st sess., S. 365, *Congressional Record* 147, no. 15, daily ed. (Feb. 15, 2001): S1503–1505; and Scott McMillion, "Senator Takes Aim at Ban on Yellowstone Snowmobiles," *BDC*, Feb. 16, 2001.

79. *ISMA et al. v. Bruce Babbitt et al.*, Dec. 6, 2000, Complaint for Declaratory and Injunctive Relief, U.S. District Court, Wyoming, found in "ISMA Info," GYC; "Snowmobile Groups File Suit over Ban," *BDC*, Dec. 8, 2000; and Jack Welch, "BlueRibbon Joins Snowmobile Manufacturers in Yellowstone Suit," *BRM*, Jan. 2000, 6. Wyoming's decision in "Wyoming Seeks to Join Suit on Snowmobile Ban," *BDC*, March 22, 2001.

80. Settlement discussions from Scott McMillion, "Snowmobile Ban Lawsuit Settlement on the Table," *BDC*, April 4, 2001; "Enzi Sees 'Change' in Park Snowmobile Ban," *CEP*, April 11, 2001; and "Park Snowmobile Ban under Reconsideration," *BGZ*, May 22,

2001. Lawsuit settlement in *ISMA et al. v. Bruce Babbitt et al.*, June 29, 2001, Civil Case 00CV-229B, Stay Order, U.S. District Court for Wyoming in Cheyenne, approved by Judge Clarence Brimmer, file "WU Settlement," GYC; "Stage Set for Lifting Snowmobile Ban," *BDC*, June 30, 2001; "NPS to Reopen Yellowstone Snowmobiling Planning Process," *BRM*, Aug. 2001, 6; and Scott McMillion, "2nd Park Winter EIS Abbreviated," *BDC*, Aug. 1, 2001.

81. "No News on Clean Machines," *BDC*, Aug. 16, 2001; William P. Horn to Iobst (Acting Superintendent of Grand Teton National Park), Aug. 7, 2001, with attached information from ISMA, Arctic Cat, and Polaris, file "ISMA 'New' Info.," GYC; Iobst to Horn, Sept. 10, 2001, and Arctic Cat Exhaust Emissions Project Engineer to Iobst, Oct. 3, 2001, both in file "WU," GYC; and "Agency Rejects Snowmobile Study," *BGZ*, Feb. 7, 2002.

82. Jack Welch, "Count Down Begins for Final Public Comments on Yellowstone Access!" *BRM*, Feb. 2002, 2, 10, and Polaris, "The Snowmobilers' Political Survival Guide," Aug. 2001, file "Winter 2002—W.U.," GYC.

83. Strategizing from GYC, "Winter Use Strategy Meeting Notes," July 31, 2001, file "Yellowstone SEIS," GYC, and "Winter Use Campaign," undated, file "[Untitled]," GYC. First letter from Rush Holt et al. to Mr. President, Sept. 26, 2001, file "WU," GYC. Scientist letter from David Wilcove et al. to Norton, Oct. 17, 2001, file "Science Letter, 10/01," GYC; "Snowmobiles Harming Wildlife, Scientists Say," *BDC*, Oct. 21, 2001; and "Experts: Snow Machines Harmful," *BGZ*, Oct. 21, 2001.

84. Express lane and prepurchased passes from Brett French, "Park Tests New Snowmobile Rules," *BGZ*, Jan. 24, 2002, and Scott McMillion, "New Rule, Old Gripes," *BDC*, Dec. 20, 2001. OSHA tests, respirators, and national press from Scott McMillion, "Park Workers Offered Respirators," *BDC*, Feb. 15, 2002, and "Park Rangers with Respirators," *NYT*, March 6, 2002. Improved health from Scott McMillion, "Respirators Protect Park Employees from Fumes," *BDC*, Feb. 19, 2002; Kathryn (Kitty) Eneboe, "Symptoms at Gate," personal statement, Feb. 25, 2002; and Pat Wimberly, untitled personal statement, Feb. 26, 2002, both in SEIS Collection, MAOF. See also Ben Long, "Yellowstone's Last Stampede," *HCN*, March 12, 2001, 16; "YNP Workers Blame Exhaust for Ailments," *BDC*, March 26, 2001; and Brodie Farquhar, "Park Workers Complain of Exhaust-Related Ailments," *CST*, March 23, 2001.

85. Deborah Schoch, "Snowmobilers Cross Line in Yellowstone," *BDC*, March 15, 2002, and "Out of Bounds," *BGZ*, March 16, 2002. Trespassing violations and ranger patrols continued the next few winters (NPS, "Multiple Snowmobilers Arrested in Closed Areas," March 20, 2003, press release, SEIS Collection, MAOF), with some violators taking illegal excursions as long as 45 miles in the park's backcountry (NPS, "$500 Reward Offered for Information on Illegal Backcountry Snowmobile Activity in Yellowstone National Park," Feb. 12, 2004, press release, Superintendent's Office files, Mammoth Hot Springs).

86. Alternatives release from Scott McMillion, "Four Alternatives for Travel in Yellowstone Park Offered," *BDC*, Jan. 6, 2002; "4 Options Listed for Snowmobiles," *BGZ*, Jan. 21, 2002; Katharine Q. Seelye, "Snowmobilers Gain against Plan for Park Ban," *NYT*, Feb. 20, 2002; Brett French, "Plan Details Economic Effects of Snowmobile Ban," *BGZ*, Feb. 23, 2002; and 67 *Federal Register* 61: 15223, March 29, 2002.

87. NPS, *Winter Use Plans Draft Supplemental Environmental Impact Statement (2002 Draft FEIS)*, [March 2002]. Reasons for lack of preferred alternative from Iobst to Assistant Secretary for Fish and Wildlife and Parks, memo, Feb. 7, 2002, file "Request for Waiver on Preferred Alternative for DSEIS; 02/07/2002," SEIS Collection, MAOF.

88. Freedom ride from Jack Welch, "2002 ISSA Yellowstone Ride for Freedom a Major Success!" *BRM*, Feb. 2002, 6. "Access Pioneers" from Clark Collins, "Land Use Decisions Are Political," *BRM*, Oct. 2002, 4. Support for cleaner snowmobiles from Christine Jourdain, "VROOOMM vs. SHHH: Noise Problem Plagues Snowmobilers," *BRM*, Dec. 1998, 8; "SAE Clean Snowmobile Challenge 2001," *BRM*, March 2001, 6; and Bill Dart, "Less Sound=More Ground II," *BRM*, July 2003, 6.

89. Coalition advocacy from Jack Welch, "Count Down [*sic*] Begins for Final Public Comments on Yellowstone Access!" *BRM*, Feb. 2002, 2, 10, and "Yellowstone Draft SEIS's Now Available: Alternative #2 Offers Best Solution," *BRM*, April 2002, 2, 17; and "Yellowstone Study Leaves Door Open to Snowmobiling," *BRM*, April 2002, 19, with "Sample Draft Yellowstone SEIS Letter" on same page. Celebration of park scenery from Colleen Kjar Durrant, "The Madison in Winter: A Yellowstone Story," *BRM*, Feb. 2002, 18–19.

90. Clark Collins of the BlueRibbon Coalition agreed that conservationists were better at generating comments, though he called their comments "hate mail" (Scott McMillion, "Industry Has Ally in Bush," *BDC*, June 27, 2002). Ten most endangered designation from Kate Himot, "Ten Most Endangered," *National Parks*, April/May 2002, 32–33, and "Group Ranks Top 10 Endangered Parks," *BDC*, March 26, 2002.

91. U.S. PIRG Education Fund involvement from "Contracted Services Agreement," fax, March 12, 2002, file "PIRG Contract, Spring 2002," GYC. Internet usage from the many solicitations I personally received, now in my personal collection (examples: GYC, March 23, 2002; NPCA, March 27, 2002; and Save Our Environment Action Center, March 27, 2002).

92. Todd Wilkinson, "Snowmobiles Must Earn Their Place in the Shrine," *BDC*, Feb. 4, 2002; "Winter Plan about Park, Not Sleds," *CST*, March 7, 2002; "Bush Should Back EPA Call for Snowmobile Ban," *(Boise) Idaho Statesman*, May 7, 2002; Ray Ring, "Looking to Rev Up Old Faithful," *CST*, May 9, 2002; Julia Page and Jackie Mathews, "Park, Towns Will Thrive without Snowmobiles," *BGZ*, May 25, 2002, guest opinion; "End Yellowstone Drone," *Salt Lake Tribune*, Feb. 24, 2002; "The Racket Is Back," *Denver Post*, Feb. 16, 2002; and "Nature Overrun," *NYT*, April 4, 2002 (the lead editorial that day).

93. NPS, *Winter Use Plans Final Supplemental Environmental Impact Statement* (hereafter *2003 Final SEIS*), Feb. 2003, 2: 368–369, and a more detailed analysis in North Wind Environmental, "Public Comment Database Summary," Oct. 2, 2002, SEIS Collection, MAOF. See also Whitney Royster, "81 Percent Back 'Bile Ban," *JHNG*, June 19, 2002; "Winter Use Comments Set Record," *CEP*, June 17, 2002; and "Comments 4–1 in Favor of Snowmobile Ban," *BDC*, June 18, 2002. Most newspaper articles (and the NPS) claimed there were 335,000 to 360,000 comments; duplicate comments account for the difference (some people sent their comments by both e-mail and U.S. mail; the NPS only included such

comments once in the SEIS analysis). Needing extra time to analyze so many comments, managers delayed the snowmobile phase-out by a year (Creachbaum and Bob Rossman to Administrative File, June 12, 2002, file "Draft Letter to Frank Walker and Steve Iobst re: Concerns of Winter Use Planning Team and Draft FSEIS Deadlines, June 12, 2002," SEIS Collection, MAOF; NPS, "Extension Approved for Final SEIS," Aug. 2, 2002, press release, SEIS Collection, MAOF; and 67 *Federal Register* 222: 69473–69478, Nov. 18, 2002).

94. Description of Lewis's managerial style from personal experience working for her and conversations with coworkers during that same era.

95. Release of snowmobile proposal from Lewis and Grand Teton Superintendent Steve Martin, "Park Service Seeks Snowmobile Trade-Off," *Denver Post,* guest commentary, Dec. 8, 2002; Mike Stark, "Strict Snowmobile Rules in Parks Vowed," *BGZ,* Oct. 9, 2002; John MacDonald, "Snowmobiling in Yellowstone," *BDC,* Nov. 12, 2002; "New Park Rules Slated for Snowmobile Use," *BGZ,* Nov. 12, 2002; Brodie Farquhar, "Greens Blast Snowmobile Plan," *CST,* Nov. 22, 2002; and NPS, "Fact Sheet—Final Supplemental Environmental Impact Statement," Nov. 12, 2002, SEIS Collection, MAOF.

96. NPS, *2003 Final SEIS,* Feb. 2003; Scott McMillion, "Final Decision: Park Service Unveils New Winter-Use Plan for Yellowstone," *BDC,* Feb. 21, 2003; NPS, "Final Supplemental Environmental Impact Statement Released for Grand Teton and Yellowstone National Parks," Feb. 20, 2003, press release, SEIS Collection, MAOF; NPS, "Decision Sets Strict Limits on Snowmobile Emissions and Numbers in Yellowstone and Grand Teton National Parks," March 25, 2003, press release, SEIS Collection, MAOF; and NPS (Karen Wade), "Winter Use Plans Record of Decision," March 25, 2003, SEIS Collection, MAOF. Lack of firm answer from NPS, "Questions and Answers/Talking Points for Final Supplemental Environmental Impact Statement," Feb. 20, 2003, e-mailed to all employees by the NPS and in author's personal collection.

97. Snowmobiler response from Rebecca Huntington, "West Wants More Sleds," *JHNG,* Dec. 11, 2002, and Carole Cloudwalker, "County Seeks Increased Sled Limits in Yellowstone," *CEP,* Oct. 20, 2003. Conservationist response from Rebecca Huntington, "Protesters Target Sleds in Teton, Yellowstone," *JHNG,* Dec. 24, 2002; Nick Gevock, "Man vs. Machine: Demonstrators Protest Continued Snowmobile Activity in Yellowstone," *BDC,* Feb. 16, 2003; Mike Stark, "Skiers Protest 'Sleds,'" *BGZ,* Feb. 16, 2003; "Snowmobile Plan All Wet," *Denver Post,* Nov. 9, 2002; "Snowmobiles Don't Belong in Yellowstone," *Great Falls Tribune,* March 16, 2003 (a three-page illustrated editorial); and William Booth, "Whining in the Wilderness," *Washington Post,* Feb. 9, 2003. Lawsuits from Scott McMillion, "Park Snowmobile Policy Finalized, Lawsuit Follows," *BDC,* March 26, 2003, and Mike Stark, "Pro-Snowmobile Rules Challenged in Court," *BGZ,* March 26, 2003. Judge Emmet Sullivan combined the two suits in September and allowed the BlueRibbon Coalition, ISMA, and the state of Wyoming to intervene (*The Fund for Animals et al. v. Gale Norton et al., [and] Greater Yellowstone Coalition et al. v. Gale Norton et al.,* Sept. 15, 2003, Civil Actions 02-2367 and 03-762, respectively, U.S. District Court, District of Columbia, Order, SEIS Collection, MAOF [hereafter *Fund for Animals v. Norton*]).

98. Public opinion from 68 *Federal Register* 238: 69269, Dec. 11, 2003; Scott McMillion, "Pro Snowmobile-Ban Mail Floods Park Service," *BDC*, Dec. 5, 2003; and "Enviros Cry Foul over Snowmobile Memo," *BDC*, Dec. 7, 2003. BlueRibbon's solicitation from Jack Welch, "Draft Rule on Snowmobile Access to Yellowstone Park Released," *BRM*, Oct. 2003, 5, 14. Final Rule from 68 *Federal Register* 238: 69268–69289, Dec. 11, 2003, and NPS, "Final Winter Use Rule for Grand Teton and Yellowstone National Parks Published in Federal Register," Dec. 11, 2003, press release, SEIS Collection, MAOF.

99. *National Park Snowmobile Restrictions Act of 2001*, 107th Cong., 1st sess., H.R. 1465; *Yellowstone Protection Act* (same title for both bills), H.R. 5044 and S. 6259, 107th Cong., 2nd sess.; and *Yellowstone Protection Act*, 108th Cong., 1st sess., March 6, 2003. See also Mike Stark, "Congressmen Unveil Snowmobile Ban Bill," *BGZ*, June 26, 2002; "Lawmakers Introduce Bill to Ban Snowmobiles," *BDC*, June 28, 2002; Ted Monoson, "Easterners Sponsor Parks Sled Ban," *CST*, March 5, 2002; Paula Clawson, "Montana Delegation against Snowmobile Ban Bill," *LVE*, March 7, 2002; Scott McMillion, "A House Divided," *BDC*, July 18, 2003; Ted Monoson, "House Strikes Sled, Bison Measures from Funding Bill," *CST*, July 18, 2003; and Scott McMillion, "Rehberg Keeps Snowmobile Ban from Passing," *BDC*, July 19, 2003. Rehberg killed another bill in 2004, using a "fact sheet" to defeat another proposed snowmobile ban (Ted Monoson, "House Kills Proposal to Ban Sleds in Parks," *BGZ*, June 18, 2004).

100. House Committee on Small Business, *Protecting Small Business and National Parks: The Goals Are Not Mutually Exclusive*, 107th Cong., 2nd sess., Jan. 26, 2002 (Seely testimony pp. 13–15 and 58–72; Mathews testimony 17–19 and letters 75–145, including the petition signed by 150 persons). See also "Yellowstone Snowmobile Ban Topic of Field Hearing," *BDC*, Jan. 20, 2002; Scott McMillion, "Phaseout [*sic*] Backers: Hearing Stacked," *BDC*, Jan. 26, 2002, and "Congressman Stands Up for Snowmobilers," *BDC*, Jan. 27, 2002; and "Committee Meets in W. Yellowstone to Discuss Snowmobile Ban Issue," *LVE*, Jan. 28, 2002. Senate Committee on Governmental Affairs, *Hearing regarding Public Health and Natural Resources: A Review of the Implementation of Our Environmental Laws*, Part 2, 107th Cong., 2nd sess., March 13, 2002, http://govt-aff.senate.gov/031302lieberman.htm, Feb. 3, 2004. "Nature as It Exists," as quoted in Sieck's testimony, is from H.R. 700, 64th Cong., 1st sess., 1916.

101. Senator Thomas made another effort to influence the outcome when he and his colleague Senator Mike Enzi (R-WY) requested in 1997 that the counties surrounding Yellowstone be designated "cooperating agencies." Under the Council on Environmental Quality (CEQ, which oversees NEPA procedures and compliance) guidelines, federal agencies can designate other governmental agencies as cooperating agencies for an EIS if they have particular expertise to contribute. In this case, Thomas and Enzi felt the counties and states had economic expertise that the NPS could utilize. This may be the official reason Thomas gave for pursuing cooperating agency status, but the ulterior motive was probably that those parties hoped to maximize their influence on the decision, even though the CEQ makes clear that the lead federal agency (the NPS, in this case) retains decision-making au-

thority. In response to the senators' request, NPS Regional Director John Cook did invite the three states and five counties nearest Yellowstone to become cooperators, along with the U.S. Forest Service, which manages most lands around the parks. Because conservationists (and the BlueRibbon Coalition) were not governmental agencies, federal regulations forbade them from being similarly invited. There was substantial friction between the cooperating agencies and the NPS, largely because most of them desired continued snowmobile use and a share in the NPS's decision-making authority, but they had little overt influence on the NPS's ultimate decisions (Yochim, "Compromising Yellowstone," 237–356; Thomas to Kathleen McGinty, Nov. 13, 1997, and McGinty to Thomas, Nov. 25, 1997, EIS Collection, MAOF; Barry to Enzi, file "Letter from Sens. Enzi, Craig, Burns, Thomas, Cubin, Hill, & Simpson to Sec. Babbitt," EIS Collection, MAOF; and 40 CFR § 1501.6. Cook to Wyoming Governor Geringer, Dec. 1, 1997, and Idaho Governor Phil Batt, Geringer, and Racicot to Cook, Feb. 10, 1998, EIS Collection, MAOF. The five counties were Park and Gallatin counties in Montana, Park and Teton counties in Wyoming, and Fremont County, Idaho).

102. Increasing political micromanaging from William R. Lowry, *The Capacity for Wonder: Preserving National Parks* (Washington, DC: Brookings Institution, 1994), 51–64, 193–201 (see also Lowry, *Preserving Public Lands for the Future: The Politics of Intergenerational Goods* (Washington, DC: Georgetown University Press, 1998). A number of ex-NPS directors support Lowry's findings: George B. Hartzog, *Battling for the National Parks* (Mt. Kisco, NY: Moyer Bell, 1988), 113–138, 249–276; James M. Ridenour, *The National Parks Compromised: Pork Barrel Politics and America's Treasures* (Merrillville, IN: ICS Books, 1994), 77–96; and William C. Everhart, *The National Park Service* (Boulder, CO: Westview Press, 1983). Lorraine Mintzmyer, transferred out of her intermountain regional director's position in 1992 for her strongly protective stance, calls for more park autonomy in "Disservice to the Parks," *National Parks,* Nov./Dec. 1992, 24–25. NPS director turnover information from Dwight T. Pitcaithley, "On the Brink of Greatness: National Parks and the Next Century," *George Wright Forum* 24, no. 2 (2007): 9–20.

103. Charles Mathesian, "The Scenic Route," *Government Executive,* June 1, 2006, 64.

104. Norton information from Ray Ring, "Rebels with a Lost Cause," *HCN,* Dec. 10, 2007. Friendship with Jourdain from "Proposed Itinerary for Secretary Norton's Winter Tour of Yellowstone National Park," Feb. 11–17, 2005, author's personal collection. Snowmobile advocacy from Seely to Norton, March 6, 2001, file "Yellowstone SEIS," GYC; SBA Office of Advocacy Representatives Susan M. Walthall, Linwood L. Rayford, III, and Austin Perez to Norton, April 16, 2001, file "SBA Comments on Final Rule, 4/16/01," EIS Collection, MAOF; and Racicot to President-Elect Bush, Jan. 10, 2001, file "MT Snowmo Reso. 2001," GYC.

105. Finley, telephone interview by author, June 24, 2003; Finley, "In Yellowstone, Uphold American Ideal," *JHNG,* May 21, 2003, "Guest Shot"; Finley, "Remarks, Greater Yellowstone Coalition, June 9, 2001," EIS Collection, MAOF; and Michael Scott, Russell Long, Kevin Collins, Charles Clusen, and Robert Ekey to Norton, April 12, 2001, file "WU Settlement," GYC. Others who agreed with Finley were Bob Ekey (personal interview by author,

April 9, 2003, Bozeman) and GYC Program Director Michael Scott (personal interview by author, April 16, 2003, Bozeman, Montana).

106. Internal and external objectives from Sacklin to Linda Miller and Jennifer Conrad, April 28, 2002, e-mail, SEIS Administrative Record, pp. 51390–51393 (quotes p. 51392), MAOF. Gale Norton interest from "Future of Winter Use, June 3–5, 2002," meeting minutes, SEIS Administrative Record pp. 51401–51425 (quote by Randy Jones p. 51401; quote by Rick Frost p. 51416), MAOF; and Kurt Repanshek, "Former Park Service Director Mainella: Interior Department Called Yellowstone Snowmobile Decisions," NationalParks Traveler.com, Nov. 29, 2007, accessed Dec. 11, 2007. Intimidation from Mike Finley, telephone interview by author, June 24, 2003.

107. First EPA letter Max Dodson to Iobst, April 23, 2002, file "EPA DSEIS Comments," GYC (quote), and "EPA: Snowmobile Ban Would Be Best for Yellowstone," LVE, April 29, 2002. Norton-Whitman lunch from Katharine Q. Seelye, "Snowmobile Letter Surprises E.P.A. Leader and Interior Chief," NYT, May 3, 2002. Second EPA letter from Robert Roberts to Iobst, May 29, 2002, file "EPA DSEIS Comments," GYC, and "EPA Softens Stance on Park Snowmobiling," BDC, June 4, 2002.

108. Office of the Secretary, FOIA Officer Sue Ellen Sloca to author, July 17, 2003, with attached CD of more than 700 pages of scanned documents, personal communication, in author's personal collection. This request was filed when I was a graduate student at the University of Wisconsin–Madison.

109. In a comment he filed on the 2007 Draft EIS on winter use in Yellowstone, Barry stated that he had "strongly supported the elimination of snowmobiling in Yellowstone Park" (Barry to Superintendent Lewis, undated, Third EIS Collection, MAOF). His memo to park staff from Barry to NPS Director, [April 2000], EIS Collection, MAOF.

110. The secretary's influence on the NPS is not new; Byron E. Pearson, in *Still the Wild River Runs: Congress, the Sierra Club, and the Fight to Save Grand Canyon* (Tucson: University of Arizona Press, 2002), illustrates that the NPS was constrained from opposing dams proposed for Grand Canyon National Park in the 1960s because Secretary of the Interior Stewart Udall supported them.

111. Finley, telephone interview by author, June 24, 2003, and "In Yellowstone, Uphold American Ideal," JHNG, May 21, 2003, "Guest Shot." Others who agreed with Finley were Bob Ekey (personal interview by author, April 9, 2003, Bozeman) and GYC Program Director Michael Scott (personal interview by author, April 16, 2003). See again Repanshek, "Former Park Service Director Mainella."

112. *Fund for Animals v. Norton,* Dec. 16, 2003, 294 F. Supp. 2d 92 (D.D.C. 2003). Sullivan history from Scott McMillion, "Judge in Park Ruling Used to Spotlight," BDC, Dec. 19, 2003. See also Rebecca Huntington, "Court to Decide Fate of Park Snowmobiles," JHNG, Oct. 8, 2003.

113. *Fund for Animals v. Norton.* The "Delay Rule" from 2002 (67 *Federal Register* 222: 69473–69478, Nov. 18, 2002) meant that the snowmobile phase-out was one year behind, so snowmobile numbers were only to be halved for the winter of 2003–2004, not elimi-

nated. See also Scott McMillion, "Snowmobile Plan Struck Down," *BDC,* Dec. 17, 2003; "Judge Strikes Down Bush Plan for Snowmobiling in Yellowstone," *BGZ,* Dec. 17, 2003; Felicity Barringer, "Judge Voids New Rule Allowing Snowmobiles in Yellowstone," *NYT,* Dec. 17, 2003; and Jack Sullivan, "Judge Orders Snowmobile Ban," *Denver Post,* Dec. 17, 2003.

114. *Fund for Animals v. Norton.* Quotes from the following pages: 180-degree reversal, p. 23; *Management Policies,* p. 19; trumps, p. 25; and final finding and "arbitrary and capricious" statement, p. 31.

115. *Fund for Animals v. Norton;* defies logic, p. 34; wholly devoid, p. 38; and flatly inadequate, p. 39. Sullivan also found the agency's five-year delay in responding to the Bluewater Network unreasonable, ordering the agency to reply to the group within two months (pp. 44–47). The agency did, but by denying the Network's petition—not a surprising outcome under Bush and Norton (Craig Manson to Russell Long, [Feb. 17, 2004], file "New Snowmobile Policy and Response to Bluewater Network Petition . . . ," EA Collection, MAOF).

116. Liberal press examples include "Banishing Snowmobiles," *NYT,* Dec. 18, 2003, and "Back to Basics at National Parks," *Chicago Tribune,* Dec. 24, 2003. Runte quote from U.S. Newswire, "Yellowstone Court Decision Draws Swift Approval," Dec. 16, 2003, http://releases.usnewswire.com/printing.asp?id=142–12162003, and Alfred Runte, *National Parks: The American Experience* (Lincoln: University of Nebraska Press, 1979).

117. "This Is a Fine Mess We've Gotten Into," *BDC,* Dec. 21, 2003; "Another Round," *LVE,* Dec. 22, 2003 (originally printed in the *Missoulian* [Missoula, Montana]); and "Park's Future Riding on Winter Rules," *BGZ,* Dec. 28, 2003.

118. Seely quote from Brett French, "Businessman Tells Workers of Ruling," *BGZ,* Dec. 17, 2003. Investments from Scott McMillion, "Burns Calls for Quick Appeal of Decision," *BDC,* Dec. 19, 2003. See also "Park Ruling a Sign People Are Getting Squeezed Out," *BDC,* Jan. 2, 2004. Some businesses did indeed close; see Whitney Royster, "Snowmobile Season in Limbo," *CST,* July 2, 2004; Carole Cloudwalker, "Businesses Hurt by YNP Winter Use Rules," *CEP,* Nov. 2, 2005; and Carol Cole to Yochim, e-mail, Oct. 19, 2004, EA Collection, MAOF, and letters therein.

119. Appeal from "Wyoming to Appeal Ruling," *BDC,* Dec. 18, 2003; Jack Welch, "Judge Limits Yellowstone Access: BRC Appeals Decision," *BRM,* Feb. 2004, 5, 9; and "Wyoming's Appeal of Snowmobile Ruling Could Take 11 Months," *BDC,* Dec. 22, 2003. Sullivan's response from *Fund for Animals v. Norton,* Dec. 23, 2003, Civil Action #02-2367, Order, http://www.dcd.uscourts.gov/02–2367a.pdf, accessed Feb. 4, 2004. Subsequent events made the appeal moot (*Fund for Animals v. Norton,* Civil Action #02-2367, Order, Feb. 16, 2005, author's personal collection). Reopened case from *ISMA et al. and State of Wyoming v. Gale Norton et al. and Greater Yellowstone Coalition et al.,* Dec. 31, 2003, Civil Action #00-CV-229-B, Order Reopening Case, EA Collection, MAOF (see also *ISMA v. Norton,* 304 F. Supp. 2d 1278, 1293 [D. WY 2004]); Mike Stark, "Snowmobile Case Surfaces in New Court," *BGZ,* Jan. 6, 2004; Ted Monoson, "Judge Reopens Snowmobile Case," *CST,* Jan. 7, 2004; and "Judge Revives Case Filed by Snowmobilers," *BDC,* Jan. 6, 2004.

120. *ISMA et al. and State of Wyoming v. Gale Norton et al. and Greater Yellowstone Coali-*

tion et al., Feb. 10, 2004, Civil Action #00-CV-229-B, Order on Plaintiff-Intervenor's Motion for Temporary Restraining Order and for Preliminary Injunction and Plaintiff ISMA's Motion for Preliminary Injunction, 304 F. Supp. 2d 1278, 1293 (D. WY 2004) (the state of Montana intervened in this suit—see p. 3); and "State AG to Fight Sled Ban," *BDC*, Jan. 10, 2004. Plaintiff's argument from pp. 6, 9, 13–21; Brimmer's logic, pp. 13–21; his order, pp. 30–31 (quote p. 31). See also the NPS's arguments against the preliminary injunction or temporary restraining order in *ISMA et al. and State of Wyoming v. Gale Norton et al. and Greater Yellowstone Coalition et al.*, Jan. 22, 2004, Civil Action #00-CV-229-B, Memorandum in Response to Plaintiff-Intervenor's Motion for Temporary Restraining Order and Preliminary Injunction, EA Collection, MAOF, in which the agency argued that the Organic Act gives it broad discretion to manage parks—making both the 2000 EIS and the 2003 SEIS legal and appropriate—but that the 2003 SEIS was its preferred option.

121. *ISMA et al. and State of Wyoming v. Gale Norton et al. and Greater Yellowstone Coalition et al.*, Oct. 14, 2004, Civil Action #00-CV-229-B, Order, 304 F. Supp. 2d 1278, 1293 (D. WY 2004), 21–29, and "Federal Judge Strikes Down Snowmobile Ban," *BDC*, Oct. 16, 2004.

122. *ISMA et al. and State of Wyoming v. Gale Norton et al. and Greater Yellowstone Coalition et al.*, Feb. 10, 2004, Civil Action #00-CV-229-B, Order, 304 F. Supp. 2d 1278, 1293 (D. WY 2004), 15. Roy A. Jordan, in "Wyoming: Its History and Common Culture" (in Jennifer Jeffries Thompson, ed., *Centennial West: Celebrations of the Northern Tier States' Heritage* [Helena, MT: Montana Historical Society, 1989], 30–35, discusses Wyoming's abrasive relationship with the federal government, as he does in "Wyoming: A New Centennial Reflection," *Annals of Wyoming* 62 (1990): 114–130.

123. Brimmer to Lewis, Feb. 13, 2004, EA Collection, MAOF, and Jim Stanford, "The Western Judge," *JHNG*, March 1, 2004.

124. Jeffrey Bissegger, "Snowmobiles in Yellowstone: Conflicting Priorities in Setting National Parks Policy and the Paradox of Judicial Activism for Recreational Business," *Journal of Land, Resources, & Environmental Law* 25 (2005): 109–118. Bissegger also used Brimmer as an illustration that liberal judges were not the only ones who could be considered activists, a direct criticism of George W. Bush's claim that many judges of the era were liberal activists.

125. "Yellowstone National Park Compendium Amendment," EA Collection, MAOF; "Grand Teton National Park/John D. Rockefeller, Jr., Memorial Parkway Compendium Amendment," Feb. 11, 2004, http://www.nps.gov/grte/winteruse/GRTE_JDR_compendium_change.pdf, accessed Feb. 12, 2004, and *ISMA et al. and State of Wyoming v. Gale Norton et al. and Greater Yellowstone Coalition et al.*, Feb. 11, 2004, Civil Action #00-CV-229-B, Notice, EA Collection, MAOF.

126. Brett French, "Fewer Snowmobiles Logged in Season's 1st Days," *BGZ*, Dec. 20, 2003; "Tough Winter Season," *BDC*, Jan. 2, 2004; Steve Lipsher, "The Brink of Beauty, the Edge of Ruin," *Denver Post*, Jan. 11, 2004; and Scott McMillion, "Park Snowmobile Visits Plunge," *BDC*, Feb. 4, 2004.

127. Finley's thinking as recalled by Ellen Petrick, Education Specialist, Yellowstone National Park, personal communication with the author, Feb. 13, 2007.

128. In my work with the agency on this issue from 2004 to 2008, I heard more than one stakeholder praise Superintendent Lewis for her more accommodating manner of dealing with the public.

CHAPTER FIVE. A NEW ERA OR MORE OF THE SAME?

1. Chandler quote from Cadence, Inc., "Public & Agency Information/Particpation [sic] Plan," Oct. 2005, Third EIS Collection, MAOF. Last quote from NPS, "Preferred Alternative Discussion: Draft Environmental Impact Statement," PowerPoint presentation given the week of June 26, 2006, to NPS and Department of the Interior representatives in Washington, D.C., Third EIS Collection, MAOF.

2. Legally, the 1990 Winter Use Plan made no changes to the 1983 snowmobile regulations, so they remained the governing rules for national parks unless otherwise specified. Had either of the recent EISs and their associated rules been upheld, they would have supplanted the 1983 regulations.

3. "Yellowstone and Grand Teton National Parks Winter Use Planning Alternatives for 2004 and Beyond," Jan. 30, 2004, EA Collection, MAOF.

4. NEPA courses of action from NPS Director's Order 12 and Director's Order 12 Handbook, found at http://www.nature.nps.gov/protectingrestoring/D012Site/ and www .nps.gov/policy/DOrders/RM12.pdf, respectively, both accessed July 20, 2006. Significant snowmobile impacts from "Preparing an Environmental Assessment to Support a Temporary Regulation on Snowmobiles," [Feb. 1, 2004], EA Collection, MAOF.

5. Interview with John Sacklin, June 1, 2007, Mammoth Hot Springs, Wyoming.

6. "Temporary Winter Use Plans Environmental Assessment Schedule as of June 30, 2004," EA Collection, MAOF; Scott McMillion, "Park Service Proposal Put on Fast Track," BDC, Sept. 8, 2004; and interview with Sacklin, June 1, 2007, Mammoth Hot Springs, Wyoming.

7. "Benefits of Commercially Guided Snowmobile Tours," [April 1, 2004]; "Short-Term Environmental Assessment Strategy," May 20, 2004; and Stephen P. Martin to Dave Freudenthal, July 27, 2004, all in EA Collection, MAOF; and interview with Sacklin, June 1, 2007, Mammoth Hot Springs. Sullivan's ruling from The Fund for Animals et al. v. Gale Norton et al. [and] Greater Yellowstone Coalition et al. v. Gale Norton et al., Memorandum Opinion and Order, June 30, 2004, EA Collection, MAOF.

8. EA begun from Scott McMillion, "Yellowstone Winter Use: The Latest Attempt at Planning for Snowmobiles Fuels Apprehension for Winter Season," BDC, June 3, 2004. Bison study from Scott McMillion, "Where the Buffalo Roam," BDC, June 9, 2004. NPS, Temporary Winter Use Plans Environmental Assessment, Aug. 2004.

9. North Wind, Inc., "Final Report: Public Comments on the Environmental Assessment . . . ," Oct. 21, 2004, EA Collection, MAOF. See also North Wind's summaries of com-

ments for Scoping and the Final Rule, both of which revealed similar anti-snowmobile majorities, also found in the EA Collection, MAOF. Several ex-NPS directors sent still another letter to Secretary Norton calling for an end to snowmobiling in Yellowstone (Nathaniel Reed, George Hartzog, Jr., Roger Kennedy, Robert Stanton, Denis Galvin, and Michael Finley to Norton, May 10, 2004, EA Collection, MAOF).

10. "Final Finding of No Significant Impact and Final Rule," Sept. 17, 2004; Sacklin to Kevin Schneider, e-mail, Sept. 21, 2004, file "Briefing Phone Call w/Region on Final FONSI"; "Talking Points for Deputy Secretary Griles," circa Oct. 14, 2004, file of same name; and Schneider to Chris Turk et al., e-mail, Oct. 22, 2004, file "Final FONSI for Review," all in EA Collection, MAOF.

11. NPS, "Temporary Winter Use Plans Finding of No Significant Impact," Nov. 2004, EA Collection, MAOF; and 69 *Federal Register* 217: 65348–65366, Nov. 10, 2004.

12. Improvements in conditions the previous winter (2003–2004) had three causes: (1) the legal confusion led to a substantial drop in snowmobile use; (2) most snowmobile rentals had converted their fleets to BAT machines in anticipation of the Supplemental EIS decision becoming reality; and (3) many visitors hired guides. Although these things may have been partly serendipity, the completed EA drew upon all three, limiting the number of snowmobiles, requiring BAT machines, and using guided tours to intentionally reduce the noise and impact of snowmobiles in the park.

13. Articles in the popular press suggesting improved conditions include Scott McMillion, "A Time of Change in Yellowstone: This Winter, the Park Is a Cleaner, Quieter and Far Less Hectic Place," *BDC*, Feb. 29, 2004; David Warner, "Bob Seibert—A Conversation," *West Yellowstone News*, Feb. 28, 2004; and Johanna Love, "Fire and Ice," *JHNG*, Feb. 1, 2006. Two resource-monitoring reports provided proof of the common perceptions: John D. Ray, "Winter Air Quality Study, 2004–2005," [2005], and Shan Burson, "Natural Soundscape Monitoring in Yellowstone National Park, Dec. 2004–March 2005," Dec. 15, 2005, both in Third EIS Collection, MAOF. Also, thanks to the cleaner snowmobiles and air, park rangers stopped wearing their gas masks (Whitney Royster, "Rangers Report Improved Health," *CST*, Feb. 5, 2004).

14. New suits from Mike Stark, "Sled Plan Faces New Lawsuit," *BGZ*, Nov. 10, 2004, and "Snowmobile Plan Draws 2 More Challenges," *BGZ*, Nov. 13, 2004. Denial of Fund for Animals suit from L. Fischer to J. Waanders, e-mail, March 16, 2006, Third EIS Collection, MAOF. Denial of GYC suit from *Fund for Animals v. Norton*, 390 F. Supp. 2d 12 (D.D.C. 2005), and Emmet Sullivan, Memorandum Opinion and Order, Sept. 28, 2005; Third EIS Collection, MAOF. Denial of Save Our Snowplanes suit from Order Upholding Agency Action, June 27, 2007, Third EIS Collection, MAOF. Save Our Snowplanes appealed the decision, as of Oct. 2008, the appeal was pending.

15. Bill Luckett, "Tourism Group Sues over Sled Ban," *CST*, Nov. 12, 2004, and Whitney Royster, "Snowplaners Use for Park Access," *CST*, March 31, 2005.

16. First two quotes from "Transcript of Administrative Hearing Proceedings before the Honorable Clarence A. Brimmer," July 19, 2005, Third EIS Collection, MAOF. See also

"Thomas Statement on Brimmer Snowmobile Decision," Feb. 11, 2004, EA Collection, MAOF. Last quote and decision (rendered on Oct. 15, 2005) from *Wyoming Lodging and Restaurant Association. v. U.S. Dept. of Interior*, 398 F. Supp. 2d 1197 (D. WY 2005); also found in Third EIS Collection, MAOF.

17. Jeffrey Bissegger, "Snowmobiles in Yellowstone," *Journal of Land, Resources, & Environmental Law* 25 (2005): 109–118.

18. Yellowstone Outdoor Recreation Planner Kevin Schneider (who also worked on this issue) actually investigated the possibilities of collaborative conservation for the snowmobile issue in a professional paper, "The Role of Collaboration in Managing National Parks," Department of Political Science Library, Montana State University–Bozeman, 2004. Note too that from this point forward, I worked directly with this issue for the NPS in Yellowstone, although almost all of the park's higher-level decision-making occurred without my direct involvement. This puts me in the position of attempting to objectively evaluate park policy-making in which I played a small role. Although I have endeavored to maintain full objectivity, the reader is advised that future historians may take a different view. Knowing historians might do just that, in the notes and bibliography of this book I have included citations for all of the known peer-reviewed works that have directly investigated this issue. Note too that while I also suggested the agency look into some form of collaboration as a way to make the EIS decision-making more durable, both Schneider and I felt that the collaborative possibilities would be limited by the polarization of the parties to the debate.

19. [Cadence, Inc.,] "Summary, First NPS Team Meeting with Cadence on Foundations for New EIS Work," April 27, 2005, Third EIS Collection, MAOF. Before hiring Cadence, the NPS had solicited advice from the U.S. Institute for Environmental Conflict Resolution (Briefing statement, "Collaborative Approach for YELL and GRTE Winter Use Plan," Jan. 19, 2005, Third EIS Collection, MAOF). Note that because this chapter records relatively recent events, it may suffer from a lack of complete documentation; not all sources were yet available. There is no way to circumvent the fact that time will probably reveal more primary sources. That said, the agency's legal requirement to generate a comprehensive administrative record (in anticipation of being sued) produced a fairly complete collection of primary sources. This chapter is based upon that collection as well as newspaper accounts and my personal experience with the issue.

20. Nedra Chandler and Nicholas Dewar, "Public Participation and Agency Cooperation in the Winter Use Planning Process for Yellowstone and Grand Teton National Parks and the John D. Rockefeller, Jr., Memorial Parkway: Summary Report of Themes and Findings," July 1, 2005, Third EIS Collection, MAOF.

21. Ibid., and Cadence, Inc., "Public & Agency Information/Particpation [*sic*] Plan," Oct. 2005, Third EIS Collection, MAOF.

22. Ibid.

23. Ibid.

24. "Secretary's Day at the Park," *BDC*, Feb. 16, 2005 (first and last quotes); Felicity Barringer, "A 3-Day Yellowstone Tour in Support of Snowmobiles," *NYT*, Feb. 17, 2005 (snow-

coach quote); and Becky Bohrer, "Norton Checks Yellowstone Snowmobile Plan," *LA Times*, Feb. 15, 2005. Jourdain's company from "Proposed Itinerary for Secretary Norton's Winter Tour of Yellowstone National Park," Feb. 11–17, 2005, author's personal collection. Norton's two letters: "Snowmobiles and Cars," *NYT*, Sept. 3, 2004, and "Gale Norton: Parks Exist for People to Enjoy, Even on Snowmobiles," *Minneapolis Star-Tribune*, Sept. 26, 2004. See also Ted Monoson, "Norton Touts Parks Works," *CST*, May 6, 2004, in which Norton expressed confidence that snowmobiling would continue in the parks.

25. Felicity Barringer, "Top Official Urged Change in How Parks Are Managed," *NYT*, Aug. 26, 2005; "Destroying the National Parks," *NYT*, Aug. 29, 2005; "Parks or Parking?" *LA Times*, Aug. 30, 2005; and Michael Shnayerson, "Who's Ruining Our National Parks," *Vanity Fair*, July 2006, www.vanityfair.com/commentary/content/printables/060612roc001? print-true, accessed June 16, 2006. Hoffman's pro-recreation and business perspectives were probably his primary motivation for making these changes, but some speculated that his proposal was an overdue reaction to his disagreements with former Yellowstone Superintendent Mike Finley (Shnayerson, cited above, and Todd Wilkinson, "Past Is Prelude: Whose Interests Should National Parks Serve?" *New West Network*, Dec. 2, 2005, www .newwest.net, accessed Dec. 2, 2005).

26. Public reaction to proposed changes in Shnayerson, "Who's Ruining Our National Parks"; President of the Outdoor Industry Association Frank Hugelmeyer and seventy-two other outdoor-industry businesses or organizations to Gale Norton, Sept. 8, 2005; "Thomas Can Save National Park Ideal," *JHNG*, Oct. 26, 2005; and Rebecca Huntington, "Senators Grill Park Service," *JHNG*, Nov. 2, 2005.

27. Hoffman's transfer (ostensibly not due to the Management Policies controversy) from Noelle Straub and Brodie Farquhar, "Hoffman Named to Different Interior Post," *CST*, March 25, 2006. Norton's resignation from U.S. Department of the Interior, "Secretary Norton Announces Departure from Interior," press release, March 10, 2006, www.doi.gov/news/06_News_Releases/060310.htm, accessed same day. New policies from Julie Cart, "Snowmobile-Friendly Plan for National Parks Rejected," *LA Times*, June 20, 2006, and Associated Press, "Revised Parks Policy Boosts Conservation," *BGZ*, June 20, 2006. Final approval from NPS, "National Park Service Finalizes 2006 Management Policies," press release, Aug. 31, 2006, http://home.nps.gov/applications/release/Detail.cfm? ID=686, accessed Jan. 7, 2007.

28. Jon Catton, personal discussion with the author, April 13, 2007, Yellowstone National Park. This interpretation differs from that of Ray Ring, who argues that such sagebrush rebels have had little long-term influence upon federal land decision-making in the West ("Rebels with a Lost Cause," *HCN*, Dec. 10, 2007). See also William R. Lowry, *The Capacity for Wonder: Preserving National Parks* (Washington, DC: Brookings Institution, 1994), and *Preserving Public Lands for the Future: The Politics of Intergenerational Goods* (Washington, DC: Georgetown University Press, 1998).

29. Public Policy Research Institute/University of Montana, "The Legal Framework for Cooperative Conservation," 12, http://cooperativeconservation.gov/library/LegalFrame

workCC.pdf, accessed July 25, 2008; and Gale Norton, http://www.doi.gov/secretary/, accessed Dec. 9, 2003.

30. Snowmobiler positions evident in Jack Welch, "Year Eight Victorious for Yellowstone N.P. Snowmobile Access," *BRM*, Aug. 2004, 5, 25; Roger Koopman, "Winter Use of Park Issue Far from Over," *West Yellowstone News*, Aug. 27, 2004; Bruce McCormack, "Guided Snowmobile Rule Insult to Public," *CEP*, Nov. 2, 2005; "Snowmobile Users Seek Looser Rules," *BGZ*, Feb. 21, 2006; and Whitney Royster, "Sled Supporters Rally for Access," *CST*, Feb. 20, 2006.

31. Mark Menlove, "You Don't Need a Motor to Experience Yellowstone Park," *LVE*, March 1, 2005; "Yellowstone's Visitor-Led Recovery," flyer from GYC, Aug. 2005, author's personal collection; Natural Resources Defense Council (NRDC), "Help Keep Snowmobiles Out of Yellowstone," Aug. 2005, author's personal collection; and "Snowmobile Deceit," *NYT*, Aug. 26, 2005. Fund for Animals interest evident in a motion to renew the organization's lawsuit, filed Sept. 15, 2006 ("Plaintiff's Renewed Motion for Summary Judgment, Memorandum in Support, and Request for Further Proceedings Pursuant to the Court's March 15, 2006 Order," Third EIS Collection, MAOF).

32. Compromises between Montana wilderness and snowmobiler advocates from Montana Wilderness Association, "The Beaverhead Strategy," http://www.wildmontana .org/, accessed July 27, 2006; and "A Compromise in the Forest," *Helena Independent-Record*, April 26, 2006. Yellowstone's prominence suggested by Brian Hawthorne, "BRC Members Rule!" *BRM*, Aug. 2004, 6–7.

33. Jay F. Kirkpatrick, "A Modest Solution," Nov. 21, 2005, Third EIS Collection, MAOF.

34. Kim Raap, "Recreationists Cry Foul at Yellowstone National Park Official's Comments," press release, Feb. 16, 2006, author's personal collection; Whitney Royster, "Park Stands Behind Employee," *CST*, Feb. 17, 2006; "Accept Apology for E-mail, Then Move On," *CST*, Feb. 21, 2006; Carole Cloudwalker, "Commissioners Want Park Official Ousted," *CEP*, Feb. 22, 2006; and "Unfortunate E-mail Taints Yellowstone Winter Plans," *BDC*, Feb. 22, 2006. Many people on all sides of the issue privately contacted Sacklin with statements of support (Sacklin, personal communication with the author, April 18, 2008). Name-calling by snowmobilers continued as well; see Jack Welch, "Yellowstone Is Open to Snowmobiles This Winter!" *BRM*, Dec. 2005, 5, 27; and Roger Koopman (an elected representative to the Montana House), "Snowmobile Flap Is the Real Air Pollution in Yellowstone," *BDC*, Feb. 21, 2004.

35. NPS, "$500 Reward Offered for Information on Illegal Backcountry Snowmobile Activity in Yellowstone National Park," press release, Feb. 12, 2004, EA Collection, MAOF; and Scott McMillion, "Untracked Snow in Yellowstone Too Tempting for Some Snowmobilers," *BDC*, Feb. 25, 2005, and "Illegal Entry," *BDC*, March 20, 2005.

36. Evidence of continued problems with snowmobile noise from Burson, "Natural Soundscape Monitoring in Yellowstone National Park, Dec. 2004–March 2005," Dec. 15, 2005, Third EIS Collection, MAOF; Burson, "Natural Soundscape Monitoring in Yellowstone National Park, Dec. 2005–March 2006," http://www.nps.gov/yell/technical/planning/

winteruse/plan/, accessed Aug. 8, 2006; Michael J. Yochim to Sacklin, Feb. 13, 2006, e-mail, Third EIS Collection, MAOF; Brodie Farquhar, "Report: No Progress in Snowmobile Emissions since '01," *CST*, Jan. 23, 2006; Mike Stark, "Study: 4-Stroke Snowmobilers Easier on Park," *BGZ*, Jan. 27, 2006; and Micah Ziegler, "Prof. Speaks Out against Yellowstone Noise Levels," *Yale [University] Daily News*, Feb. 8, 2006. Retreat from cleaner emissions requirements in Mike Stark, "Plan Allows 720 Sleds a Day in Park," *BGZ*, Nov. 21, 2006, and NPS, *2007 FEIS*, vol. 1: 60–64.

37. BAT snowmobiles were not only being sold in Yellowstone but also becoming popular in the upper Midwest, although two-stroke machines remained the lion's share of the market there (Kate Miller, Superintendent of Voyageurs National Park, personal communication, Sept. 23, 2005, and Jim Williams, Assistant Director of International Wolf Center, Ely, Minnesota, personal communication, Sept. 22, 2005).

38. New Snowlodge and cost from Scott McMillion, "A Winter Visit to Yellowstone Doesn't Mean You'll Be Roughin' It," *BDC*, Feb. 22, 2000, and Brett French, "What Price for Paradise?" *BGZ*, Feb. 14, 2000. Snowlodge rates from Xanterra Parks & Resorts, "Old Faithful Snow Lodge & Cabins: Winter Accommodations," http://www.travelyellowstone.com/, accessed Aug. 8, 2006.

39. Beginning new EIS from Scott McMillion, "Yellowstone Winter Use Will Get Another Study," *BDC*, June 25, 2005, and Rebecca Huntington, "Yellowstone Revs Up Snowmobile Study," *JHNG*, Aug. 10, 2005. Calls for compromise or other solutions from John Baden, "Trust May Offer Hope for Ending Park Quagmire," *BDC*, Feb. 25, 2004; "Compromise Is the Best Path to Our Future," *West Yellowstone News*, March 5, 2004; "Who'll Be the Judge?" *CST*, Aug. 29, 2004; and Todd Wilkinson, "Snowmobile Policy Flipped, and Flopped," *JHNG*, Oct. 27, 2004.

40. "Yellowstone National Park 2005–2006 Winter Summary," "Yellowstone National Park 2004–2005 Winter Summary," and "Cumulative Snowmobile and Snowcoach Statistics (Dec. 17, 2003–March 14, 2004)," all in Third EIS Collection, MAOF. New EIS information from NPS, "Winter Use Plans Draft Environmental Impact Statement," Nov. 2006, 34–36, 128–135, Third EIS Collection, MAOF. Public reaction samples from Brodie Farquhar, "New Federal Winter Use Study Won't Change Yellowstone," Nov. 21, 2006, http:// www.newwest.net/, accessed Jan. 5, 2007; and "Snowmobile Rules Have Been Effective So Far," *CST*, Nov. 22, 2006; but see also "Ban Yellowstone's Snowmobiles," *LA Times*, Nov. 24, 2006.

41. Tim Stevens to Winter Use Planning Team, June 4, 2007, and Stevens et al. to Winter Use Planning Team, June 4, 2007, both in Third EIS Collection, MAOF.

42. Burson, "Natural Soundscape Monitoring in Yellowstone National Park, Dec. 2005–March 2006," and Burson, "Natural Soundscape Monitoring in Yellowstone National Park, Dec. 2006–March 2007," both available at http://www.nps.gov/yell/technical/plan ning/winteruse/plan/, accessed Oct. 30, 2007 (hereafter "Burson, soundscape monitoring reports"); Gary A. Bishop, Daniel A. Burgard, Thomas R. Dalton, and Donald H. Stedman, "In-Use Emission Measurements of Snowmobiles and Snowcoaches in Yellowstone National Park, Jan. 2006," http://www.nps.gov/yell/technical/planning/winteruse/plan/re

ports/bishopreport11_05.pdf, accessed Aug. 8, 2006; and Gary A. Bishop, Ryan Stadt-muller, and Donald H. Stedman, "Portable Emission Measurements of Snowcoaches and Snowmobiles in Yellowstone National Park," January 2007, Third EIS Collection, MAOF.

43. NPS, "Winter Use Plans Draft Environmental Impact Statement," cooperating agency review draft, Nov. 2006, 30, Third EIS Collection, MAOF. See also Stark, "Plan Allows 720 Sleds a Day in Park." The high numbers of snowmobilers historically (795 per day) relative to snowcoaches (only about 20 per day) certainly made the agency's previous focus upon snowmobiles justifiable.

44. Continued noise problems from Burson, soundscape monitoring reports.

45. "Why 540 Snowmobiles? (and Why Not More . . . or Less?)," briefing, July 2007, and NPS, Record of Decision, Nov. 20, 2007, both in Third EIS collection, MAOF; Burson, soundscape monitoring reports; and NPS, *2007 FEIS*, vol. 1: 60–64, and vol. 2, Appendix E.

46. NPS, Record of Decision, Nov. 20, 2007, Third EIS Collection, MAOF.

47. Cadence, Inc., "Public & Agency Information/Particpation [*sic*] Plan," Oct. 2005, Third EIS Collection, MAOF. Stakeholder meetings from NPS, "Public Involvement Update for YELL and GRTE Winter Use Plan," Briefing Statement, Aug. 1, 2006, Third EIS Collection, MAOF.

48. Promoting snowcoaches from Randy Roberson: "Guest Opinion: Yellowstone's Snow Season Looks Good," *BGZ*, Dec. 3, 2005. Placemats advertising diversity and history obtained at Clyde Seely's Holiday Inn Restaurant in Jan. 2006 and in author's personal collection; David Warner, "Heritage Tourism—A Path to a Diversified Town Economy," *West Yellowstone News*, Jan. 28, 2005; Mike Stark, "Winter Business in Park Changes," *BGZ*, Nov. 30, 2005; and "Yellowstone Adapts to Changing Rules, Desires," *Great Falls Tribune*, Dec. 29, 2005. Increase in West Yellowstone tourism from NPS, "Winter Use Plans Draft Environmental Impact Statement," Cooperating Agency Review Draft, Nov. 2006, 132, Third EIS Collection, MAOF.

49. University of Calgary, Faculty of Environmental Design, "The Ecology of Bison Movements and Distribution in and beyond Yellowstone National Park," 2005, Third EIS Collection, MAOF, and Mary Ann Franke, "Do Groomed Roads Increase Bison Mileage?" *Yellowstone Science* 13 (Fall 2005): 15–24.

50. Big Sky Institute, "Bison, Snow and Winter Use: A Stakeholder Workshop to Identify Potential Winter Use Management Effects Studies for the Road Corridor from Madison Junction to Mammoth Hot Springs," Jan. 18–19, 2006, Third EIS Collection, MAOF, and Robert A. Garrott and P. J. White, "Evaluating Key Uncertainties regarding Road Grooming and Bison Movements," May 23, 2007, Third EIS Collection, MAOF.

51. Social vs. biological issue in P. J. White and Troy Davis, "Wildlife Responses to Motorized Winter Recreation in Yellowstone," July 15, 2005, 15, and White and Davis, "Wildlife Response to Winter Recreation in Yellowstone National Park," July 14, 2004, 22, both in Third EIS Collection, MAOF. Both research proposals in Wayne A. Freimund, Michael Patterson, Shelley Walker, and Melissa Baker, "Winter Visitor Experiences in Yellowstone National Park: Visitor Perceptions of the Natural Soundscape and of Interactions with Bison," May 21, 2006, Third EIS Collection, MAOF.

52. Aaron Wildavsky and Naomi Caiden, *The New Politics of the Budgetary Process*, 5th ed. (New York: Pearson-Longman, 2004).

53. NPS, *2007 FEIS*, vol. 1 (fuel consumption analysis pp. 79–80; other environmental effects in Chapter 3 (buses are a component of Alternative 6). Xanterra's website (https://www.travelyellowstone.com/old-faithful-snow-lodge-cabins–1700.html, accessed Jan. 5, 2007) provides an idea of the relative costs of snowcoach and snowmobile transportation: A 100-mile bus tour in the summer (the "Circle of Fire") cost $50 in 2006, while the same tour cost $115 by snowcoach in the winter of 2006–2007. A snowmobile rental that same winter cost $210 (for one or two people).

54. Amy McNamara and others to Winter Use Planning Team, March 23, 2006, file "Feedback on Prelim. Alt's . . . included in summary report by N. Dewar," Third EIS Collection, MAOF. Plowing had a few promoters; see Ken Sinay, "Snow Plowing Idea Deserves Another Look," *BDC*, June 8, 2004, and William Oldroyd, testimony at public hearing on Winter Use Plans Draft Environmental Impact Statement, West Yellowstone, Montana, May 17, 2007, Third EIS Collection, MAOF.

55. Private conversations with two prominent conservationists involved in this issue by telephone on Sept. 9, 2007, and in person in Bozeman, Montana, Oct. 9, 2007. See also Stevens to Winter Use Planning Team, June 4, 2007, and Stevens et al. to Winter Use Planning Team, June 4, 2007, both in Third EIS Collection, MAOF.

56. D. J. Schubert to Yellowstone National Park, Nov. 16, 2007, Third EIS Collection, MAOF.

57. NPS, "Winter Use Plans Draft Environmental Impact Statement," cooperating agency review draft, Nov. 2006, 34.

58. "Near Miss Report Form," Feb. 18, 2004; Brad Ross, Bruce Sefton, and Michael P. Keator, "Sylvan Pass Avalanche Control and Grooming Operations," PowerPoint program, May 15, 2004; State of Montana, Department of Military Affairs, "Potential Environmental and Safety Impacts Associated with the Use of Ordnance for Avalanche Control at Sylvan Pass," June 2004; Occupational Safety and Health Administration, "Sylvan Pass, Yellowstone National Park," unpublished report to NPS, 2001; and Steve Swanke to Chief Ranger, July 12, 2004, all in Third EIS Collection, MAOF.

59. Mike Stark, "Avalanche Strategy," *BGZ*, Sept. 4, 2004; NPS, *2007 FEIS*, vol. 1: 159; and the following from Third EIS Collection, MAOF: Swanke to Chief Ranger, July 12, 2004; "Yellowstone National Park—Avalanche Control and Forecasting Budget," Nov. 1, 2005; "CRO Avalanche Control Meeting Agenda, July 12, 2006"; Freudenthal to Sacklin, June 4, 2007; and NPS, "Sylvan Pass Operational Risk Management Assessment," Oct. 2007.

60. NPS, *2007 FEIS*, vol. 2: F-8 to F-10, and NPS, "Sylvan Pass Operational Risk Management Assessment," Oct. 2007, Third EIS Collection, MAOF.

61. NPS, *2007 FEIS*, vol. 1: 159 and vol. 2: F-7. U.S. 550 travel volumes from Yochim to Sacklin and others, e-mail, Jan. 22, 2007, Third EIS Collection, MAOF.

62. Although the NPS and the U.S. Forest Service had given permission to a private party to plow it in the winter of 1984–1985, that party had not done so (Stephen P. Mealey

and others, "Decision Notice and Finding of No Significant Impact," Nov. 1984; "1984 Environmental Assessment: U.S. Highway 212"; and Jerry L. Rogers to Ron Marlenee, Dec. 26, 1984, all in Third EIS Collection, MAOF).

63. The quid-pro-quo opportunity was evident as early as 2004; see Ross, Sefton, and Keator, "Sylvan Pass Avalanche Control and Grooming Operations." Reconstruction of Cooke Pass from Central Federal Lands Highway Division, "Beartooth Highway Reconstruction Project," http://www.cflhd.gov/projects/WYBeartooth.cfm, accessed Aug. 8, 2006. Proposal to close Sylvan Pass from NPS, "Winter Use Plans Draft Environmental Impact Statement," cooperating agency review draft, Nov. 2006, 34.

64. See Ruffin Prevost, "Deadline Near for Report on Sylvan Pass," *BGZ*, Sept. 14, 2007, and Bruce McCormack, "Northeast Access Can't Replace Sylvan," *CEP*, Sept. 17, 2007, for confirmation of this NPS fear.

65. Ecosystem Research Group, "Comment Document for Cooperating Agency Internal Review, . . ." Jan. 5, 2007; Cody Mayor Roger Sedam et al. to Suzanne Lewis, Dec. 5, 2006; Idaho Governor C.L. "Butch" Otter to Lewis, Jan. 4, 2007; Temple Stevenson to Lewis, Jan. 5, 2007; and Ken Volker to Sacklin, Dec. 18, 2006, all in Third EIS Collection, MAOF. Further opposition from Mike Stark, "Lawmakers Push to Keep Pass Open," *BGZ*, May 3, 2007; Ruffin Prevost, "500 Attend Cody Forum on Sylvan Pass Proposals," *BGZ*, March 23, 2007; and Craig Thomas, Michael B. Enzi, and Barbara Cubin to Winter Use Planning Team, May 2, 2007, and Freudenthal to Lewis, May 3, 2007, both in Third EIS collection, MAOF.

66. Liza J. Nicholas, *Becoming Western: Stories of Culture and Identity in the Cowboy State* (Lincoln: University of Nebraska Press, 2006). See especially Chapter 2, "The West, the East, Buffalo Bill, and a Horse," pp. 33–65. Travels of Buffalo Bill from Louis S. Warren, *Buffalo Bill's America: William Cody and the Wild West Show* (New York: Alfred A. Knopf, 2005). See also Comment Form from Kathleen Thompson, n.d., Third EIS Collection, MAOF, in which this docent at the Buffalo Bill Historical Center argued that "Buffalo Bill Cody, as you know(,) was instrumental in forming a coalition to support East Gate to Greater Yellowstone(.) Our community deserves to carry this tradition for generations to come."

67. Colin Simpson to Sacklin, June 5, 2007, and Lee Whittlesey to Yochim (refuting Simpson's statement), e-mail, Sept. 25, 2007, both in Third EIS Collection, MAOF; Robert E. Bonner, *William F. Cody's Wyoming Empire: The Buffalo Bill Nobody Knows* (Norman: University of Oklahoma Press, 2007), 5, 243; and Whitney Royster, "Final Plan: Close Sylvan in Winter," *CST*, Sept. 22, 2007 (Cubin's quote).

68. NPS, Record of Decision, Nov. 20, 2007; Jim Drinkard, "White House Reverses Experts on Yellowstone Policy," *San Jose [CA] Mercury News*, July 24, 2008 (quotes); "White House Overruled Experts on Sylvan Pass," *BDC*, July 25, 2008; and Cory Hatch, "Parks Sled Plan in Limbo," *JHNG*, Nov. 20, 2007.

69. NPS, *2007 FEIS*, vol. 1: 60–64; Cory Hatch, "Feds Hire Mediator for Sylvan Pass Fight," *JHNG*, Oct. 17, 2007; NPS, Record of Decision, Nov. 5, 2007, Third EIS Collection,

MAOF; 72 *Federal Register* 239: 70781–70804, Dec. 13, 2007; and National Park Service, "Winter Use Plans Record of Decision Amendment—Sylvan Pass Management," July 16, 2008, MAOF.

70. Michael J. Yochim, "Compromising Yellowstone: The Interest Group–National Park Service Relationship in Modern Policy-Making" (Ph.D. dissertation, University of Wisconsin–Madison, 2004), 94–152 (see also pp. 32–93 therein).

71. See again William T. Borrie, Wayne A. Freimund, and Mae A. Davenport, "Winter Visitors to Yellowstone National Park," *Human Ecology Review* 9 (2002): 41–48; Mae A. Davenport and William T. Borrie, "The Appropriateness of Snowmobiling in National Parks," *Environmental Management* 35 (2005): 151–160; Judith Layzer, *The Environmental Case: Translating Values into Policy* (Washington, DC: CQ Press, 2006); and Yochim, "Compromising Yellowstone."

CONCLUSION: YELLOWSTONE'S WONDERLAND, ALICE'S WONDERLAND

1. Shan Burson, "Natural Soundscape Monitoring in Yellowstone National Park, Dec. 2007–March 2008," June 30, 2008, unpublished report to NPS, http://www.nps.gov/yell/parkmgmt/winterusetechnicaldocuments.htm, accessed Nov. 3, 2008.

2. I am indebted to Paul Schullery for some of these ideas; see his *Searching for Yellowstone: Ecology and Wonder in the Last Wilderness* (Boston: Houghton Mifflin, 1997), 254. Quote from "Mild Autumn Fans Hopes of Partisans," *BGZ*, Nov. 9, 1958.

3. See Schullery, *Searching for Yellowstone*, 261.

4. I borrow the phrase "windshield wilderness" from David Louter, *Windshield Wilderness: Cars, Roads, and Nature in Washington's National Parks* (Seattle: University of Washington Press, 2006).

5. In discussing how society lays its values on the land, I am influenced by Lynne Heasley's ideas in *A Thousand Pieces of Paradise: Landscape and Property in the Kickapoo Valley* (Madison: University of Wisconsin Press, 2005).

6. The quote is, of course, from Lewis Carroll's book, but it was also used by NPS Deputy Director Sue Masica to describe the high-level policy deliberations that took place late in 2007 over the NPS's proposed closure of Sylvan Pass (Masica to Mary Bomar, e-mail, Oct. 26, 2007, file "Discussions with CEQ/OMB regarding Decision, 1025–11/6/07," Third EIS Collection, MAOF).

7. Dwight T. Pitcaithley, "On the Brink of Greatness: National Parks and the Next Century," *George Wright Forum* 24, no. 2 (2007): 9–20. See also Lorraine Mintzmyer, "Disservice to the Parks," *National Parks*, Nov./Dec. 1992, 24–25.

8. Smithsonian Institution, "The Board of Regents," http://www.si.edu/about/regents.htm, accessed Nov. 5, 2007. Public trusts are still another possibility; see John A. Baden, "Parks Best Managed by Trusts," *BDC*, Nov. 16, 2005.

9. William R. Lowry, *The Capacity for Wonder: Preserving National Parks* (Washington, DC: Brookings Institution, 1994), 210–219.

10. Suzanne Lewis, "The Role of Science in National Park Service Decision-Making," *George Wright Forum* 24 (2007): 36–40.

11. T. H. Watkins, "Call It Silence," *National Parks,* Sept/Oct. 1999, 41–42 (quotes p. 42). See also Joseph Sax, *Mountains without Handrails: Reflections on the National Parks* (Ann Arbor: University of Michigan Press, 1980), and Judith L. Meyer, *The Spirit of Yellowstone* (Lanham, MD: Rowman & Littlefield, 2003), 112–116. Both Sax and Meyer articulated much the same perspective.

Bibliography

ABBREVIATIONS

MAOF   Management Assistant's Office Files, National Park Service, Mammoth Hot Springs, Yellowstone National Park, Wyoming. Note that these files may be transferred to the Yellowstone National Park Archives in Gardiner, Montana, at any time as part of routine government archiving.

NPS   National Park Service.

YNPA   National Archives, Yellowstone National Park, Gardiner, Montana.

YNPR   Yellowstone National Park Research Library, Gardiner, Montana.

ARCHIVAL COLLECTIONS

Author's personal collection (from close to twenty years of working and researching in Yellowstone).

Executive secretary's office, Xanterra Parks & Resorts, Mammoth Hot Springs, Wyoming.

Gale W. McGee Collection, Accession #9800, American Heritage Center, University of Wyoming, Laramie.

Glacier National Park Archives, West Glacier, Montana.

Greater Yellowstone Coalition files, Greater Yellowstone Coalition, Bozeman, Montana.

Lassen National Park files, Mineral, California.

Management Assistant's Office Files, National Park Service, Yellowstone National Park, Wyoming. These include the Environmental Impact Statement Collection (EIS Collection), the Supplemental Environmental Impact Statement Collection (SEIS Collection), the Research Collection, the Temporary Environmental Assessment (EA) Collection, the Third EIS Collection, the 2008 Environmental Assessment Collection, the EIS Administrative Record, the SEIS Administrative Record, and the Temporary EA Administrative Record.

Milward Simpson papers, American Heritage Center, University of Wyoming, Laramie.

Montana Historical Society, Helena, Montana.

Mount Rainier National Park files, Ashford, Washington.

Noranda Collection, Greater Yellowstone Coalition, Bozeman, Montana.

Park County Historical Society, Cody, Wyoming.

Record Group 79, National Archives, College Park, Maryland.

Superintendent's Office Files, National Park Service, Yellowstone National Park, Wyoming.

Vertical Files, Yellowstone National Park Research Library, Gardiner, Montana.

Wilderness Society Collection, CONS 130, Conservation Collection, Denver Public Library, Denver, Colorado.

Wyoming State Archives, Cheyenne.

Yellowstone Center for Resources files, National Park Service, Yellowstone National Park, Wyoming.

Yellowstone Historic Center archives, West Yellowstone, Montana.

Yellowstone National Park Collection, National Archives, Yellowstone National Park, Gardiner, Montana.

Yellowstone National Park Museum Collection, Yellowstone National Park, Gardiner, Montana.

BOOKS AND ARTICLES

Abbey, Edward. *Desert Solitaire: A Season in the Wilderness.* New York: Ballantine Books, 1968.

Albanese, Catherine L. *Nature Religion in America: From the Algonkian Indians to the New Age.* Chicago: University of Chicago Press, 1990.

Aune, Keith. "Impacts of Winter Recreationists on Wildlife in a Portion of Yellowstone National Park." Master's thesis, Montana State University–Bozeman, 1981.

Barker, Rocky. *Scorched Earth: How the Fires of Yellowstone Changed America.* Washington, DC: Island Press, 2005.

Bartlett, Richard A. *Yellowstone: A Wilderness Besieged.* Tucson: University of Arizona Press, 1985.

Belasco, Warren James. *Americans on the Road: From Autocamp to Motel, 1910–1945.* Cambridge, MA: MIT Press, 1979.

Biel, Alice Wondrak. *Do (Not) Feed the Bears: The Fitful History of Wildlife and Tourists in Yellowstone.* Lawrence: University Press of Kansas, 2006.

Bissegger, Jeffrey. "Snowmobiles in Yellowstone: Conflicting Priorities in Setting National Parks Policy and the Paradox of Judicial Activism for Recreational Business." *Journal of Land, Resources, & Environmental Law* 25 (2005): 109–118.

Bjornlie, Daniel. "Ecological Effects of Winter Road Grooming on Bison in Yellowstone National Park." Master's thesis, Montana State University–Bozeman, May 2000.

Blevins, Bruce. *Park County, Wyoming: Facts and Maps through Time.* N.p.: WIM Marketing, 1999.

Bonner, Robert E. *William F. Cody's Wyoming Empire: The Buffalo Bill Nobody Knows.* Norman: University of Oklahoma Press, 2007.

Borrie, William T., Wayne A. Freimund, and Mae A. Davenport. "Winter Visitors to Yellowstone National Park: Their Value Orientations and Support for Management Actions." *Human Ecology Review* 9 (2002): 41–48.

Buchholtz, C. W. *Rocky Mountain National Park: A History.* Niwot: University Press of Colorado, 1983.

Cassirer, Frances, David J. Freddy, and Ernest D. Ables. "Elk Responses to Disturbance by Cross-Country Skiers in Yellowstone National Park." *Wildlife Society Bulletin* 20 (1992): 375–381.

Chamberlin, Agnes. *The Cody Club: A History of Cody Country Chamber of Commerce* (1940). Jeannie Cook and Joanita Monteith, eds. Cody, WY: Yellowstone Printing & Design, 1999.

Chase, Alston. *Playing God in Yellowstone.* New York: Harcourt Brace Jovanovich, 1986.

Clifford, Hal. *Downhill Slide: Why the Corporate Ski Industry Is Bad for Skiing, Ski Towns, and the Environment.* San Francisco: Sierra Club Books, 2002.

Cohen, Michael P. *The History of the Sierra Club.* San Francisco: Sierra Club Books, 1988.

Coleman, Annie Gilbert. *Ski Style: Sport and Culture in the Rockies.* Lawrence: University Press of Kansas, 2004.

Consolo Murphy, Sue, and Beth Kaeding. "Fishing Bridge: 25 Years of Controversy regarding Grizzly Bear Management in Yellowstone National Park." *Ursus* 10 (1998): 385–393.

Cook, Jeannie, Lynn Johnson Houze, Bob Edgar, and Paul Fees. *Buffalo Bill's Town in the Rockies: A Pictorial History of Cody, Wyoming.* Virginia Beach, VA: Donning, 1996.

Craighead, Frank C. *Track of the Grizzly.* San Francisco: Sierra Club Books, 1979.

Davenport, Mae, and William T. Borrie. "The Appropriateness of Snowmobiling in National Parks: An Investigation of the Meanings of Snowmobiling Experiences in Yellowstone National Park." *Environmental Management* 35 (2005): 151–160.

Demars, Stanford E. *The Tourist in Yosemite, 1855–1985.* Salt Lake City: University of Utah Press, 1991.

Dilsaver, Lary. *America's National Park System: The Critical Documents.* Lanham, MD: Rowman & Littlefield, 1994.

———. *Cumberland Island National Seashore: A History of Conservation Conflict.* Charlottesville: University of Virginia Press, 2004.

Dilsaver, Lary M., and William C. Tweed. *Challenge of the Big Trees: A Resource History of Sequoia and Kings Canyon National Parks.* Three Rivers, CA: Sequoia Natural History Association, 1990.

Duffy, Robert J. *The Green Agenda in American Politics: New Strategies for the Twenty-First Century.* Lawrence: University Press of Kansas, 2003.

Dunlap, Thomas R. *Faith in Nature: Environmentalism as Religious Quest.* Seattle: University of Washington Press, 2004.

Dustin, Daniel L., and Ingrid E. Schneider. "The Science of Politics/The Politics of Science: Examining the Snowmobile Controversy in Yellowstone National Park." *Environmental Management* 34 (2005): 761–767.

Everhart, W. C. *The National Park Service.* Boulder, CO: Westview Press, 1983.

Fawcett, Darcy L. "Colonial Status: The Search for Independence in West Yellowstone, Montana." Professional paper, Montana State University, 1993.

Flores, Dan. *The Natural West: Environmental History in the Great Plains and Rocky Mountains.* Norman: University of Oklahoma Press, 2001.

Foresta, Ronald A. *America's National Parks and Their Keepers.* Washington, DC: Resources for the Future, 1984.

Fox, Stephen. *The American Conservation Movement: John Muir and His Legacy.* Madison: University of Wisconsin Press, 1981.

Franke, Mary Ann. "Do Groomed Roads Increase Bison Mileage?" *Yellowstone Science* 13 (Fall 2005): 15–24.

———. *To Save the Wild Bison: Life on the Edge in Yellowstone.* Norman: University of Oklahoma Press, 2005.

———. *Yellowstone in the Afterglow: Lessons from the Fires.* Mammoth Hot Springs, WY: National Park Service, 2000.

Frome, Michael. *Regreening the National Parks.* Tucson: University of Arizona Press, 1992.

Gottlieb, Robert. *Forcing the Spring: The Transformation of the American Environmental Movement.* Washington, DC: Island Press, 1993.

Graber, Linda. *Wilderness as Sacred Space.* Washington, DC: American Association of Geographers, 1976.

Haines, Aubrey L. *The Yellowstone Story: A History of Our First National Park.* Revised edition, vols. 1 and 2. Yellowstone National Park: Yellowstone Association for Natural Science, History & Education, in cooperation with the University Press of Colorado, 1996.

Hardin, Garrett. "The Tragedy of the Commons." *Science* 162 (1968): 1243–1248.

Hardy, Amanda. "Bison and Elk Responses to Winter Recreation in Yellowstone National Park." Master's thesis, Montana State University–Bozeman, 2001.

Harmon, Rick. *Crater Lake National Park: A History.* Corvallis: Oregon State University Press, 2002.

Hartzog, G. B., Jr. *Battling for the National Parks.* Mt. Kisco, NY: Moyer Bell, 1988.

Harvey, Mark. "Managing the Wild." *Environmental History* 10 (2005): 700–701.

Heasley, Lynne. *A Thousand Pieces of Paradise: Landscape and Property in the Kickapoo Valley.* Madison: University of Wisconsin Press, 2005.

Hess, Karl, Jr. *Rocky Times in Rocky Mountain National Park: An Unnatural History.* Niwot: University Press of Colorado, 1993.

Hummel, Don. *Stealing the National Parks: The Destruction of Concessions and Park Access.* Bellevue, WA: Free Enterprise Press, 1987.

Ingham, L. Allister. *As the Snow Flies: A History of Snowmobile Development in North America.* Lanigan, Saskatchewan, Canada: Snowmobile Research Publishing, 2000.

Irvine, Amy. *Making a Difference: Stories of How Our Outdoor Industry and Individuals Are Working to Preserve America's Natural Places.* Guilford, CT: Falcon Press, 2001.

Isenberg, Andrew C. *The Destruction of the Bison: An Environmental History, 1750–1920.* New York: Cambridge University Press, 2000.

Jacoby Karl. *Crimes against Nature: Squatters, Poachers, Thieves, and the Hidden History of American Conservation.* Berkeley: University of California Press, 2001.

Jakle, John A. *The Tourist: Travel in Twentieth-Century North America.* Lincoln: University of Nebraska Press, 1985.

Jordan, Roy. "Wyoming: A New Centennial Reflection." *Annals of Wyoming* 62 (1990): 114–130.

————. "Wyoming: Its History and Common Culture." In [Jennifer Jeffries Thompson, ed.], *Centennial West: Celebrations of the Northern Tier States' Heritage* (Helena, MT: Montana Historical Society, 1989), 30–35.

Jurale, James A. "History of Winter Use in Yellowstone National Park." Master's Thesis, University of Wyoming, 1986.

Kay, Charles. "Aboriginal Overkill: The Role of Native Americans in Structuring Western Ecosystems." *Human Nature* 5 (1994): 359–398.

————. "Are Ecosystems Structured from the Top-Down or Bottom-Up? A New Look at an Old Debate." *Wildlife Society Bulletin* 26 (1998): 484–498.

Kemmis, Daniel. *This Sovereign Land: A New Vision for Governing the West.* Washington, DC: Island Press, 2001.

Kensel, W. Hudson. *Pahaska Tepee: Buffalo Bill's Old Hunting Lodge and Hotel, A History, 1901–1946.* Cody, WY: Buffalo Bill Historical Center, 1987.

Lacasse, Roger. *Joseph-Armand Bombardier: An Inventor's Dream Come True.* N.p.: Libre Expression, 1988.

Langston, Nancy. *Forest Dreams, Forest Nightmares: The Paradox of Old Growth in the Inland West.* Seattle: University of Washington Press, 1995.

Lavigne, Jean E. "Constructing Yellowstone: Nature and Environmental Politics in the Rocky Mountain West." Ph.D. dissertation, University of Kentucky, 2003.

Layzer, Judith. *The Environmental Case: Translating Values into Policy.* Washington, DC: CQ Press, 2006.

Lewis, Suzanne. "The Role of Science in National Park Service Decision-Making." *George Wright Forum* 24 (2007): 36–40.

Lien, Carsten. *Olympic Battleground: The Power Politics of Timber Preservation.* San Francisco: Sierra Club Books, 1991.

Louter, David. *Windshield Wilderness: Cars, Roads, and Nature in Washington's National Parks.* Seattle: University of Washington Press, 2006.

Lowry, William R. *The Capacity for Wonder: Preserving National Parks.* Washington, DC: Brookings Institution, 1994.

————. *Preserving Public Lands for the Future: The Politics of Intergenerational Goods.* Washington, DC: Georgetown University Press, 1998.

Magoc, Chris J. *Yellowstone: The Creation and Selling of an American Landscape.* Albuquerque: University of New Mexico Press, 1999.

Manning, Robert E., David W. Lime, Marilyn Hof, and Wayne A. Freimund. "The Visitor Experience and Resource Protection (VERP) Process: The Application of Carrying Capacity to Arches National Park." *George Wright Forum* 12 (1995): 45–54.

Marx, Leo. *The Machine in the Garden: Technology and the Pastoral Ideal in America.* New York: Oxford University Press, 1964.

McBeth, Mark K., and Elizabeth A. Shanahan. "Public Opinion for Sale: The Role of Policy Marketers in Greater Yellowstone Policy Conflict." *Policy Sciences* 37 (2004): 319–339.

McBeth, Mark K., Elizabeth A. Shanahan, and Michael D. Jones. "The Science of Storytelling: Measuring Policy Beliefs in Greater Yellowstone." *Society and Natural Resources* 18 (2005): 413–429.

Meadow, Robert, Richard P. Reading, Mike Phillips, Mark Mehringer, and Brian J. Miller. "The Influence of Persuasive Arguments on Public Attitudes toward a Proposed Wolf Restoration in the Southern Rockies." *Wildlife Society Bulletin* 33 (2005): 154–163.

Meagher, Mary. *The Bison of Yellowstone National Park.* National Park Service Scientific Monograph No. 1, Washington, DC: U. S. Government Printing Office, 1973.

———. "Evaluation of Boundary Control for Bison of Yellowstone National Park." *Wildlife Society Bulletin* 17 (1989): 15–19.

Meeks, Harold A. *On the Road to Yellowstone: The Yellowstone Trail and American Highways, 1900–1930.* Missoula, MT: Pictorial Histories Publishing, 2000.

Meyer, Judith. *The Spirit of Yellowstone.* Lanham, MD: Rowman & Littlefield, 1996.

Miles, John C. *Guardians of the Parks: A History of the National Parks and Conservation Association.* Washington, DC: Taylor & Francis, 1995.

Morehouse, Barbara J. *A Place Called Grand Canyon: Contested Geographies.* Tucson: University of Arizona Press, 1996.

Morrison, Micah. *Fire in Paradise: The Yellowstone Fires and the Politics of Environmentalism.* New York: HarperCollins, 1993.

Murray, Ester Johansson. *A History of the North Fork of the Shoshone River.* Cody, WY: Lone Eagle MultiMedia, 1996.

Nabokov, Peter. *Restoring a Presence: American Indians and Yellowstone National Park.* Norman: University of Oklahoma Press, 2004.

Nicholas, Liza J. *Becoming Western: Stories of Culture and Identity in the Cowboy State.* Lincoln: University of Nebraska Press, 2006.

Nykerk, Sandra. "Pilgrims and Rituals in Yellowstone National Park: Touristic Encounters with the Sacred." Directed Interdisciplinary Studies Bachelor's Honors Thesis, Montana State University–Bozeman, 2000.

Park County Story Committee. *The Park County Story.* Dallas: Taylor, 1980.

Pearson, Byron E. *Still the Wild River Runs: Congress, the Sierra Club, and the Fight to Save Grand Canyon.* Tucson: University of Arizona Press, 2002.

Perkins, Marlin. "Winter Comes to Yellowstone." *Wild Kingdom*, March 14, 1965, available at YNPR.

Pitcaithley, Dwight T. "On the Brink of Greatness: National Parks and the Next Century." *George Wright Forum* 24 (2007): 9–20.

Plater, Zygmunt J. B., Robert H. Abrams, and William Goldfarb. *Environmental Law and Policy: A Coursebook on Nature, Law, and Society.* St. Paul: West Publishing, 1992.

Polzin, Paul E., and Tat P. Fong. "Snowmobiling in Montana: An Economic Study." *Montana Business Quarterly*, Winter 1988, 3–10.

Pritchard, James A. *Preserving Yellowstone's Natural Conditions: Science and the Perception of Nature.* Lincoln: University of Nebraska Press, 1999.

Quinn, Ruth. *Weaver of Dreams: The Life and Architecture of Robert C. Reamer*. Gardiner, MT: Leslie & Ruth Quinn, 2004.

Reese, Rick. *Greater Yellowstone: The National Park & Adjacent Wildlands*. Helena, MT: American & World Geographic Publishing, 1991.

Reich, Leonard S. "Ski-Dogs, Pol-Cats, and the Mechanization of Winter: The Development of Recreational Snowmobiling in North America." *Technology and Culture* 40, no. 3 (1999): 484–516.

Ridenour, James M. *The National Parks Compromised: Pork Barrel Politics and America's Treasures*. Merrillville, IN: ICS Books, 1994.

Righter, Robert W. *Crucible for Conservation: The Struggle for Grand Teton National Park*. [Boulder]: Colorado Associated University Press, 1982.

Rolston, Holmes. "Biology and Philosophy in Yellowstone." *Biology and Philosophy* 5 (1990): 241–258.

Rothman, Hal K. *Devil's Bargains: Tourism in the Twentieth-Century American West*. Lawrence: University Press of Kansas, 1998.

Runte, Alfred. *National Parks: The American Experience*. Lincoln: University of Nebraska Press, 1979.

———. *Yosemite: The Embattled Wilderness*. Lincoln: University of Nebraska Press, 1990.

Sarewitz, Daniel. "How Science Makes Environmental Controversies Worse." *Environmental Science & Policy* 7 (2004): 385–403.

Sax, Joseph. *Mountains without Handrails*. Ann Arbor: University of Michigan Press. 1980.

Schneider, Kevin B. "The Role of Collaboration in Managing National Parks." Master's professional paper, Montana State University–Bozeman, 2004.

Schrepfer, Susan R. *The Fight to Save the Redwoods: A History of Environmental Reform, 1917–1978*. Madison: University of Wisconsin Press, 1983.

Schullery, Paul. *Searching for Yellowstone: Ecology and Wonder in the Last Wilderness*. Boston: Houghton Mifflin, 1997.

———. *Yellowstone's Ski Pioneers: Peril and Heroism on the Winter Trail*. Worland, WY: High Plains Publishing, 1995.

Sellars, Richard West. *Preserving Nature in the National Parks: A History*. New Haven, CT: Yale University Press, 1997.

Shelton, Peter. *Climb to Conquer: The Untold Story of World War II's 10th Mountain Division Ski Troops*. New York: Scribner, 2003.

Smith, Phyllis. *Bozeman and the Gallatin Valley: A History*. Helena, MT: Two Dot Press, 1996.

Spence, Mark David. *Dispossessing the Wilderness: Indian Removal and the Making of the National Parks*. New York: Oxford University Press, 1999.

Sylvester, James T., and Marlene Nesary. "Snowmobiling in Montana: An Update." *Montana Business Quarterly*, Winter 1994, 3–8.

Tuan, Yi-Fu. *Space and Place: The Perspective of Experience*. Minneapolis: University of Minnesota Press, 1977.

Tuite, James J. *Snowmobiles and Snowmobiling.* New York: Cowles, 1969.

Turner, Tom. *Justice on Earth: Earthjustice and the People It Has Served.* White River Junction, VT: Chelsea Green, 2002.

Vale, Thomas R. *The American Wilderness: Reflections on Nature Protection in the United States.* Charlottesville: University of Virginia Press, 2005.

Vale, Thomas R., and Geraldine Vale. *Walking with Muir across Yosemite.* Madison: University of Wisconsin Press, 1998.

Varley, John, and Paul Schullery. "Reaching the Real Public in the Public Involvement Process: Practical Lessons in Ecosystem Management." *George Wright Forum* 13 (1996): 72, 74.

Warren, Louis S. *Buffalo Bill's America: William Cody and the Wild West Show.* New York: Alfred A. Knopf, 2005.

Western, Samuel. *Pushed Off the Mountain—Sold Down the River.* Moose, WY: Homestead, 2002.

Whiteley, Lee. *The Yellowstone Highway: Denver to the Park, Past and Present.* Boulder, CO: Johnson Printing, 2001.

Whiteley, Lee, and Jane Whiteley. *The Playground Trail, The National Park-to-Park Highway: To and through the National Parks of the West in 1920.* Boulder, CO: Johnson Printing, 2003.

Whittlesey, Lee H. "Cows All Over the Place." *Wyoming Annals* 66 (Winter 1994–1995): 42–57.

Wildavsky, Aaron, and Naomi Caiden. *The New Politics of the Budgetary Process,* 5th ed. New York: Pearson-Longman, 2004.

Yochim, Michael J. "Aboriginal Overkill Overstated: Errors in Charles Kay's Hypothesis." *Human Nature* 12 (2001): 141–167.

———. "Compromising Yellowstone: The Interest Group–National Park Service Relationship in Modern Policy-Making." Ph.D. dissertation, University of Wisconsin–Madison, 2004.

———. "The Development of Snowmobile Policy in Yellowstone National Park." Master's thesis, University of Montana, 1998.

———. "The Development of Snowmobile Policy in Yellowstone National Park." *Yellowstone Science* 7 (Spring 1999): 2–10.

———. "Snow Machines in the Gardens." *Montana: The Magazine of Western History* 53 (Autumn 2003): 2–15.

———. "A Water Wilderness: Battles over Motorboats on Yellowstone Lake." *Historical Geography* 35 (2007): 185–213.

GOVERNMENT DOCUMENTS

Code of Federal Regulations (CFR).

Congressional Record.

Conservation Law Foundation of New England v. Clark. 590 F. Supp. 1467 (1984), 1467–1490.

Executive Order 11644, February 8, 1972, 42 U.S.C.A. § 4321.

Executive Order 11989, May 24, 1977, 42 U.S.C.A. § 4321.

Federal Register.

Fund for Animals et al. v. Gale Norton et al. [and] Greater Yellowstone Coalition et al. v. Gale Norton et al. Dec. 16, 2003. 294 F. Supp. 2d 92 (D.D.C. 2003).

Fund for Animals v. Norton. Sept. 28, 2005. 390 F. Supp. 2d 12 (D.D.C. 2005).

Government Executive.

Greater Yellowstone Winter Visitor Use Management Working Group, Winter Visitor Use Management: A Multi-Agency Assessment, March 1999.

ISMA et al. and State of WY v. Gale Norton et al. and Greater Yellowstone Coalition et al. Oct. 14, 2004. 304 F. Supp. 2d 1278, 1293 (D. WY 2004), 21–29.

National Park Service. Bison Management for the State of Montana and Yellowstone National Park, Executive Summary. Aug. 2000.

———. Environmental Assessment: Temporary Closure of a Winter Road. Nov. 1997.

———. Temporary Winter Use Plans Environmental Assessment. Aug. 2004.

———. Winter Use Plan Draft Environmental Impact Statement. July 1999.

———. Winter Use Plan Environmental Assessment, Nov. 1990.

———. Winter Use Plans Draft Environmental Impact Statement. March 2007.

———. Winter Use Plans Draft Supplemental Environmental Impact Statement. [March 2002.]

———. Winter Use Plans Final Environmental Impact Statement. [Oct. 2000.]

———. Winter Use Plans Final Environmental Impact Statement. 2007.

———. Winter Use Plans Final Supplemental Environmental Impact Statement. Feb. 2003.

Sierra Club v. Clark, 756 F. Supp. 2d 1276.

State Highway Commission. Seventh Biennial Report of the State Highway Commission of the State of Wyoming. [Cheyenne]: WY Labor Journal, 1930.

Superintendent's Annual Reports, and Superintendent's Monthly Reports. YNPR.

U.S. Department of Transportation, Federal Highway Administration and Wyoming Highway Department. Final Environmental Impact Statement: Wyoming Highway Project FLH 18-4, Clarks Fork Canyon Road, Park County, Wyoming, 1973.

U.S. House Committee on Resources, Subcommittee on National Parks & Public Lands. Oversight Hearing on Snowmobile Recreation in National Parks, Particularly Yellowstone National Park. 106th Cong., 2nd sess., May 25, 2000.

U.S. House Committee on Small Business, Subcommittee on Tax, Finance, and Exports of the Committee on Small Business. Impact of Banning Snowmobiles inside National Parks on Small Business. 106th Cong., 2nd sess., July 13, 2000.

———. Protecting Small Business and National Parks: The Goals Are Not Mutually Exclusive. 107th Cong., 2nd sess., Jan. 26, 2002.

U.S. Senate Committee on Appropriations. *Winter Operation of Roads in Yellowstone National Park.* 90th Cong., 2nd sess., 1968.

U.S. Senate Committee on Energy and Natural Resources. *Snowmobile Activities in the National Park System and Miscellaneous National Heritage Bills.* 106th Cong., 2nd sess., 2000.

U.S. Senate Committee on Governmental Affairs. *Hearing regarding Public Health and Natural Resources: A Review of the Implementation of Our Environmental Laws, Part II.* 107th Cong., 2nd sess., March 13, 2002.

U.S. Senate Committee on Interior and Insular Affairs. *Snowmobiles and Other Off-Road Vehicles: A Study of the Effects of the Rapidly Expanding Use of All Terrain Vehicles on the Public Lands.* 92nd Cong., 1st sess., May 21,1971.

Wyoming Lodging and Restaurant Association v. U.S. Dept. of Interior. Oct. 15, 2005. 398 F. Supp. 2d 1197 (D. WY 2005).

Yellowstone National Park, U.S. Fish and Wildlife Service, University of Wyoming, University of Idaho, Interagency Grizzly Bear Study Team, and University of Minnesota Cooperative Park Studies Unit. "Wolves for Yellowstone? A Report to the United States Congress." May 1990.

PERIODICALS, NEWSPAPERS, AND NEWSLETTERS

Amicus Journal (periodical of the Natural Resources Defense Council)

Audubon

Backcountry

Billings Gazette, Billings, Montana

BlueRibbon Magazine (newsletter of the BlueRibbon Coalition, Pocatello, Idaho)

Bozeman Courier, Bozeman, Montana

Bozeman Daily Chronicle, Bozeman, Montana

Casper Star Tribune, Casper, Wyoming (before 1961, *Casper Morning Star*)

Casper Tribune-Herald, Casper, Wyoming

Chicago Tribune

Christian Science Monitor

City Sledder (published in Minnetonka, Minnesota)

Cody Enterprise, Cody, Wyoming

Collier's

Commentary Newsletter (in-house newsletter published by Xanterra Parks & Resorts in Yellowstone, available at YNPA)

Daily Telegraph, Port Deposit, Maryland (http://www.portdeposit.com/History/MilwardSimpson.htm)

Defenders (periodical of Defenders of Wildlife)

Denver Post

Deseret News and Telegram (now *Deseret News*), Salt Lake City

Fresno Bee, Fresno, California

Greater Yellowstone Report (newsletter of the Greater Yellowstone Coalition, Bozeman, Montana)

Great Falls Tribune, Great Falls, Montana

Helena Independent (later the *Helena Independent Record*), Helena, Montana

High Country News

Idaho Falls Post-Register, Idaho Falls, Idaho

Idaho Statesman, Boise, Idaho

Illustrated

Jackson Hole Courier, Jackson, Wyoming

Jackson Hole News & Guide, Jackson, Wyoming

Life

Livingston Enterprise, Livingston, Montana

Living Wilderness

Look

Los Angeles Times

Lovell Chronicle, Lovell, Wyoming

Minneapolis Star-Tribune

Missoulian, Missoula, Montana

National Parks (previously *National Parks
& Conservation Magazine*)

National Wildlife

Natural History

New West Network

New York Times

Outdoor America (periodical of the Izaak
Walton League)

Parade

Park County News, Livingston, Montana

Park Science (an NPS publication available
at MAOF and elsewhere)

Popular Gardening & Living Outdoors

Salt Lake Tribune, Salt Lake City, Utah

San Francisco Chronicle

Seattle Post-Intelligencer

SnoWest Magazine

Snowmobile

Snowmobile West

Snow Travel

Union Pacific Magazine

USA Today

Vanity Fair

Washington Post

West Yellowstone News, West Yellowstone,
Montana

Wilderness, including *Wilderness Society's
Quarterly Newsletter*

Wisconsin State Journal, Madison

Wyoming State Tribune, Cheyenne

Wyoming Wildlife

Yale Daily News, Yale University, New
Haven, Connecticut

Index

catalytic converters, 258n81

CDST. *See* Continental Divide Snowmobile Trail

Chandler, Nedra, 188, 189, 197

Chapman, Oscar, 38

Cheney, Dick, 207, 208

Chittenden, Hyram, 206

"Citizen's' Solution for Winter Access to Yellowstone," 131–132, 133

Clean Air Act, 115

Clinton, Bill, 120, 127

Cody, Wyoming

  Buffalo Bill and, 206

  Fishing Bridge controversy and, 93

  relationship to Yellowstone, 20–21, 52

  road plowing and, 21–22, 47, 51, 63

  Sylvan Pass controversy and, 205, 206–207

Cody Club, 22, 23, 27, 29, 35–36, 37, 47

Cody Country Chamber of Commerce, 110, 117, 190

Cody Enterprise, 29

Collier's, 39

Collins, Clark, 100

Colorado state highway department, 48

commercial guide restriction, 155(photo), 181

Committee on Interior and Insular Affairs, 61, 77

Congress

  NPS funding and, 217

  snowmobile ban and, 145–146, 156–157

Congressional Research Service, 97

conservation biology, 96

conservationists

  biased use of scientific studies, 139–140

  entrenched position of, 209

  Fund for Animals lawsuit decision and, 168

  high-profile letters organized by, 152(table)

  language and imagery used by, 135–136

  negative views of snowmobiles, 133

  notions of freedom, 266n39

  the press and, 132

  response to snowmobile ban, 144

reverence for nature, 7, 133–135

  snowcoach-only option and, 200–201, 209, 211

  snowmobile policy and, 81–82, 85

  snowmobiling in Yellowstone and, 65–66, 120

  Supplemental EIS and, 150–151, 153

  Winter Use Plan and, 103, 111, 112–113

  See also Greater Yellowstone Coalition

Continental Divide Snowmobile Trail (CDST)

  "Citizen's Solution" on, 131

  closed in Grand Teton, 178, 196–197

  conservationists request an EIS for, 103

  EIS on, 146

  through Grand Teton, 99, 105, 108, 253n37

  impact on winter visitation, 114

  path and building of, 104, 105–106

  proposal of and plan for, 99

  Alan Simpson and, 105–106

  in winter use debate, 112

  in 1990 Winter Use Plan, 102, 108, 109, 111

  Yellowstone concessionaires and, 253n37

Cook, Adena, 118

Cook, John, 277n101

Cooke City, Montana, 17, 24, 63

Cooke Pass, 204–205

cooperating agencies, 276n101

Council on Environmental Quality, 111

court cases

  against the Environmental Assessment, 181–183, 188

  appeal of Judge Sullivan's decision, 169–170

  overview of, 171(figure)

  on winter use issue, 184–187(table)

  winter use program lawsuit, 123, 126–127, 129, 130, 167–169

Craig, Larry, 145

Crandall, Derrick, 79

Crater Lake National Park, 78

cross-country skiing

  impact of snowmobiles on, 58, 238n15

  at Shoshone Geyser Basin, 2–3, 4–5

  at Upper Geyser Basin, 104(photo)